MEXICO'S
Lake Chapala & Ajijic

THE INSIDER'S GUIDE

Expanded
Second Edition
Includes Jocotepec

Teresa A. Kendrick

Contributors:
Don Adams, Zofia Barisas, Tony Burton, Daniel Jackson Garcia, Mary McDermott, John A. Miller, Gerry Mugford, Dale Hoyt Palfrey and Carol Wheeler

www.chapalaguide.com • ajijic@chapalaguide.com

Mexico's Lake Chapala and Ajijic

The Insider's Guide

SECOND EDITION
First Printing - June 2005

Published by
Mexico Travelers Information (MTI)
P.O. Box 26091
Austin, Texas USA
78755-0091

Some photographs have been used by permission and are the property of the original copyright owners.

ISBN: 0-9675248-3-0

Author: Teresa A. Kendrick

Contributors: Don Adams, Zofia Barisas, Tony Burton, Daniel Jackson Garcia, Mary McDermott, John A. Miller, Gerry Mugford, Dale Hoyt Palfrey, and Carol Wheeler

Production & Design: Marianne Carlson

Front Cover Design: Allan Turnipseed

Front Cover Photograph: Pablo Fernandez del Valle Ochoa

Back Cover Photographs: Dale Hoyt Palfrey

Available online at www.chapalaguide.com and www.amazon.com and other locations.

TABLE OF CONTENTS

TABLE OF CONTENTS (CONT.)

Preface

Since the first edition of this book was published in 2000 the Lakeside area has seen many changes. Once sleepy, the area now bustles with traffic, visitors, new residents, commerce and the sounds of construction. The dramatic recovery of Lake Chapala following the rainy season of 2004 lured many Guadalajara residents back to family vacation homes. Many decided to stay and make Lakeside their primary home. Weekend tourism is steady and half-year tourism is robust.

The foreign community continues to grow dramatically. Their contributions to the area are substantial and many charities and cultural groups have been the fortunate beneficiaries of their energy and expertise. The area now boasts many more first world services and products sold by English speaking businesspeople.

There have been growing pains. The congestion of traffic on the main Chapala to Jocotepec highway frustrates drivers used to having the village roads to themselves. The cost of living has grown, too. Mexico, especially this area, is no longer the fantastic bargain it once was. Prices for gasoline, telephone, electricity, real estate and food have all risen dramatically. In general, goods are expensive and services are reasonable. The reverse is true north of the border. Real estate is booming as is construction and development.

The task of keeping up with change has been formidable. I've been fortunate to welcome the research and writing of authors Don Adams and Zofia Barisas. Because of their work I have proudly expanded the guide to include Jocotepec and the services industry. Their labor didn't end there, though. Their excellent research enriched the entire book. Our investigative method stayed true: door to door visits, personal interviews and constant telephone work. However, printing a guide in the midst of such rapid change means that some of the listings will have changed by the time this comes off the press.

In this new edition we've welcomed back Dale Hoyt Palfrey who updated us on Lake Chapala, Lakeside Law, *fiestas* and provided us with a wonderful walking tour of Chapala. The scholarship of writers Tony Burton, Carol Wheeler, Gerry Mugford Fowler, and John Miller remains from the first edition. We would also like to thank Daniel Jackson Garcia, Pete Johanson, Samuel Kovac, Laura Leming, Robin Lawrason, Mary McDermott and Dr. Amelia Stevens for their contributions, advice and expertise. Our layout saint, Marianne Carlson accomplished the extremely difficult task of bringing it all together. Allan Turnipseed designed the guide's stunning cover.

And finally, I'd like to thank Mr. John and Margaret Cornes for their ongoing support of this project. Without them the guide would not exist.

T.A.K., June 2005
www.chapalaguide.com;
ajijic@chapalaguide.com

Who Are We?

Writers

TERESA A. KENDRICK made Mexico her home in 1994. A former journalist and writer specializing in the arts, she has long been involved in Mexican art and culture. She is a former columnist with the Guadalajara Colony Reporter and is a frequent contributor to online magazines and newspapers including the Miami Herald International, Mexico Edition. She is one of the writers featured in the anthology, "Agave Marias", available in September 2005.

DON ADAMS, author of "Head for Mexico—The Renegade Guide", is a former columnist for Mexico Connect Internet Magazine where he shared Best Columnist honors for 2003. Readers also selected one of his humorous writings as Best Column and a research work as Best Series. He is a contributor to the Miami Herald International, Mexico Edition, and an avid reader and researcher. After more than 30 years of traveling within the Mexico, he is now living in Cuyutlán, Colima on one of the state's beautiful volcanic beaches.

ZOFIA BARISAS grew up in Quebec. She studied Interior Design in Toronto and later worked in house renovation and landscaping. She has traveled and lived in many parts of the world. She now lives in Jocotepec where she writes and paints. Some of her short stories appear in the Lakeside Writers anthology, "Agave Marias", which becomes available in Ajijic in September 2005.

TONY BURTON, author of the highly acclaimed "Western Mexico—A Traveller's Treasury" (3rd edition, Perception Press, 2001, also in Spanish) is a writer, educator and naturalist who lived and worked eighteen years in Mexico, including ten years on the shores of Lake Chapala. Busy working on two new books, he resides currently in British Columbia and is a regular contributor to Mexico Connect website.

DALE HOYT PALFREY, a full-time resident of Ajijic, Jalisco, since 1973, followed in the footsteps of grandparents who put down roots in the Lake Chapala area during the early 1950s. She recently relinquished a post in international relations at the University of Guadalajara to devote her time to freelance work as a bilingual journalist and translator. An avid Mexicophile, her pet project at present entails active research for an upcoming book on the country's many colorful fiestas.

MARY MCDERMOTT is an avid birder and writer who recently walked away from a popular column on birdwatching in the Ajijic-based Lake Chapala Review. She now divides her time between her home in Ajijic, and in Cuyutlán, Colima. She is a frequent traveler and very active in dog rescue.

JOHN A. MILLER is a former resident of Ajijic who retired here after a career as a trust and investment banker in Philadelphia. In addition to his professional activities, he was very active in a number of charities and educational organizations. Other interests include the study of genealogy, cooking, writing and music. He has since returned to Philadelphia where he has resumed his volunteer work.

GERRY MUGFORD FOWLER is a language teacher who works for the Universidad de Guadalajara and Universidad del Valle de Atemajac. He writes an ongoing column about the subject he finds most absorbing, language and its usage, for the Guadalajara Colony Reporter. Gerry is happily married and has two wonderful children.

ANTHROPOLOGIST CAROL WHEELER ESPARZA has spent more than 21 years in West Central Mexico, where she has authored and edited English-language publications since 1981. She is director of Perception Press of Saint Augustine, Florida, a publishing house specializing in works on Mexico.

Photographers

DALE HOYT PALFREY—See Writers.

PABLO FERNANDEZ DEL VALLE OCHOA is from the town of Tlaquepaque just outside Guadalajara. Pablo is an industrial designer who has been working as a commercial photographer since 1992. His client list includes Cemex, Urrea Herramientas, Mexlub, IBM, and Hewlett Packard, among others. When not on commercial shoots, he loves to photograph landscapes. His work has been published in Geomundo and Concejo Nacionál de la Fauna.

JOHN FROST is a former Californian who first came to Jocotepec in 1966 with his wife, author Joan Van Every Frost. A veteran of the darkroom since age 14, John earned a degree in Graphic Art following military service in the pacific during WWII, before settling into photography work in the mid-1950s. Since 1979 he has extensively photographed Mexico's mid-Pacific coast, the volcanoes of Colima and Lake Chapala from the air. His aerial work has been included in university exhibitions throughout Mexico.

Researchers

DANIEL JACKSON is a lakeside jeweler who is an avid hiker and outdoorsman. He is married to Viridiana Rivera de Jackson, an Ajijic native. Their favorite time of year to hike is in the rainy season when the arroyos are full of water and the flowers are in bloom.

LAURA LEMING lived in Ajijic from 2002-2004. While in Ajijic, she was a web designer, creating websites for local businesses, authors and media relations firms in Guadalajara. She is currently working on updates for the Area Metropolitan Guide for the five Municipalities of Guadalajara and also works in the financial industry as a Training Technical writer. While she enjoys her life in Texas, Ajijic will always hold a special place in her heart.

Layout Designer

MARIANNE CARLSON is co-owner of Galería Maestros del Arte in Ajijic, a gourd artist, and vendor of Mexican miniatures from her website www.mexicoetc.com. Her far-reaching connections in the world of Mexican artists allows her to attract important artists to the annual Feria Maestros del Arte art exhibition. In her spare time she does layout work for writers.

Cover Designer

ALLAN TURNIPSEED Having traveled Mexico extensively since 1970, Allan Turnipseed finally achieved his lifelong dream of living here by moving to Lake Chapala in 2004. In his thirty-year career as a graphic designer in the U.S. from modest beginnings as a freelance production artist to an award-winning studio/agency, he designed numerous projects. He brought his design skills to catalogs and collateral materials, to videos and to book covers. His clients included prestigious and some not-so-well-known clients ranging from interior designers, to clothing designers and to those working in high tech. He now hopes to begin another career creating fine art pieces in the artistic environment of Lakeside.

Spanish Edit

ISABEL FUENTE is the owner of Mexico Cultural Journeys. As a bonded, licensed tour guide she plans and escorts guests from all over the world on tours that unlock the secrets of Mexico. She speaks English and French as fluently as her native language, Spanish. She is best remembered for her warm enthusiasm and the delight with which she shares the "pearls" of her country.

Dale Hoyt Palfrey

1

Lake Chapala, Ajijic and the North Shore Area

with
TONY BURTON, DALE HOYT PALFREY and MARY MCDERMOTT

Climate and Geography by TONY BURTON

WINTER WARMTH

The single major attraction of the Lake Chapala area is undoubtedly its semitropical climate, rated among the finest in the world. The ameliorating effects of the lake, situated at an altitude of 1,525 meters (5,000 feet), help ensure that temperatures remain pleasantly warm all year, with an annual average temperature of 19.9°C (67.8°F). This figure masks seasonal changes, ranging from average lows of 12°C (53.6°F) in December-January-February to average highs of 29°C (84.2°F) in May-June, immediately before the onset of the rainy season.

SUMMER RAINS

The rainy season, usually stretching from early June through late September, heralds slightly cooler daytime temperatures. Within days, the hillsides turn green with the new growth of luxuriant vegetation. Average annual rainfall (snow is virtually unknown at Lakeside) totals about 875 mm, or 34.4 inches. The wettest month is July. Many

Mexico uses the
Celsius (Centigrade) Thermometer

Fahrenheit		Celsius
0°	equals	-18°
32°	water freezes	0°
50°	cool weather	10°
68°	comfortable weather	20°
88°	hot weather	30°
98.6°	body temperature	37°
100°	very hot weather	40°
212°	water boils	100°

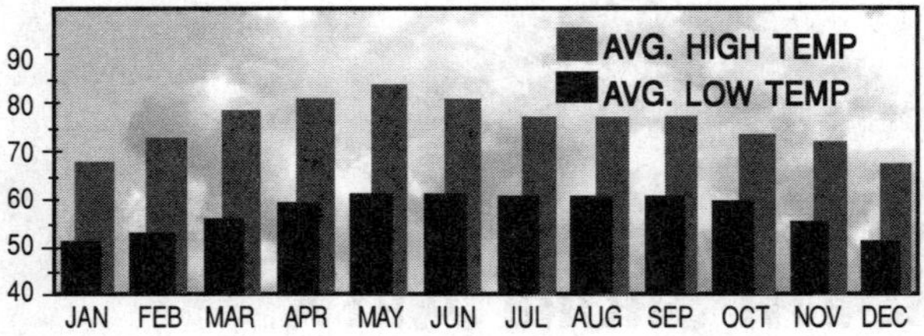

***Almost every day** in the Lake Chapala region, altitude 5,000 feet, brings sunshine and moderate temperatures.*

"snowbird" visitors spend their summers in Canada, the U.S. or Europe and their winters in Mexico. Ironically, in visiting the lakeside region between December and March, they see the Chapala landscape at its least attractive.

GARDENS AND FLOWERS

The balmy subtropical (latitude 20° N) temperatures of a Chapala "winter" allow for the year-round growth of most garden plants. While the hillsides towering above the residential areas look brown and dry, with brightly colored, winter-flowering trees scattered here and there, the cultivated and manicured gardens closer to the lakeside are a riot of color even in January. A year-round supply of fresh flowers for table decorations is taken for granted in most homes. During and immediately after the summer rainy season, local hillsides provide colorful competition for the gardens as a profusion of wildflowers scents the air and thrills the spirit.

WINDS AND WAVES

Winds are fairly predictable in strength, rarely exceeding 15 km/hour and posing little risk for well-prepared fishermen or those participating in aquatic sports.

Several different winds affect the region. The prevailing wind is the *Mexicano* which blows from east to west. The next most frequent is the *Abajeño* which blows from the opposite direction, followed by the *Sureño*, which comes from the south. Other named winds include the *Guaracheño* blowing from the southeast and the *Colimote* from the southwest.

GEOGRAPHY

The Lake Size and Depth

The lake is about 75 kilometers (50 miles) long from east to west with a maximum north-south width of about 20 kilometers (12.5 miles). Its large surface area (1,050 square kilometers or 405 square miles) makes it the largest natural lake in Mexico and the third largest in Latin America, after Lake Titicaca in the Andes and Lake Nicaragua in Central America. Despite its size, Lake Chapala is quite shallow, with an average depth of only slightly over four meters (13 feet) and a maximum depth of less than 30 meters (97.5 feet).

Lake Changes

Lake Chapala has not always been its present size. Thousands of years ago, some experts believe that it formed part of a much larger lake, usually referred to as the Mexican Inland Sea. Even at the time of the Spanish Conquest in the 16th century, the lake was considerably larger than today, with its eastern shoreline some 40 kilometers further east. The building of embankments limiting the lake to its present size enabled an extensive area of valuable farmland, the Ciénega de Chapala, to be drained at the start of the 20th century. At this time, several towns, including Sahuayo, Jiquilpan, Venustiano Carranza and Pajacuarán lost their lakeshore positions.

Lake Origin

The main mountain ranges surrounding the lake formed as a result of repeated volcanic eruptions about five million years ago, during the Pliocene period. The lake occupies a tectonic rift valley, and is the largest of a series of lakes scattered through the Neovolcanic Axis, a wide belt of high, volcanic terrain stretching west-east across Mexico. Signs of past vulcanism are everywhere. Some of the prominent peaks, such as Mount García on the southern shore, still have clear craters

***Three of the four sides** of Lake Chapala are enclosed by mountain massifs.*

Pablo Fernandez del Valle

near their summits. Eighty kilometers (50 miles) further south is the still-active Colima Volcano. Fortunately, it is sufficiently far enough away to pose no conceivable threat to the Chapala region.

Islands in the Lake

The main islands in the lake — Scorpion Island *(Isla de los Alacranes)* and Mezcala Island *(Isla del Presidio)* — are also of volcanic origin, as is the former island, now a promontory, on which nestles the village of Petatán on the southern shore of the lake. Incidentally, Scorpion Island is named for its shape, rather than for any abundance of scorpions!

Geothermal Spas

The Lake Chapala region's volcanic origins have brought an unexpected bonus, especially along the northern shore in the vicinity of Chapala, Ajijic, San Juan Cosalá and Jocotepec. Geothermal activity in these areas means that some subdivisions are able to pipe naturally thermal water directly into homes. In addition, several well-appointed spas have been developed around hot springs, enabling visitors and residents alike to benefit from the undoubted medicinal and curative properties of water which leaves the ground at temperatures of up to 85°C (185°F). Such spas include the Monte Carlo hotel in Chapala and the lakeshore spa in San Juan Cosalá, where a sporadically operating geyser spurts warm water high into the air.

THE NORTHERN SHORE

Jocotepec & San Juan Cosalá

Starting from the northwestern corner of the lake and traveling clockwise, Cerro Los Agraciados is the prominent hill rising behind the town of Jocotepec. North of Cerro Los Agraciados, beyond a small interior valley, is the highest peak in the Chapala area, Cerro Viejo, part of a ridge known as Sierra el Madroño. Cerro Viejo's summit is 2,960 meters (9,711 feet) above sea level.

East of Cerro Los Agraciados is Sierra Las Vigas (sometimes referred to as Sierra Tecuán), with the village of San Juan Cosalá at its foot.

Ajijic & Chapala

Next comes the Sierra Travesaño, which rises behind the villages of Ajijic and San Antonio Tlayacapán. During the rainy season, the vegetation on both the Sierra Las Vigas and the Sierra Travesaño turns bright green. At this time of year, the beauty of these hills is further enhanced by the numerous waterfalls that tumble down their flanks toward the lake.

San Nicolás de Ibarra & Vista del Lago

Continuing further east, the Chapala-Guadalajara highway cuts through a low pass between the Sierra Travesaño (to the west) and the Cerro San Francisco. The highest part of Cerro San Francisco, over 2,030 meters (6,660 feet) above sea level, is behind the small village of San Nicolás de Ibarra. Next comes the 2,350-meter (7,710-foot) Cerro Punta Grande, or the Sierra of Mezcala, the steep and imposing backdrop to Mezcala village.

Ocotlán & Jamay

Still further east, well beyond the reach of vehicles, the steep slopes of Cerro Grande descend abruptly into the lake immediately west of the course of the Santiago River and the town of Ocotlán. The final prominence on the northern side of the lake is the 1,970-meter (6,463-foot) high Cerro Gomeño, behind Jamay.

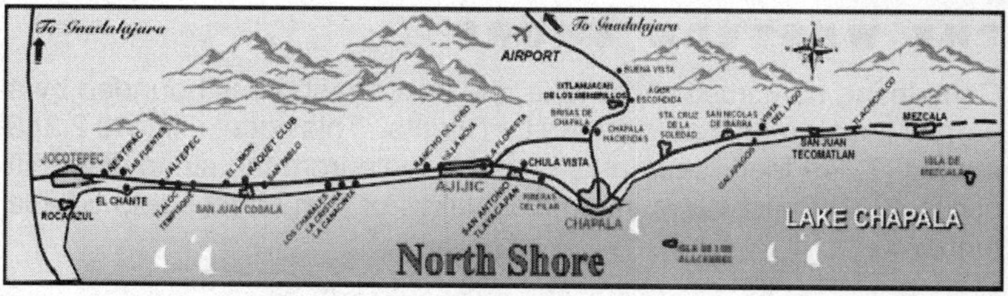

THE EASTERN SHORE

The eastern side of the lake lacks any highland. Instead, we find the flat, deliberately drained Ciénega of Chapala which has only isolated small hills which represent former islands in the original, larger, pre-reclamation lake. This region, between La Barca and Sahuayo, is crossed by the meandering Lerma River on its way towards the lake.

THE SOUTHERN SHORE

Petatán & Tizapán el Alto

On the southern shore continuing clockwise, now along federal highway 15, Cerro El Talayote overlooks the lakeside village of La Palma and Cojumatlán bay. A short distance beyond the town of Cojumatlán is the former island of Petatán, now reached by a causeway with paved road. Westward from here, the lower slopes of Cerro Buenos Aires, the northernmost extension of the Sierra del Tigre, provide some outstanding lakeside scenery as far as the city of Tizapán el Alto.

Mismaloya & Cerro El Alto

Behind the tiny fishing village of Mismaloya is Cerro Las Coronas, which extends as far west as the road which leaves highway 15 and climbs the lake's southern escarpment to the pretty mountain town of Mazamitla. Still further west, Cerro El Alto is the backdrop to the small lakeshore community of San Nicolás de Acuña.

Cerro Garcia

The southwestern corner of the lake basin is guarded by Cerro García, whose summit at 2,750 meters (9,072 feet) above sea level, is more than 1,230 meters (4,035 feet) above the lake level. García, which has the villages of San Luis Soyatlán and San Cristóbal Zapotitlán reclining at its foot, is a very prominent and attractive landmark from virtually everywhere on the northwestern shore.

THE WESTERN SHORE

Completing our circuit of the lake, the western shore is bounded by a narrow escarpment called Sierra La Difunta. This ridge, rising to 2,240 meters (7,349 feet), separates Lake Chapala from the steep-sided rift occupied by the shallow, intermittent lakes of San Marcos and Sayula further west.

Ecological Zones

The Lake Chapala region has a richly diversified fauna and flora. The variety of altitude, relief and climate around the lake has given rise to several distinct ecological zones, including the lake and lakeshore, the lower slopes of the surrounding hills and the upper slopes of the lake basin.

ALTERED VEGETATION

With only a few exceptions, the area in close proximity to the lake has been greatly modified by agriculture and human settlement. The hills which surround the lake were, until recent times, forested with oaks and pines but only isolated remnants of that original vegetation now remain, mostly on the highest, least accessible slopes. Reforestation projects have had some success in restoring lost woodland in various parts of the Chapala basin, although regrettably some of the species planted do not belong to the native flora of the area.

ALL KINDS OF ANIMALS

The native fauna has also been depleted in historic times, especially on the lower slopes, though several larger mammals such as white-tailed deer, coyotes, skunks, raccoons and opossums can all still be seen. Habitat conservation programs and restrictions on hunting should help ensure that no more large animals join the Mexican wolf and the puma, or cougar, in becoming extinct in the region. Fortunately, most birds and innumerable smaller animals, such as frogs, toads, bats, butterflies and moths, are all present in healthy numbers and show no signs of decline.

A complete list of fauna and flora is clearly impossible in the confines of this chapter and so the following sections merely highlight some of the more interesting, unusual and colorful plants and animals in the region.

Flora and Fauna

LAKE FLORA

The aquatic and sub-aquatic vegetation found in and around the lake includes bulrushes, common reeds, cattails, sedges, floating water-spangles, waterlily, water-milfoil, pondweed, duckweed and water hyacinth. Trees at the water's edge include willows and *amezquite* as well as numerous introduced species, such as eucalyptus and Ficus.

Tony Burton

LAKE FAUNA

Fish

The lake is home to almost 40 different species of fish, several of which are found only in this region. Native species include the catfish, the *charal*, the virtually extinct *popocha*

Tony Burton

Birding on Lake Chapala

By Mary McDermott

The Lake Chapala area is home to a wide variety of species of birds, and provides the interested observer with many opportunities to experience Mexican avian activity.

Although some birds will be instantly recognizable from sightings in the United States and Canada, there is a large number of endemic species here (those found only in Mexico). From the comfort of one's terrace or garden, you will be able to see the antics of the violet-crowned hummingbird, found only in Western Mexico. Instantly recognizable, due to its creamy white breast, one has to be patient to get a glimpse of its pretty purple crown, as these are very active little creatures. Far easier to spot, is the crimson-colored Vermilion Flycatcher, with its contrasting black wings. The Great Kiskadee, a large yellow, white and brown bird with a black eye line and a raucous cry, is common in our gardens here.

Along the lake front, look for the large wading birds such as the Great Egret, Great Blue Heron, and Black-Crowned Night Heron. In November of each year, we have the return of the American White Pelican from its breeding grounds in the Northern United States and Canada. These massive white birds are graceful in their soaring flights around the lake and against the mountains. They travel in cohesive social groups and work together communally to fish the waters of Lake Chapala. Their return to our shores annually is cause for celebration for the improving health of the lake.

Observing birds is one of the best ways to connect with the natural world, and to develop an appreciation for conserving our environment. Like all animals, birds require a safe place to live, and a steady supply of food to ensure survival. Many birds in the Lake Chapala area depend on fish as their main diet, supplemented by small amphibians and water vegetation. A century ago, Chapala provided a sustainable habitat for many different species of waterfowl, who found refuge in its marshes at the east end. Although those marshes no longer exist, having been drained to create farmland, one can still encounter a variety of bird life on its shores. As Lake Chapala continues to recover, one can hope to find even more over the coming years.

and the whitefish.

Other Aquatic Life

The lake also harbors a freshwater turtle species, one kind of water snake and several species of frogs, toads, mollusks and crabs, though the latter are now much harder to find than they were 30 years ago. In addition, of course, the lake is home to numerous insect species ranging from fleets of water boatmen to dragonflies, the occasional mosquito and seasonal swarms of tiny non-biting insects known locally as *bobos* (fools).

Birds

The lakeside fauna includes numerous species of aquatic birds, both native and migratory. American coots, egrets, herons, gulls, and cormorants are common all year, while diverse species of ducks and geese, together with stately flocks of white pelicans, arrive at the beginning of every winter.

The white pelicans congregate, in the hundreds, near the former island of Petatán. By far the largest birds in the region, they fish in groups, fanning out into a semi-circle and then slowly closing in on their lunches.

The eye-catching northern jacana or lily-trotter is a wading bird with dramatic yellow flashes on its wings. Three different species of white herons—the great egret, cattle egret and snowy egret—can also usually be seen somewhere near the water. The cattle egret first arrived in Mexico as recently as 1880 and can claim to be the first non-Mexican visitor to so fall in love with the area's climate, beauty and people that it settled here permanently!

Exploring the lake shore will allow you to see several colorful flycatchers including the vermillion flycatcher and the great kiskadee, as well as black-crowned night herons, grebes, ibises, mallards, teals, pintails, gadwalls, shovellers, tree ducks, avocets, gulls and terns.

GARDEN FLORA

Local gardeners make full use of several Mexican natives, including the poinsettia, chrysanthemums, sunflowers, cosmos, zinnias, calla lilies, and dahlias, the national flower. They also grow hundreds of introduced species, some of which have now escaped to grow wild throughout the region. Introduced species include ornamentals like the bougainvillea, violet-flowering jacaranda, African tulip tree, Indian laurel, yellow-flowering primavera and monkey-puzzle, as well as fruit trees like mangos, oranges, pomegranates and various kinds of palms including the coconut palm.

Tony Burton

Many gardens in the Chapala area are delightful. Masses of brightly colored bougainvillea, white, purple and red, cascade down one garden wall and a tangle of flame vine (*llamaradas*) with its brilliant red flowers spreads over the opposite wall. Hibiscus bushes with huge double-headed flowers, unusually-shaped bird of paradise flowers and the golden chalice (*copa de oro*) vine with its handsome golden flowers on glossy evergreen leaves, provide contrasting colors. Flower beds range from the whimsically tropical to the formal and neat.

In one corner of the garden, towering poinsettia plants grow so high that they need cutting back each year. The poinsettia or *nochebuena* is, of course, the pre-eminent Mexican contribution to Christmas decorations in many parts of the world.

The common names of many plants in the region are highly imaginative. For example, as you stroll across your friend's "lawn" in Ajijic, you might actually be walking not on grass but on rat's ears! On account of the shape of its leaves, this name is given to *Dichondra*, a ground cover that remains green year-round. It thrives in warm temperatures but needs heavy watering during the dry season.

Xeriscaping

In recent years an increasing number of gardeners actively practice xeriscaping (dry-gardening). Judicious choice and placement of plants makes far less demand on water than traditional gardening techniques. From an environmental standpoint, this is particularly welcome, given the low lake levels of the past decade.

GARDEN FAUNA

Hummingbird feeders in many Lakeside homes provide opportunities to marvel at the extraordinary flying abilities of hummingbirds, the stunt flyers of the bird world. Hummingbirds have to eat about half their own weight in sugars, mainly derived from nectar, each day. A human equivalent would require a daily intake of about 130 kilos (286 pounds) of hamburger meat!

Tony Burton

You may even find hummingbirds nesting somewhere in your garden. Their nests are fascinating: very small, beautifully constructed using mosses, lichens, cobwebs and other fine material, and so well camouflaged that they are virtually impossible to distinguish from their supporting leaves and twigs.

And garden pests? Well, perhaps the most serious is the leaf-cutter ant. An army of leaf-cutters can reduce an entire tree to bare twigs and branches during a single overnight chomping session. Fortunately, the ants tend to be selective and local gardeners have a variety of natural, as well as chemical, means of counterattack.

HOUSEHOLD BEASTIES

This account would be incomplete if no mention was made of some of the household pests that may be encountered.

***A variety** of harmless and vividly colored lizards bask in the sunshine.*

Cockroaches

Cockroaches, one of the insect world's great scavengers, will live and breed almost anywhere. Very few households can honestly say they never see any! Flies and mosquitoes tend to be few in number and seasonal; most houses are screened to prevent their easy entry.

Scorpions

Scorpions are quite common, but your chances of seeing one largely depend on how many rocks you turn over and how high up the mountainside you live. The local scorpions are not especially venomous, but local pharmacies and doctors' offices carry supplies of antidote, just in case.

Others

The spiders in the area include the black widow and the occasional tarantula. The tarantula is not poisonous, but can bite. Snakes are also sometimes seen, but usually as roadkills. The greatest potential hazard in gardens is being stung by red ants, bees, wasps or hornets as they go about their daily chores such as pollination.

FLORA OF THE LOWER SLOPES

On the lower slopes the vegetation, closely connected to the climate and the altitude, is typical of the semiarid zones of central Mexico. Among the trees commonly found thriving in this subtropical scrub are huge, white-trunked *amates*, kapoks, ape's earrings, *guamúchiles*, *guajes* and mesquites.

Paintings on *amate* paper, usually brightly colored naive scenes of village life, are a popular tourist souvenir. There are several fine *amates* alongside the lakeshore highways.

In early spring, another tall tree bears showy yellow flowers, even though it is leafless. This is the *primavera*, one of the most striking trees in the entire region.

Tony Burton

Tony Burton

Tony Burton

***Almost any** variety of flowering plants thrive in Jalisco's semi-tropical climate.*

The occasional kapok tree with its telltale seed pods which split open to reveal masses of seeds encased in balls of cottony fibers, also enlivens the lower slopes. The kapok tree belongs to the Bombax family, which includes several trees which have spectacular flowers and are cultivated as ornamentals.

Alongside the trees, castor oil plants tower up to six or seven meters high, and acacia bushes provide a thorny barrier to climbing the slopes.

Wildflowers on the lower slopes include the pretty bi-colored lantana, various colors of morning glory vines and trees, and, in the more disturbed areas, the prickle poppy, milkweed and several kinds of groundsel.

The cooked root of one morning glory is best known as *camote*, a kind of sweet potato, which is served everywhere from the best restaurants to the humblest homes. While some people buy cultivated *camotes* from food stores, others scour (and excavate) the upper slopes of the hills behind Ajijic in search of equally tasty wild *camotes*.

Close cousins of the morning glories include *cuscuta* or angel's hair, a notorious parasite, and wild *jícama*, the sweet, watery root of a woody vine which bears mauve or purplish bracts.

A beautiful tropical milkweed, with yellow and red flowers, grows wild in the Chapala area. Easy to find growing on vacant lots and wasteground, the milkweed, locally called *señorita*, attracts bees, wasps and monarch butterflies. This region's year-round resident non-migratory population of monarchs is totally dependent on milkweed. Fortunately, tropical milkweed flowers are so pretty that many Lakeside gardeners now encourage the plant in their gardens.

Elsewhere on the lower slopes, occasional cacti, including the flat-padded prickly pear, with its delectable fruit the *tuna*, and *agaves* add further variety to the fascinating mix of native and introduced flora. The *agaves* are native to the New World and the source of several commercial products, including *tequila*, Mexico's national drink.

FAUNA OF THE LOWER SLOPES

The lower slopes are home to dozens of different birds including grackles, anis, kingbirds, flycatchers, chickadees, finches and orioles. Both great-tailed grackles and groove-billed anis are large, black and noisy. Anis have shorter, hooked and markedly grooved beaks.

Several different kingbirds are found in the Chapala region, including Cassins, the thick-billed, the western and the tropical. Like most flycatchers, tropical kingbirds are often seen sitting on an exposed perch, waiting for insects to fly within range.

Among animals in this zone are opossums, armadillos, skunks, shrews, jackrabbits, cottontail rabbits, squirrels and weasels, as well as lizards and insects such as grasshoppers, cicadas, dragonflies, beetles and ants. All these creatures are found higher up the mountainsides as well.

The opossum or *tlacuache*, which is the size of a house cat, is nocturnal and most often seen by the light of vehicle headlights. Alternatively, you may hear it scampering across your roof tiles.

CULTIVATED CROPS

Some parts of the lower slopes are cultivated. One unusual local crop is the vegetable pear or *chayote*, a vine which, when mature, looks like a grapevine spreading on improvised trellises, casting deep shade over the ground below. The *chayote* is particularly delicious when oven-baked with cheese and fillings.

Tony Burton

***A canopy** of chayote vines (above).*

Many other crops are cultivated on the small truck farms in the area. The staple is corn, grown on even the steepest and rockiest slopes, but the summer rains allow for a wide variety of fruits and vegetables to be grown. When the Spanish first settled this area in the 16th century, they planted groves of orange trees and for a while Chapala was famous for its production of orange blossom. Today, most lakeside gardens provide their owners with a ready supply of all kinds of citrus fruit, mangos, avocados, papaya and bananas.

FLORA OF THE UPPER SLOPES

On the higher ground, different species of Ficus, together with peeling-bark *burseras* and *tepeguajes,* are common. The highest, least disturbed areas near Mezcala, on Mount García and Cerro Alto, as well as in the Vigas and Travesaño ranges, remain as pine-oak forests. Here, besides pine, oak and *madrone* trees, two-meter-tall thistles, several brightly colored Salvia species, Indian paintbrush and delicate wild geraniums all add their splash of seasonal color and enchantment. Beautiful blue lupines, instantly recognizable, are just one of several plants that will be very familiar to Europeans and North Americans.

On the larger trees, epiphytic air plants, or bromeliads, make their home. Some of these bromeliads bear giant red flowers in the early part of the year. Wild orchids can also be found. On a smaller scale, numerous branching lichens, which grow prolifically on tree trunks throughout the region, attest to the cleanliness of the mountain air.

FAUNA OF THE UPPER SLOPES

In addition to the animals who live on the lower slopes, the more remote and less accessible areas of the upper slopes are a suitable habitat for several larger mammals. Bobcats are occasionally sighted in such areas, as are white-tailed deer, gray foxes, raccoons and ring-tailed cats. The local populations of several of these larger animals are now considered endangered, as the direct result of hunting and loss of habitat.

General Information About the Lake Chapala Area by DALE HOYT PALFREY

The region surrounding Lake Chapala comprises eight municipalities in the state of Jalisco and four in the state of Michoacán. Most of the area's visitors and residents from abroad gravitate to the northshore municipalities of Ajijic, Chapala and Jocotepec. Under the jurisdiction of Chapala, the municipal seat, are five *delegaciones*; the villages San Nicolás de Ibarra and Santa Cruz de la Soledad to the east, San Antonio Tlayacapán and Ajijic to the west, and the remote Atotonilquillo to the northeast. Among the communities administered by Jocotepec are San Juan Cosalá, El Chante and Nestipac.

POPULATION

In Mexico's 1990 national census, the total population of the Municipality of Chapala was officially registered at 36,000 inhabitants. Current estimates indicate there are now some 20,000 residents in Chapala alone, 15,000 in Ajijic, 3,000 in San Juan Cosalá, and 16,000 in Jocotepec, which would bring the entire northshore population to approximately 60,000. About half the population is under 20 years of age.

Around 12,000 *North Americans currently reside in the area.*

Records at the United States Consulate Gen-

Lake Chapala: An Ecological Update

by Dale Palfrey

Lake Chapala has undergone a dramatic transformation since the start of the new millennium. In June, 2002 the lake stood at the lowest level recorded since 1955, holding less than 15 per cent of its full water storage capacity. The dire situation prompted a number of environmental activists to warn of Chapala's imminent demise, a prediction that fortunately proved dead wrong. Abundant precipitation during the 2003 and 2004 rainy seasons has brought the lake back to around 75% full capacity and the highest level registered since the early 1980's.

The decade-long crisis effectively spurred government agencies, politicians and diverse citizen groups into paying much closer attention to Mexico's largest lake.

In 2001 SEMARNAT, the federal government's environmental protection agency, launched a comprehensive plan for the Lerma-Chapala Basin that lays out short- and long-term goals for natural resource conservation and sustainable development in the region. The program not only targets restoring Lake Chapala to optimum conditions, but also aims to resolve general problems of over-exploitation, waste and contamination of water resources, massive deforestation and soil degradation, taking into account related issues such as poverty and migration in rural communities, population growth in urban areas, industrial development and overall economic growth.

Some key actions are already under way as this book goes to press. With 30 million pesos budgeted for 2004, state and federal agencies have implemented a project to reduce and control the recurrent problem of water hyacinth infestation in Lake Chapala. Additional funding is going into construction and upgrades for sewage treatment facilities serving lake shore communities. A new network of cutting-edge instruments installed along the Lerma River to monitor water and weather conditions will give government, scientists and the general public greater access to critical information. And, after several years of strident negotiations, water users in the five Lerma-Chapala Basin states appear to have finally hammered out terms for a new and more equitable water distribution pact.

In 2002 Lake Chapala was incorporated into the Living Lakes organization, an international network dedicated to preserving lakes and wetlands that operates under the auspices of the Global Nature Fund. Membership should translate into greater worldwide attention on Chapala, corporate funding for specific projects and permanent pressure on Mexican authorities to keep lake conservation high up on the nation's environmental agenda.

Internet resources for more information on Lake Chapala:

www.semarnat.gob.mx
www.livinglakes.org
www.amigosdelago.org
www.mexconnect.com

eral in Guadalajara show more than 40,000 U.S. citizens registered as residents of its consular district that includes the states of Jalisco, Colima and Nayarit. Unofficial estimates put the number of U.S. citizens residing full- or part-time in the Lake Chapala area at about 6,000 and an equivalent figure for Canadian citizens. The numbers peak during the December-April high season when thousands of "snowbirds" migrate from points north to enjoy the area's temperate climate. The foreign population, including natives of Great Britain, a variety of European nations and Japan, has been increasing steadily over the past decade.

TIME ZONE

Central Standard Time

Guadalajara and the Lakeside area observe Daylight Savings Time, on the same schedule as the U.S. and Canada.

ELECTRICITY

Current in Mexico is 110 volts, 60 cycles, the same as in the United States and Canada. The same flat-prong plugs and sockets are used, though grounded 3-prong plugs and sockets are less common and, in many cases, must be installed.

Dale Hoyt Palfrey

The Alcantar Family & Friends *salute the Traditional Posada Ajijic anniversary.*

Dale Hoyt Palfrey

The words "Generation Gap" *have little meaning in Mexico. Grandparents mingle with young marrieds, teens play with toddlers, and everyone indulges children.*

Dale Hoyt Palfrey

2

How to Be a Good Visitor to the Area

with CAROL WHEELER ESPARZA,
GERRY MUGFORD FOWLER

Cultural Etiquette

by CAROL WHEELER ESPARZA

Latin American culture is different from our Anglo Saxon tradition. The Spanish adventurers who founded Mexico City in 1520 did so on the site of an already flourishing Mexico city—then called Tenochtitlán—which astonished the conquistadors with its wide avenues and magnificent monuments. While English settlers in the U.S. largely killed off the Indian population or segregated them on reservations, the conquering Spaniards intermarried with indigenous peoples of Mexico to form a unique *mestizo* population whose customs meld both traditions.

While you may not share Mexican values and customs, a good guest should be aware of them. Don't be daunted. It can take years in any environment to become aware of the subtleties that govern our behavior.

NETWORKING

Mexican culture is founded on church and family. Large, extended families are the norm. Although this is gradually changing, traditionally it has not been unusual for a couple to marry and have eight, ten or even more children. Every generation brings numerous aunts, uncles, cousins, second cousins, nieces, nephews, etc., to the family. A great many of these remain near their places of birth throughout their lives, thus forming a natural network of individuals who help each other in all manner of business, social, personal and political situations.

In addition to the incorporation of in-laws and all their relatives whenever a marriage takes place, the family is extended even further through voluntarily acquired relationships such as *compadres*, *padrinos* and *ahijados*. No matter what need may arise, one will probably already have someone in the family to call upon, or a friend or acquaintance

***A Mexican bride** often has multiple* padrinos *who bear the costs for the wedding dress, the invitations, the reception, flowers, etc.*

who is willing to help out and thus become one more extension of the family.

COMPADRES

The Catholic faith provides the backdrop for most of the rites of passage in a person's life—christening, First Communion, marriage—and all these call for godparents. Parents and godparents (or *padrinos)* become *compadres*—literally "co-parents." Christening godparents take on the responsibility of raising the godchild *(ahijado)* if orphaned. But daily life in Mexico is marked by many more milestones which require *padrinos* of varying importance.

When a newborn leaves the home for the first time, it is taken to the church and presented to the Virgin Mary; this requires *padrinos.* A girl's 15th birthday signifies her coming of age. A special Mass is offered to give thanks, and she is presented to society as a *señorita* in a gala party called a *quinceañera;* this, too, requires godparents. A family moves to a new home or opens a new business, the priest comes with holy water to bless it, and there must be *padrinos.* Graduation from college, high school, junior high and even primary school also calls for a special Mass, as well as a pair of very influential godparents—politicians perhaps—for the entire graduating class.

In every case, the *padrinos*' role is an important one. They are always older, more successful, wealthier, more powerful. They occupy a place of honor and help defray costs of the event. They also acquire lifelong obligations. You may, at some time, be invited to act as godparents. Do not take it lightly.

Y'ALL COME

Mexicans are rarely segregated by age. Grandparents mingle with young marrieds, teens play with toddlers, and everyone indulges children. While an occasional invitation may specify "no children," this is the exception, not the rule. Except for the most formal gatherings, RSVP is not accorded great importance. It is usually wisest to accept an invitation when offered, even when you know in advance you may not attend. Better to have something "come up" that prevents your going than to offend your host with a flat refusal.

When you are the host, be prepared to throw on a few extra plates. I have often invited two or four people to a sit-down dinner and had them arrive with an extra cousin and his wife, mother or grandmother, perhaps some nephews staying over for the weekend, or simply a friend or two my guests thought I'd enjoy meeting. How to handle it? Accept it graciously. There's a saying in Spanish—"add some more water to the beans"—and quickly set up a buffet instead. More can be merrier. (Of course it helps to cook extra just in case.)

SHARE AND SHARE ALIKE

Another area where inclusiveness can be surprising is at restaurants. When dining with a group, it is very rare to be presented with separate checks (although some Lakeside eateries have developed the cultural sensitivity to ask). Usually the bill is divided equally among diners, no matter who ordered what, and each pays without quibbling.

If a Mexican friend invites you to dine, he expects to pay. In fact, it is considered an honor to pay the bill for the entire group, and occasionally two or more would-be hosts will vie for the privilege of picking up the tab. (This clearly demonstrates his purchasing power and will eventually bring favors in return.) Should you find yourself dining in a group, you'll save face by paying an equal share. Over time, among friends, it all usually evens out; however, if it matters to you, be sure to insist on a separate check beforehand.

SOCIAL SKILLS

Many Mexicans find North Americans, foreigners and other strangers fascinating, so don't be surprised—or unnerved—if you notice the Mexicans (especially saucer-eyed children) staring at you. What might be considered rude north of the border is merely an acceptable display of curiosity south of it.

Meeting and greeting rituals between close friends or family members are a delight. When greeting someone in passing, making eye contact and smiling are not enough. You need to say "hello," or "good day." Better yet, pause and shake hands the Mexican way. We usually greet one another and say goodbye to each other with a kiss on the cheek. It is a very ritualized kiss, and I still don't get it right all the time. Women exchange it with women and men.

It works this way. We shake hands. Then, while our hands are still clasped,

I extend my right cheek to you, and you place your right cheek against mine. Then we both go "kiss" in the air, somewhere vaguely in the area of our ears, but without touching lip to anything. Men do not exchange a kiss on the cheek with other men, not even with brothers or father or sons. They have a special kind of embrace instead. First they shake hands. Then they place their hands on the shoulder blades of the person and pat one another's back three times. Only three, neither more nor less (under extremely fraternal circumstances, like Christmas, this may be six times, in sets of three). Our right arm is above the other's left arm. Then we shake hands once again, while looking into each other's eyes and smiling warmly.

PERSONAL SPACE

After the greetings are over, Mexicans remain up-close. While the average North American needs an arm's length between himself and others to feel comfortable, personal space in Mexico is about half that. (Nomadic Arabs, an anthropology professor assures us, get much closer, close enough to breathe on one another. But that would be too close in Mexico.)

When standing in line at the bank or supermarket, stand close to the person ahead of you. If you don't, someone could assume you are not in line at all and slip in before you. It has happened more than once. The up-close personal space rule also applies when driving. Do drive defensively, but don't be surprised if someone cuts you off; it appears like there is plenty of room.

MAN-WOMAN: DEFINING LIMITS

Though ages mingle, sexes do not. Although restrictions are looser than they once were, many young people still date with chaperones, and a serious relationship, called a *noviazgo*, leads to marriage. American women are often considered easy marks for Don Juans. Many Mexicans' conceptions of Americans come from movies. Looking a man in the eye and smiling can be taken as an invitation. A rule of thumb that works well for me is this: always address persons of the opposite sex as "*Usted*," the formal form of address. It sets very clear limits to the degree of familiarity permitted.

DRESS FOR RESPECT

A Mexican friend once stated, "Mexicans dress better than gringos." Indeed! But if you take socioeconomic levels into consideration, it is probably true. You will rarely—if ever—see mature Mexicans in shorts and sloppy T-shirts or halter tops or bra-less. If you want to be respected, dress decently, whatever the occasion.

WHAT YOU SEE ISN'T WHAT YOU GET

In the "Labyrinth of Solitude," Octavio Paz described his people as "inward." Here, houses offer an austere facade to the street; the beautiful things, the personal treasures, the gardens, are all inside. Similarly, the Mexican attempts to present a seamless, socially-correct appearance at all times. No matter what he may be feeling, he will strive to maintain his composure. You will find him unfailingly polite.

The *gringo*—so outward, his feelings manifest on the surface—is disconcerting, especially when rude or angry or too forthright. Losing your temper is never a good idea. You will get much farther with good manners. In fact, a saying in Spanish admonishes "he who gets angry loses." Remember, you are guests here. When in Rome, do as the Romans, and when in doubt, take the high road.

Spanish Language Primer

by GERRY MUGFORD FOWLER

Language and culture are inseparable, thus the difference between Spanish and English is not merely a matter of different words. Comprehending Spanish helps us understand what makes our Mexican neighbors tick.

Foreign visitors will find it rewarding to explore, understand and accept Mexico's differing concepts of such things as time, etiquette, family structure, etc.—at least *during* your travels into Mexico. Learning the language is a good way to begin understanding their values, appreciating different ways of thinking, and helping to rectify unrealistic stereotypes.

Whether you want to become a proficient Spanish-speaker or just get by on survival Spanish, it is important to master the language to some extent. This "Spanish Language Primer" offers both a guide to survival Spanish and insights into different aspects of the Mexican culture. This objective includes surveying the language aspects of greetings, travel, hotel accommo-

Sounds

a (ah)	as in *cha-cha*
e (eh)	as in *bet*
i (ee)	as in *beep*
o (oh)	as in *ocean*
u (ooh)	as in *boom.*
h (silent)	
j (h)	as in *hello*
ll (y)	as in *yes*
ñ (ny)	as in *canyon*
qu (k)	as in *king*
v (b)	*as in back*
z (s)	as in *salt*

dation, restaurants and shopping.

A large number of instructive books, tapes and even videos are available at bookstores for those who wish to use them in learning Spanish. When purchasing one, try to avoid versions geared toward *Castillian* Spanish, which is spoken in *Spain,* rather than that spoken in Mexico. As in all countries, colloquialisms and commonly-used terms vary from region to region. For that reason—if none other—listening carefully to those who are fluent in a language is still the best teacher.

THE BASICS

One of the most common reasons Mexicans fail to understand one's early efforts at speaking Spanish is pronunciation. Begin by learning the five primary sounds: ***a*** (ah), ***e*** (eh), ***i*** (ee), ***o*** (oh), ***u*** (ooh); then seven others that are a bit different from English: ***h*** (silent), ***j*** (h), ***ll*** (y), ***ñ*** (ny), ***qu*** (k), ***v*** (b), and ***z*** (s).

Try reading some Spanish text aloud and you'll have the hang of it in no time. Listen carefully to how your Mexican acquaintances speak, and try to mimic their pronunciation. It is helpful to remember that there are *no exceptions* to the Spanish rules of pronunciation, unlike English. *Poco a poco* (little by little), listening and practicing will pay off.

Beware of simply nodding in agreement or saying *"Sí"* when you don't understand what someone just said. Since you don't know what you may be agreeing to, it may be preferable to simply admit, *"No entiendo"* (I don't understand). If someone is speaking too rapidly, respond with, *"Más despacio, por favor"* (Slower, please).

USING COGNATES

Spanish is full of words called cognates that look or sound the same (or almost the same) as those in English. Learning these words can make communicating in Spanish easier. For example, hot dog is still *hot dog, taxi* is *taxi,* and sofa is *sofa.* Hotels are full of cognates, starting off with the word *el hotel* and including *la recepción* (reception), *el lobby, el bar, el bellboy,* and *el*

Examples of Cognates

el album	*el lobby*
el bar	*el mínimo*
la cámara	*el patio*
el cassette	*la pizza*
el closet	*la recepción*
el costo	*el shampoo*
el club	*el sofá*
la diferencia	*el show*
el depósito	*la tableta*
la foto	*el total*
el hotel	*el VCR*

restaurante.

The names of people, cities, companies and brand names also are usually the same in both English and Spanish. For example, Kleenex is *Kleenex,* Ford is *Ford,* and Coke is *Coca.* Simply apply the Spanish rules of pronunciation.

GREETINGS & FAREWELLS

The commonplace Spanish-language greeting *"hola"* is very close to the English-language "hello" or "hi." For good-bye, you can say *"adiós."* So does that deal with greetings and farewells in Spanish? Well hold your *caballos* (horses); it's not quite as simple as that!

Adiós is an especially handy word because it covers many situations and, unlike *"Buenos Días"* (Good morning), *"Buenas tardes"* (Good afternoon/evening) or *"Buenas noches"* (Good night), it does not convey a sense of time. Although *adiós* may mean good-bye, it also is used extensively as a greeting in passing *IF one does not plan on stopping to talk.*

Perhaps one of the important aspects to remember about greetings is signaling the appropriate level of formality or informality. Even as Mexico undergoes rapid social and cultural change, marks of respect are important, as they define and smooth over social relationships.

Spanish often expresses informality through the word *tu* and formality through *usted.* So a formal greeting is *"¿Cómo está usted?"* while an informal greeting is *"¿Cómo estás?"* (The *tu* is not used in this instance. Personal pronouns are not always necessary as the Spanish verb conjugation usually makes the person ob-

Greeting Vocabulary

Hello	***Hola***
Good-bye (or Hello in passing)	***Adiós***
Good morning	***Buenos días***
Good afternoon	***Buenas tardes***
Good night	***Buenas noches***
How are you?	***¿Cómo está?***
How nice to see you!	***¡Gusto en verte!***
Nice to meet you	***¡Mucho gusto!***
Thanks so much	***Muchas gracias.***
You're very kind	***¡Muy amable!***
See you later	***Hasta luego.***
Go well!	***¡Que le vaya bien!***
How's it going?	***¿Que tal?***

vious.) The most common way to say, "Nice to meet you!" is *"¡Mucho gusto!"*

Use formal greetings when talking to strangers, officials or people in authority, and senior citizens. English-language speakers are often seen as being too direct and informal. But be ready for more informal salutations such as, *"¡Qué pasa!" "¡Qué tal!" "¡Qué hay!" "¡Quiúbole!"* and *"¡Qué onda!"*

You may frequently hear the phrase, *"¡Que le vaya bién!"* when leaving a restaurant, exiting a taxi or saying good-bye. Although it doesn't translate well, it is a courteous and commonly used phrase that basically means, "Go well." You can respond with *"¡Muchas gracias!"* (Thank you very much!) or *"¡Muy amable!"* (You're very kind).

Another important aspect about *saludos* (greetings) and *despedidas* (farewells) is that Mexicans give them time and due consideration. Mexicans are often interested in ritual greetings every time they meet—not just a cursory nod or wave of the hand. Men often give each other solid handshakes. Women kiss on the cheeks when they meet. Take the time to engage in greeting rituals; it can help smooth a difficult language encounter.

TRAVEL

Don't expect to have an easy linguistic ride when it comes to using public transportation; some—but certainly not all—taxi drivers or bus drivers speak English. Whenever you are a visitor to another country, the obligation is yours to try to speak *el idioma* (the language). Mexicans tend to admire people with a sincere interest in learning their language and are usually very tolerant of language errors, unlike a greater percentage of English-language speakers.

You will need to acquire basic travel language, including words such as *carro* (car), *avión* (plane), *ferrocarril* (train), *taxi* or *sitio* (taxi) and *camión* (bus). Since attempting to roll those double R's in Spanish—as in *carro* and *ferrocarril*—can tie your tongue in knots, try to use the synonyms: *el coche* and *el tren.*

Buses

Part of the secret of being a successful communicator is anticipating possible language difficulties and taking corrective action in order to get your message across. Meanwhile, the word *camión* can sometimes be confusing, because *camión* can also refer to various types of trucks. To differentiate between the different types of *camiones,* buses are sometimes called *camiones de transporte público.* There are also *los minibuses* (smaller buses), sometimes also called *combis.* In Guadalajara, there are *los camiones de lujo* (luxury buses which have air-conditioning and television).

Travel Vocabulary

airport	***aeropuerto***
airplane	***avión***
ticket	***boleto***
bus or truck	***camión***
car	***carro, coche***
downtown	***El Centro***
train	***ferrocarril, tren***
street corner	***la esquina***
bus stop	***la parada***
fare	***pasaje***
town	***pueblo***
taxi	***taxi, sitio***
taxi driver	***taxista***
trip	***viaje***

Local buses are an extremely attractive means of getting around town, as taxi fares can become quite expensive after awhile. Furthermore, buses are a good way to keep in contact with the people, see a slice of life not found in luxury hotels, and provide a golden opportunity to hear the language close-up.

There are two *terminales de autobuses* (bus stations) in the greater Guadalajara area. The first and oldest terminal, located near *El Centro* (downtown), is commonly referred to as *La Central Vieja.* It offers service between Guadalajara and the surrounding villages, including Ajijic, Chapala and Jocotepec. Buses arrive and leave here every half-hour or so, the last one being at 9:30 p.m. Most buses here are *Segundas* (second-class buses) which stop any time someone wants to get on or off. If you wish to pay a little more, you can request a *boleto* (ticket) on a *Primera* (first-class bus), which goes *directo* (direct) to downtown Chapala, Ajijic and Jocotepec without all the mid-transit stops. Passengers sit in any available seat. Occasionally, when buses are particularly crowded, passengers stand in the aisles until seats become available.

The second and larger terminal, *La Nueva Central Camionera,* is in Tonalá, a suburb on the eastern edge of Guadalajara. At *"La Nueva Central,"* interstate buses arrive from and depart to various destinations throughout *el país* (the country). These cross-country buses are often an easy and inexpensive way to see Mexico. Unlike the buses at *La Central Vieja,* here your bus ticket guarantees your own selected seat. The better *líneas* (bus lines) have videos, snacks, air conditioning and a restroom.

To find a city bus in Guadalajara, you need *una parada* (a bus stop). Sometimes these are marked, or *los camiones* may stop at *la esquina* (a street corner). In more rural areas, buses respond much like a taxi, pulling over anywhere on their route for a passenger who wishes to board or get off.

In Guadalajara, you simply pay a standard fare, no questions asked. At Lakeside, you may need to tell the driver your destination, as *el pasaje* (the fare) sometimes depends on the distance traveled. Secondly, you may have a choice between shuttles and *camiones*. Shuttles may meander through residential areas, providing a pleasant and free sightseeing trip within *el pueblo (the town),* while buses may take a more direct route.

Hotel Vocabulary

swimming pool	***alberca***
remote control	***control***
room	***cuarto***
deposit	***depósito***
cash	***efectivo***
luggage	***equipaje***
room	***habitación***
check-out time	***hora de salida***
the bill	***la cuenta***
key	***llave***
luggage	***maleta(s)***
a tip	***propina***
service	***servicio***
credit card	***tarjeta de crédito***

When you have paid, you should be given *un boleto* (a ticket). Make sure you hold onto it for the duration of your ride, as sometimes mid-route inspections take place. Hold onto your valuables as well; as in every country, there may be pickpockets around. (For more information, see Chapter 13: Getting Around.)

Trains

Although many of their passenger routes have recently been discontinued, trains can also be another tourist attraction, especially the Tequila Train that takes enthusiasts from Guadalajara to the nearby town of Tequila, and offers traditional Mexican fare along with *mariachi* music during *el viaje* (the journey). Another international favorite is the train through the spectacular Copper Canyon in northern Mexico.

Taxis

You can hail *un taxi* on the street or phone *un sitio* (taxi stand). When the taxi arrives, you need to be able to respond to the question, *"¿A dónde va?"* (Where are you going?). Always agree on *el pasaje* (the fare) before you start your journey: *"¿Cuánto va a cobrar?"* (How much are you going to charge?). This can be a difficult bargaining process. Try to find out well in advance what an acceptable fare would be, perhaps by asking your hotel receptionist.

On the bright side, there is a good chance that *el taxista* (the taxi driver) does know some English. It is not uncommon for *taxistas* to have worked and saved money in the U.S. to come back and start their own *negocios* (businesses) in Mexico. Mexicans are generally an enterprising people with deep family ties. Many have *el sueño* (the dream) of returning to their family roots and starting their own businesses.

HOTEL ACCOMMODATIONS

Hotels *usually* have English-speaking staff, but don't count on it. Linguistic savvy is important. It may be helpful—whenever available—to refer to the different categories of hotels through their "star rating" which go from *una estrella* (one) to *cinco estrellas* (five stars). Top luxury hotels are known as *hoteles de gran turismo* with prices to match. The higher the star rating, the more likely the hotel is to have bilingual individuals on their staff.

Registering is usually a simple business—paying depends on your personal finances. A room is *un cuarto* or *una habitación* as in *"¿Tiene un cuarto?"* (Do you have a room?). You will need to decide whether you need *una habitación individual* (a single room) or *una habitación doble* (a double room). You may be asked to sign *un voucher en blanco* (a blank credit card voucher) to open your hotel account. If you object to this procedure, you may be asked to leave a cash deposit. You will be given *la llave del cuarto* (the room key) and perhaps *un control* (a TV remote) and may be asked if you have any luggage *"¿Tiene equipaje?"*

El bellboy, or *el botones* will take you to your room. Tipping is a strong and continuing custom in Mexico and it is appreciated rather than expected, so don't forget *la propina* (the tip). Notice that the spoken word "tip" is usually only used to mean 'a piece of advice.' Check-out time is *la hora de salida* and you need to ask for *la cuenta* (the bill). When it comes to paying, you can usually pay by *tarjeta de crédito* (credit card)

MEXICAN MANNERS

Be careful not to try to buy goodwill with tips that are inappropriate or other gifts of money or goods that only emphasize your economic status. Instead, learn and consistently give the gift of courtesy. Take the time to learn Mexican manners. It will allow you to assimilate into Mexican society, be it village or city, faster than anything else will.

or *en efectivo* (cash).

RESTAURANTS

Fruta *(fruit) and* burrito *are* cognates, *Spanish words that look or sound the same (or almost the same) as those used by English-speakers.*

You have probably been given enough warnings about the spiciness of *la comida mexicana* (Mexican food) and what it can do to your stomach. But remember that people the world over suffer digestive upsets when they travel. It takes time to get used to another country's food or water. If you eat sensibly, that is, eat spicy foods in moderation, patronize reputable restaurants and avoid street food vendors, you can usually avoid the worst of problems. If in doubt about the water, ask for *una botella de agua* (a bottle of water). Then hold onto your *sombrero* (hat) as you enjoy a taste-exploding culinary ride.

The main meals of the day are divided into *el desayuno* (breakfast), *la comida* (main meal) and *la cena* (supper). Mexico is a rapidly changing country—both economically and socially—so stories about two-hour meals followed by *la siesta* (the afternoon nap) do not always reflect the economic reality of a hard-working country where the work day can start at 7 a.m. and finish twelve hours later.

Pollo con arroz *(chicken with rice) and* camarones *(shrimp) are typical favorites in Mexico.*

When eating out, remember that Mexicans often eat at different times than Americans or Canadians. For instance, *la comida* is usually served after 2 p.m. Be prepared for crowded restaurants during important celebrations such as *el Día de los Madres* (Mother's Day), May 10th, when *la comida* honors mothers, or *el Día del Amor y la Amistad*, February 14th, which celebrates both *los novios* (sweethearts) and *la amistad* (friendship).

To order food, you need *una carta* or *un menú* (a menu). Attracting a waiter's attention can be difficult. Snapping *los dedos* (the fingers) is a big mistake—Mexicans make a sucking sound with the lips. Foreigners are advised to catch a waiter's attention by signaling or through eye contact. The waiter will approach and usually ask, *"¿Gustan algo para tomar?"* (Would you like something to drink?) *La carta* can be divided up into *antojitos* (appetizers), *el plato fuerte* (main meal) and *el postre* (dessert). Unadventurous diners can look for the cognates: sirloin, T-bone, *hamburguesa*, hot dogs and pizza. This is not to say that there isn't first-class international *comida* in the area; there is, but do also try traditional Mexican food.

Restaurant Vocabulary

appetizers	***antojitos***
purified water	***agua purificada***
beverages	***bebidas***
snacks	***botanas***
a menu	***una carta***
beef	***carne de res***
pork	***cerdo (or puerco)***
supper	***cena***
lunch or food	***comida***
the bill/check	***la cuenta***
cutlery	***cubiertos***
breakfast	***desayuno***
chicken	***pollo***
dessert	***postre***
afternoon nap	***siesta***
vegetables	***verduras***

Traditional breakfasts are often quite heavy on the stomach and include such delights as *chilaquiles* (a fried *tortilla*-and-tomato dish), *menudo* (tripe), *gorditas* ("little fat ones" made of *masa,* cornmeal-flour, filled with meat, potato, etc.) and *huevos rancheros* (fried eggs with a *chile* sauce). For a light breakfast, dive into the rich selection of *frutas* (fruit) that Mexico offers ranging from *la papaya* and *la sandía* (watermelon) to the more exotic kiwi.

For the main meal, there are enticing offerings from all the different regions of Mexico. Jalisco is renown for *pozole* (hominy and pork stew) and *birria* (goat-meat stew). It's probably best to avoid another Jalisco favorite: *las tortas ahogadas* (a meat-filled bread roll dipped in a red-hot burning *chile* sauce). Take a gastronomic stroll around Mexico and try *cochinita pibil* (pork) from Yucatán, *mole poblano* (chicken in a dark chocolate-*chile* sauce) from Puebla *or huachinango a la Veracruzana* (red snapper from Veracruz).

At the same time, don't forget the simple and tasty offerings such as the traditional *sopas secas* (literally 'dry soups'), *guacamole,* and an array of appetizers including *queso fundido* (melted cheese). If there is any room left, there is always *el postre,* with standard favorites such as

Shopping Vocabulary

Store that sells milk, cheese and eggs	***cremería***
bakery	***panadería***
bookstore	***librería***
butcher's shop	***carnicería***
cake bakery	***pastelería***
candy store	***dulcería***
hardware store	***ferretería***
office/school supply	***papelería***
pharmacy	***farmacia***
service station	***gasolinera***
street market, usually held once weekly	***tianguis***
supermarket	***supermercado***

bag	***bolsa***
box/small box/cash register	***caja/cajita***
can	***lata***
expensive	***caro***
groceries	***abarrotes***
inexpensive	***barato***
size	***tamaño***

At your service (or, May I help you?)	***A sus órdenes.***
Do you have change?	***¿Tiene cambio?***
Excuse me, when getting someone's attention	***¡Disculpe!***
How much does it cost?	***¿Cuanto cuesta?***
I'm just looking.	***Estoy viendo.***
I don't have change.	***No hay cambio.***
I don't understand.	***No entiendo.***
"With your permission," used when maneuvering through a crowd.	***¡Con permiso!***

chongos, cajeta de membrillo, flan and *jericalla.*

Supper often consists of *masa*-based dishes including *tacos, flautas* (flutes), *quesadillas* (cheese-filled tortillas), and *sincronizadas* (cheese-

and ham-filled tortillas). If someone orders *una gringa*, they are asking for a cheese-meat-and-*tortilla* dish and not an American or Canadian woman, and *un sope* doesn't mean soup but a thick *tortilla* with a rich dressing of *frijoles* (beans) and other ingredients. *Pozole* is also eaten at night.

When it comes to eating habits and customs, there are notable differences between Mexico and north of the border. Mexicans have no qualms about eating with their hands. Obviously *cubiertos* (cutlery) are used in more formal situations, but *tortillas* and *tostadas* (crispy fried tortillas) are more practical and can save on the washing up. *Chile, sal* (salt) and *limón* (lime) are popular condiments for everything from soup to fruit. If you are invited *a comer* (to eat), this means at midday or, most likely around 2 p.m. *A cenar* means at night.

When it comes to drinks, you need to separate the alcoholic from the non-alcoholic. Many Mexicans drink *aguas frescas* (fruit-flavored waters) during *la comida*. In restaurants you can order it by the glass or by *la jarra* (the pitcher). Popular flavors include: *fresa* (strawberry), *melón* (melon), *sandía* (watermelon) and *jamaica* (blossoms from a particular hibiscus bush). There is also *agua de horchata* (a rice-based drink). On the warm drink front, especially at night, there is *atole* (a corn-based drink), chocolate and *café* (coffee). Black coffee is often called *café americano* and *café de olla* is a rich sweetened coffee with cinnamon sticks from *la olla* (pot).

On the alcoholic front, there is obviously *tequila* which is served straight or in a variety of forms such as with a *sangrita* chaser (a spicy *tomato*-based non-alcoholic drink), and Squirt (*tequila* with salt, lime, and a grapefruit-based soft drink). Other popular drinks range from *sangría* (a wine-based refreshment) and brandy to *cerveza* (beer) and a host of prepared drinks.

At some point during your visit to the restaurant, you may wish to use their bathroom facilities. To be directed to the restroom, simply ask, *¿Dónde está el baño?* (Where is the bathroom?) or *¿Puedo usar el baño, por favor?* (May I use the bathroom, please?).

SHOPPING

Ir de compras (to go shopping) in Mexico is an engaging experience from *la tienda de abarrotes* (the corner store) and *el tianguis* (the street market) to the traditional arts and crafts *mercados* (markets) and *ferias* (fairs). From *equipales* (leather chairs) and wide-brimmed *sombreros* to *huaraches* and *sarapes*, street markets are brimming with bargains and a sense of history. While it is a common practice to haggle over prices, bargaining is a subtle practice and can easily lead to offense if the price being offered is too low.

With the spread of *super-mercados*, shopping language need not be extensive but *la tienda de abarrotes* (the corner store) is still very strong in Mexico, so you will need to build up a basic list of grocery vocabulary. Shoppers typically ask basic questions such *as, "¿Cuánto cuesta?"* (How much does it cost?) and *"¡Disculpe! ¿Puede ayudarme?"* (Excuse me! Can you help me?). You might also hear or need the phrase: *"¿Tiene cambio?"* (Do you have any change?).

You do have one advantage on your side: cognates. Remember, cognates are words that are similar or nearly similar in both languages. On the food side there is *la fruta* (fruit), *el té* (tea), *la crema* (cream), *la sardina* (sardine), *el salmón* (salmon), *el vinagre* (vinegar), *la pasta* (pasta) and *la pera* (pear). You also need to be careful about not mixing up some Spanish words. For instance, *el jamón* (ham) is not to be confused with *el jabón* (soap). However, watch out for the false cognates (words that look similar but are not). Examples are *atún* which is tuna while the Spanish *tuna* is prickly pear and *la sopa* is not soap but soup.

A shop assistant may come up to you and ask, *"¿Le ayudo en algo?"* (Can I help you with something?). Or, they may say, *"A sus órdenes"* (At your service). If you don't want any help a polite answer *is: "No gracias, estoy viendo"* (No, thanks, I'm just looking).

Hopefully, this grammar primer lays the groundwork for surviving in Spanish and illustrates that understanding underlying cultural values is just as important as understanding *el idioma*. Mexico is a very traditional country where *la gente* (people) welcome *visitantes* (visitors),

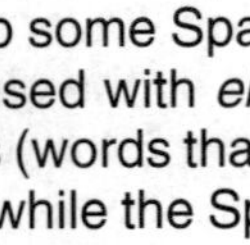

Lana (wool, money) - Typically "Expensive!"

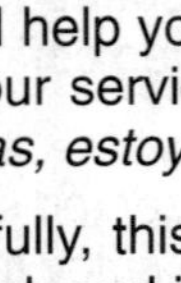

No, ni modo (no, no way) - Discourages pesky peddlers faster than anything else.

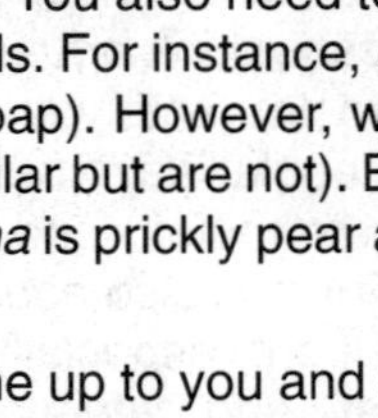

¡Ojo! (Eye!) - The meaning depends on the situation. In reference to another person, "Watch out for him," "Be careful," or "He's sharp!"

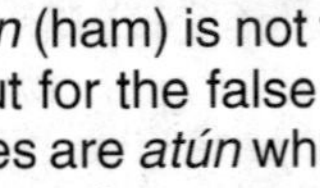

Momentito (a moment) - Be right back, or a little bit.

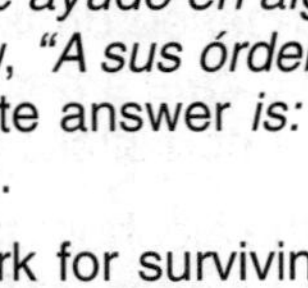

Adelante (ahead) - "Move forward" or "Come here. Can be very confusing to *gringos*.

but they always appreciate respect *(respeto)* and *entendimiento* (understanding).

USING "SIGN LANGUAGE"

Hand signals and body language are often universal, and Mexicans tend to use them liberally. This form of nonverbal communication is an easy, fun and useful way to send messages. With just a little practice, you'll quickly be able to communicate with nonverbals.

A few of the most commonly used hand signals are shown here from *The People's Guide to Mexico,* © 1998 by by Carl Franz and Lorena Havens, published by John Muir Publications, Santa Fe, NM 87504 (www.peoplesguide.com):

Lakeside Spanish Instruction

James Dean 376 766-4070	Beginning and advanced students. Privada Jesus Garcia #11, San Antonio. Tlayacapán. dmdean@mexconnect.com
Noemy Lafitte 376 766-0641	For beginners.
Darrell Schmidt 376 766-5194	Camino Real #47, La Floresta. *Recommended.*
Laura Reyes 376 766-2924	Beginning and advanced students. Individuals and groups. Aprender2004@prodigy.net.mx
Spanish Ajijic 376 766-2287	Survival Spanish, beginner, intermediate and advanced courses; conversation, reading and writing. Zaragoza #80, Ajijic. spanishajijic@yahoo.com.mx; www.geocities/com/spanishajijic/spanishajijic.html
Spanish Superlearning Ajijic 376 766-4869	Accelerated learning for all levels with Dr. Barbara Lotito. Call for schedules. spanishsuperlearning@yahoo.com

Spanish at the Lake Chapala Society. Look for listings on their bulletin boards at 16 de Septiembre #16-A in Ajijic or in local newspapers.

Guadalajara Spanish Instruction

Berlitz 01 33 3630-3987 01 33 3641-2074	Total immersion courses and weekly instruction. Two locations in Guadalajara: Ave. Vallarta and Ave. Providencia. www.berlitz.com
Instituto Cultural Mexicano Norte-american de Jalisco, A.C. 01 33 3825-5838 01 33 3825-5666 01 33 3825-4101	The only institution recognized by the US government in Guadalajara, this 55 year-old binational cultural center offers year-round programs for all levels. Enrique Diaz de Leon Sur # 300, Col. Moderna, Guadalajara. cultural@guadalajara.net; www.guadalajara .net/~cultural
Worldwide Teachers Institute of Guada-lajara,C.T.E.F.L. 01 33 3613-5226 01 33 3614-4883	Certificates in teaching English as a Foreign Language. The Boston TEFL Certificate Method three-week immersion course of 150 hours, offered monthly in Guadalajara. The school features full- and part-time certification courses, a limited enrollment, guidance for placement throughout the world, supervised teacher training, *posada* accommodations, and scholarships for Mexican citizens and FM3 visa holders. Madero 616, Zona Centro, Guadalajara.

Internet Spanish Instruction

Foreign Languages for Travelers	www.travlang.com/languages/ is an Internet site that can provide you with traveler's Spanish.

From cozy B&Bs *to established hotels, the visitor has many options on the Northshore of Lake Chapala.*

3

Accommodations, Rentals and Real Estate

with ZOFIA BARISAS

Accommodations

Visitors will find every kind of accommodation on the Northshore, from large hotels offering many amenities to cozy B&Bs suitable for the more independent traveler.

Your credit card might hold your reservation but may not be accepted for your stay, especially in smaller establishments. Almost exclusively, the Lakeside area is a cash society. Be sure to ask if you must pay in cash or if a personal check would be accepted. Travelers checks might be welcome but a passport is required to cash them. The best strategy is to bring along your ATM card and withdraw cash from your home account using your PIN number. The ATM machine will dispense *pesos.* Be aware that a 15% sales tax (called IVA) and a 2% hospitality tax will be added to your bill unless the rate clearly states that the tax has been included.

Inquire about the location of your hotel or B&B. Is it within walking distance of the village plaza, shops, currency exchange houses, and restaurants? If not, ask if the staff can help you arrange taxis, especially for your return trip to the airport. If it is important for your comfort, check the availability of cable or satellite television, whether the water is purified in the taps or bottled, and whether secured parking is available. You'll want a fan in your room during the warm months of April, May and June, as air conditioning and central heating are rarely used in this part of Mexico. Mexican beds typically do not have box springs. A mattress is placed either on a concrete slab or wooden platform. If you're a light sleeper, be sure to pack earplugs. Village life can be noisy in the early morning and sometimes late at night. I recommend Mack's Wax® earplugs. They can save your vacation.

Hotel Casa Grande
In Mexico:
01 800 361-0300
Local:
01 33 3678-9000
Internationally:
01 888 306-2487

Guadalajara Airport/Hidalgo International. $90 US and up. 189 rooms/suites. Non-smoking and deluxe rooms Amenities: satellite TV, spa and fitness gym, meeting rooms, computer rooms, bilingual staff. Can make reservations online.
cchica@mail.udg.mx;
www.casagrande.com.mx

AJIJIC HOTELS & B&Bs

Birds of Paradise
01152 376 766-1308

Libramiento #100, Ajijic. $175 to $380 US weekly for one and two bedroom condos with kitchen and TV; some with telephones. Amenities: pool, jacuzzi, clubhouse, gym, secured parking, convenience store, and guest laundry. Ask about discounts. English spoken. Visa, MasterCard, and American Express credit cards accepted for online reservations. Check for rental availability on their website.
www.birdsofparadisecondos.com

Casablanca Hotel
01152 376 766-4440

16 de Septiembre #29, Ajijic. $55 to $67 US, includes tax and breakfast. 8 rooms, some with fully-stocked kitchenettes. Amenities: free high-speed Internet service, wheelchair access, cable TV, and laundry service. Secure parking can be arranged. Near the Lake Chapala Society, the plaza, restaurants, banking, shopping, galleries, bus and taxi service, and the outdoor market. English spoken.
hotelcasablancaajijic@hotmail.com;
www.casablancaajijic.com

Casa Flores B&B
01152 376 766-1164

Zaragoza #38, Ajijic. $45 to $60 US, includes tax and breakfast. 5 rooms with cable TV, box springs, patios or terraces. Amenities: guest refrigerator, lap pool, secure parking, and mountain views. 3 blocks from the plaza, restaurants, banking, shopping, galleries, bus and taxi service. Airport pickup by prior arrangement. English spoken. innkeeper@casafloresmexico.com;

www.casafloresmexico.com

Casamalcolm B&B
01152 376 766-3570

Donato Guerra #15, Ajijic. $75 US, 2-night minimum. Includes tax and breakfast. Monthly discounts. 3 rooms with queen-sized or twin beds. Amenities include purified water, extra-large closets, chaise lounges for sunbathing, kimonos, fine beds and linens and complimentary glass of wine. Each room has a balcony or patio. Within walking distance of the plaza, restaurants, banking, shopping, galleries, bus and taxi service, the outdoor market.English spoken. Casamalcolm@yahoo.com

Casa Tres Leones
01152 376 766-0361

Emiliano Zapata #10, Ajijic. $60 to $80 US, includes tax and breakfast. 8 suites and 3 efficiency apartments with purified drinking water in taps, private terraces and patios, heated towel racks. Amenities: pool, Internet access, secure parking; ask about pets and children. Close to public transportation and within walking distance of Ajijic. Long-term rentals available. English spoken. treslyones@laguna.com.mx; www.mexconnect.com/amex/ctl/index.html

Danza del Sol
01152 376 766-0640
fax 376 766-0220

Zaragoza #165, Ajijic. 650 *pesos* for doubles, 1000 to 1400 *pesos,* up to 6 guests (includes tax). 45 rooms with full kitchen and patio, cable TV. Amenities: pool, tennis courts, gym and spa. Within walking distance of restaurants and bus service. Some English spoken. www.realdechapala.com

Hotel Ajijic Plaza Suites
01152 376 766-0383

Colón #33, Ajijic. $50 US, includes tax. 10 suites with king or twin beds. Amenities: Escencias Spa, restaurant, pool, boutique, video library, secure valet parking and handicapped accessibility. Located across from the plaza, near banking, shopping, restaurants, bus and taxi service, and cybercafes. Pets accepted. Weekly rates available. Can be noisy during November

festivals. English spoken.
ajijichotel@yahoo.com; www.ajijichotel.com

Hotel La Estancia
01152 376 766-0717

Morelos #13, Ajijic. 500 *pesos*, includes tax and breakfast. 8 rooms with king or twin beds, cable TV. Amenities: restaurant. Located on Ajijic's main street, a block and a half from the pier, near banking, shopping, galleries, bus and taxi service. Small pets okay. hotelestanciaajijic@hotmail.com

Hotel Mis Amores
01152 376 766-4640
01152 376 766-4641
01152 376 766-4642

Hidalgo #22, Ajijic. 600 *pesos* singles, 700 *pesos* doubles + tax. Breakfast included. 12 rooms with cable TV, minibar, coffeemaker,and fan. Located 1 block from the plaza, restaurants, banking, shopping, galleries, bus and taxi service. Some English spoken.
hotelmisamores@yahoo.com

Italo Hotel
01152 376 766-2221
fax 376 766-4273

Guadalupe Victoria #10, Ajijic. 248 to 329 *pesos* + tax for singles, and up. 22 rooms, some with jacuzzi. Basic hotel with restaurant, bar, pool, and meeting facilities. Located near the plaza, cybercafes, banking, bus and taxi service and shopping. Weekly rates available. Can be noisy. Some English spoken.

La Nueva Posada
01152 376 766-1344
01152 376 766-1444

Donato Guerra #9, Ajijic. $65 US + tax, breakfast included. 16 rooms with cable TV, Internet access, long distance phone lines. One and two bedroom garden villas available for daily, monthly rates. Amenities: La Rusa restaurant, bar, meeting facilities, pool, book kiosk, secure parking, wheelchair accessibility. Within walking distance of the plaza, restaurants, banking, shopping, galleries, bus and taxi service, the outdoor market. English spoken.
nuevaposada@laguna.com.mx;
www.mexconnect.com/amex/np/

La Paloma B&B
01152 376 766-4140
Tollfree from US & Canada
1 877 237-1980

Juan Alvarez #56, Ajijic. $41 US and up, includes tax and gourmet breakfast. 7 rooms; single, queen, and king-sized beds. Some with TV. Amenities include a heated pool, guest kitchen, full-time coffee and tea bar, luxurious towels, robes, and down comforters, book and video libraries. Within walking distance of the plaza, restaurants, banking, shopping, galleries, bus and taxi service, the outdoor market. Airport pickup and delivery. www.lapalomabb.com

Las Casitas
01152 376 766-1145

Carretera Pte. #20, Ajijic. 395 *pesos* for doubles, includes tax. 11 rooms. Amenities: pool, secure parking. Within walking distance of shopping, restaurants, the plaza. Weekly discounts available. English spoken.

Los Artistas B&B
01152 376 766-1027
fax 376 766-1762

Constitución #105, Ajijic. 600 to 900 *pesos*, includes tax and breakfast. 7 rooms. Amenities: pool, gardens, secure parking, with telephone and guest refrigerator in common area. Located 6 blocks from the plaza and within walking distance of restaurants, shopping, galleries, cybercafes, horseback riding, banking, bus and taxi service. Discounts available. English spoken.
www.losartistas.com;
losartistas@laguna.com.mx

Posada Las Calandrias
01152 376 766-1052

Carretera Pte. #8, Ajijic. 290 *pesos* for 1 bedroom bungalow with double bed and kitchenette; 550 *pesos* for 2 bedroom unit with kitchenette, + tax. Amenities: pool and secure parking. Some English spoken. Visa, Mastercard accepted.

Real de Chapala
01152 376 766-0014
01152 376 766-0021

Paseo del Prado #29, Ajijic. 1295 to 1395 *pesos*, suites 2000 *pesos* + tax. 79 rooms. Amenities: restaurant, bar, pool, boutique, billiards, tennis courts, meeting facilities for 30, 60 and for groups up to 500. Close to horseback riding. Some English spoken. www.realdechapala.com

Swan Inn
01152 376 766-2354
01152 376 766-0917

16 de Septiembre #18, Ajijic. $55 to $75 US + tax. Breakfast included. 6 rooms, 2 *casitas;* with fans, electric blankets. Amenities include pool, guest lounge, and cooking kitchenette. Located near the Lake Chapala Society, shopping, galleries, banking, the plaza, taxi and bus service. Discounts available. English spoken.
swaninnajijic@hotmail.com;
www.swaninnajijic.com

Villa del Angel
01152 376 766 0783

Juárez Privada #3, Las Salvias, Ajijic.$75 US and up includes tax. Suites with king or queen-sized beds in exceptional European-style boutique hotel. Amenities: pool, outdoor kitchen for guests, extensive gardens, views and private chapel for events. Good parking. Within walking distance of restaurants, shopping, bus service. Visa, Mastercard, and American Express accepted. www.villadelangel.com.

Villas Ajijic
01152 376 766-0983

Linda Vista #14, Ajijic. 500 to 600 *pesos* for single or doubles, 850 to 1400 for suites, includes tax. 10 rooms, with ceiling fans, cable TV, full-sized bathrooms. Amenities: pool, volleyball, trampolines, activities for children. Within walking distance of restaurants, shopping, bus service.

Villas Eucaliptos
01152 376 766-1400
fax 376 766-2821

16 de Septiembre #127, Ajijic. $50 to $60 US includes tax. Breakfast included. Five rooms, with TV, refrigerators, electric kettles, microwaves. Amenities include offstreet parking and pool. Close to restaurants, cinema, shopping, galleries, cybercafes and horseback riding, and within walking distance of banking, the plaza, taxi and bus service. Discounts available. English spoken. mrram@laguna.com.mx; www.villaeucaliptos.com

Villas del Sol
01152 376 766-1152

Carretera Ajijic-Jocotepec #119, Ajijic. $45 US daily, $250 weekly, $610 monthly for fully-equipped, one bedroom condos with full kitchens, dining/living rooms, TV. Two bedroom condos $700 US includes tax. Amenities include secure parking, pool. Near bus route and restaurants. axixic@infosel.net.mx; www.chapala.com (look under income properties "Villas del Sol")

CHAPALA HOTELS AND B&Bs

Brisas de Chapala
01152 376 765-2590
01152 376 765-2591

KM. #39, Guadalajara-Chapala Carretera, Chapala. 349 *pesos* and up, includes tax. 40 basic rooms with TV. Amenities: pool. Taxi service can be arranged. Some English spoken.

Candilejas
01152 376 765-2279

Lopez Cotilla #363, Chapala. 180 to 250 *pesos*, includes tax. 9 basic rooms, without TV. Behind Chapala market and near shopping, restaurants, taxi and bus service.

Chapala Haciendas
01152 376 765-2720

Km. #40, Guadalajara-Chapala Carretera, Chapala. 250 *pesos* for doubles to 350 *pesos* for quads, includes tax. 16 basic rooms. Amenities: restaurant, pool. Discounted weekly rates. Car needed. English spoken.

Hydidees Hideaway
01152 376 765-2165
01152 376 765-4388

Juárez #499, Chapala. $350 US per month for a fully furnished 2 bedroom, 1 bath apartment with kitchen, living room, laundry, cable TV. 2 apartments. Amenities: near Chapala pier, boardwalk, and market, banking, restaurants, shopping, taxi and bus service. English spoken.

Lake Chapala Inn
01152 376 765-4786
fax 376 765-5174

Paseo Ramón Corona #23, Chapala. $50 US + tax, includes breakfast. 4 rooms with TV, telephone, hair dryers, views. Amenities: lap pool, library and music rooms, laundry, secured parking, airport pickup by arrangement. Located near restaurants, banking, shopping, bus and taxi service. Long-term rentals available. Discounts. English spoken. chapalainn@laguna.com.mx www.mexconnect.com/amex/chapalainn-index.html

Las Palmitas
01152 376 765-3070

Juárez #531, Chapala. 150 *pesos* single, 190 *pesos* double + tax. 14 rooms with queen beds and cable TV. Near the Chapala market, shopping, restaurants, bus and taxi service.

Quinta Quetzalcoatl
01152 376 765-3653

Zaragoza #307, Chapala. $69 and $75 US per night, includes tax and breakfast for two people. 5 rooms with deluxe accommodations plus three *casitas* for long-term rentals. Amenities include pool and gardens. Located within walking distance of shopping, banking, restaurants, the plaza, taxi and bus service. English spoken. qqinnchapala@yahoo.com

Villa Montecarlo
01152 376 765-2216
01152 376 765-2122
01152 376 765-3366

Hidalgo #296, Chapala. 500 *pesos* and up Sunday through Thursday, 1580 *pesos* and up Friday and Saturday. 48 rooms. Amenities: pool, jacuzzi, restaurant, meeting spaces. Located within walking distance of shopping, banking, restaurants, the plaza, taxi and bus service. Some English spoken.

JOCOTEPEC HOTELS AND B&Bs

Hotel La Quinta
01152 387 763-1400

Matamoros #87-A, next to the bus station, Jocotepec. 150 *pesos* for double bed, 200 *pesos* for room with two single beds. 11 rooms.

Los Dos
01152 387 763-0657

Calle Rico #191 Norte, off the Jocotepec-Nestipac Carretera (12 miles west of Ajijic). $50 to $90 US + tax, breakfast included. 2 apartments, 1 *casita* with kitchenettes, balcony or patio, TV. Amenities: secure parking, quiet mountain views. Seasonal rates. English spoken.
rauchlosdos@compuserve.com;
www.mexconnect.com/MEX/losdos/bungalows.html

Posada del Pescador
01152 387 763-2245
Tel/fax 387 763-0021

Miguel Arana #611, on the Chapala-Jocotepec Carretera at Km. #26, Jocotepec. 400 *pesos* for suites, 600 *pesos* for 2 person bungalows with kitchens, fireplaces, and up, includes tax. 23 rooms, 6 suites. Amenities: Large pool, volleyball, secured covered parking, maid service, small convenience store. Half kilometer from banking, plaza, shopping, taxi and bus service.Travelers checks accepted. Discounts. English spoken.
pdelpescador@hotmail.com
http://www.mexconnect.com/amex/pescador

Real del Monte Hotel Bar
01152 387 763-1580

Jose Santana Ote. #55, Jocotepec. Sparkly clean, cheerful, all rooms upstairs. 14 rooms. Private bathrooms with hot water, cable TV. No bar, despite the name, and no restaurant.

Villas Posada del Sol
No telephone.

Km. #26, Chapala-Jocotepec Carretera, Jocotepec. 200 *pesos* for 2 person bungalow, 350 *pesos* for 4 person bungalow with kitchenette, includes tax. 7 units. Amenities: secure parking. Half kilometer from banking, plaza, shopping, taxi and bus service.

SAN ANTONIO TLAYACAPÁN HOTELS AND B&Bs

El Sueño Guest Suites
01152 376 766-1648
$55 to $75 US, tax included. Suites include kitchenettes, fans, cable TV and twin beds. Amenities: spa services, offstreet parking, laundry facilities, and a 30 x 11 foot gravel RV pad. Within walking distance of restaurants, bus. info@elsueno.ca; www.elsueno.ca

SAN JUAN COSALÁ HOTELS

Bungalows Mama Chuy's
01152 387 761-0022
La Puerta #100, San Juan Cosalá. 730 *pesos* single or double, includes tax & breakfast. 10 rooms with cable TV. Amenities: restaurant, pool, tennis courts. Weekly and monthly rates. English spoken.

Bungalows Villa Chelo
01152 387 761-0013
Zaragoza #102 Pte. y La Puesta, San Juan Cosalá. 695 *pesos*, tax included. 2 rooms. Amenities: restaurant, pool, tennis courts, meeting facilities. Discounts.

Condominio Cosalá
01152 387 761-0321
01152 387 761-0322
01152 387 761-0323
Km. #13.5, Chapala-Jocotepec Carretera. 700 up to 1275 *pesos*, tax included. 33 rooms with kitchenettes. Amenities: restaurant, pool, tennis courts. Some English spoken.

Hotel Spa Balneario San Juan Cosalá ***(formerly Villa Bordeaux)***
01152 387 761-0302
Carretera Chapala-Jocotepec Km. 13 (enter through "Ruben's Grill"). 700 *pesos* per room for two and up, tax included. Marble bath and changing rooms, gym, steam rooms, massage area, beautiful swimming pool and a hot pool and a fabulous view of the Lake. Also a library and restaurant with seafood and Mexican-style entrees.

Hotel Villa Bordeaux
01152 387 761-0321
01152 387 761-0322
01152 387 761-0323
Km. #13.5, Chapala-Jocotepec Carretera. 700 up to 1275 *pesos*, tax included. 33 rooms with kitchenettes. Amenities: restaurant, pool, tennis courts. Some English spoken.

Villas Buenaventura Resort & Mineral Spa
01152 387 761-0202
01152 387 761-0303
fax 387 761-0364

Km. #13.5, Chapala-Jocotepec Carretera. 1100 *pesos* + tax and up. 20 bungalows, 6 indoor Jacuzzis for rent by hour with 2-hour minimum. Amenities: restaurant, pool, tennis courts. Located near Balneario San Juan Cosalá Thermal Spa, bus line, grocery shopping, restaurants, Raquet Club. English spoken.

Rentals and Real Estate

In past years publicity about the Lakeside area touted the low cost of living to be had by visitors and residents. Following the dramatic influx of foreigners and the resulting glut of real estate agencies, real estate prices now hover at resort levels. Opposite of the American and Canadian economies, goods are expensive in Mexico, services are not. Some costs, such as gasoline, telephone, and imported products are far more expensive than you'd expect.

If your plans include an extended stay, you will want to consider rentals. Beware of rental rumors that claim 4-bedroom, 4 bath homes with pool, staff, gardens and view can be rented for $500 US, utilities included! Not so, regardless of what you may have read in publications that are out-of-date, merely promotional hogwash or the result of irresponsible drive-by writers who don't do their homework. Rental agencies and real estate companies that offer rentals are the fastest route for first-time visitors. Even though they claim turn-key service, they can't deliver in a way you'd expect, but some agencies get closer than others. Rentals require various deposits, signed leases, and may offer only three-month, six-month or one-year contracts on some properties, especially in the high season, November through March, when the demand is exceptional.

You will probably find yourself in one of two kinds of rental situations. You'll either rent from an agency or real estate company, or rent from an independent landlord. In Mexico, unless a sanitation or health risk is involved, landlords are not obligated to make repairs or improvements to their property. These problems are the responsibility of the tenant. So if you rent from an independent, especially a Mexican landlord, be sure that everything works. If you rent through a rental agency you will have much more leverage if repairs are needed.

Once you're here, rentals can be found via the bulletin board system:

flyers posted at the Ajijic Post Office, the Lake Chapala Society, Farmacia Guadalajara, El Torito and Super Lake grocery stores, in the classified sections of the Guadalajara Colony Reporter, the Ojo del Lago and Lake Chapala Review magazines, and of course, by word of mouth.

If the purpose of your visit is to buy real estate, look for two distinctions that can guide you to the more professional agencies. GIL (*Grupo Inmobiliario del Lago*) is the local organization of realtors, and AMPI *(Asociación Mexicana de Profesionales Inmobiliaria)* is the national real estate organization that has international affiliations. Are agents licensed? Sort of. Are agencies regulated by the government? Not really. Do local agencies self-regulate? They try to.

Most agencies offer a multiple listing service that means your agent has access to properties listed by other agencies. Go to the website www.mlsmexico.com to view properties. They may not show them to you, though, unless you prompt them, because their commission will be less. Home tours can be a good way for buyers to view properties in all kinds of neighborhoods and villages. As everywhere, agent and agency-hopping is frowned upon. If you do purchase a property it will most certainly be for cash as mortgages are very rare. Make sure that your contract is in English and never buy *ejido* land, no matter what anyone tells you. Another source to look to for services online is www.lakeside.com.mx

REAL ESTATE OFFICES

Ajijic

A-1 Eager & Asociados	Donato Guerra #16; 376 766-1917, 376 766-1918, fax 376 766-2211; eager_asoc@laguna.com.mx; www.eagerrealty.com
Ajijic Real Estate	Morelos #4; 376 766-2077, fax 376 766-2331; email@ajijic.com; www.ajijic.com
Coldwell Banker	Carr. Ote. 38-B; 376 766-1152, 376 766-3676, fax 376 766-2124; axixic@infosel.net.mx; www.ajijic.com
Continental Realty	Calle Colón #12; 376 766-1994, 376 766-2145,fax 376 766-1272; kaybee@laguna.com.mx

Hernandez Realty Group	Carr. Chapala-Ajijic #36-38; 376 766-2103; www.Hernandez.rg.com
Realty Professionals	Carr. Ote. #60-A; 376 766-4004, tel/fax 376 766-0300; info@realtyprofessionals.com.mx; www.realtyprofessionals.com.mx
Re/Max Ajijic	Carr. Ote. #52; 376 766-2190, 376 766-2173, 376 766-2148, fax 376 766-1933 www.remax-ajijic.com

Chapala

Coldwell Banker	Hidalgo #223; 376 765-2877, 376 765-3676, fax 376 765-3528; chapala@infosel.net.mx; www.chapala.com
Re/Max Fenix	Carr. Chapala-Ajijic #159A; 376 766-1776, fax 376 766-1779; remax-fenix@laguna.com.mx; www.ajijic-chapala.com
Sierra Vista Realty	Hidalgo #236, Local 7; Tel/fax: 376 765-2383; ricardomarin_1@hotmail.com

Chula Vista

Century 21 Vistas Realty	Calle Chula Vista #10-A; 376 766-2612, 376 766-2613, 376 766-2614; c21vistas@laguna.com.mx; www.century21vistas.com

San Antonio Tlayacapán

El Parque	Allen W. Lloyd #149; info@elparque.info; www.elparque.info

HOUSE RENTAL & MANAGEMENT AGENCIES

Ajijic Rentals	Colón #1, Ajijic. 376 766-1716; rentals@prodigy.net.mx; www.ajijicrentals.com
Hernandez Realty Rental Group	Colón #2, Ajijic. 376 766-3030, 376 766-3737

Ribera Rental Center Hidalgo #69-A, Riberas del Pilar. 376 765-3838, fax 376 765-5038; riverarental@prodigy.net.mx

Roma Property Management and Rentals Constitución #57-A, Ajijic. Open Monday through Friday, 9 a.m. to 5 p.m., Saturday 9 a.m. to 3 p.m. 376 766-3163, 376 766-5171. *Recommended.* mexrealy@prodigy.net.mx

Rebecca Arrendondo 376 766-3313

MOVING COMPANIES

Lake Chapala Moving 376 765-6134 Worldwide service to and from Lake Chapala, on-line do-it-yourself quotes and moves, local moves, and packing services. English spoken. Carr. Chapala-Jocotepec #144, San Antonio Tlaycapán. www.lakechapalamoving.com

Strom Moving of Ajijic 376 766-4049 International, national and local moves, small or large loads, personally at the border for each crossing, guaranteed. They'll drive your vehicle in or out of Mexico, various insurance packages available, professional packing available. Buy packing materials at their store on the Carr. Pte. #258, Ajijic, in the Plaza La Huerta across from Villa Nova. English spoken. *Recommended.* strom@laguna.com.mx; www.strommoving.com

The Movers Lakeside 376 766-3571 English spoken. themoverslakeside@yahoo.com

LOCAL MOVING SERVICE

Barbara's Bazaar 376 766-3636 Independencia #7, Ajijic. English spoken.

Carlos' Bazaar 376 766-3939 Marcos Castellanos #22, Ajijic. English spoken.

STORAGE

La Floresta Self-Storage Rental Spaces
376 766-0661
01152 376 766-1045

Storage units: 5'x5', 5'x10', 10'x10', 10'x 20' (all 8 feet high), as well as storage space for cars, motorhomes and boats. and boats. Very secure with 24-hour guard, security alarm system, high voltage fence, and electronic card access. Office hours Monday through Friday 9 a.m. to 5 p.m., Saturday 10 a.m. to 2 p.m. Access hours: 7 a.m. to 7 p.m. year-round. Carr. Chapala-Ajijic #40, Plaza La Floresta near the traffic light by the Libramiento, Ajijic.

Dale Hoyt Palfrey

Dale Hoyt Palfrey

Pablo Fernandez del Valle

Dale Hoyt Palfrey

4

Food, Drink and Nightlife

with ZOFIA BARISAS, DON ADAMS

Price Ranges In Pesos

$$	$45 - $60 per entree
$$$	$65 - $90 per entree
$$$$	$90 & up per entree

Be prepared to pay cash for your dinner; few places accept credit cards. Tipping: 10 and sometimes15% is customary.

Restaurants abound on the Northshore of Lake Chapala. Visitors can choose from humble *fondas* serving home-cooked Mexican favorites to gracefully appointed restaurants serving everything from Northern-Mex to Austrian-German, French, Italian, Chinese and Japanese-style cuisine. Many places have adopted an international menu to appeal to foreign residents, visitors and well-heeled Mexican weekenders.

Some of the traditional foods from this part of Mexico include *caldo michi* (fish soup), the sardine-sized *charal*, *caviar de carpa* (still available in restaurants in Jamay), *birria de carpa* (oven-baked carp), *bagre* (catfish), *pozole* (hominy and pork stew), and *birria* (baked goat, a favorite in Jocotepec). With the exception of the *charales* and the *caviar de carpa* the seafood you find served in Lakeside restaurants comes from Mexico's coasts, trucked into Guadalajara's seafood market and picked up by chefs in the early morning hours.

Restaurants can open with great fanfare and close when you least expect it in Ajijic's saturated restaurant scene. During the slow season, May through October, owners shorten their hours or close altogether if business is slow only to reopen when business picks up again. During major holidays, Semana Santa and Semana de Pascua (the two weeks either side of Easter), Christmas, and New Years, Lakeside resembles the resort town it always has been and reservations are prudent. You might be interested to know that several of the oldest restaurants in Ajijic are La Traditional Posada Ajijic, the Nueva Posada, Bruno's Circus, Trattoria de Axixic, and Johanna's.

Getting restaurants to commit to opening days and times is nearly impossible. Many follow a schedle for the high season, November through March, and adjust to another schedule for the low months.

Restaurants

AJIJIC

Armandos Hideaway
376 766-0039

Located on the Ajijic Plaza, Armando's continues to serve international dishes with professional flair. Wonderful for people-watching, you'll enjoy attentive service and their full bar. The lunch and dinner menu includes well-flavored soups as well as excellent filet mignon, pork chops, shrimp, red snapper, brochettes, and *fajitas*. Red meat eaters will enjoy the flambéed Steak Mostaza. Finish off dinner with the Crepes Suzette. $$-$$$ Open 12 p.m. to 9 p.m. Closed Wednesday. Jardín #1-A, Ajijic.

Axixque Meson
376 766-1588

Restaurant and bar featuring Mexican menu with specials such as *paella* (rice dish with vegetables and meat or fish). $$ Open daily 8:30 a.m. to 5 p.m. Carretera Chapala-Jocotepec #424, Plaza Rancho del Oro, Ajijic.

Borselino's
376 766-2368

This restaurant serves a Sunday brunch in a pretty garden setting. Full bar. $$-$$$ Open Sunday, 10 a.m. to 1 p.m. by reservation. Closed Monday, Tuesday and Wednesday. 16 de Septiembre #5-A, Ajijic.

Bruno's El Circo
376 766-1674

Bruno continues to serve up excellent grilled steaks, chicken, sausage and pork chop dinners with the best baked potatoes in town. Their lunch menu offers stir fry dishes, grilled meat sandwiches and salads. Order up drinks from their full bar. Reservations are essential in the high season as seating is limited. $$-$$$$ Open for lunch 12:30 to 3 p.m. and for dinner, 5 to 8 p.m. Closed Sunday. Carretera Ote. #20, Ajijic.

Mexican Manners

It is courteous when leaving a restaurant to wish the diners at tables nearby "*Buen Provecho*" in a well modulated voice as you pass by. Accompanied by a smile, one wish is generally enough.

Bruno's Hideaway
376 766-0632

Serving a similar menu as Bruno's El Circo above, the Hideaway also offers tasty appetizers, salmon, and daily specials for diners eating indoors or on the patio. A brisk bar trade, scruffy charm, and occasional live music keeps things lively. $-$$$$ Open Thursday through Saturday 4 p.m. until late, Sunday from 2 p.m. on; dinner served until 9:30 p.m. On the Ajijic-Jocotepec *carretera* near La Canacinta, across from the Japanese nursery.

Café In Acalli
376 766 4857

This little café serves very reasonable breakfasts and lunches, inside or out. Scruffy, but earnest, it is well-located along gallery row, 16 de Septiembre, not far from the Lake Chapala Society. $ Open 9 a.m. to 5 p.m. Monday through Saturday. 16 de Septiembre #6A, Ajijic.

Chinese Buffet/ Restaurant Chung
376 766-4804

Calories for the strapped budget. Chinese buffet 35 *pesos*, with shrimp, 50. $$ Open daily noon to 6 p.m. In Plaza la Huerta, Ajijic (Rancho del Oro).

Danny's Restaurant and Bar
376 766-2222

American-style breakfasts and lunches. Hamburgers, chili and *chilaquiles* are favorites. Open Monday through Saturday 8 a.m. to 4 p.m., Sunday 8 a.m. to 1 p.m. breakfast only. Carretera Chapala-Ajijic #2-A, Ajijic (near the corner of Colón and the Ajijic *carretera*).

David's Cafe
376 766-3074

Cozy café for breakfast, lunch and other light fare one-half block from the Ajijic plaza. Great for smoothies, hot cakes, waffles, burgers and club sandwiches. $$ Open Daily 8:00 a.m. to 4 p.m. Closed Wednesday. Hidalgo #21, Ajijic.

Dominos Pizza
376 766-3690
Take out and delivery.

Donas
Popular breakfast, donut and coffee shop. Breakfast prices are competitive but you pay well for their substantial donuts. Open Monday through Friday 7 a.m. to 7 p.m., Saturday & Sundays 7:00 a.m. to 8:00 p.m. Carretera Ote. #49, Ajijic.

El Sarape
376 766-1599
This restaurant on the *carretera* exudes colorful easy-going charm while delivering the best Tex-Mex, Arizona-Mex, and northern Mexican dishes around. If you're an aficionado of border-Mex, this is the place to go for *machaca* beef *chimichangas*, *flautas* and *albondigas* soup. You'll find a good hamburger, grilled steaks, ribs and chicken. They serve the tallest glass of iced tea around and give you as many refills as you can handle Their full bar can handle your harder drinks, too. Reservations suggested on weekends in the high season. $$-$$$ Open 11 a.m. to 9 p.m. daily. Carretera *Pte.* 26-A, Ajijic.
www.chapala.com/elsarape.html

Fonda Doña Lola
376 766-4455
This open-air, country-style *campestre* restaurant serves reasonably-priced breakfasts and lunches until 5 p.m. $$ Open daily 8 a.m. to 5 p.m., closed Thursday. Carretera Pte. #36 (across from Casa del Waffle).

Golden Fried Chicken
376 766-2426
More a fast food restaurant than a sit down, Golden is found inside the Tobolandia Water park, just west of the junction of the Libramiento and the Ajijic *carretera* at the traffic light. They serve breakfast: eggs, yogurt, hot cakes, *licuados* (smoothies), and tortas. For lunch and dinner choose from fried chicken, hamburgers, chicken burgers,

DID THE WAITER FORGET SOMETHING?

The menu	*El menú, por favor.*
Toothpicks	*Hay palillos?*
Silverware	*Deme un cubierto, por favor.*
Salt Shaker	*Deme un salero, por favor.*
Pepper	*Deme un pimintero, por favor.*
Ashtray	*Un cenizero, por favor.*
Sugar/Cream	*Hay azúcar? Hay crema?*
Bill	*Traígame la cuenta, por favor.*

"burritas", hot dogs and *tortas de pierna.* $$-$$$ Open Monday through Sunday 9 a.m. to noon for breakfast, until 9 p.m. for lunch and dinner. At Tobolandia, Ajijic.

Johanna's Restaurant
376 766-0437

Johanna's gives her clients exceptional Austrian-German cuisine in a spotless, cheerful and cozy setting. Take a moment to check out the reviews on their wall of fame. Their traditional dinner menu includes bratwursts, veal, trout, pork chops, duck, rabbit, and *sauerbraten* as well as *borscht, reibekuchen* (potato pancakes), and *spåtzle* (noodles). Their wine list is extensive. German, Dutch and Mexican beers are available. Reservations are essential during the high season. $$$ Open 12:30 p.m. to 8 p.m. Tuesday through Sunday. Closed Monday. Blvd. Ajijic #118-A, Ajijic (in upper La Floresta opposite the Auditorium).

Jose's Illusion
376 766-5142

This bistro serves a full menu of delicious Greek and Mediterranean dishes: *hummos,* stuffed grape leaves, salads, pizzas, *spanakopita, moussaka, gyros* in pita bread, pastas and lamb, beef and seafood served several ways. Try the excellent new Thai entrees. Courses are well-crafted and well-priced. Beer and wine served. Carretera Pte. #123, Ajijic (near Villa Nova) $-$$$ Open Monday through Saturday 11 a.m. to

9 p.m. Closed Sundays.

La Bodega
376 766-1002

Serving lunch and dinner, the casual furnishings of this terrace restaurant belie a pricey menu. *Botanas*, salads, soup, as well as pasta, chicken, fish and beef entrées are offered, including one for vegetarians. If you like spicy, try shrimp prepared Diabla Felix style and cool off with a slice of Angelwings cake—baklava over a light cheesecake. Full bar available. Check listings for live music in the evenings. $$-$$$ Open noon to 10 p.m. Tuesday through Friday, Saturday noon to 11 p.m., Sunday 8 a.m. to 10 p.m. 16 de Septiembre #124, Ajijic. VISA accepted. labodega@hotmail.com

La Rusa Restaurant
La Nueva Posada
376 766-1344
376 766-1444

Landmark destination on the Northshore for meals, holiday events and meetings. Appreciated for its consistent service and competitively-priced international menu, La Rusa also creates holiday meals for the community. Try their 'comfort meal' menu or order from their regular breakfast, lunch and dinner menu. The bar is a prime meeting place and you can order your favorite liquid refreshments. Wheelchair access. $$$ Open 8 a.m. to 9 p.m. Sunday through Thursday; Friday and Saturday until 10 p.m. Donato Guerra #9, Ajijic.

La Taverna Dei Quattro Mori
376 766-2848

Italian chefs Maria Grazia and Guiliano serve up their version of the real thing—homemade pasta, gnocci, seafood dishes, chicken cacciatora, lamb, and Italian sausages—in this homegrown restaurant on the *carretera* on the west side of Ajijic. Entrées are well priced from 55 to 85 *pesos;* salads and sides are extra. Pastas are made on the spot so expect to wait for them, quite a while if they're busy. Their bar offers Italian wines, liquors and coffees. $$$ Open from 1 to 9 p.m. daily. Plaza de la Huerta, Ajijic.

La Traditional Posada Ajijic
376 766-0744

"If these walls could talk . . ." Known as the Old Posada, this landmark near the Ajijic pier has been the watering hole for local and foreign characters for decades. It has recently been revived to offer a menu of sandwiches, salads, soup, burgers and dinner items. $$-$$$ The restaurant is open from noon to 8:30 p.m. daily, and until 9 p.m. Friday and Saturday. Live music and sometimes dancing on weekends until 1:30 a.m. Morelos #1, Ajijic.

La Trattoria de Axixic
376 766-3796

After changing owners a few times in the last couple of years, La Trattoria has returned to serving somewhat-better-than-average Italian fare and other favorites for a decent price. Service is good, happy hours are popular and the bar business is brisk. Watch for live music performances on the weekends. $$-$$$$ Open noon to 10:30 p.m. Monday through Saturday, Sunday noon to 8:30 p.m. Carretera Ote. #30, Ajijic.

La Traviata
376 766-4467

One of several Italian restaurants that opened in 2003, this one offers a no-surprise menu of pastas, meat courses and desserts. The ambience is charming but meals tend to lack flavor. Beer and wine are available. A private dining area is available with advance notice. $$-$$$$ Open noon to 10 p.m. Monday through Thursday, until 9 p.m. Friday and Saturday. Carretera Pte. #35, Ajijic.

Loncheria El Tepalo
376 766-0727

(Formerly Arraiga Brothers) On the south side of the plaza, this typical Mexican *lonchería* is great for breakfast and lunch with a Mexican menu featuring Aztec soup, fresh juices and hamburgers. Good for people-watching, teenagers and tourists. Makes deliveries near the plaza. $$-$$$ Open daily 8 a.m. to 5 p.m., Saturday and Sunday 8 a.m. to 6 p.m. Parroquia #2, Ajijic.

Los Telares (The Looms)
376 766-0666
376 766-0428

Once one of the best places to dine in Ajijic, *Los Telares* suffered roller coaster times after the death of its founder. Their menu offers breakfast, lunch and dinner entrées in a beautiful indoor-outdoor setting. Full bar. Open 9 a.m. to 9 p.m. daily. Morelos #6, Ajijic.

Manix
376 766-0061

This quiet, cozy restaurant is an excellent place to recover from hoards of guests. You can always count on consistently good service and excellent entrées from their efficient staff and immaculate kitchen. Osso Buco, Veal Valdostana and Shrimp Curry are some of their established favorites. Their menu is organized into daily specials. Expect to pay top prices. Full bar. $$$$ Open noon to 9 p.m. Ocampo #57, Ajijic.

Media Luna Bistro Café
376 766 0932

This café has been growing in popularity due to its excellent location and food. Serving upscale breakfasts, lunches, and dinners with international flair, their home-made pastries, soups, and sandwiches are especially good. They roast their own coffee and have a wide selection of quality wines and beer. $$ Open Monday through Saturday 9 a.m. to 9 p.m. Carr. Chapala-Jocotepec Ote. #103, Ajijic.

Melanie's
376 766-1688

On Ocampo's restaurant row, Melanie's offers international cuisine with a French flair. Their menu includes fish, beef and chicken entrées and their extensive Sunday brunch offers more than 40 items, including dishes suitable for vegetarians. The brunch is free for kids and it's on from 10 a.m. to 3 p.m. every Sunday. Order drinks from their full bar and stay for the live music on the weekends. $$-$$$$ Open noon to 11 p.m. daily. Closed Monday and Tuesday. Ocampo #30, Ajijic.

Michael's Bakery & Coffee Shop
Sidewalk café with specialty coffee drinks, teas and pastries inside Bugambilias shopping center. $ Open daily 8:30 a.m. to 7 p.m. Plaza Bugambilias is next to El Torito grocery on the main highway in Ajijic.

Mi Pueblo Pizza
376 766-2270
Acceptable pizza with free delivery. $-$$ Open 6 to 10 p.m. Sunday through Wednesday, 6 to 11 p.m. Friday and Saturday. Closed Thursday. Guadalupe Victoria #15, Ajijic. Across from the Italo Hotel, near the church.

Min Wah
376 766-0686
This Cantonese restaurant, complete with Chinese zodiac place mats and fortune cookies, serves 80 well-known dishes, many suitable for vegetarians, to take out or eat in. You may order full dinners or *a la carte;* both offer generous portions. They stock a full bar. A wheelchair ramp and plenty of offstreet parking are available. $$-$$$$ Open 8 a.m. to 9 p.m. daily. Callejón del Tepalo #6, Ajijic.

Panino's Deli
376 766-3822
Excellent deli serving fresh sandwiches, soups, side salads, daily specials, beer and wine. Dine inside or out. Catering available. Closed for the month of May. $$ Open 11 a.m. to 5 p.m. Monday through Friday, 11 a.m. to 3 p.m. Saturday. Carretera Ote. #1, Plaza La Montaña, Ajijic. (At the traffic light at Colón.)

Pastelería Miky
376 766-1651
Delectable high quality pastries and specialty coffee drinks to eat in or take out. $$-$$$ Open Tuesday through Sunday 8 a.m. to 8 p.m. Will deliver. Boulevard Ajijic #62, La Floresta (across from Tobolandia on the "Avenue of Trees" as you enter Ajijic from the *Libramiento* or bypass).

Pedro's Gourmet
376 766-4747
Pedro's gets top marks for creating delicious, unusual dishes at a great price. Their international menu and daily specials will take your taste buds for a ride. Try the sam-

pler platter with seven of the day's creations or order oysters, shrimp, lobster tails, barbecue, steaks and other dishes from their varied menu. Full bar. All menu items can be made to go. Wheelchair access. $$-$$$ Open noon to 9 p.m. Tuesday through Saturday. Reservations recommended. Ocampo #71, Ajijic.

Que Taco Bar
376 766-4155

The ambience here is impossible to beat - mellow music, great views, the owner's habit of bowing and saying "Why Not" every time you order—so stay and order from their original, if slightly quirky, menu. It offers Mexican-style beef, chicken, shrimp, mushroom and cheese dishes. Several, like the mushroom burger, are suitable for vegetarians. Other favorites include the grilled brochettes, "nightmares" and "balloons." Enjoy their full bar but be careful on the stairs, especially if you've tipped a few. Watch for superb live jazz on Friday nights. $$-$$$ Open noon to 10 p.m. Tuesday through Thursday, Friday and Saturday noon to midnight. Carretera Chapala-Jocotepec #14, Ajijic (just past La Canacinta).

Salvador's
376 766-2301

North American-style menu with daily specials, salad bar and full bar. Occasional live music. $-$$ Open daily 8 a.m. to 8 p.m. Carretera Ote. #58 (next to El Torito grocery), Ajijic.

Secret Garden
376 766-5213

Fresh, very clean, and economical are the hallmarks of this well-run natural food restaurant a half block from the Ajijic plaza. Try their breakfasts with juice or coffee for a mere 35 *pesos*. Order veggie burgers, excellent *nachos*, three kinds of homemade soup, fruit and garden salads, yogurt shakes, sandwiches, upscale pastries, organic coffee and teas, including chai, for prices not found anywhere else in town. Look for daily specials and a lunch menu that are equally well priced. Everything is homemade; their *flan* is the best in town. Unwind in their peaceful garden and mingle with young weekend lovelies from Guada-lajara. $ Open 9 a.m. to 6 p.m., Monday through Friday (closed Wednesday), Saturday, and Sunday 9 a.m. to 9 p.m. Hidalgo #8, Ajijic.

Señor Sushi
376 766-4606

This tiny sushi bar and restaurant serves sushi, teriyaki, tempura, teppan yaki, shish kebobs and rice and noodle bowls. Suitable for vegetarians. They offer saki, Japanese Sapporo beer, Mexican beer and wine. To go orders by phone; platters and sushi-rolling demonstrations can be ordered for parties. $-$$$$ Open noon to 10 p.m., closed Tuesday. Carretera Pte.-Jocotepec #439-A, Ajijic (just east of La Canacinta). www.senorsushi.com.mx

Susazón
376 766-4314

Quality and imported frozen foods and meals to go. Also serves breakfast, lunch and early dinners. Specialty coffee drinks. Open 8:30 a.m. to 5 p.m. daily. Boulevard Ajijic #39-C, Ajijic.

Super Burrito
376 766-2233

Modest cafe serves super *burritos*, hamburgers, sandwiches, Mexican pizza, *quesadillas* and seafood. Delivery available. $$-$$$ Open 9 a.m. to 9 p.m. daily except Tuesday. Encarnación Rosas #76, Ajijic (upper Ajijic).

Tio Domingo
376 766-2453

This grass-roots favorite offers a limited but delicious menu of international dishes served outside in their garden dining room. Order the ribs or one of their other scrumptious entrées and finish your meal with flambéed dessert crepes. $$$-$$$$ Open 1 p.m. to 9 p.m. Friday through Tuesday. Closed Wednesday and Thursday. Ocampo #404, Ajijic.

Valenciana's Pizza
376 766-2046

Pizza parlor with delivery service. $$-$$$ Open daily noon to 10 p.m. Plaza Montaña #1, Ajijic.

Villa del Arte
376 766-2772

Exceptional, trendy, beautifully presented Italian cuisine made perfect in this classy former gallery. Appetizer, lunch and dinner menu boasts prawns, mussels, clams, pasta, chicken, pizza, and steaks. Try the Vivaldi Ribeye served with beef paté and brandy or the Sor Juana chicken breast in marinara sauce with balsamic vinegar. Finish with one of their pastries, specialty coffees, or an after dinner drink from their full bar. Expect to pay top prices and enjoy every bit of it. $$$-$$$$ Open noon to 9:30 p.m. Monday through Saturday. Rio Bravo #7, Ajijic (across the *carretera* from Villa Nova).

The Waffle House

Pricey, hearty American and Mexican-style breakfasts including 12 varieties of waffles, pancakes, blintzes, biscuits and shakes in an attractive, efficient environment. Their newsstand carries many current publications. $$-$$$ Open every day except Tuesday, 8 a.m. to 2 p.m. Carretera Pte. #75, Ajijic.

CHAPALA

Alfredo's California Restaurant & Bar
376 765-2245

Operating on the idea that more is better, Alfredo's extensive menu lists more than 200 items for breakfast, lunch and dinner and is geared for the homesick gringo palette. Check out their popular Sunday brunch from 8 a.m. to 1 p.m. that includes free champagne. Occasionally there's live music in second-floor lounge and always a full bar. $-$$$$ Open 8 a.m. to 8 p.m., closed Tuesday. They offer delivery within the Chapala area. Madero #116, Chapala.

American Legion Post 7 Grill
376 765-2259

Inside the Chapala American legion is a popular and well-priced grill that serves reasonably priced breakfasts, lunches and dinners. On Tuesdays, steak sandwiches are on special, and according to regulars, they make a killer hamburger. $-$$$ Open Monday through Saturday 9 a.m. to 3:30 p.m. Morelos #114, Chapala.

Café Paris
376 765-2343

This sidewalk café is perfect for people-watching in downtown Chapala. Good place for breakfast, lunch, and for simple afternoon coffee and dessert. $$-$$$ Open daily 9 a.m. to 10 p.m. Madero #421, Chapala.

El Superior
376 765-2180

Serves breakfast, lunch and dinner of typical regional and gringo fare; *Enchiladas Suizas* are a favorite. Patio seating in front, courteous service. $$-$$$ Open daily 8 a.m. to 8 p.m. On Madero #419, corner of Hidalgo at the light in Chapala.

La Leña

Restaurant and bar featuring grilled steaks from Sonora, and open-air dining in a relaxed atmosphere. Good barbeque ribs, generous portions. $$ -$$$ Open daily 2 p.m. to 10 p.m. Madero #236-C, Chapala.

Los Cazadores (Braniff House)
376 765-2162

Mexican food, seafood and steaks are served up in this historic 19th century mansion where you can watch the comings and goings along the Chapala Pier. $$-$$$$ Open noon to 7 p.m. Tuesday through Thursday, noon to 11 p.m. Friday and Saturday, though hours vary widely. Paseo Ramón Corona #18, Chapala. VISA, Mastercard, American Express accepted.

Mariscos Guicho
376 765-3232

Like its neighbor, Cozumel, Guichos serves shrimp, rock lobster, prawns, red trout, fish fillets, snapper and bubbling *molcajetes* without the raucous noise—or atmosphere, but it's all on the pricey side considering it's served on scruffy plastic plates. *Margaritas* and white wine available. Free delivery in the Chapala area. $$-$$$$ Open daily 11 a.m. to 8 p.m., except Tuesday. On the Chapala Malecón (boardwalk) next to Restaurant Cozumel.

Pensando En Ti Decent breakfast and lunch fare at a reasonable price. $$ Open 8:30 a.m. to 4:30 p.m. Sunday through Friday. Closed Saturday. Madero #112, near the American Legion.

Restaurant Cozumel
376 765-4606
This weary Lakeside favorite serves a large selection of seafood (their cheese-stuffed, bacon-wrapped shrimp are a specialty), steaks, *margaritas*, and bar drinks. Live music on Wednesday and Friday. $$$$ Reservations suggested on Wednesdays. Open Tuesday through Sunday 10 a.m. to 10 p.m. On Paseo Ramón Corona #22-A (on the east end of the Chapala Malecón or boardwalk), Chapala.

The Coffee Tree Offers fresh roasted coffee and coffee drinks, pastries, pies, and cookies. USA Today on sale. $ Open Monday through Saturday 9 a.m. to 4 p.m. Hidalgo #236, Plaza las Palmas, Chapala.

Tomas Restaurant Bar
376 765-3897
After 2 p.m. the kitchen serves up tasty steaks and seafood for very reasonable prices. To get to the upstairs dining room you'll need to go past the bar and through the kitchen. $-$$$ Open Tuesday through Saturday 2 p.m. to 10 p.m. Alvaro Obregón #1.

Veneciana's Pizza
376 765-4182
Pizza pies from 44 to 86 *pesos;* will deliver. Open Tuesday through Sunday 1 p.m. to 10 p.m. Morelos #209, Chapala.

RIBERAS DEL PILAR

Chicken Lick'n Deli/Restaurant
376 765-4399
Offers prime chicken dishes, including fried chicken, and deli sandwiches and sides. Great place for lunch and take out. Call early for fried chicken dinners. $$ Open Monday through Friday 9 a.m. to 5 p.m. Saturday 9 a.m. to 3 p.m.Closed Sunday. Carretera Ajijic-Chapala #101, Riberas del Pilar.

•

Mom's Deli & Restaurant
376 765-5719

Great homemade soups, salads, hot and cold sandwiches, pastries and well-priced daily specials. Catering available. $$ Open 11:30 a.m. to 3:30 p.m. Monday through Friday, 11:30 to 2:30 p.m. Saturday. Deli open 9 a.m. to 4 p.m. Monday through Friday, Saturday until 3. Closed Sundays. Hidalgo #79-I, Plaza Máscaras (behind the kiosk).

SAN ANTONIO TLAYACAPÁN

Diana's
376 766-0097

Full-course, Italian and international meals for lunch and dinner, reasonably priced. Full bar. Catering available. Open Tuesday through Saturday 12:30 p.m. to 10:00 p.m. Independencia #124. Reservations needed during high season or on American Thanksgiving and Christmas.

Mario's
376 766-1452

Sparkly-clean *fonda* featuring good regional fare, as well as hamburgers, french fries and exceptional specials. Their proud, courteous owners serve breakfast and lunch until 5 p.m. $$ Open Tuesday through Sunday 9 a.m. to 5 p.m. Closed Monday. Ramón Corona #132 (just off the plaza).

Tony's
376 766-4069

This *equipal* table-and-chair restaurant squeezed between Tony's Meat Market and the Hernandez Brothers garage serves local Mexican food and good barbecued ribs. Their salad bar is one of the freshest in town. Service is prompt and friendly. Watch a little TV while you dine or listen to Tony try on some Sinatra. It's, *um,* memorable. Fill up on drinks from their full bar. $$ Open noon to 10 p.m. Closed Wednesday. Carretera Chapala-Jocotepec #28 (near Super Lake grocery store).

SAN JUAN COSALÁ

Sometimes locals will refer to the seafood restaurants that hug the lake in San Juan Cosalá as those at *Piedra Barrenada*. In fact you'll see a sign saying as much as the road curves and the *ciclopista*, the bike path, rises up and over the cliff. The rocky foothills came so close to the lake there that rock cutters were required to make room for the road. If you look closely the rock (*piedra*) of the cliff has been cut away leaving rippled layers (*barrenada*) where the stone saws hacked away at the rock.

Doña Chila One of the beach restaurants you see as the Chapala-Jocotepec highway winds its way west. A good place for drinks and Mexican-style beach fare (the seafood is from the Pacific coast), it also offers a good view of the lake and weekend windsurfers, boaters, and jet-skiers. Great for teens and visitors looking to unwind. $$$ Open daily 10 a.m. to 7 p.m. Carretera Chapala-Jocotepec Km 62.

Restaurante Las Ollas
387 761-0444
Lakefront beach restaurant serving drinks, seafood and typical Mexican fare. Great place for lunch with great views of the lake. $$$ Open daily 11 a.m. to 8 p.m. Carretera Chapala-Jocotepec Km. 62.

Restaurante Minera One of the beach restaurants serving typical Mexican food and specializing in barbecue. Great place to watch the sunset over drinks. $$ Open daily 11 a.m. to 8 p.m. Carretera Chapala-Jocotepec Km. 62.

Villa Bordeaux - Reuben's Grill
387 761-0606
Located on the west side of the thermal baths in San Juan Cosalá, their menu features shrimp, chicken and beef entrées. Hour-long Survival Spanish Lessons with owner, Reuben, are free with the purchase of breakfast on Saturday mornings at 9:50 a.m. $-$$$ Open 8:30 a.m. to 9 p.m. daily. La Paz Ote. #418 (just inside the Balneario complex from the *carretera*).

JOCOTEPEC

El Cantarito Lamb, pork, chicken, sausage, and Cornish hens slowly cooked on long skewers above beds of oak coals. Served with handmade *tortillas*, fresh *salsa*, beer or soft drinks. $$-

$$$ Open Saturday and Sunday 10 a.m. to 6 p.m. Carr. Guadalajara-Morelia, the old highway to Guadalajara. Turn right (north) at the "T" (south is towards Mazamitla, north is toward Guadalajara) in Jocotepec, go one half kilometer. El Cantarito is on the left.

Gil's Pizza
387 763-1336

Good homemade pizza and soft drinks on the Jocotepec plaza. Jocotepec delivery available. $-$$$$ Open daily, noon to 11 p.m. Hidalgo #28-A.

Jando's

Old-style diner serving eggs, hamburgers, stews and *pozole* every day after 2 p.m. $-$$ Open daily 7:30 a.m. to 11 p.m. Miguel Arana #126, a block and a half before the plaza.

La Carreta

A Jocotepec landmark, this restaurant near the church is popular with locals and out-of-town visitors. Mexican grilled meat dishes with traditional accompaniments make up the menu. The building offers diners a glimpse of the past but sometimes the meat can be too tough to chew. Beer, wine, *tequila* and other mixed drinks are available. $$ - $$$ Open Thursday through Tuesday 1:30 p.m. to 8 p.m. Closed Wednesday. Hidalgo #75.

Lucy's Deli
387 763-2687

Between Las Fuentes and Jocotepec, Lucy's Deli offers a well-priced breakfast and lunch menu that includes sub sandwiches, pizza and daily specials. Their bakery produces 12 different kinds of breads and rolls. They serve soft drinks, beer and wine. $-$$ Well worth the trip but don't be in a hurry. Open daily 9 a.m. to 9 p.m. On the Ajijic-Jocotepec *carretera* between Las Fuentes and Jocotepec.

Mi Pueblito

Spotless, budget restaurant on the main street going into Jocotepec from points east, about 4 blocks from the bank. $-$$ Open 9 a.m. to 10 p.m. except Thursdays when they open at noon. Closed Sundays and last Wednesday of every month. English spoken. Miguel Arana #253.

Tom's Pizza delivered with congenial sass by longtime "Joco" character Tom. Soft drinks and beer are available. $-$$$ Open Tuesday through Sunday noon to 4:30 p.m. Call ahead for special orders. Closed the month of May. At Vicente Guerrero and Highway 15 to Guadalajara.

RESTAURANTS ON HIGHWAY 35 GOING NORTH TO GUADALAJARA FROM CHAPALA

El As del Oros
01 33 3688-1561

This country-style restaurant and bar features meats cooked in a huge open pit. They roast pork, beef, sausage, chicken, goat, and lamb for midday *comidas* served with vegetables, breads, *tortillas*. They have a well-priced breakfast buffet at 44 *pesos* per person with *café de olla*, eggs to order including custom omelets, with hotcakes, cereal, substantial meat dishes, fresh fruit, juices, beans, rice and *molletes*. *Tequila* and beer. $-$$$ Open daily for breakfast buffet from 8 a.m. to 1 p.m., lunch and early dinner until 8 p.m. Chapala-Guadalajara Highway Km. 15, Tlajomulco de Zuñiga (about 30 minutes north of Chapala on the west side of the highway). Some English spoken.

Fonda Argentina
01 33 3870-3648

Delicious five-course meals with South American flair for 95 *pesos* per person. Open daily from 10 a.m. to 10 p.m. $$-$$$ At the intersection of the Chapala-Guadalajara Highway, Km. 35, west side of the south-bound lane.

Los Burritos de Moyahua

Behind the serving line in this 24-hour truck stop is an army of cooks working to feed its many customers throughout the day. Pick up trays and slide them along the buffet to choose from 8 kinds of *burritos*, barbecued ribs, *chiles rellenos* and other daily specials; *jericallas* and *flans;* fresh cheese wedges (*panela*); pastries, candies; cold beer, soft drinks, bottled water and delicious *café de olla*, sweetened coffee flavored with cinnamon. The *café de olla* and freshly made-on-the-spot *tortillas* are worth the trip alone, but read the inspirational signs posted throughout both dining areas.They're someone's labor of love. $$-$$$ Just beyond the intersection of the Chapala-Guadalajara Highway Km. 15, on the west side of the south-bound lane.

Good for Your Soul Food

Plaza, market and street eating is part of the social fabric of Mexico. After mass ends Sunday on the Ajijic plaza you'll find neighborhood vendors selling everything from cakes and pies to hot dogs, freshly fried potato chips, roasted corn and garbanzos in season. In 2004 the municipality of Chapala banned street vendors from setting up on the sidewalks in front of businesses. Although hotly contested, the result was the disappearance of many streetside *taco*, burger and hot dog stands that propped up late-night diners who created the village's lively street life. Some *taco* wagons that could claim terra firma away from the sidewalks and onto the streets stayed open. Sundays and holidays on the Chapala pier bring out vendors selling dried or deep fried *charales*, ice cream and other snacks. The plaza in San Antonio Tlayacapán boasts two food carts, and an indoor-outdoor *cenaduría* (informal supper place) on the plaza. *Birrierías*, serving baked goat, line the north and south sides of the plaza in Jocotepec. *Rosticerías* selling roasted whole chicken dinners are in every village and are ready to serve take-home plates by 1 or 2 in the afternoon, but be alert, they sell out quickly. Festivals are an excuse to sample local fare, so dive in. But if you're new or suffer from a touchy stomach, be careful or abstain completely. If you're not accustomed to *comida corrida*, street food, an eating spree could land you groaning in the bathroom for a few days. The time to be most prudent is during the hot months of April and May when temperatures climb into the 80's and 90's F. , 30's and 40's C. It's best to visit *taco* stands during the evening instead of the day when the sun's heat can easily spoil food and *salsas.* Vigorous sightseeing in the sun can bring on diarrhea from heat exhaustion, too, so be sure to drink plenty of water.

Bing Ice Cream Ice cream, shakes, sundaes, the works. Colón #25, Ajijic (across from the plaza); Madero #200-A, Chapala (near the pier).

Birriería El Saucito *Birria,* stewed or baked goat, and *menudo*, tripe stew, are often the last stop before heading home after all-night *tequila* sessions. *Tacos* and "special orders" also avail-

Tepache

One of the most refreshing drinks on a hot day is the slightly fermented infusion of pineapple called *tepache*, originating in the state of Jalisco. It should be made in a large earthenware jug or pot and served ice cold or over ice cubes. If you are using the *piloncillo*, soak it beforehand for a couple of hours in one and a half cups of water to soften it.

1 very ripe pineapple (about 2 pounds)
2 whole cloves
2 whole allspice
4-inch piece cinnamon bark
9 and a half cups of water
1 pound *piloncillo* or dark brown sugar
1 cup light beer

Remove the stem and base of the pineapple and scrub the outside well. Cut into 1 and a half-inch cubes, skin and flesh together. Crush the spices roughly and add them, together with the pineapple and 8 cups of the water, to a large earthenware jug. Cover and set in the sun or a warm place until the mixture begins to ferment and become bubbly on top—about 3 days, depending on the temperature.

Put 1 and a half cups of water and the sugar into a saucepan and bring to a simmer. Simmer, stirring from time to time, until the sugar has melted. Let it cool slightly, then add it to the pineapple infusion, along with the beer, and stir well. Cover the jug and leave in a warm place for one or two days longer, until it has fermented. Strain and serve very cold. Makes about 2 quarts. Add bicarbonate of soda, stir and there's your delicious alka seltzer, Jalisco-style.*
From, *Recipes from the Regional Cooks of Mexico* by Diana Kennedy © 1978. *Author's note.

able. Open 8 a.m. Sunday, on the *carretera*, across from Plaza Montaña near the traffic light at Colón. Carr. Ote. #6, Ajijic.

Birriería el Tartamudo
One of two *birria* restaurants of the same name (*tartamudo* means 'stutterer') on the south side of the square across the street from the plaza that serve the traditional baked dish with *tortillas*, described above. Open daily 9:30 a.m. to 5 p.m. Miguel Arana #14, Jocotepec. Some English spoken.

Birriería La Playita
Traditional baked goat meat served in a spiced tomato broth with handmade *tortillas*. Instant coffee, beer, soft drinks, alcoholic beverages available. Open daily 8:30 a.m. to 5 p.m. Miguel Arana #28, on the south side of the square, across the street from the plaza. Some English spoken.

Cenaduría Doña Elvira
376 766-3612
Across the street from Mario's in San Antonio Tlay., this dinner place serves 5 *peso tacos*, *tostadas*, *tamales de pollo* and *mole*, and bowls of *pozole* starting at 20 *pesos*. Soft drinks and *aguas frescas*. Open Saturday and Sunday 7 p.m. to 11 p.m. Ramón Corona #127 & 127-A, San Antonio Tlayacapán.

Cenaduría Elba
376 765-5026
An all-time favorite. Open since 1973, this clean, well-run operation presents you with a menu to look over and mark up for the cook. They offer the largest selection of down-home favorites of any *cenaduría* we've found. Dinner for two with three drinks, a hot dog, two *sopes*, and *jericalla* dessert cost 47 *pesos*, about $4.25 US. For upset stomachs ask for a *tepache*, the fermented pineapple and beer drink served with bicarbonate of soda. It works like alka seltzer, only better. They serve beer, soft drinks and *aguas frescas*. Open daily 7 p.m. to 11:30 p.m. Zaragoza #343, Chapala. *Recommended.*

Cenaduría Lono You'll spy this place in the evenings by the *taco* wagon out front. They serve traditional tripe stew, *menudo*, and *pozole* Sundays starting at 7:30 a.m. In the evenings it's *tacos* with all the trimmings. Eat inside behind the wagon. Open Monday through Sunday 7:30 p.m. until they deplete their supplies of food or customers. González Gallo #74, San Antonio Tlayacapán.

Cenaduría Lupita Taquería A secret place the locals love for delicious, clean Mexican food including *pozole* on weekends, *sopas*, *flautas*, *enchiladas*, and *tostadas*. $ Open Monday through Friday 7 to 10 p.m., Saturday 3 to 10 p.m., Sunday 4 to 10 p.m. Hours for *pozole* Saturday 3 to 5 p.m. On Porfírio Díaz #92, San Juan Cosalá (street that runs on the south side of the church).

Cenaduría Memo´s Excellent *pozole, sopes,* and *tostadas*. Down home *Jalisience* food served family style. Open daily 6:30 p.m. to 12 p.m. Hidalgo #25, Ajijic.

Cenaduría Pachita Sitting down in this busy, friendly *cenaduría* is like eating in your grandmother's farm kitchen 50 years ago. Wedge yourself into a table by sacks of corn and choose from the menu: delicious beef *enchiladas*, *pozole*, *tostadas* and *tacos* and *tostadas* of *frijoles*, potatoes, *requesón* (a fresh, crumbled far-mer's cheese), *picadillo* (ground meat cooked with peppers and potatoes), and meat. Bring your own container for *pozole* to go. Soft drinks and *aguas frescas* are available. Open 6:30 p.m. to 11 p.m. daily. Flavio Romero de V. #439-A, Chapala.

Churros Aldama Serves fried and sugared "*churros*." Open Monday through Friday 9:30 a.m. to 2:00 p.m., 6:30 p.m. to 10:00 p.m. Madero # 461, Chapala.

Dale Hoyt Palfrey

El Potrero
01 33 31090-8673

This Sonora-style restaurant probably belongs in the restaurant section but their menu of country favorites lands it here. Order their *Parillada Mexicana* (Mexican grill) for two and get ready for a terrific meal of sirloin steak, barbecued ribs, chicken *fajitas*, *carne adobada*, *chorizo*, *quesadillas*, french fries, and Mexican *frijoles* from the pot served with handmade *tortillas*. A feast for 180 *pesos*. Drinks include *aguas frescas*, soft drinks and beer, *tequila*, rum, brandy and *margaritas*. Open noon to 6 p.m. daily. Aquiles Serdan #11, Ajijic (next to El Sarape on the *carretera*).

Lonchería San Antonio

This place on the plaza serves breakfasts, burgers, *lonches*, club sandwiches, *burritos*, *quesadillas*, and fresh juices. Open daily 8 a.m. to 4 p.m. San Antonio Plaza #2B (on the north side), San Antonio Tlayacapán.

Miky & Mike Pizza and Snacks
376 765-6573

Surprisingly good pizza by the slice or whole. Home delivery in Chapala. On López Cotilla on the north side of the Chapala plaza.

Nieves Arrañaga Tejuino Bulk ice cream for scooping, iced cappucino and *tejuino*. Carr. Pte. #1, Ajijic (near the traffic light on Colón). In Jocotepec across from the plaza. They deliver for events.

Nieves Chavez Sixteen flavors of ice cream *de garrafa*, made in big wooden buckets the old-fashioned way, using all natural ingredients and without preservatives, artificial colorings or flavors. They also serve *tejuino*, an unusual and hearty cold corn drink with salt and lime, and *aguas frescas*, fruit juices made with water and sugar. Open daily 9 a.m. to 9 p.m. Hidalgo Sur #150, Jocotepec. *Recommended.*

Nieves El Nevado de Toluca Don Chui prepares the original, authentic ice cream *de garrafa* of Jocotepec in 15 flavors. There are no preservatives, food coloring, or artificial flavoring used. Hidalgo Sur #158, Jocotepec.

Tacos Don Emilio 387 763-2301 This large place has one wall open to the street. Tongue, beef, pork *tacos* with all the usual toppings of cilantro, onion, and *salsas*. Local home delivery. Open daily 10 a.m. to 8 p.m. except Wednesday. José Santana #67, Jocotepec.

Tacos El Compadre We like this guy's style—cowboy hat, dark glasses at night, boots, western wear and a big belt buckle. But most of all we like how welcome he makes us feel at his outdoor *taco* wagon. He and his family sell *tacos* of all kinds, including *al pastor*, tongue, and beef with a good selection of toppings and *salsas*. Ask for a roasted *chile* and live a little. Soft drinks and *aguas frescas* will help with the burn. Open daily 5 p.m. to 1 a.m., except Tuesday. On Hidalgo going north. Look for the banner, "El Compadre."

Tacos La Doña *Tacos* 5 *pesos* and up. Choose from brains (*sesos*), lips (*labios*), tongue (*lengua*), and others with the usual toppings. Soft drinks.

Open 7 p.m. to 11 p.m., closed Tuesday. López Cotilla #283, Chapala.

Tacos San Antonio
376 766-2952

Tacos, tortas, sopes, quesadillas, and *vampiritos* are on the handwritten posterboard menu. These nice folks serve *aguas frescas* and soft drinks, and will allow you to bring your own beer. If you're good, the owner may mold a *burro* out of a *tortilla* for you, complete with ears and jaunty snout. Prices are higher than other places, though. Open Monday through Saturday 9 a.m. to 2 a.m., Sunday 9 a.m. to 6:30 p.m. San José #249A-D, San Antonio Tlayacapán.

Tamale Lady by La Farmacia Guadalajara

This woman sets up a table in the parking lof of Farmacia Guadalajara, next to Lloyd on the south side of the *carretera* in Ajijic. She offers delicious homemade *tamales* to go: beef, chicken, pork, cheese and green *poblano chiles* (*rajas*), and even scrumptious strawberry tamales. Ask for hot *atole*, if you like the taste of vanilla and cinnamon. It's all good. She'll be there nearly every evening from roughly 7:30 p.m. until 10:30 or until she sells out. Don't look for her on Sundays, though. *Recommended.*

The Hole in the Wall

Our name for this unsigned (and difficult to spot) homegrown restaurant in the Seis Esquinas neighborhood, west of Ajijic, that serves homemade *tamales, empanadas, tostadas, sopes* and *atole*, a bracing, sweet corn drink served hot. $ Open Monday, Tuesday and Saturday 7 p.m. to approx. 10 p.m. Hidalgo #96, Ajijic. *Recommended.*

Taqueria Jessica

This clean place on the *carretera* across from Bruno's offers 8 kind of *tacos* including tripe, tongue, sausage, and beef; 3 kinds of *tortas*; and *quesadillas* with all the trimmings: radishes, onions, cilantro, spicy red and sweet green *salsas*, and *frijoles*. Beer, soft drinks, and *aguas frescas* are available. We liked that the bowls of *salsa* on the tables were covered with foil. Open daily 3 p.m. to 2 a.m. except Wednesday. Carr. Pte. #23, Ajijic. *Recommended.*

Mmm What's That?

Aguas Frescas - freshly squeezed fruit juices, herbs, and flavorings mixed with water, sugar and ice.
Al pastor - meat cooked with a barbecue sauce.
Antojitos - appetizer or snack.
Asado or *asada* means broiled or grilled meat.
Atole - warm drink made from white corn *masa*, sweetened with *piloncillo* and spiced with cinnamon and vanilla bean.
Azúcar - sugar.
Birria - in Jalisco, stewed (cooked on top of the stove) or baked young goat (*chivito*) in a mild tomato base. Served with *tortillas* or *bolillos*.
Bolillos - oval-shaped sandwich roll made with white flour. The crust is baked medium hard and the center is soft.
Borrego or *cordero* - lamb. Chefs we asked preferred the term *cordero*.
Botana - another name for an appetizer or snack.
Buches - fried chicken necks.
Buñuelo - an open, lacy fritter made from wheat flour, deep fried and sugared. A Christmas tradition in this part of Mexico.
Burrito - a filled and wrapped flour tortilla.
Cabeza - pork head.
Cajeta - a caramel paste or thick sauce made from goat or cow's milk and sugar.
Calabaza or *calabacitas* - generic term for many kinds of squash.
Caldo - in broth.
Canela - Ceylon cinnamon whose flavor is considered milder and sweeter than the Cassia variety common north of the border.
Capirotada - bread pudding. One of the favorite Lenten desserts made with *bolillos*, raisin, sugar, cinnamon and almonds.
Carne Asada - beef, sliced thin and grilled.
Carnitas - chopped, steamed pork cooked in lard.
Cerdo or *puerco* - pork.
Ceviche - raw fish marinated and "cooked" in lime juice. The acid in the lime juice firms the flesh and turns it opaque, so the texture tastes cooked.

Chalupa - corn *tortilla* dough formed into small ovals or rounds with the rims pinched up. Serves as boats for appetizer fillings.
Champiñones - mushrooms.
Chayote - pear-shaped, green vegetables related to the squash family. Very subtle flavor.
Chicharrón - fried pork rind.
Chícharros - peas.
Chilaquile - casserole made with day old *tortillas* and combined with any or all of the following: eggs, sausage, chicken or meat, onion, red or green *salsa*, and topped with crumbled cheese.
Chimichanga - large flour *tortilla* stuffed, folded and fried.
Chorizo - Mexican sausage made from pork leftovers and *chiles*.
Churros - rope-shaped, deep-fried fritter about 10" long (25 cm) rolled in sugar while hot. You can buy pieces instead of the entire coil.
Cilantro - a green herb, also known as Chinese parsley.
Crema - Mexican cream that is thick and slightly sour used to garnish *enchiladas*, *tacos*, *tamales* and other snacks.
Dona - donut.
Elote - corn, also corn on the cob roasted over an outdoor brazier and topped with salt, *chile* and lime juice. It's not sweet corn, however, and it can be tough. Sometimes made into ice cream!
Empanadas - pastry turnovers filled with fruit or meats.
Enchilada - filled corn *tortilla*, folded, rolled or stacked, and covered with sauce and often baked.
Epazote - a green herb used in bean dishes, *tamales*, sauces, stews and other dishes. Also used as a tea for poor digestion and to keep the body clear of parasites.
Escabeche - means pickled. You'll find meats, fish, and vegetables pickled in vinegar, spices and oil.
Flan - a baked custard made with milk and eggs, originally from Spain.
Flautas or taquitos - corn *tortilla* rolled around beef or chicken or other fillings and fried.
Flor de la calabaza - the yellow flower of the squash cooked in dishes or battered and deep fried.
Frijoles - cooked dried beans.
Frijoles refritos - cooked beans, mashed and refried in a skillet with lard added.
Gordita or sope - appetizer made from corn *tortilla* dough shaped into patties, fried and filled with beans, meat or chicken.

Guacamole - mashed avocados combined with onion, *serrano chiles*, cilantro, lime juice and salt.

Harina - flour.

Horchata - a cold drink made by soaking and grinding uncooked white rice and blending it with water, almonds, sugar, cinnamon, and ice. Sometimes made with ground melon seeds instead of rice. Used for settling upset stomachs or curing hangovers.

Huitlacoche or *cuitlacoche* - a black fungus that grows on corn during the rainy season. Considered a delicacy and used to top soups, eggs, or as a filler for crepes.

Jamaica - a cold and sweetened tea made from the hibiscus flower.

Jericalla - a gelatin-based dessert made with condensed milk.

Jícama - big beige-colored, root vegetable shaped like a turnip with a crisp sweet taste. Around here it is peeled, sliced and eaten raw with ground red *chile* and a squeeze of *limón*.

Lengua - beef tongue used in *tacos* or sliced as a meat entrée.

Limón - Mexican lime.

Lonches - *bolillos* made into cold sandwiches with meat, lettuce, tomato, and a slice of onion.

Machaca - beef that has been dried and shredded and then reconstituted for fillings.

Mamey - unusual brown fruit with a skin somewhat like a kiwi, a shape like an avocado, a creamy texture and banana-like taste. Sometimes made into ice creams and pies.

Masa - fresh dough made of processed dried corn for making corn *tortillas*, *tamales* and other *masa* dishes. Dried *masa* is further dehydrated into a flour called *masa harina*.

Menudo - a hominy soup made with the chunks of the stomach lining of the cow.

Michelada - beer mixed with *chile* sauce and lime.

Mole - the Náhuatl word for sauce. It refers to a number of traditional sauces from different regions of the country.

Molletes - *bolillos* topped with refried beans and melted cheese.

Nieve or helado - ice cream dipped out into cups or cones or made into ice cream bars, *paletas*. *Aguas* are sherbets, *cremas* are made with milk. The traditional ice creams are made without artificial flavorings or preservatives.

Nopales - paddles from the prickly pear cactus, peeled, with the spines cut off, sliced into strips and served raw or slightly pickled in cold salads or for cooking. Its edible fruit is called a *tuna*.

Pan de Muerto - Day of the Dead bread. Round sweet bread decorated with a skull and crossbones to honor deceased family and friends.

Pan - bread.
Papa - potato.
Pasteles - pastries.
Pay - pie.
Picadillo - sautéed ground meat made from beef, pork or chicken, and tomatoes, onions, garlic and other regional flavorings. Often used as a stuffing.
Piloncillo - unrefined cane sugar shaped into cones or slabs. It traditionally sweetens *café de olla*, coffee boiled in the pot with sticks of cinnamon.
Pitallas or *pitayas* - fruit of an upright cactus, similar to the *tuna* of the *nopal* cactus. Seasonal delight, available in June, July and sometimes August.
Pollo - chicken.
Pozole - hominy soup with pork broth and chunks, sometimes made with shrimp or other meat, served with radishes, chopped cilantro and onion. A tradition at the New Year and Christmas.
Quesadillas - a corn or flour *tortilla* grilled with white cheese inside and typically served folded over.
Raspados - fruit drinks made with shaved ice not unlike snow cones.
Res - beef.
Rompope - cooked eggnog drink made with milk, sugar, egg yolks, vanilla and rum.
Salsa Verde - cooked or raw green sauce.
Sangrita - a drink to accompany *tequila* made from orange juice, grenadine, *chiles*, and sometimes tomato juice.
Sopa seca - "dry soup"; rice and pasta dishes. The liquid the rice or pasta begins cooking with is completely absorbed, making it dry.
Taco - corn *tortilla* folded around a filling, sometimes briefly fried. If fried it's called *taco dorado*, literally golden *taco*.
Tamal - *tortilla* dough filled with any kind of meat, vegetable or fruit, wrapped in corn husks and steamed. Note that one of them is a *tamal;* two or more of them are *tamales*.
Tamarindo - bean of the tamarind tree that is warmed in water, peeled, soaked for at least four hours, sieved, and mixed with sugar, water and ice.
Tejuino - a white corn drink made by boiling *maiz* with *piloncillo* to produce a dark base which is then ground, iced, and stirred with salt and lime juice depending on who makes it. Sometimes topped with a scoops of lime sherbet instead of the salt and lime juice.

Tomatillo - small green tart fruit with a papery husk that looks like a little tomato. Used in cooked and raw sauces.
Torta - Mexican sandwich made here with *bolillos*. Also can be a pie or a tart.
Tortas Ahogadas - meat-filled *bolillos* drowned (*ahogada*) in hot and a very spicy au jus.
Tortilla - thin flat round bread made of *masa*, a specially treated dried corn. Corn *tortillas* are Mexico's bread. Flour *tortillas* are eaten in northern Mexico.
Tostada - fried corn *tortilla* chips or whole fried *tortillas* used as an edible plate for scooping up *salsa*, *guacamole* or for piling with beans, cheese and other vegetables.
Totopes - *tortillas* cut in wedges and fried for chips.
Tripas - beef or pork intestines.

Alcoholic Beverages

Una copita, por favor (a cup, please) is the expression to use to order a drink, although Lakeside waiters are savvy enough not to bring you the entire bottle when you say, "*Tequila, por favor!*" Most visitors are familiar with Mexican beers such as Corona, Bohemia, Estrella, Modelo and others but might not know that Mexico produces rum, brandy, Kahlua, and wine along with its well-known beers and *tequila*.

TEQUILA

It might surprise you to know that the entire world's supply of genuine *tequila* is still made from the blue agave grown in Jalisco, primarily in the town of Tequila! Only in recent years have Mexicans considered drinking *tequila de rigeur*. The change came as fine *tequilas* produced from the hearts of the blue agave were introduced as drinks to be sipped and savored, not downed in shots or mixed into *margaritas*.

Cuervo Gold may be the world's most popular *tequila* but it is tinted with caramel and not 100 percent blue agave. If the bottle you buy does not say 100 percent blue agave, you can bet that it is just over half blue agave and as much as 49 percent sugar. In general, most *tequilas* are distilled at 110 proof, or 55 percent alcohol by volume, and then diluted with water. Once distilled, the substance is made into one of four types of *tequila:* Silver, unaged and sometimes called *blanco* or white, is good for sipping chilled over ice like vodka or mixed with Squirt, a lemon-lime soft drink; Gold, unaged *tequila* colored with caramel, good for mixed drinks; *Reposado*, or rested *tequila* is a pale yellowish color and is aged from 60 days to a year and preferred for cocktails; and *Añejo, tequila* aged in wooden barrels for more than a year (but not more than four), that is gold in color and elicits the qualities of Cognac.

MEXICAN WINE

Mexico produces some good wines—the reds being considered superior to the whites. Most wineries are located in northern Baja and central Mexico near Zacatecas, Aguascalientes, Dolores Hidalgo, and San Juan del Río. *Omar Khayyam's Mexican Vinos for Gringos* by David Ramirez is a comprehensive guide to Mexican wines and is usually available at *Libros y Revistas de Chapala,* a Spanish- and English-language bookstore on Madero #230 in Chapala.

The area's best selection of wine from Mexico, South America, and elsewhere can be found at La Paz Vinos y Licores, next to the Super Lake grocery store on the Carretera Pte. #145 in San Antonio Tlayacapán. (They are open daily 10 a.m. to 10 p.m.)

Bars & Night Spots

American Legion Post 7
376 765-2259
Bar is open Monday through Saturday 11 a.m. to 8 p.m. Morelos #114, Chapala. English spoken.

El BarCo
Sit down bar and package store popular with young weekend warriors from Guadalajara. Look for live music on the weekends. Hours and days vary. Carretera Ajijic-Jocotepec #33-A, next to the Pemex Station, Ajijic.

El Camaleón
376 766-1897
2 for 1 Happy Hour, national drinks, 5 to 7 p.m. daily. Constitución #29, Ajijic.

La Barra Roja (Formerly the Beer Saloon)
Beer and mixed drinks. 2 for 1 Happy Hour 5 to 8 p.m. Open daily 2 p.m. to 1 a.m. Closed Tuesday. Morelos #11, Ajijic, 1 block from the Ajijic pier.

La Cantina de Don Manuel
Open since 1920, this *cantina* is clean, quiet and suitable for men and women. 2 for 1 drinks on Tuesday and Thursday, all day. Open daily 8 a.m. to midnight. Morelos

#196, Chapala. English spoken. *Recommended.*

La Nueva Posada Hotel Bar
376 766-1444
376 766-1344

Open until 9 p.m. Sunday through Thursday; Friday and Saturday until 10 p.m. Donato Guerra #9, Ajijic. English spoken. *Recommended.*

La Playita Bar

On the street on the south side of the plaza in Jocotepec between the *birria* restaurants. *Equipal* chairs and tables let you sit and view the plaza and mountains. Open daily 9 a.m. to 11 p.m. Miguel Arana #26, Jocotepec.

"Las Piedritas"

Locals call this "*el bar de las piedritas*" the bar of the little stones, even though it isn't marked by any sign. It's the only building on the street with pebbles embedded in the cement. The dark, grotto-like interior is lit by lamps studded with colored marbles.

The back is open to a small, walled-in courtyard. Teachers bring school children to view the hundreds of artifacts collected by its owner, Salvador Aguilar, on display in glass cases. Coffee, tea, juices, soft drinks, beer, wine, liquor are available as well as hamburgers, *burritos*, and *lonches*. Quiet place for families and couples. Open daily 8 p.m. to 11:30 p.m. Jose Santana #27, east of Hidalgo Sur, Jocotepec. English spoken. *Recommended.*

La Tradicional Posada Ajijic
376 766-0744

Malecón #1, on the Ajijic pier. English spoken.

Los Caballos Locos

Popular sports bar with draft beer, mixed drinks, juke box, cable and satellite TV, dancing and snacks. Good late-night place with a view of the Chapala pier and boardwalk. Open Monday through Saturday noon to 1 a.m. Av. Ramón Corona #8, Chapala. Some English spoken. *Recommended.*

Some of the Mexican Favorites
(based on Ramirez' recommendations)

Red Wines	White Wines
Chateau Domecq Vino Tinto	Don Angel Sauvignon Blanc
Domecq Cabernet Sauvignon X-A	Casa Madero Chardonney
Don Angel Cabernet Sauvignon	L.A. Cetto Chardonney
L.A. Cetto Petit Sirah	Pedro Domecq Blanc de Blanc
Los Reyes Reserva Real Vino Tinto	Santo Tomás Vino Blanco
Santo Tomás Barbera	
Valmar Cabernet Savignon	

Maria Felix Bar
376 766-0014

Named after the late film actress, this elegant hotel bar boasts beautiful views of the hotel grounds from its patio. Beautifully appointed with photos of 1930s film stars. Until 11 p.m., Paseo del Prado #20, Ajijic in Lower La Floresta. English spoken. *Recommended.*

The Music Box (La Caja Musical)
376 766-4672

Draft beer, wine, full bar including more than 40 varieties of *tequila*. Great jukebox and clean bathrooms. Open daily 10 a.m. to midnight. On the east side of the Ajijic plaza. English spoken. *Recommended.*

Tomas in Chapala
376 765-3897

The bar at this popular watering hole next to the soccer ring in Chapala opens at noon and closes at 10 p.m. everyday except Sunday and Monday. The kitchen opens at 2 and stops serving around 9:30 p.m. Alvaro Obregón #1, Chapala. English spoken. *Recommended.*

Tom's Bar
376 766-0355

Draft beer, wine, full bar. Happy Hour 5 to 6 p.m. with 2 for 1 national drinks and wine. Very tasty lunch and dinner specials from noon to 10 p.m. by Chef Andrew. Open daily 11 a.m. to 1 a.m. Constitución #32, Ajijic. English spoken. *Recommended.*

Botaneros/Bordellos

Centro Botanero Rafa Bar with 3 or 4 women who will dance and have drinks with customers. Open 11 a.m. to 11 p.m. Closed Tuesday and Wednesday. At the Crossroads where Vicente Guerrero ends at its west end, turn right. It's the second building on the right, Jocotepec.

Chivi's Bar Bar, music, and full strip show featuring about fifteen women. Rows of small rooms on two floors, across a paved yard available for agreed-upon activities. Frequented by locals and gringos. Shows Friday, Saturday and Sunday starting at 10 p.m. or when the dancers arrive. Bar open daily from 7 p.m. to 3 a.m., Tuesday 10 p.m. to 2 a.m. Vicente Guerrero on the way to the Old Highway 15 to Guadalajara, Jocotepec. Look for sign on left. Building deeply recessed from street, next to construction material store.

Liquor Stores

Package liquor stores usually open around 10 a.m. and close by 10 p.m. Be forewarned that most liquor stores cannot legally sell alcoholic beverages on political holidays beginning at approximately 8 p.m. the previous day, although cut-off times can vary from town to town. Stock up early the day before *Día de Independencia*, September 16 or *Día de la Revolución*, November 20, for example, and especially on national, state and local voting days. For a list of holidays see Calendar of Events, Chapter 7. When buying beer from a *depósito*, you'll pay a deposit in advance and receive a slip of paper with the date and amount of your purchase. You have several days to return the bottles to be reimbursed. After that date, you're out of luck.

AJIJIC

La Despensa
376 766-1448

Wines and liquors. Open Monday through Thursday 8 a.m. to 9 p.m., Friday and Saturday 8 a.m. to 10 p.m., Sunday 8 a.m. to 3 p.m. Carretera Ote. #13-A, Ajijic.

Super La Playa
376 766-3816
376 766-3817

Part of a Guadalajara chain of the same name, La Playa offers a large selection of imported wines, liquor, beer, soft drinks and beach snacks. Open 9 a.m. to 8 p.m. daily, until 8:30 p.m. on Saturday. Carretera Pte. #240, Ajijic.

Super Mercado El Torito Vinos y Licores
376 766-2202

Domestic and imported wines and liquors, beer. Chips, nuts and other snacks. Open daily 8 a.m. to 10 p.m. Some English spoken. Carretera Ote. #56, next to El Torito grocery.

Vinos y Licores

Beer, wine, liquor, cigarettes, soft drinks, snack items. Open daily 10 a.m. to 11 p.m. Located on the east side of the plaza in Ajijic.

Vinos y Licores Beto

Beer, wine, liquor, cigarettes. Will handle table and chair rentals for parties. Open daily 9:30 a.m. to 10 p.m. Carretera Pte. #2, Ajijic. At the traffic light at Colón and the highway.

CHAPALA

Cervecentro Chapala

Beer, wine coolers, cigarettes. Open daily 10 a.m. to 8 p.m. Madero #200-C, Chapala.

El Despacho
376 765-5931

Discount beer, liquor & wines. They also sell snack foods, cold meats and cheeses, telephone cards, cigars and cigarettes. Open daily 9 a.m. to midnight. Madero #409, Chapala. *Recommended.*

La Despensa
376 765-4433

Wines and liquors. Open Monday through Thursday 8 a.m. to 9 p.m., Friday and Saturday 8 a.m. to 10 p.m., Sunday 8 a.m. to 3 p.m. Madero #453, Chapala.

OXXO

The 7-11 of Mexico, OXXO sells beer, soft drinks, snacks, sandwiches of all kinds. Open 24 hours on the west side of Chapala Pier. Other OXXO locations are at the Pemex gas station on the *Libramiento* and on the main *carretera* across from Chula Vista.

CHULA VISTA

Thursday's Modelorama Carries the following discounted beers: Negro Modelo, Modelo Light, Modelo Especial, Corona, Victoria, Cerveza Montejo (from Mérida), León, Pacifico, Estrella, O'Donls Amber, Bud and Bud Light. They stock a small selection of liquors, convenience foods, Sara Lee frozen cakes, and soft drinks. Open daily 8 a.m. to 9 p.m. Chula Vista #1, Chula Vista.

JOCOTEPEC

Casa Hoyos In business for more than 30 years, Saul Hoyos sells liquor, beer, wine and packaged snacks. Home delivery near Jocotepec. Open daily 9 a.m. to 3:30 p.m., 5 p.m. to 11 p.m. Miguel Arana #109, Jocotepec.

Vinos y Licores 387 763-0034 Beer, wine, liquor, soft drinks, snack items, cigarettes. 9 a.m. to 2 a.m. daily. Miguel Arana #105, Jocotepec.

SAN ANTONIO TLAYACAPAN

Cerveza Corona de Chapala Corona retail shop that sells brand name novelties, beer, kegs and who will rent party tents, tables, chairs and coolers. Open daily 8 a.m. to 8 p.m. Carretera Chapala-Ajijic #136, San Antonio Tlayacapán (opposite Super Lake).

La Paz Vinos y Licores The area's best selection of *tequila*, national and imported wines, liquors, beer, soft drinks, mixers, cigars and cigarettes. Open daily 10 a.m. to 10 p.m. Next to Super Lake grocery store. Carretera Pte. #145, San Antonio Tlayacapán.

Sol Distributorship 376 766-2800 Across from the Coca Cola distributorship on the north side of the *carretera* in San Antonio Tlayacapán, this shop sells XX Lager, Tecate, Superior, Bohemia, Indio, and Carta Blanca.

SAN JUAN COSALÁ

Vinos y Licores Beer, wine, liquor, soft drinks and snack items. Open daily 8 a.m. to 10 p.m. On Porfirio Díaz #10, San Juan Cosalá.

Cigarettes/Tobacco

You can find the following cigarettes at Lakeside though not in all *abarrotes*, the corner Mom and Pop stores. Try La Paz Liquors and Super Lake in San Antonio Tlayacapán, Super Guba in Chapala, and El Torito in Ajijic as well as some of the better stocked liquor stores and OXXO's to get your brand: Camel and Camel Lights; Salem; Viceroy and Viceroy Lights; L&M and L&M Lights; Raleigh, Montana and Montana Lights; Boots and Boots Light; Benson & Hedges 100's, Menthol and Lights; Faros; Delicados; and Marlboro lights, Menthol and Menthol Lights.

El Despacho
376 765-5931
Open daily 9 a.m. to midnight. Madero #409, Chapala (near the pier).

El Torito
376 766-2202
Open 7:30 a.m. to 10 p.m. Carretera Ote. #56, Ajijic (Plaza Bugambilias).

La Paz Vinos y Licores
Open daily 10 a.m. to 10 p.m. Next to Super Lake grocery store. Carretera Pte. #145, San Antonio Tlayacapán.

OXXO
24-hour OXXOs, Mexican 7-11s, can be found at the Pemex gas station on the *Libramiento* (bypass), on the main Chapala-Jocotepec *carretera* across from Chula Vista, and at the pier in Chapala.

Super Lake
Open daily 8 a.m. to 9 p.m. *Carretera* Pte. #145, San Antonio Tlayacapán (across from Corona Beer Distributorship).

Super La Playa
376 766-3816
376 766-3817
Open 9 a.m. to 8 p.m. daily, until 8:30 p.m. on Saturday. Carretera Pte. #240, Ajijic.

***The easiest way to** get* pesos *is via ATM machines using ATM bank cards or credit cards with PIN numbers.*

5

Money Matters

with

JOHN A. MILLER and ZOFIA BARISAS

Mexican Currency and Coins

The *peso* is the basic monetary unit of Mexico. Each *peso* is divided into 100 *centavos*. Notes of 20, 50, 100, 200 and 500 *peso* denominations are in common circulation, and there are coins of 10, 20, and 50 *centavos* as well as of 1, 2, 5, 10, and 20 *pesos*. A ten-*peso* note is no longer in circulation and a 5-*centavo* coin is rarely seen as are 50-*peso* coins.

Each coin is distinguished by size, metal and shape and each note is distinguished by size and color. In addition, each coin and note is clearly marked with it value shown in numbers.

While *centavo* coins are given in change they are seldom required when paying for goods and service and are not appropriate as tips for waiters.

PRICES

In the Lakeside area most prices are quoted in *pesos*, or *moneda nacional*. When written, prices in the national currency are indicated in several possible ways. The price of 100 *pesos* might be shown as:

$100.00	100 *pesos*	$100.00p
$100.00mn	$100 MN	N$100

or any combination of these. Hotels, bed and breakfast establishments, and some gift shops and galleries may quote their prices in U.S. dollars instead of or in addition to *pesos*. This can be confusing, since the symbol for the *peso* is nearly the same as the dollar. While the dollar is often shown by a double line in the "S" symbol, this cannot always be relied upon. In almost all cases, however, written prices that are being quoted in dollars will be shown as:

US$100	$100US	$100USD

When prices are spoken, most persons in the Lakeside area are careful to specify dollars or *pesos*. No one will be annoyed by your question if you feel uncertain. Even in halting Spanish you need only say "*Pesos ó dólares* (DOE-lah-rehs), *por favor*."

While there is a sales or value-added tax on most products, it is almost always included in the stated price. When it is not included, the price marker will indicate *"+IVA"* or *"más IVA."* If a price sign says *"IVA incluido"* it is included.

A WORD ABOUT TIPPING

Tipping in Mexico is an inexact science, as it is almost everywhere. In the Lake Chapala area, probably because of the large number of North Americans, tipping is more widely expected than it is in rural or isolated areas, yet it is not in such demand as it is in the resort areas of Mexico.

Tipping at Hotels

On arrival, be prepared to tip a porter at the airport the equivalent of 10 to 15 *pesos* per bag. Bellmen receive 20 to 30 *pesos*. Taxi drivers do not demand tips as they often do in U.S. cities, but since the fare is often a few *pesos* under the next higher coin or note denomination allowing the driver to keep the change from the next higher coin or note is both courteous and convenient. Other than the chambermaid at your hotel, who should be tipped the equivalent of US$1 per night per person, very few other individuals you will come in contact with will expect a tip and none will demand one—Mexicans are far too courteous to do so.

Tipping at Restaurants

Ah yes, restaurants! As in the U.S., waiters expect tips and indeed depend on them for a major portion of their income. Contrary to the foregoing advice to give a U.S. dollar equivalent to porters and chambermaids, use a standard percentage for restaurants: ten percent in ordinary restaurants and about fifteen percent in good restaurants. In *fondas*, or rustic, home-style restaurants, no tip is expected. It is never necessary to give more than fifteen percent in the Lakeside area unless you have been particularly demanding and hope to return to the restaurant.

Miscellaneous Recommended Tips

Mexicans tip bag boys and girls at grocery stores up to three *pesos*, since they earn no salary. It is also customary to tip gas station attendants who fill your tank two *pesos* or so and to tip the person who might wash your windshield or put air in your tires. If that person is the same as the one who fills your tank, a couple more *pesos* will be appropriate.

If you plan to vacation in the area for an extended stay you'll find that the locals tip the main traffic police officer about 100 *pesos* during the Christmas or Easter holidays and on Mailman's Day, November 12, the postman receives a tip as well.

Exchanging Money

We have referred to the "equivalent of US$1" above, but just what is the *peso* worth? This is impossible to state in print, since the *peso* fluctuates against the dollar and other international currencies on a daily basis. At this writing (early 2005) the *peso* is worth a little more than US10 cents (1.09) and about 8 and a half cents (.86) Canadian. To make figuring easier let's say that the equivalent of US$1 is about ten *pesos*.

THE EXCHANGE RATE

The daily exchange rate is posted in a variety of places, and the exact rate varies among some of those places. For example, the rate quoted in most banks will be about the same, the rate quoted in the *casas de cambio* (literally "houses of change") may be a little higher. The rates quoted in shops that are willing to accept dollars will differ considerably from each other but will normally be lower than the bank rates, and the rates quoted in hotels will almost always be the lowest in the area. The exchange rate also varies depending on whether you are exchanging your dollars for *pesos* or cashing in your *pesos* at the end of your visit. This difference is expressed as the "buy" or "sell" rate and is usually posted in each location. Normally you will be concerned with the "buy" or *"compra"* rate, since the institution is "buying" your dollars. A rate quoted as "*compra:* 10.94" and *"vende:* 11.21*"* means that the institution will give you 1094 *pesos* in exchange for your US$100 but will charge you 1,121 *pesos* if you want to buy US$100 from them. If only one rate is posted, it is the "buy" rate since exchanging dollars for *pesos* is the most frequent transaction in most locations, and the comparative listings mentioned above are also based on the "buy" rate.

Exchange Documentation Required

The documentation required to change money will vary with the form of money that you present and the type of institution you visit. All banks and *casas de cambio* will exchange actual dollar notes without documentation. Changing travelers' cheques will usually require your passport. It is very difficult to cash a personal check, except perhaps in the hotel in which you are a guest. The easiest way to get *pesos* is via ATM machines using ATM bank cards or credit cards with PIN numbers.

ATM SCAMS

Don't let strangers help you "remove" a stuck ATM card that requires you to re-key in your PIN number. It's a well-practiced scam, especially in Guadalajara, by con artists who have rigged the slot to temporarily jam the card. It's best to look for and use machines that ask you to swipe your card instead of insert it.

ATM MACHINES

Normally you will be able to withdraw about US$200 to $400 worth of *pesos* per card per day. You have to do your own conversion according to the day's rate, since the machines require you to enter the *peso* amount that you wish to withdraw. It is not a good idea to depend entirely on the machines, though, since their own cash supplies some-

ATM VOCABULARY

Insert or swipe your card.	*Introduzca su tarjeta.*
Enter your PIN number.	*Teclée su numero confidencial (or) Teclée su numero NIP*
Indicate a cash withdrawal	*Retiro de efectivo*
from your checking account or,	*Cuenta de cheques*
from your credit card or,	*Tarjeta de crédito*
or from your debit card.	*Tarjeta de débito*
Respond yes or no if you'd like a receipt.	*Desea usted un recibo impreso?*
Would you like another transaction?	*Desea otra transacción?*

ATM CHARGES*

All banks in Mexico charge service fees for transactions made with cards issued by other financial institutions.

To withdraw	7.50 *pesos*,
Balance Inquiry:	3.00 *pesos*.

Some Mexican banks charge their *own* customers for using their ATMs:

Banamex	10 *pesos*
BBVA Bancomer	20 *pesos*
HSBC	17.50 *pesos*
Santander Serfin	19.50 *pesos*
Scotiabank Inverlat	18 *pesos*
Banorte	19 *pesos*
Inbursa	13 *pesos*

*Courtesy Guadalajara Colony Reporter July 2004

times are not promptly replenished and can be frequently out of service.

The ATM Transaction

To use the ATM machine, it will be helpful to know the Spanish terms for some parts of the transaction although, depending on what card you use, many of the machines will give you an option for English or Spanish instructions. The card itself is called a *tarjeta.* You may be required to insert the card first into the door of the ATM *cajero* or kiosk where the machine is located. After you insert the card a buzzer will sound and the door will allow itself to be opened.

Be sure to remove your card at the end of the transaction if you inserted it, since the institution that operates the ATM will have no idea where to find you while you are in Mexico.

The ATM machines in this area all accept the same cards: Visa, Mastercard, Cirrus, Plus and Red system cards in addition to the card of the bank owning the machine if you have an account there. Some machines accept Diner's Club cards, but none accept American Express. The machines are normally available 24 hours a day.

ATM Locations

Travelers will find ATM machines at the Miguel Hidalgo International Airport in Guadalajara; in Ajijic at BBVA Bancomer bank, Farmacia

Guadalajara, and at La Floresta Self Storage at the junction of the *Libramiento* and the *carretera*; in San Antonio Tlayacapán at Super Lake grocery store; in Chapala at both entrances of Mercado Soriana, and at the Santander Serfin, HSBC, BBVA Bancomer, and Banamex bank branches; in Jocotepec at two Santander Serfin locations; one on the highway to Guadalajara at the Ixtlahuacán de los Membrillos OXXO.

CELLPHONES BANNED IN BANKS

Don't use or answer your cellphone while in a Lakeside or Guadalajara bank. It's illegal. "Rabbit Hunters" once robbed customers carrying large withdrawals. A confederate inside the bank would observe customers receiving large payments and call a partner outside and describe the victims as they exited.

BANKS

A 2004 article in the Guadalajara Colony Reporter revealed that Mexican banks are the most expensive in the world. For travelers, services are limited except that all of them at Lakeside now have ATM machines. For travelers who stay long-term, a bank account might have some advantages. If so, Lakeside banks are listed below:

LOCATIONS OF BANKS

Ajijic

BBVA Bancomer
376 766-0546

Will change U.S. and Canadian dollars for *pesos* for non-account holders with driver's license or passport. Will cash American Express, Visa and Thomas Cook travelers' cheques with passport, drivers license or FM-3. For money changing and travelers' cheque cashing services, hours are 8:30 a.m. to 3 p.m. Monday through Friday. General banking hours are Monday through Friday 8:30 a.m. to 4 p.m. Parroquia #2, at the southwest corner of the main plaza.

Chapala

Banamex
376 765-3918

Will change U.S. dollars into *pesos* for non-account holders. Will cash American Express travelers' cheques only with passport. Money exchange Monday though Friday 8 a.m. to 6 p.m, general banking hours 8 a.m. to 7 p.m. Monday through Friday, Saturday until 3. Madero #222, just north of the main intersection.

Santander Serfin
376 765-2310

Will change U.S. dollars into *pesos* for non-account holders. An account is required to change Canadian dollars. American Express travelers' cheques cashed with passport. Open 9 a.m. to 4 p.m. Monday through Friday. Hidalgo #210, on the *carretera* from Ajijic to Chapala, just west of the town's main intersection.

HSBC
376 765-4110

Will change U.S. dollars only into *pesos* for non-account holders with passport. Will cash American Express travelers' checks. Total daily limit $500. Open Monday through Friday 8 a.m. to 7 p.m. Bank has controlled access doors. The outer door will not open until the inner door has closed completely. Madero #208, next to the Municipal building.

> HSBC are the initials for the Hong Kong and Shanghai Banking Corporation, a British Bank. HSBC is the world's second largest bank after Citibank. HSBC purchased Banamex three years ago.

Jocotepec

Santander Serfin
387 763-0806
387 763-0075 fax

Will exchange Canadian and U.S. dollars for *pesos* for non-account holders and can cash American Express travelers' cheques with passport. Open Monday through Friday 9 a.m. to 3 p.m. Matamoros #42, at the intersection of the Chapala-Jocotepec highway and Matamoros, at the second traffic light.

INVESTMENT HOUSES

Chapala

Operadora de Fondos Lloyd/Lloyd
376 765-2149
fax 376 765-4545

This investment house caters well to long-term visitors who wish to buy into one of their seven investment funds, six of which carry a AAA1 rating from Standard and Poor's. The most popu-

Did you know that Allen W. Lloyd who founded Lloyd Funds was originally from Ohio, U.S.A? He moved to Mexico in the early 1950's and married Martha Manjarrez, a widow with four children. They opened a small 12-room hotel in Jocotepec, "La Quinta," that proved to be so popular with tourists from the U.S. and Canada that guests looked for ways to spend more time in Mexico. The question of how to extend their car insurance lead to even more extensive discussions on how to invest. After meeting with Mexican bankers, representatives of the Stock Exchange and executives in the insurance industry, Lloyd decided that providing investment and insurance services to foreigners would be more profitable than running a hotel. In 1960 he sold La Quinta in Jocotepec and set up offices in Guadalajara. By 1965 he incorporated under the name of Allen W. Lloyd y Asociados, S.A. That same year he opened his first branch in Chapala, managed by his stepson, Terence O'Rourke. Now 12 corporations operate under the Lloyd umbrella. The investment division has 14 branch offices in Mexico, from the first in Chapala, to Zapopan, Puerto Vallarta, Mexico City, Querétaro, San Miguel de Allende, Nuevo Laredo, Tijuana, León, and Ajijic.

lar fixed income money market fund for individuals, AWLASA, allows account holders (*cuenta-habientes*) to buy and sell funds the same day up to $50,000 *pesos*. 24-hour notice is required for sums greater than $50,000. But sell your shares before 11 a.m. to avoid paying a commission and before 1 p.m. to receive your money the same day. Very user friendly, literature and staff are bilingual and helpful. Download and print your monthly statements from their website www.lloyd.com.mx Profits made from funds are not taxable by the Mexican government, although they may be subject to taxes in your home country. They can exchange pounds sterling, U.S. and Canadian dollars, and cash travelers' cheques with photo I.D. including driver's license and passport. Some locations also offer Mexican automobile insurance and travel services. Open Monday through Friday 9 a.m. to 5 p.m.

Madero #232, one half block north of the main intersection.

Ajijic

***Operadora de Fondos Lloyd*/Lloyd**
376 766-3110-13
fax 376 766-3115

The Ajijic branch offers the same services as the Chapala branch, see above. Carretera Chapala-Jocotepec #40, near Farmacia Guadalajara.

MultiValores
376 766-2499
376 766-0912

This Mexican firm offers investors eight Mexican mutual funds and is regulated by the National Banking and Securities Commission (CNBV, Comisión Nacional Bancaria y de Valores). English spoken. Carretera Oriente #33B, Ajijic. Online investing at www.multivalores-operadora.com.mx

NO-CHARGE DEBIT CARDS

Lloyd/*Operadora de Fondos Lloyd*

Lloyd now offers a debit card called *monedero electrónico* (electronic purse) for account holders that can be used fee-free at 18,000 Scotiabank automatic tellers in Mexico. The card accesses funds from a static, non-interest bearing account set up for that purpose.

CASAS DE CAMBIO

The exchange agencies are usually very small, staffed by one person and identified by such terms as *"dólares"* or *"cambio"* painted on the outside walls. The exception is the one at the Hidalgo International Airport in Guadalajara that has a more internationally standard sign. For every transaction we recommend that you take your passport, even for the exchange of dollars into *pesos*. Requirements at each change house are different.

Ajijic

***Casa de Cambio*/Consultoría Internacional**
376 766-2382
fax 376 766-1642

Money changing services. Open Monday through Friday 10 a.m. to 4 p.m., Carr. Pte. #61, Ajijic (near the Waffle House).

Epsilon Divisas
376 766-2213

This conveniently located *casa de cambio* will change both Canadian and U.S. dollars for *pesos*, and cash American Express travelers' cheques with a passport. They claim to have no limit on the amount of money you can exchange at one time. If your Spanish is good you can call them and ask the exchange rate from your hotel room. Open Monday through Friday 8:30 a.m. to 5 p.m., Saturday 8:30 a.m. to 4 p.m. Colón #27, on the west side of the plaza, kitty-corner from BBVA Bancomer bank, a few doors down from the police station.

Chapala

Epsilon Divisas 376 765-2915 — Will exchange both U.S. and Canadian dollars for *pesos* and will cash American Express travelers' cheques with passport. Open Monday through Friday 8:30 a.m. to 5 p.m., Saturday 8:30 a.m. to 4 p.m. Av. Hidalgo #202, Chapala.

Compra Venta Dólares — Inside Mercado Soriana. Exchange of Canadian and U.S. dollars for *pesos* only. Open Monday through Friday 10 a.m. to 3 p.m., 4 p.m. to 8 p.m. Madero #699, north of the Pemex station, Chapala.

Jocotepec

Farmacia Blanca — On Hidalgo Eje Sur, a block south of the plaza, changes money and can send money to the U.S.

Vinos y Licores — This liquor store one block before the plaza on Miguel Arana at the corner of Guadalupe Victoria also changes money. Miguel Arana #101 and #105.

SHOPS THAT WILL CHANGE DOLLARS

Several shops will change dollars for you. Whether they will do so or not on any given day depends on their cash supply and the owners' guess as to whether having dollars on hand is a useful short-term investment strategy. Two of them are:

El Torito Grocery Store	Open daily 8 a.m. to 10 p.m. Carretera Ote. #56, Plaza Bugambilias, Ajijic.
Super Lake Grocery Store	Open daily 8 a.m. to 9 p.m. Carretera Pte. #145, across from Corona Beer Distributorship, San Antonio Tlayacapán.

Alternatives to Cash

CREDIT CARDS

While your credit card will come in handy in a few places in the Lakeside area, **it is not the preferred method of payment.** Lakeside operates primarily as a cash society. The vendors who do accept it pay large fees and must sometimes have the cardholder confirm the purchase by phone before the credit card company will allow the purchase. For most transactions it is wise to be prepared to pay cash.

The most accepted credit card is VISA, followed by Mastercard. Rarely is American Express accepted. Be sure that the price on the credit card receipt is clearly marked in *pesos* if that is the way the price was quoted.

TRAVELERS' CHEQUES

A few of the hotels, Hotel Mis Amores in Ajijic, for example, are happy to accept travelers' cheques, *"cheques de viajero,"* from major companies from their guests. But with the ease and availability of ATM machines, most travelers will find using their credit or debit cards to pull out a day's worth of spending money preferable to standing in bank lines to cash travelers' cheques.

EMERGENCIES

In general, it is always advisable to have two or three different forms of money with you: *pesos*, U.S. dollars, a credit card, a debit card, and travelers' cheques, especially if your stay is a long one.

If your emergency is due to lost or stolen credit cards or travelers' cheques, use the phone and report immediately the card or cheque numbers that you have carefully recorded and stored separately from your actual cards. In some cases it will be possible to get a replacement card while in Mexico; for example, there is an American Express Bank office at Circunvalación Agustin Yañez #2537 in Guadalajara, near Minerva Circle. Other bank branches are in Mexico City,

CONSUMER FRAUD

If you are the victim of consumer fraud, Mexico has an agency for foreigners to gain recourse. PROFECO is Mexico's federal consumer protection agency. It once operated a regional office in Chapala but complaints are now routed through their website www.profeco.gob.mx. They explain how to submit a complaint:

"ATTENTION TO FOREIGNERS"

Profeco is committed to always provide the best service. We extend our protection to the people who do not live in Mexico and acquire any product or service from a Mexican supplier and are not satisfied with the good or service. This is a totally free service and does not require the presence of the consumer in the procedure. The complaint can be submitted in any Profeco office, Embassy, Consulate or any other official representation. The Profeco address is Av. José Vasconcelos No. 208, 6º Piso, Col. Condesa, México D. F. C.P. 06140

The information you must submit is: your name, complete address, telephone and fax numbers, and office hours for contact; supplier's name and address; a short letter explaining exactly the reason for the complaint and the amount requested; copies of all documents as evidence of the transactions, and all other available documents to support the claim. For further information you can contact us at the following numbers: 55-68-8722; 01 800 468-8722 or E-mail: extranjeros@profeco.gob.mx

Monterrey, and Puebla. For the Guadalajara office dial 01 33 3818-2300, for English stay on the line.

MONEY FROM U.S. TO MEXICO

"Banamex" Orlandi de Mexico, S.A. de C.V.
387 763-2469

Even though the sign says Banamex, this is a wire transfer service that allows money to be sent from the U.S. to Mexico. Commission fees are paid by the sender. For more information call toll free 1-800-515-5505. Miguel Arana #148-A, across the street from the Santander Serfin bank, Jocotepec. Some English is spoken.

Sigue
376 766-5317
Inside Turismo Sonrisa Travel Agency, is this money transfer service. Open Monday through Friday, 9 a.m. to 6 p.m., Saturday 9 a.m. to 2 p.m. Carr. Ote. #60, (Across from Telmex), Ajijic.

As a very last resort, the U.S. Consulate in Guadalajara, Progreso #175, Guadalajara, telephone 01 33 3268-2100 or fax 01 33 3268-2200, will advance U.S. citizens some funds, but you will never travel out of the country again until the loan is repaid! If your emergency is after 4:30 p.m. the number for assistance is 01 33 3826-5553.

INTERNET ACCESS

Aside from actual money in hand, many travelers are concerned with monitoring their bank accounts and investment portfolios while on holiday. Internet cafes can be found near the plazas in Chapala, Ajijic, and Jocotepec. Two are:

The CIA
The Café Internet Ajijic is open Monday through Friday, 8:30 a.m. to 5 p.m., Saturday 8:30 a.m. to 2 p.m. Carr. Ajijic #58C, across from Telmex, in Ajijic. English spoken.

Cyber Centro
Open Monday through Saturday 10 a.m. to 2 p.m., 4 p.m. to 8 p.m., Sunday 10 a.m. to 3 p.m. Morelos #77, one short block north of the plaza, in Jocotepec.
Cybercentro_jocotepec@hotmail.com

"Niña con la Llave" (Girl with the Key) by photographer Xill Fessenden.

World-class artists *can be found along the Northshore.*

Shopping: Galleries, Folk Arts & Crafts, Boutiques

with Laura Leming

Mexico's rich and longstanding tradition of craftwork and the serious pursuit of art thrives at Lakeside. The Lake acts as a giant natural mirror, reflecting the blue skies found at this altitude. This brilliant natural light inspires artists and craftspeople from all over the world.

A small group of artists in Jocotepec, San Juan Cosalá and in Chapala form strong communities on the western and eastern ends of the Lake respectively, but Ajijic is the main destination for artists. An international community of painters, photographers, printmakers, glass artists, jewelry makers, and weavers gather and work, inspired by Mexican traditions, personal visions, or the superb natural beauty of the area. Exhibitions change frequently, so gallery openings educate collectors and art lovers about the wide range of accomplished art that can be purchased for modest prices.

Dale Hoyt Palfrey

Artist Jesus Lopez Vega *(above) is one of many accomplished artists who live and work in the Lakeside area.*

For those interested in a self-guided gallery trek we've included a map of galleries.

Art Classes and Galleries

Many artists in the Lakeside area offer classes for adults and sometimes children. Arrangements can be made by contacting the artists in their studios or galleries. Some of them are listed below.

Karl Barnhardt Artist Karl Barnhardt will teach you to draw well in two weeks. This exceptional teacher delivers on his promise. Classes Monday 10 a.m. to noon, Tuesday, Thursday and Friday 9 a.m. to 12:30 p.m. Upstairs in the San Andrés Plaza, Suite E, next to LagunaNet Internet Service Provider. (San Andrés is just west of El Torito grocery.)

Emilio Galindo
376 766-0964
376 766-2771
Instruction in Watercolors.

Efren Gonzalez Art Gallery
376 766-4093
Home instruction in painting. Bugambilias Plaza upstairs.

Estela Hidalgo
376 766-1125
Classes in stone and bronze sculpture, large scale. www.hidalgo55sculptor.com

Luisa Julian
376 766-1292
Instruction in oil painting. Studio Arts Gallery, Ramón Corona #11, Ajijic.

Dimitar Krustev
376 766-3381
Gallery and studio, classical portraiture, lessons in portrait painting and drawing. Alvaro Obregón #5, Ajijic.

Enrique and Belva Velazquez
376 766-0162
Instruction in watercolor. 16 de Septiembre #7, Ajijic.

Dale Hoyt Palfrey

If an address is on the Carretera Chapala-Jocotepec it means that it's located on the main highway that runs from Chapala to Jocotepec. If the address specifies Carretera Chapala-Jocotepec Oriente #123, often abbreviated to read Carr. Ote. #123, it means that it's east of the stop light at Colón, toward Chapala. If it reads Carretera Poniente #123, abbreviated, Carr. Pte. #123, it means it's west of Colón toward Jocotepec. If an address includes Norte (north) it is often abbreviated to Nte., and Sur means south. An easy way to keep oriented is to remember that as long as you are on the Northshore, the lake is south and the mountains are north.

ART GALLERIES

Ajijic Society for the Arts (ASA)

Holds Art in the Garden exhibitions, some judged, some not, with works for sale. Watch for notices of upcoming shows in the Riberas Arts section of the Guadalajara Colony Reporter. The group meets the first Monday of every month, 10 a.m. at La Nueva Posada hotel, Donato Guerra #9, Ajijic.

Art Studio Antonio Cardenas
376 766-1478
376 766-0545

Gallery and studio. Oils, watercolors and mixed media. Open Monday through Saturday, 10 a.m.to 6 p.m. 16 de Septiembre #33, Ajijic.

Casa Hoy
01 33 3812-1160
01 33 3812-1161
01 33 3827-0378

Thirty dealers selling Mexican and European antiques, religious art, high quality folk art and hand created items, primitives and rustic furniture, old west and authentic hacienda treasures, contemporary art, lithographs, and original bronzes. Locator service for hard-to-find items. Open Monday through Friday, 10 a.m. to 9 p.m., weekends by appointment. Francia #1933, Col. Moderna, Guadalajara. English spoken. *Recommended.*

Centro de Arte y Cultura
376 766-0337

Gallery featuring the work of Dionisio Morales, Isidro Xilonzóchitl, Janice Kimball, Georg Rauch, Francisco Rojas and other fine artists. Look for Kimball's studio in the back where she sponsors a Huichol beader.

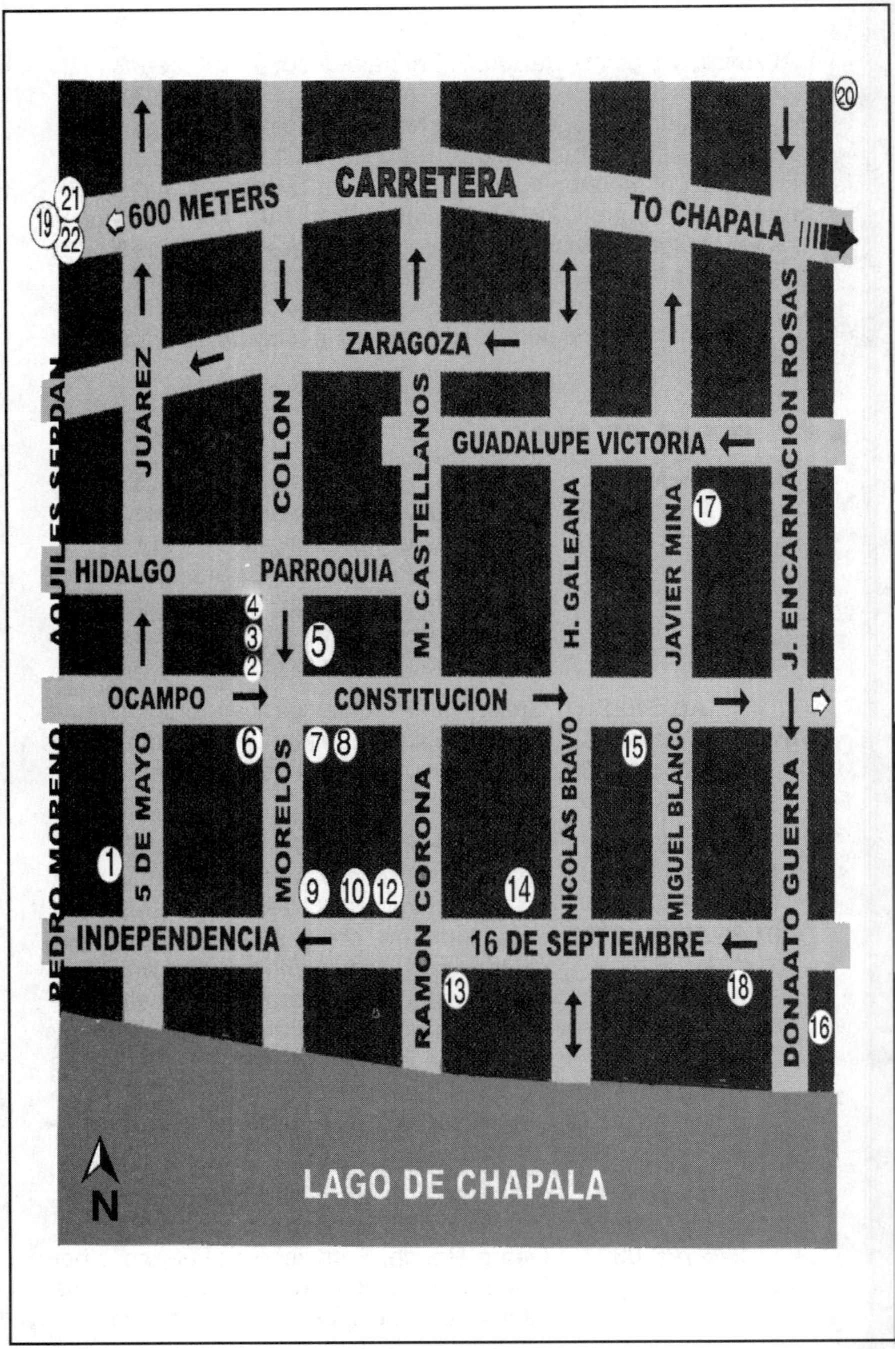
CARRETERA
600 METERS
TO CHAPALA
ZARAGOZA
GUADALUPE VICTORIA
HIDALGO
PARROQUIA
OCAMPO
CONSTITUCION
INDEPENDENCIA
16 DE SEPTIEMBRE
AQUILES SERDAN
PEDRO MORENO
JUAREZ
5 DE MAYO
COLON
MORELOS
M. CASTELLANOS
RAMON CORONA
H. GALEANA
NICOLAS BRAVO
JAVIER MINA
MIGUEL BLANCO
J. ENCARNACION ROSAS
DONAATO GUERRA
LAGO DE CHAPALA
N
1
2
3
4
5
6
7
8
9
10
12
13
14
15
16
17
18
19
20
21
22

Map of Local Art Galleries

(For hours and exact addresses, see page listings)

1. Ute Hagen, 5 de Mayo #11
2. Lakeside's Best, Colón #1
3. Galería DiPaola, Colón #13
4. Centro de Arte y Cultura, Colón #13
5. Tao, Colón #8
6. Los Telares Looms, Ocampo #2
7. The Gathering Place, Constitución #16
8. Centro Fotografico, Xill Fessenden, Constitución #16
9. Arte Estudio de Belva y Enrique Velazquez, 16 de Septiembre #7
10. Maestros del Arte, 16 de Septiembre #13
12. El Gallo-Ken Gosh, 16 de Septiembre #23
13. Cathy's Art Gallery, Cathy Chalvignac, 16 de Septiembre #22
14. Arte Estudio Antonio Cardenas, 16 de Septiembre #33
15. Galería de Arte Zaragoza, Javier Zaragoza, Constitución #50
16. Expositor Arte y Espíritu Huichol, Donato Guerra #7
17. Estela Hidalgo, by appointment
18. C. Jordan English, by appointment
19. Dimitar Krustev, Alvaro Obregón #5
20. Efren Gonzalez, Plaza Bugambilias, level 2
21. Villa del Arte, Javier Ramos, Rio Zula #7A
22. Galería Axixic, Jesus Lopez Vega, Rio Zula #11
23. Sergio Cuevas, San Juan Cosalá
24. Claudette Gasser, San Juan Cosalá
25. Laura O. Wagner, Jocotepec area
26. Georg Rauch, Jocotepec
27. Rommy, La Cristina

Open daily, 10 a.m. to 6 p.m. Colón #13, Ajijic. centroarteycultura@hotmail.com

Centro Fotografo Gallery — Xill Fessenden art photography, paintings, folk art and other fine work. Exceptional photography by Xill. Constitución #16, Ajijic.

Cathy Chalvignac
376 766-1153 — Art Gallery and studio. Hyper-real portraits in acrylics. Canvas and coconut purses. Open most of the day Monday through Sunday. 16 de Septiembre #22, Casa del Encanto (next to the Swan Inn, next to the Lake Chapala Society), Ajijic. cathy_chalvignac@hotmail.com

Sergio Cuevas
387 761-0202
387 761-0303 — Stoneware and glass sculptures. La Paz #423, San Juan Cosalá.

Jose Duran Arquitecto/Artist Gallery
376 766-0717
Hotel and Gallery. Watercolors, T-shirts of his original work, calendars, cards, jewelry, handpainted clothing. Open daily 10 a. m. to 4 p.m. Morelos #13, Ajijic.

Eclipse Galería
01 33 5305-1414
Gallery of artist Anselmo Avalos who organizes the Regatta de Globos, balloon racing event, each September. Large paper balloons are crafted and launched using traditional methods. Watch the newspapers for classes in balloon construction, dates for racing trials and the main event in September. Galeana #5, Ajijic.

C. Jordan English Art Studio
01 33 3495-8401
Gallery and Studio. Abstracts in acrylics and other media. By appointment. Ceagleflying@yahoo.com

Galería Artesanal Torres
376 765-5813
Artesanía in blown glass, iron, clay. Very good prices. Open Monday through Saturday 9 a.m. to 2 p.m., 4 p.m. to 6 p.m., Sunday 10 a.m. to 2 p.m. Madero #551, Chapala.

Galería Di Paola
376 766-1010
fax 376 766-2401
Gallery and book store. Changing exhibitions and photography by Maria Di Paola Blum, paintings, sculptures, silver, amber, and semi-precious stone jewelry, largest selection of books about Mexico in English. Visa & MC accepted. Open Monday through Saturday, 10 a.m. to 2 p.m., 4 p.m. to 6 p.m. Colón # 11, Ajijic. English, Italian and French spoken. dipaolablum@yahoo.it; www.lakeside.com.mx/business/galeriadipaola.htm

Paulette Gasser Studio
387 761-0296
Exceptionally fine stoneware ceramics. Look for her work at The Gathering Place, Constitución #14, Ajijic.

The Gathering Place Galería
376 766-1706
This gallery highlights women artists working in traditional Mexican forms such as the Cocucho ceramists, as well as international artists working in a wide variety of mediums. Look for work by Xill Fessenden, Cathy Chalvignac, Jill Flyer, Paulette Gasser, Ute Hagen, Gloria Coronado and many others.

Their grounds and tea room provide a venue for programs and events. Open daily 11 a.m. to 4 p.m. except Tuesday. Constitución #14, Ajijic.

Efren Gonzalez Art Gallery
376 766-4903

Gallery and Studio. Accomplished oils, watercolors, pastels, largest selection of art supplies Lakeside. Open daily 10 a.m. to 4 p.m. Plaza Bugambilias, 2nd floor. Ask about lessons.

Ken Gosh
376 766-4171

El Gallo Gallery, open 10 a.m. to 1 p.m. daily. Closed Sunday and Wednesday. Ramón Corona #23, Ajijic (across from the Lake Chapala Society). Ask about lessons. kgosh365@hotmail.com

Ute Hagen Studio
376 766-1852

Vibrant acrylics of Mexican themes. 5 de Mayo #11,Ajijic. ute@prodigy.net.mx

Instituto de la Artesanía Jaliscience
376 766-0548

Open Monday through Friday 10 a.m. to 6 p.m., Saturday 10 a.m. to 4 p.m., Sunday 10 a.m. to 3 p.m. Carr. Chapala-Jocotepec Km. 6.5 (next to the Auditorio de la Ribera in Lower La Floresta) Ajijic.

Luisa Julian Studio Art Gallery

Striking acrylics and oils, often with a floral theme. Open Monday through Saturday 10 a.m. to 2 p.m. Ramón Corona #11, Ajijic.

Dimitar Krustev
376 766-3381

Gallery and studio, classical portraiture, lessons in portrait painting and drawing. Alvaro Obregón #5, Ajijic.

Lakeside's Best

Jewelry by Daniel Van Waeyenberg, Carmen Bermel, Diane Pearl, paintings by Gerry Krause, as well as changing exhibitions of work by accomplished Lakeside artists. Open Monday through Saturday, 10 a.m. to 3 p.m. Colón #1, Ajijic.

Maestros del Arte
376 766-4133
376 766-1089

Promoting Mexico's *artesanías* (hand crafts) is the primary focus of the gallery. Also look for gourd art by Marianne Carlson, gift items and other unusual art objects. Open Monday, Tuesday, Thursday-Saturday 11 a.m. to 2 p.m. 16 de Septiembre #13, Ajijic.

mariannecarlson@mexicoetc.com;
www.mexicoetc.com

Feria Maestros del Arte

Every November brings the Maestros del Arte fair to Ajijic. Master artists from Jalisco, Michoácan and other states sell authentic art and *artesanía* for collectors and art lovers. Organized by Marianne Carlson of Galería Maestros del Arte, 16 de Septiembre #13, Ajijic, the fair lasts 3 days and connects buyers with master artists of Mexico. Contact Marianne Carlson (376) 766-4133; mariannecarlson@mexicoetc.com for more information. *Recommended.*

Museo Regional de la Ceramica
17th and 18th century master ceramists on display. (Neo-classical building built in the mid 1800's.) Open Tuesday through Saturday 10 a.m. to 6 p.m., Sunday 10 a.m. to 3 p.m. Independencia #237, Tlaquepaque.

Javier Ramos
376 766-0979
Accomplished oil portraits of the draped figure, still lifes. Rio Zula #7A, Ajijic.

Georg Rauch
387 763-0657
International artist with original oils and museum quality giclee reproductions on canvas. Studio visits by appt.
rauchlosdos@yahoo.com;
www.mexconnect.com/MEX/losdos/losdos.html

Rommy Custom Designs
376 766-2033
376 766-3437
Texas 956 624-1445
Original and reproduction fine art finishes, trompe l'oeil, gold leafing, pergamino paper; oil, acrylic and watercolor paintings; decorative painting around fireplaces, domes and murals; planning, construction and remodeling of rooms and homes. Trained as an engineer, Roman Guevara can provide perspective drawings and blueprints to scale. One minute past La Cristina (toward Jocotepec) on the north side of the highway. romyart@prodigy.net.mx; www.romycustomdesign.com

Hilary Stewardson Portraits in pastels, including animal portraits. hstewardson@hotmail.com

Tao
376 766-1290
Terra Designs: handworked silver jewelry by Lauri Jenson; fine Oaxacan black pottery, wall art, sculptures, gifts, handmade candles and other exceptional items. Open Monday and Tuesday, 10 a.m. to 2 p.m., Thursday, Friday, Saturday and Sunday, 10 a.m. to 4 p.m. Colón #8, Ajijic.

Libby Townsend Jewelry Look for announcements about her work in local newspapers.

Jesus Lopez Vega Galería Axixic Exceptional acrylics, watercolors and other work with mythical themes. Rio Zula, Ajijic.

Arte Estudio de Belva & Enrique Velazquez
376 766-0162
Gallery and studio. Watercolors, fine art, pen and ink, calendars, cards, art supplies and classes. Open Monday through Saturday, 10 a.m. to 1:30 p.m. 16 de Septiembre #7, Ajijic. belva@laguna.com.mx; www.mexconnect.com/amex/chaprev/cprv11001.html

Laura O. Wagner
387 763-2188
Accomplished oil paintings; faisanes@laguna.com.mx

Robert Burns Wilson
376 766-1292
Bronzes and hammered copper busts. Complex patinas make this artist's work stand out. At the Studio Arts Gallery, Ramón Corona #11, Ajijic.

Galería de Arte Javier Zaragoza
376 766-2857
376 766-0573
Portraits in oil. Ask about painting sessions with live models each Friday at Ocampo #200, just off Rio Zula one door west of Galería Axixic. Space is limited. The Zaragoza studio is open Tuesday through Saturday 10 a.m. to 1 p.m. Constitución #50, Ajijic.

ART SUPPLIES

Efren Gonzalez Gallery They stock the largest inventory of supplies for artists. Open Monday through Friday 10 a.m. to 4 p.m., second floor, Plaza Bugambilias (next to El Torito grocery) in Ajijic.

Garden of Eden

This card and gift shop also carries a supply of artist's materials. Open Monday through Friday 9 a.m. to 2 p.m., 3 p.m. to 7 p.m., Saturday 9 a.m. to 2 p.m., 3 p.m. to 6 p.m. Plaza Bugambilias, downstairs, Local #4, Ajijic (plaza next to El Torito grocery store).

CERAMICS

***Arte en Barro/* Art in Clay**
376 766-0385

Talavera pottery and decorative items, tin mirrors with ceramic surrounds, clay chimneys, address plaques, flowerpots, all kinds of accessories. Wholesale and retail work. Open Monday through Friday 10 a.m. to 6 p.m., Saturday 10 a.m. to 2 p.m. Carr. Ote. #39-B (next to Telmex), Ajijic.

Bellagio Furniture & Decorative Accessories
376 766-4030

Factory outlet gallery for interior design objects, gifts and custom work. Distinct sophisticated finishes on clay. Open Monday through Saturday 10 a.m. to 4 p.m. Carr. Pte. #30, Ajijic.

Hand loomed textiles can be found in Ajijic at Telares Los Reyes.

Pablo Fernandez del Valle

Casa Mexicana
376 765-4383

Furniture and accessories. Mostly all kinds of ceramics, some Talavera-style, that are lead-free and dishwasher safe. Also furniture gifts and crafts for all budgets. Open Monday through Saturday, 10 a.m. to 6 p.m. Madero #409, Chapala.

HAND-LOOMED GOODS

Telares Los Reyes
376 766-0508

Wholesale and retail sales of hand loomed articles. Jackets, shawls, bedspreads, cushions, table cloths and napkins, fabrics for curtains and drapes. Open Monday through Saturday 10 a.m. to 6 p.m., Sunday 11 a.m. to 3 p.m. Ocampo #2, Ajijic.
virginiap@prodigy.net.mx
www.telareslosreyes.com

HUICHOL ART

Expositor Arte y Espíritu Huichol
376 766-1717

Stunning gallery of Huichol indigenous art including large beaded and yarn works. Open 9 a.m. to 7 p.m. On Donato Guerra #7, across from the Nueva Posada Hotel, Ajijic.

MEXICAN SANDALS/HUARACHES

Rugged handmade *huaraches*, belts, leather car seats, horse tack, dog harnesses and collars can be found in this shop. Open daily 8 a.m. to 9 p.m. Miguel Arana #107, Jocotepec. Some English spoken.

LEATHER

La Pioneros los Piel
376 766-3768

Leather Factory. Handmade leather shoes, purses, belts, crocheted purses, hats, handwoven scarves, tablecloths. Shoes in larger sizes. Open Monday through Saturday 10 a.m. to 2 p.m., 4 p.m. to 6 p.m. 16 de Septiembre #1-C, Ajijic.

Soaring Eagles Designs
376 766-2903
376 766-4253

Leather boutique with art. One-of-a-kind southwestern style clothing of denim and/or leather, including vests, skirts, jackets, hat , bands, dusters, belts and more. Also custom silver jewelry and original paintings.

Shopping Vocabulary

I am only looking.	*Estoy sólo mirando/Estoy viendo.*
Can you help me?	*¿Puede usted atenderme?*
Can you show me this?	*¿Puede usted enseñarme esto?*
Can you show me something?	*¿Puede usted enseñarme algo?*
I like it.	*Me gusta.*
I'll take it.	*Me lo llevo.*
It's not really what I want.	*No es realmente lo que quiero.*
It's too expensive.	*Es demasiado caro.*
How much is it?	*¿Cuánto es?*
Can I pay by traveler's check?	*¿Puedo pagar con cheque de viajero?*
Do you accept credit cards?	*¿Aceptan tarjetas de crédito?*
I'd like a dress.	*Quiero un vestido.*
I'd like a pair of blue jeans.	*Quiero un pantalón de mezclilla.*
. . . pullover/*una sudadera.*	**. . . shirt**/*una camisa.*
. . . pair of shoes/*un par de zapatos.*	**. . . shorts**/*shorts.*
. . . skirt/*una falda.*	**. . . socks**/*unos calcetines.*
. . . man's suit/*un traje.*	**. . . woman's suit**/*traje de señora.*
. . . tie/*una corbata.*	**. . . pantyhose**/*unas medias.*

. . . pair of trousers or pants/*unos pantalones.*

I don't like the color.	*No me gusta el color.*
I'd like something in black.	*Quiero algo en negro.*

. . . Blue/*azul.*	**. . . brown**/*café.*	**. . . green**/*verde.*
. . . gray/*gris.*	**. . . mauve**/*malva.*	**. . . orange**/*anaranjado.*
. . . pink/*rosa.*	**. . . red**/*rojo.*	**. . . violet**/*violeta.*
. . . white/*blanco.*	**. . . yellow**/*amarillo.*	**. . . beige**/*beige.*

Do you have a better quality?	*¿Tiene algo de mejor calidad?*
What is it made of?	*¿De qué está hecho?*
Can I try it on?	*¿Puedo probármelo?*
Where is the fitting room?	*¿Dónde está el probador?*
It fits very well.	*Queda muy bien.*
It doesn't fit.	*No queda bien.*
It's too short.	*Es demasiado corto.*
It's too long.	*Es demasiado largo.*
It's too tight.	*Es demasiado ajustado.*
It's too loose.	*Es demasiado flojo(a)/ancho(a).*

Open Monday through Saturday 10 a.m. to 1 p.m., 3 p.m. to 6 p.m. Ocampo #30, Ajijic. lindagailmj@msn.com

Piteado

Embroidered leather belts with dried maguey fibers are very stylish among Mexican cowboys. Extremely time consuming, there are about 50 stitches made in each inch of leather. Fine belts can cost as much as $1000 US. Most feature Aztec designs, some less regal. Look for them at the San Juan de Dios market in Guadalajara or sometimes at Lakeside markets.

SILVER JEWELRY AND FINE CUSTOM JEWELRY

Alfonso's Silver Star Jewelry Boutique
376 766-1240
Manufacturing and repair of gold and silver jewelry, exclusive custom designs. Open Monday through Saturday, 10 a.m. to 6 p.m. Morelos #13-B. bere_q@hotmail.com

Daniel Jackson Garcia
376 766-2223
Master jeweler with 20 years experience. He designs, remakes, and repairs gold and silver jewelry; re-sets stones, sizes rings and has excellent stone suppliers. Ask about watch and clock repairs. Call for an appointment. Hidalgo #29-A, Ajijic. Fluent English spoken. *Recommended.*

Arati Para Ti
376 766-0130
Silver jewelry with semi-precious stones, scarves, Mexican artifacts, Feng Shui objects. Open Monday through Saturday, 10 a.m. to 2 p.m., 4 p.m. to 6 p.m. Morelos #3, Ajijic.

Kafri de Mexico Jewelry
376 766-4156
Exquisite silver jewelry by the Mexican designer Daniel Espinosa Studio franchise. Chameleon collection and Carlos Albert collection featured. Open daily 10 a.m. to 3 p.m. Constitución #2-A, Ajijic. kafridemexico@hotmail.com

Lakeside's Best
Jewelry by Daniel Van Waeyenberg, Carmen Bermel, Diane Pearl and other Lakeside artists. Open Monday through Saturday, 10 a.m. to 3 p.m. Colón #1, Ajijic.

Tao
376 766-1290

Terra Designs: handworked silver jewelry by Lauri Jenson. Open Monday and Tuesday, 10 a.m. to 2 p.m., Thursday, Friday, Saturday and Sunday, 10 a.m. to 4 p.m. Colón #8, Ajijic.

Taxco Silver by Lourdes
376 766-2368

Custom-made and one-of-a-kind silver jewelry with precious and semi-precious stones. All silver mined in Taxco, Mexico. Open Tuesday through Saturday 10 a.m. to 3 p.m. 16 de Septiembre #4C, Ajijic. borsanipa@yahoo.com.mx

Jewelry Shopper's Vocabulary

Could I see that, please?	*¿Me muestra eso, por favor?*
Do you have anything in gold?	*¿Tiene usted algo en oro?*
Is it real silver?	*¿Es de plata auténtica?*
I'd like a bracelet.	*Quiero una pulsera.*
I'd like a chain/cross/necklace.	*Quiero una cadena/cruz/collar.*
I'd like an anklet.	*Quiero una pulsera para el tobillo.*

SERAPES AND RUGS

Sarapes y Tapetes de Lana
387 763-1155

Woolen *sarapes* and rugs by Salvador Moya Mendez. Look for his work on the plaza every Saturday and Sunday from 9:30 a.m. to 3 p.m. He has a wide range of designs and prices are very reasonable. Privada Independencia Norte #9, Jocotepec.

Sarapes y Tapetes Luis Vasquez

Luis Vasquez shows off his rugs and serapes on the plaza benches each Saturday and Sunday morning until mid-afternoon. Available in both wool and acrylic, in different sizes, designs and colors. Others can be seen at his home on Degollado #77, Jocotepec.

SOMBREROS

Sombreros Leon

Leonardo Hoyos has been bringing Mexican hats, *sombreros*, from Sahuayo, Michocán to Jocotepec for more than 15 years. He also duplicates keys on the premises. Open daily 9 a.m. to 3 p.m., 4 p.m. to 9 p.m. Miguel Arana #121, Jocotepec. Some English spoken.

SOUVENIRS

The Original Ajijic T-Shirt
376 766-4397

"Ajijic" and custom t-shirts, hats, mugs, stickers, gifts, and paintings by Bruno Mariscal. Open 9 a.m. to 6 p.m. Monday through Saturday. Morelos #13-A, Ajijic.

The Truth About Lead Glazing

Lead, tin, cadmium, and copper oxide glazing is an integral part of the traditional ceramics of Mexico. Although the danger of poisons leaching from tableware is extremely small, demand from European and North American buyers have encouraged artists to search for new glazes that will provide them with the same traditional colors. Acid-based foods such as tomatoes, lime juice, and coffee can potentially break down the integrity of the glaze *over time* if the object has not been fired at more than 1000° C.

If you are selecting Talavera tableware, for example, for everyday use and have a history of heavy metal poisoning, be sure to buy the best quality you can afford. It is likely to have been fired at optimum temperatures, allowing the glaze to fully fuse.

STAINED GLASS

Aimar Vitrales Stained Glass Gallery
376 766-1875

Call for appointment. Libertad #6, near Six Corners, Ajijic. aimarvitrales@hotmail.com

Bob & Kathie Coull
376 766-2875

Las Golondrias Studio, custom work and instruction. Independencia #100, San Antonio Tlayacapán.
treetops@laguna.com.mx

Size Conversion Chart*

WOMEN				MEN					
Dresses *(Vestidos)* (In Mexico women's blouse sizes are the same as in the U.S.)		**Shoes** *(Zapatos)*		**Shirts** *(Camisas)* (T-shirts and other casual shirts or jackets may bear the U.S. sizes S, M, L, or XL, or their Spanish equivalent C, M, G or XG)		**Jackets** *(Chamarras)*		**Shoes** *(Zapatos)*	
U.S.	Mex.	U.S.	Mex.	U.S.	Mex.	U.S.	Mex.	U.S.	Mex.
6	32	5	3 or 23	14	37	32	40	6	24
7	33	5½	3½ or 23½	14½	38	34	42	7	25
8	34	6	4 or 24	15	39	36	44	8	26
9	35	6½	4½ or 24½	15½	40	38	46	9	27
10	36	7	5 or 25	16	41	40	48	10	28
11	37	7½	5½ pr 25½	16½	42	42	50	11	29
12	38	8	2 or 26	17	43	44	52		
13	39	8½	6½ or 26½	17½	44				
14	40	9	7 or 27	18	45				
		9½	7½ or 27½						

*Be sure to try everything on. Sizes vary because north of the border patterns were originally figured in inches, not centimeters, which is the Mexican standard.

Jacqueline Stewart
376 766-4533

Jacqueline Stewart, accomplished glass artist and watercolorist who prefers wildlife studies. By appointment only. Call for more information.

Shopping

BOUTIQUES

La Flor de la Laguna
376 766-1037

Boutique and folkart. Custom designs for casual wear, jewelry, ceramics, pewter, copper, wall art. Open Monday through Friday 10 a.m. to 2 p.m., 4 p.m. to 6 p.m., Saturday 10 a.m. to 2 p.m. Morelos #17, Ajijic.

Lois Cugini's OPUS Boutique
376 766-1790

Boutique featuring a good selection of Mexican fine clothing lines such as Alejandro Julian, Tachi Castillo, Dunes, Victor Rojo and Maria O'Campo Designs. Jewelry by

Luisa Conti, Claudia Gonzalez and Oliver. Excellent variety of gifts and folk art. Open Monday through Saturday, 10 a.m. 6 p.m. Morelos #15, Ajijic.
loiscugi@laguna.com.mx

Mi Mexico
376 766-0133
Mexican folk art, clothing, pottery, and interior art of all kinds, Ajijic/San Miguel sandals, and jewelry. Open Monday through Saturday 10 a.m. to 6 p.m., Sunday 11 a.m. to 3 p.m. Moralos #8, Ajijic.

MEN'S AND WOMEN'S CLOTHING

Alma Gutierrez Boutique
376 766-1066
Hand-painted casual wear, designer evening wear and special orders for all sizes. Open Monday through Saturday, 10 a.m. to 5 p.m. Constitución #59, Ajijic.
almagv@hotmail.com

Ana R. Designs
376 766-3977
Painted and appliqued manta clothing and other styles. 16 de Septiembre #1. Ajijic.
lopezana13@hotmail.com;
www.ana-r.com

Boutique Evolution
Buckaroo brand jeans, swimsuits and beach wear for young men and women. In Plaza Montaña, Carr. Chapala-Jocotepec at the traffic light at Colón.

Boutique Luz
376 766-2218
Clothing for children through young men and women. Including bathing suits, surf shorts, bras, underwear, men's socks and underwear, belts, sunglasses, watches, purses, backpacks, original perfumes and personal electronics. Men's sizes up to 42 and 44, women's up to XL and XXL. Open Monday through Friday 10 a.m. to 2 p.m., 4 p.m. to 9 p.m., Saturday 10 a.m. to 9 p.m., Sunday 10 a.m. to 4 p.m. Ocampo #6, Ajijic.

Fiaga Boutique & Galería
376 766-1816
Custom designer wear, evening wear made of cotton/linen blends in small and large sizes. Open Monday through Saturday 9 a.m. to 3 p.m., 4 p.m. to 6 p.m. Morelos #7, Ajijic. www.chapala.com/fiaga.html

Shopping Hours/*Horario de Tiendas*

Many businesses observe *siesta*, approximately from 2 p.m. to 4 p.m., when they will close their doors for lunch and then reopen and remain open until 7, 8 or 9 p.m. Grocery stores, real estate companies, restaurants and businesses geared to travelers will stay open throughout the day without observing *siesta* but may close as early as 3 p.m. *Siesta* hours in some villages are observed more traditionally than in others—Chapala, for example, is more traditional than Ajijic—so be sure to make a note of the times that businesses close and reopen, especially if you are on foot.

GA Boutique
376 766-4936
Casual wear for young women. Open Monday through Saturday 10 a.m. to 7 p.m., Sunday 10 a.m. to 5 p.m. Ocampo #8, Ajijic.

Heidi's Fashions/ Bear with Me
376 766-4721
376 766-5167
Clothing for the relaxed lifestyle, custom, ready to wear. Styles from elegant to casual. Open Monday through Saturday 10 a.m. to 2 p.m., 4 p.m. to 6 p.m. Hidalgo #10, Ajijic. heidisfashions@hotmail.com; www.heidisfashions.tripod.com

La Pulgita
376 766-2885
Toys, clothing for girls and boys, stockings, purses and belts, bras, adult clothing with a youthful orientation. Men's shoes up to size 12 U.S./Canadian, women's shoes up to size 8 U.S./Canadian. Open Monday through Friday 10 a.m. to 2 p.m., 4 p.m. to 9 p.m., Saturday 10 a.m. to 9 p.m., Sunday 10 a.m. to 7 p.m. Ocampo #4, Ajijic.

La Sala de Smokee
044 376 769-0853
376 765-4803
Boutique and consignment. Lakeside's newest and largest clothing and consignment store; accessories, jewelry, name brands, artwork, sculptures and more. Open Monday through Friday 9:30 a.m. to 4 p.m., Saturday 10 a.m. to 4 p.m. Plaza Bugambilias, downstairs, next to El Torito grocery, Ajijic. In Chapala, on Juárez behind the market.

Luisa's Boutique
376 765-5515
Men's and women's clothing and accessories. Encarnación Rosas #8, Chapala.

Luz Boutique
376 766-2218

Casual and formal clothing, designer perfumes and accessories. Open Monday through Friday 10 a.m. to 2 p.m., 4 p.m. to 9 p.m., Saturday 10 a.m. to 9 p.m., Sunday 10 a.m. 7 p.m. Ocampo #6, just west of Colon, Ajijic.

Studio G

Stylish shoe store for women, with leather handbags and jackets. Open Monday through Saturday 9 a.m. to 2 p.m., 4 p.m. to 7 p.m. Guadalupe Victoria Sur #78, Jocotepec.

SHOES

Flexi Shoes

High quality Flexi-brand shoes for men and women. Men's sizes up to 12 and 1/2 U.S. and Canadian sizes, women's up to size 10. Open Monday through Saturday 10 a.m. to 3 p.m., 5 p.m. to 9 p.m. López Cotilla #278-B, Chapala.

Sport Tennis
376 765-5333

Flexi, Hush Puppies, Nike, Adidas, New Balance, Skechers, Reebok, Rider beach shoes, and children's shoes. Women's shoes to size 10 U.S. and Canadian. Open Monday through Friday 10 a.m. to 3 p.m., 5 p.m. to 8 p.m., Saturday 10 a.m. to 8 p.m., Sunday 10 a.m. to 7:30 p.m. Madero #413, Chapala.

Zapatería La Bodeguita

Shoes for women, men and children. Boots in some exotic skins for men. Open daily 9 a.m. to 8 p.m. Hidalgo Sur #92, Jocotepec.

RELIGIOUS GIFTS

Ceramica "Cuquis"
376 766-1086

Gifts and clothing for weddings, baptisms, *quinceañeras*, and communions. Open Monday through Thursday 10 a.m. to 2 p.m., 4 p.m. to 9 p.m., Friday and Saturday 10 a.m. to 2 p.m., Sunday noon to 2 p.m. Colón Sur #4, Ajijic.

Numbers/Numeros

1 *uno*	2 *dos*	3 *tres*	4 *cuatro*	5 *cinco*
6 seis	7 *siete*	8 *ocho*	9 *nueve*	10 *diez*
11 *once*	12 *doce*	13 *trece*	14 *catorce*	15 *quince*
16 *diez y seis*	17 *diez y siete*	18 *diez y ocho*	19 *diez y nueve*	20 *veinte*
25 *veinte y cinco*	30 *treinta*	35 *treinta y cinco*	40 *cuarenta*	50 *cincuenta*
55 *cincuenta y cinco*	60 *sesenta*	65 *sesenta y cinco*	70 *setenta*	75 *setenta y cinco*
80 *ochenta*	85 *ochenta y cinco*	90 *noventa*	95 *noventa y cinco*	100 *cien*
200 *doscientos*	300 *trescientos*	400 *cuatrocientos*	500 *quinientos*	600 *seiscientos*
700 *setecientos*	800 *ochocientos*	900 *novecientos*	1000 *mil*	1,000,000 *millón*

CARD AND GIFT SHOP

Garden of Eden

Greeting cards in English and Spanish, stuffed animals, toys, artist supplies, designer party supplies, candles, greeting balloons, dolls, gift wrap. Open Monday through Friday 9 a.m. to 2 p.m., 3 p.m. to 7 p.m., Saturday 9 a.m. to 2 p.m., 3 p.m. to 6 p.m. Plaza Bugambilias, downstairs, Local #4, Ajijic (plaza next to El Torito grocery store).

COMPREHENSIVE BUSINESS DESIGNERS

Itzáes Deseñadores
01 33 3638-0936

From floor plan to signage to business cards, Maricela Silva will do it all. Monte Atlas #1612, Colonia Independencia, Guadalajara.

FRAMING SHOPS

Vidriería Gonzalez
376 766-1356

Quality custom framing, shadow boxes, and good selection of prints and photos by local artists for sale. Excellent service, but due to their extremely high volume of work they can get backlogged. They're good about telling you if there's a wait. Owner Ricardo Gonzalez is Ajijic's current mayor. Open Monday through Friday 9 a.m. to 2 p.m., 3 p.m. to 7 p.m., Saturday 9 a.m. to 2 p.m. Guadalupe Victoria #38, Ajijic. glezglezrica@hotmail.com Some English spoken. *Recommended.*

Greca
01 33 1519-5811

Frame shop and embroidery shop in one. More than 500 frames to choose from, standard and non-reflecting glass available. Embroidery classes are 10 *pesos* per class, materials available for purchase. Open Monday through Saturday 9:30 a.m. to 2 p.m., 4 p.m. to 7:30 p.m. Sunday 9:30 a.m. to 2 p.m. Guadalupe Victoria #88-B, Jocotepec.

Dale Hoyt Palfrey

Lighting castillos during *the fiestas of San Antonio Tlayacapán.*

7

Things to See and Do

Events, Fiestas, Indoor Pursuits, Worship

with

DALE HOYT PALFREY, ZOFIA BARISAS and ROBIN LAWRASON

A wealth of things to see and do can be found in the Lake Chapala area. Local events, *fiestas*, and a large variety of clubs, churches and social organizations all help make one's stay pleasurable, rewarding and stimulating.

Fiesta Time

BY DALE HOYT PALFREY

The hundreds of colorful, noisy *fiestas* that crowd Mexico's calendar are among the country's most intriguing attributes. The Jalisco tourism department lists nearly 200 different events in its catalogue of the state's most important local festivities, fairs and religious pilgrimages. This chapter is intended as a basic introduction to celebrations you'll be likely to encounter in and near the Lake Chapala area.

National civic holidays are often marked by parades, public ceremonies and other special events. On the calendar shown below, major holidays marked with an asterisk (*) indicate the dates when employees are entitled to a paid holiday and banks, government offices, schools and some businesses shut down operations.

Local religious festivities may last for several days, or even weeks, with crowds flooding village streets and plazas to celebrate with processions, fireworks, street markets, rodeos and general carousing. Loud rockets startling you from slumber at dawn are a sure sign that an important celebration is underway. With most of the hubbub concentrated after dark, business often carries on much as usual during working hours, except perhaps on the main *fiesta* day.

Some religious celebrations are moveable feasts that are not fixed to a specific date. Many major Roman Catholic festivities and related customs are observed nationwide. Mexico also recognizes various social and occupational groups with specific secular celebrations.

FIESTAS PATRONALES

All Mexican towns and most *barrios* (neighborhoods) recognize a particular religious patron, usually a saint, that is honored once a year with special festivities. Frequently the celebration runs for a nine-day period, referred to as a *novenario,* that culminates on the day the church calendar designates to the patron in question. The *fiestas patronales* are important both in a religious sense and as a social phenomenon through which local inhabitants break away from everyday routines, let their hair down and reaffirm community identity.

Organizational responsibilities and costs of the celebration are largely shouldered by occupational guilds—called *gremios*—or an individual steward—known as the *mayordomo* or *carguero*. The most extravagant festivity is often seen on the date sponsored by *hijos ausentes*—absent native sons and daughters who work in the U.S.A.

Celebrations generally start at daybreak with religious observances hailed by a barrage of deafening sky rockets. Traditional processions that often feature an icon of the patron accompanied by colorful floats, costumed dancers, blaring bands and prancing horses, may occur on one or more dates at various times of day. Afternoon activities may center at the local *lienzo charro* or *plaza de toros* (bullring) where crowds gather for cowpoke contests that are commonly fueled by live music, dancing and prodigious drinking. After dark, following church services, people cluster around the village plaza to socialize and relish a fair-like offering of typical foods, drinks, assorted trinkets, games and mechanical rides. The evening usually climaxes with a dazzling fireworks display.

FIESTA CALENDAR

This abbreviated index of national and local celebrations—arranged as best as possible in chronological order—will guide you in figuring out what all the fuss is about on key *fiesta* days. The dates listed for *fiestas patronales* indicate the religious patron's special day when the celebration reaches its grand finale. Check local English language publications for articles offering more in-depth details.

January 1: *Año Nuevo* (New Year's) * Like most countries, Mexico starts the New Year by taking a day off to rest up from New Year's Eve celebrations.

January, third Sunday: Jocotepec celebrates *fiestas patronales* honoring *El Señor del Monte* (Lord of the Mount).

Dale Hoyt Palfrey

"El torito" *will be laced with firecrackers.*

January 6: *Día de los Santos Reyes* (Three Kings Day-Epiphany) Close on the heels of Christmas, children throughout Mexico anxiously await the day they wake up to find gifts delivered not by Santa Claus, but by the Magi. All age groups traditionally celebrate Epiphany by sampling *rosca de reyes,* a large, crown-shaped bread decorated with jewel-colored candied fruits. Whoever cuts off a slice with a tiny baby doll baked inside is designated as a godparent who will take charge of a party and other customs linked to Candlemas, celebrated February 2.

January 20: Ajijic's *Barrio de San Sebastián* honors patron Saint Sebastian with communal feasting and a spirited block party.

February 2: *Día de la Candelaria* (Candlemas). To mark the conclusion of the Christmas season, families remove figures of the baby Jesus from household Nativity scenes. Godparents (see January 6 above) provide a new outfit for the Christ Child and host the obligatory *tamale* feast. Religious services feature special blessings for infants, seeds for Spring planting, candles and other devotional items.

February-March, variable dates: *Carnaval* (Mardi Gras) is celebrated with unbridled revelry in the days immediately prior to Ash Wednesday and the start of Lent. Festivities in Chapala and Ajijic are noted for a string of colorful parades, rodeos, and big public dances. *Martes de Carnaval* (Shrove Tuesday) falls between February 3 and March 9.

February 5: *Día de la Constitución* * The promulgation of Mexico's Constitution (1857 and 1917) is observed.

February 24: *Día de la Bandera* Mexican Flag Day.

March 18: *Conmemoración de la Expropiación Petrolera* * The nationalization of the petroleum industry (1938) is commemorated.

March 21: *Natalicio de Benito Juárez* * Benito Juárez, a famous

Mexican president and national hero, is remembered on his birthday.

March-April, variable dates: *Semana Santa* (Holy Week) marks the end of the 40-day period of Lent. On the previous Friday many householders in Chapala, San Antonio Tlayacapán and Ajijic display elaborate doorstep altars venerating *La Virgen de Dolores* (Our Lady of Sorrows). Ajijic's *Pasión de Cristo* (Passion Play) troupe enthralls hoards of spectators with a spectacular dramatization of the Easter story staged in various episodes running from Palm Sunday through Good Friday. Most other towns mark Good Friday with the *Vía Crucis* (Way of the Cross), a procession reenacting the climb to Calvary and Christ's Crucifixion. Easter Sunday falls between March 22 and April 25.

April 30: *Día del Niño* (Children's Day) Mexican youngsters enjoy a day of festivity with gifts and special activities organized by families, businesses, schools and social agencies.

May: The faithful dedicate the entire month to the blessed Virgin Mary. Young children, decked out in their First Communion finery, parade to the church every afternoon bearing floral offerings for *La Virgen*.

May 1: *Día del Trabajo* * On Mexico's equivalent to Labor Day, all salaried workers enjoy a paid holiday. Labor union affiliates gather in most major cities for public demonstrations. The date coincides with the church's veneration of *San José Obrero* (Saint Joseph), patron of workers.

May, first Sunday: Jocotepec honors the town's second major patron, *El Señor del Guaje* (Lord of the Guaje tree) with special devotions and an impressive afternoon procession.

May 3: *Día de la Santa Cruz* (Day of the Holy Cross) is celebrated by all Mexican masons and builders with feasting and lots of loud fireworks. Crosses fixed at the highest point of every construction site and those permanently set along village streets and on neighboring hilltops are festooned with streamers, flags and flowers. Costumed troupes perform ritual dances around midday in Mezcala, while rowdy night time festivities rock Ajijic. Look for shrines laden with food, flowers and candles displayed in many neighborhoods. The date also marks the close of *fiestas patronales* in Santa Cruz de la Soledad.

May 5: *Conmemoración de la Batalla de Puebla* The nation marks the anniversary of its crushing victory over the French army at Puebla de los Angeles (1862). Curiously, *Cinco de Mayo* festivities held in

Latino communities north of the border are a much bigger deal than the sedate observances hallowing national sovereignty held in most parts of Mexico.

May 10: *Día de las Madres* (Mother's Day) is invariably celebrated on this date. Though neither a civic nor religious holiday, it counts among the most widely and fervently celebrated dates on Mexico's calendar. Families honor their matriarchs with early morning serenades, noisy fireworks, floral bouquets, gifts and special meals. Youngsters lovingly entertain their moms with cultural pageants organized by their school teachers.

Dale Hoyt Palfrey

***Ajijic's annual Passion Play** attracts international attention.*

May-June, variable date: Corpus Christi falls 60 days after Easter. The following Sunday marks the end of *fiestas patronales* in Jamay, celebrated with the *Desfile de los Gremios,* a remarkably colorful midday parade.

June 13: San Antonio Tlayacapán celebrates *fiestas patronales* honoring Saint Anthony of Padua. As the festivities usually coincide with the start of the summer rainy season, seasoned locals carry umbrellas.

June, variable date: *Día del Padre* (Father's Day) falls on the third Sunday of the month. Family gatherings held in Dad's honor usually lack the exuberant fanfare associated with Mother's Day.

June 29: Both San Juan Cosalá and San Juan Tecomatlán celebrate *fiestas patronales* honoring Saint John the Baptist. The festivities are often interrupted by a sudden downpours.

July 16: *Nuestra Señora del Carmen* (Our Lady of Mount Carmel) is widely honored all over Mexico. Local festivities center in the Chapala *barrio* of the same name.

July 25: Ixtlahuacán de los Membrillos celebrates *fiestas patronales* honoring Santo Santiago (Saint James the Greater), a widely popular patron distinguished as the first Christian saint to appear on Mexican shores. Colorful representations in Tonalá (near Guadalajara) feature Santiago battling evil pagan forces as represented by garishly masked Tastoán dancers.

August 15: Mezcala celebrates *fiestas patronales* honoring patroness *La Virgen de la Asunción* (Virgin of the Assumption).

September 1: *El Informe Presidencial* Mexico's commander-in-chief delivers his annual State of the Union address.

September 16: *Día de la Independencia* * Celebration of Mexico's Independence Day is marked with parades across the nation, including Chapala, Ajijic and Jocotepec. Lively festivities begin the previous evening as local officials reenact the *Grito de Dolores*, Padre Miguel Hidalgo's 1810 call for insurgency against Spanish rule.

October 7: *La Virgen del Rosario* (Virgin of the Rosary) is venerated in many localities. Ajijic honors its earliest religious patron throughout the entire month, capped off October 31 with a picturesque procession through the town and an evening of festivities at the central plaza.

October 4: Chapala celebrates *fiestas patronales* honoring *San Francisco de Asís* (Saint Francis of Assisi).

October 12: *Día de la Raza* Observances recall Columbus' arrival to the Americas as an event that spawned the fusion of Indian and European cultures and the birth of modern Mexico's Mestizo race. *La Virgen de Zapopan*, trusted as a divine protector against disease and natural disaster, is honored on this date with a massive pilgrimage that essentially shuts down normal business in the Guadalajara metro area all day long.

November 1-2: *Día de todos Santos* and *Día de los Muertos* (All Saints' Day and All Souls' Day) are marked by unique and surprisingly festive practices derived from a synthesis of pre-Hispanic rituals and Christian customs. Mexican people honor their dead by decorating family grave sites and attending memorial services held in local cemeteries. Colorful offerings of typical foods, marigold blossoms, candy skulls and other symbolic items laid out to honor and entice departed souls are seen on the traditional altars displayed at many homes, schools and public venues.

November 12: *Día del Cartero* (Mailman's Day) is an occasion to show appreciation to the postmaster and local mail carriers with a gift

FIESTA PYROTECHNICS

The deafening sky rockets that so often herald Mexican festivities are an anathema to a lot of foreigners who object to the constant commotion or perceive them as a huge waste of money for people of limited means. An appreciation of the finer points may help take the edge off your encounters with Mexican-style fireworks.

According to conventional wisdom, no *fiesta* is truly complete without an abundance of *pólvora* (gunpowder) and *juegos pirotécnicos* (firework displays). Introduced to Mexico after the Spanish conquest, their use in festivities originated with the concept that the heaven-sent explosions represent a palpable manifestation of faith to alert the Almighty or honored religious patron and spook evil spirits. For the folks footing the bill, the noisy custom may be a question of pride in the sense that the degree of racket and expense somehow equates to the sponsor's fidelity.

Unlike their cautious northern neighbors, Mexican fiesta-goers tend to like getting up-close and personal when it comes to pyrotechnics. Yes, accidents do happen. Without getting into statistics, countless injuries and deaths have resulted from firework mishaps, including one in which famed muralist José Clemente Orozco lost an arm in his boyhood. But the latent danger is every bit as alluring as all the color and magic.

A main menu of pyrotechnic devices includes:

cohetes de trueno - booming sky rockets that signal religious rites and mark the pilgrims' progress in processions.

cohetes de luces - hissing rockets that pop gently before releasing a spray of colored starlights.

bomba - a rocket that sets off a huge spherical starburst tinted in brilliant hues, alternately known as a *bola*.

salvo - a barrage of 20-odd rockets ignited in rapid succession.

el castillo - the *fiesta* centerpiece, an intricate contraption made up of split-reed figures latched to a tall vertical pole, detonated in stages comprising a phantasmagoric array of fulminating Catherine wheels, *giranadoles*, Roman candles, fizgigs and other devices that whirl, fizzle, crackle and delight.

torito - a reed and papier mâché figure shaped like a bull, laced with firecrackers and formed to fit over the head of a runner who charges through *fiesta* crowds as the explosives whiz off in all directions.

buscapiés - firecrackers known as "foot-seekers' that emit a distinctive whistle as they ricochet helter-skelter along the ground.

los judas - crude papier mâché effigies, often tagged with the names of infamous public figures that are threaded with powerful firecrackers, strung up in public and blown to smithereens; a custom practiced on the eve of Easter Sunday representing Judas Iscariot's suicidal hanging, and by extension, the obliteration of evil forces.

globos - blessedly silent, but otherwise closely related to the above, are the rainbow-hued hot air balloons fashioned from tissue paper in myriad shapes and sizes; especially popular in Ajijic where they are set afloat en masse during aerial regattas linked to Independence Day festivities.

or gratuity, along with a word of thanks.

November 20: *Día de la Revolución Mexicana* * The official celebration of the start of the Mexican Revolution (1910) is marked by colorful civic parades held nationwide, including Chapala, Ajijic and Jocotepec.

November 22: *Día de Santa Cecilia* (Saint Cecilia's Day), the patroness of musicians is feted with boisterous celebration by Mariachi bands, melody-makers and music lovers in general. The date coincides with the start of Ajijic's *fiestas patronales.*

November 30: Ajijic celebrates *fiestas patronales* honoring *San Andrés* (Saint Andrew the Apostle).

December 6: San Nicolás de Ibarra, near the Vista del Lago subdivision, celebrates *fiestas patronales* honoring Saint Nicholas.

December 12: *Día de Nuestra Señora de Guadalupe.* The dark-skinned Virgin of Guadalupe, patroness of all Latin Americans, is honored across Mexico with colorful processions, fireworks and lively street fairs. Neighborhoods surrounding churches dedicated to *La Guadalupana* may celebrate with prolonged festivities. Many local families ornament their homes with altars hallowing *La Virgen Morena.*

December 16-24: *Las Posadas* are holiday parties celebrating the Christmas season. Children join in traditional neighborhood processions that represent the Holy Family's search for shelter in Bethlehem, a custom best exemplified by the candlelight parades held each evening in San Antonio Tlayacapán. *Posada* gatherings often culminate with the boisterous breaking of brightly decorated *piñatas* stuffed with sweets and seasonal fruits.

December 24: *Noche Buena* (Christmas Eve) is the occasion Mexico sets aside to celebrate the Nativity. Catholic families may attend a late night *Misa de Gallo* (Rooster's Mass) before gathering at home for a holiday feast. Gift exchanges, *piñata*-smashing and joyful socializing frequently stretch out into the wee hours. While Christmas trees are now common, home holiday decorating usually centers on the *nacimiento* (creche). In these often elaborate nativity scene displays, the manger is left empty until December 24 when the image of the Baby Jesus is tenderly laid in place at a key moment in the *Noche Buena* festivities.

December 25: *Navidad* * (Christmas) is usually a laid-back day of rest for Mexican families. Housewives dish out *el recalentón*—a savory repast made up of leftovers from the previous evening's feast.

December 28: *Día de los Santos Inocentes* (Day of the Holy Innocents), Mexico's equivalent to April Fool's Day, is marked by pulling jokes and pranks on friends and relations.

December 31: *Año Nuevo* (New Year's Eve) is celebrated with late night supper parties. Eating 12 grapes as the clock strikes midnight, donning a specific color of underwear or welcoming in the New Year with a pocket full of cash are among the customs practiced to propitiate good fortune in the coming months.

Clubs, Organizations and Indoor Entertainment

CLUBS AND ORGANIZATIONS

Especially during the winter season, November through April, Lakeside swells with clubs and service organizations that bring together people with similar interests, concerns, and skills. Check the Bulletin Board section of the Guadalajara Colony Reporter for meeting announcements, as well as listings in The Ojo del Lago and Lake Chapala Review magazines. Many events are held in private homes, the Auditorium in La Floresta, at the Little Theater in San Antonio Tlayacapán, at restaurants, hotels, and on the grounds of the Lake Chapala Society.

Dale Hoyt Palfrey

LCS is an important *resource for foreigners.*

The Lake Chapala Society
376 766-1140

Pablo Fernandez del Valle

The Lake Chapala Society was founded in Chapala in January 1955 by 31 English-speaking residents as a cultural, social and benevolent society. In 1989, Neill James, a pioneer in the foreign community, bequeathed her estate to the Society and it moved to its present location on 16 de Septiembre #16-A in Ajijic. For more information about their activities visit their website; www.lakechapalasociety.org

To take advantage of the services of the Lake Chapala Society, including the use of the English-language library and video rental service, you must become a member, although you can attend some events there without joining. If your stay is long enough, you'll want to belong as it is the most useful organization for the English-speaking visitor. The offices are open Monday through Friday 10 a.m. to 2 p.m. and annual membership fees are currently 450 *pesos* for families and 350 *pesos* for individuals. Part-time memberships are available. Affiliation entitles members to a large number of useful services, including help with immigration, IMSS (the Mexican Health Care system), wills, trusts and post life planning. Membership also includes your name, address and phone number in the LCS yearly directory.

Canadian Club

Geared to Canadians but open to everyone, this lively group offers a popular travel program, keeps current with Mexican laws that affect immigration, wills, property and tax matters, and promotes Canadian good will and spirit. Visit their website at www.canadianclubmx.com.

LIBRARIES

American Legion
376 765-2259

The American Legion has a lending library for members. Morelos #114, Chapala.

***Biblioteca de Jocotepec/* Jocotepec Library**

Inaugurated in November 2003, the new Jocotepec library is behind *La Casa de Cultura* on the southwest corner of the plaza. A very pleasant space, it looks onto a small courtyard and shares a grassy area with an ancient church wall. Every Thursday the library schedules children's story time. The library holds a small number of English books and some English and French magazines. It is open Monday through Friday 10 a.m. to 1 p.m., 2 p.m. to 8 p.m., Saturday 8 a.m. to 2 p.m. Occasionally it closes Monday mornings. Some English is spoken. The library is entered through the south side, at the corner of Hidalgo Sur and Corona.

Higher Shelf Library

A collection of self-realization and spiritually-minded books is available for lending Monday through Thursday from 9 a.m. to 9 p.m. at Guerrero #190-A, at Mi Casa Hotel, Chapala.

The Lake Chapala Society (LCS)

LCS houses a library of more than 30,000 books in English. Lending privileges are to members only. Open Monday through Friday, 10 a.m. to 2 p.m. 16 de Septiembre #16-A, Ajijic.

Talking Books Library

LCS loans special Talking Books audio cassettes and the machines that play them to U.S. citizens who are visually impaired or handicapped. Provided by the Library of Congress in Washington, D.C., the service is free. For non-U.S. citizens, commercial books on tape are available. Open Thursday 10 a.m. to 1 p.m. 16 de Septiembre #16-A, Ajijic.

COOKING SCHOOL

School of Mexican Culinary Arts
01 33 3647-5239
01 33 3647-4621

Sign up for culinary classes with Rose Marie Plaschinski, who began her career at the Cordon Bleu in Paris, studied at the Culinary Institute of America in New York, and attended UNAM in Mexico city to master the historical recipes of Mexico.

BRIDGE

Lake Chapala Duplicate Bridge Club
376 766-0705, 376 766-3924

ACBL sanctioned games. About one-third of the members are Life Masters. There are member and non-member fees and dues. Tuesday, Thursday and Friday 1:20 p.m. to 5:30 p.m. Carr. Chapala-Jocotepec #77-1, Riberas del Pilar, one block east of the Máscaras Clinic. English spoken. www.chapalabridge.com

SPANISH LANGUAGE CLASSES

Spanish Classes at the American Legion

Beginning classes 11 a.m., Intermediate Spanish 1 p.m., at the American Legion Post 7. Morelos #114, Chapala on Monday. Free to members.

Spanish Classes at the Lake Chapala Society

Beginning Spanish 2 p.m. Friday, Advanced beginners, 2 p.m. Wednesday, Advanced speakers 10 a.m. Thursday. Free to members.

Darrell Schmidt
376 766-5194

Beginning, Intermediate and Advanced classes. Camino Real #47, La Floresta. *Recommended.*

Spanish Superlearning Ajijic
376 766-1022

Accelerated learning for all levels with Dr. Barbara Lotito. Call for schedules. Spanishsuperlearning@yahoo.com

Laura Reyes, Hilda Ortiz
376 766-2924
376 765-5958

Beginning and advanced learners. Individual and group classes. aprender2004@prodigy.net.mx

Classes in Guadalajara

Berlitz
01 33 3630-3987
01 33 3641-2074

Courses begin every week and intensive courses are held each Saturday. www.berlitz.com

Instituto Cultural Mexicano Norte-american de Jalisco, AC
01 33 3825-5838
01 33 3825-5666
01 33 3825-4101

Learn Spanish in a bi-national cultural center, the only institution recognized by the U.S. government in Guadalajara. The Instituto has been in operation since 1949. instructors use communicative techniques in a year-round program offering all levels in small groups. Enrique Díaz de León Sur #300, Col. Moderna, Guadalajara. cultural@guadalajara.net; www.guadalajara .net/~~cultural

ENGLISH AS A SECOND LANGUAGE TRAINING

Worldwide Teachers Institute of Guadalajara
01 33 3613-5226
01 33 3614-4883

The Institute graduates students with C.T.E.F.L. certificates for teaching English as a Foreign Language. Their Boston TEFL Certificate Method is a three-week immersion course (150 hrs) that's offered each month in Guadalajara that emphasizes practice rather than theory. They help with accommodations and scholarships for Mexican citizens and FM-3 holders. After graduation they assist with placement in worldwide locations. Madero #616, Zona Centro CP 44100, Guadalajara. Teflmexi@hotmail.com; www.eltschools.com; Boston Web Page: www.bostonTEFL.com

RADIO STATIONS

FM Stations

88.1 Jacobo Zabludovsky, Mexico's "Walter Cronkite", continues to deliver the news via radio from 1 to 5 p.m., Monday through Friday.

89.9 Oldies and contemporary tunes in an all-day listening format. Classics from the early '60's to the late '80's.

93.8 Classical and opera music, as well as ultra-contemporary techno music in English and Spanish, and classic and contemporary

	multi-national music.
95.5	Music in English, Ballads
99.5	Musical Favorites in English
101.9	Romantic Ballads
105.9	Oldies in English

TELEVISION

Mexican TV channels broadcasting from Guadalajara and available via a rooftop antenna are characterized by news and interview programs, movies (occasionally in English with Spanish subtitles), variety shows, sports, and the ever popular prime-time soaps, *novelas*. For programming in English, basic and expanded cable service is available, along with C-Band satellite and mini-satellite systems.

WHAT'S 4DTV?

4DTV uses a specialized digital receiver and the big dish (eight to ten feet, although the bigger 18 foot dishes can also be used) to receive approximately 345 video channels and 120 music channels. If pointed toward the satellite AnikE2, says Pete Johanson who writes the Tech Talk column for the Guadalajara Colony Reporter, you can pick up the Star Choice programming out of Canada.

CABLE TV SERVICE

Telecable Jocotepec
387 763-0543

Forty-nine channels, many in English. Prompt installation and service; if bill paid within first 10 days of month a free GUIA (TV guide in Spanish) is given. Payments can be made with debit card. Installation can be arranged through the Riberas del Pilar office for those who speak no Spanish. (See below.) Open Monday through Friday 9 a.m. to 2 p.m., 4 p.m. to 6 p.m., Saturday 9 a.m. to 1 p.m. In the Ramírez Rábago furniture store on Miguel Arana #171, at the very back, Jocotepec.

Telecable Riberas del Pilar
376 765-4550

Cable television broadcasting, up to 58 channels, more than two-thirds of them in Spanish, is available through Telecable. American channels in English include Discovery, ESPN 2, Fox, Headline News, TBS, TNT, WGN and others in English with Spanish subtitles. Open 8 a.m. to 6 p.m., Monday through Saturday. Av. Hidalgo #88, Riberas del Pilar (on the main *carretera* just west of the Máscaras Clinic.)

SATELLITE TV SERVICE

Satellite & Electronics Service Center/ *Electronica y Servicio*
376 766-1351

Sales and installation of 4DTV, Sky TV and C-band satellite subscriptions. They also repair TVs, VCRs, microwaves, fax machines, stereos, CD players, camcorders, and DVD players. Open Monday through Saturday, 9 a.m. to 2 p.m., 3 to 6 p.m. Carr. Chapala-Jocotepec #146, San Antonio Tlayacapán (across from Super Lake grocery store).

Satellite Source
376 766-4327

Offers programming for C-Band dishes and for small dishes; 4DTV. English spoken.
visionxsat@yahoo.com

Satellite Systems of Ajijic
376 766-1117
376 766-3371

Sales, installation and service of 4DTV, C-Band satellite dishes, receivers, and subscriptions including Canadian Star Choice satellite systems and packages. They also install phone, fax and stereo hookups, intercom systems, and voltage regulators. They'll match any other offer. Monday through Friday 9 a.m. to 2, 3:30 to 5 p.m. Las Flores #2-A, Ajijic. English spoken. *Recommended.*
satelites2002@prodigy.net.mx

Star Choice

Canadian-based Star Choice launched one of the world's most powerful satellites in 2001 that reaches all of Mexico and much of Central America. For information on equipment and programming, email Jim Forman, a satellite dealer from Duncan,

British Columbia, at info@ultravisionsatellite.com

VIDEO/DVD RENTAL

Shops renting videos and DVDs are common but permission to rent tends to be geared toward residents or long-term visitors. Here are several options:

Maxivideo Paco Video rental, some for sale. Good choice of English movies with Spanish subtitles and new releases, Spanish language movies with no subtitles. Two-day rentals for DVDs are 20 *pesos*, newer videos 15 *pesos*, older videos 10 *pesos*. Open daily 9 a.m. to 9 p.m. Hidalgo Sur #149, Jocotepec.

Video & DVD Sales G & S Cyber 376 766-4233 You can buy DVDs of movies in English, in English with Spanish subtitles, and Spanish for 25 *pesos*, downloaded from the Internet. Plus you can get tapes duplicated and surf the net for the best price in town, 10 *pesos* an hour. Plus you can rent computers by the hour. Open Monday through Saturday 10 a.m. to 9 p.m., Sunday 4 p.m. to 8 p.m. Aldama #24, Ajijic. English spoken. graceesquedah@hotmail.com

Video Centro Ajijic 376 766-0619 For membership, one must show proof of a local address (telephone or electricity receipt) and two personal references. Open daily 9:30 a.m. to 8 p.m. On the Ajijic-Chapala Carretera #6-B, in Ajijic. Spanish spoken.

Video Centro Chapala 376 765-4183 For membership one must show proof of a local address (telephone or electricity receipt) and three personal references with addresses. Open daily 9 a.m. to 8:30 p.m. Madero #469, Chapala.

Video Club Chiru Good selection of old and current films in English with Spanish subtitles. Cartoon movies all dubbed in Spanish and some foreign films with Spanish subtitles. Open daily 10 a.m. to 2 p.m., 4 p.m. to 9 p.m.

Morelos #20, just east of the main market, Jocotepec.

Video Tape Library at The Lake Chapala Society

The Tape Worm Video Club rents its 6,000 VHS tapes and DVDs for adults and children to its members, 10 a.m. to 2 p.m. Monday through Saturday. The best of the Short Subjects from the Ajijic Film Festival *(Ajijic Festival Internacionál de Cine),* 1999-2002, are part of their collection. 16 de Septiembre #16-A, Ajijic. Look for the video catalog on their website, www.lakechapalasociety.org

CINEMA

Cinemas Bugambilias
376 766-3729

Lakeside's Cinemas Bugambilias opened in November 1999 just in time for the first annual Ajijic International Film Festival (now defunct). This tri-plex usually shows two first-run films in English with Spanish subtitles and one Spanish-only film. Movie-goers will enjoy their full snack bar and discount Wednesdays when ticket prices are cheaper. Check the Guadalajara Colony Reporter newspaper for listings and times or visit their website, www.cba.com.mx. Daily matinees at 3 p.m. Films change every Friday. Upstairs in the Plaza Bugambilias next to El Torito grocery store in Ajijic. Carr. Ote. #54-C.

Movie Buff?

Want to know something about the movie showing at the theater? Go to www.allmovie.com

MUSIC

Music Appreciation Society/ Charleton Bullock
376 766-1582

MAS brings world-class ballet, musicians, ensembles, opera, as well as national music and dance to the Auditorio de Riberas del Pilar (Lakeside Auditorium) in La Floresta. Season tickets and performance-only tickets are sold for events.

Viva la Musica!
Suzanne Forrest
376 766-0908

This group organizes concerts for up-and-coming musicians, as well as bus trips to Guadalajara and other places for concerts and dinners.

COMMUNITY THEATRE

Lakeside Little Theatre Box Office
376 766-0954

In 2004 the Lakeside Little Theatre celebrated 40 years of performances. Its first play, "The Saddle Bag Saloon" was written, choreographed and staged by Betty Kuzell who rallied her friends to organize the theatre into offering an official season by its 10th year. The theatre, off Allen W. Lloyd Boulevard in San Antonio Tlayacapán, was built in 1987 and seats 112 patrons.The stage measures 25 feet across and 55 feet deep and the orchestra pit accommodates as many as six musicians. The theatre season runs October through April, with season tickets in high demand. A typical season consists of seven plays. Musicals are especially popular and garner ten performances, two more than other plays. Many of LLT's actors, directors and choreographers are seasoned professionals who have had careers in many parts of the world. Too shy to get onstage? Hardworking armies of volunteers are needed backstage for productions; or let yourself get bitten by the acting bug gently by signing up for one of the workshops offered each year.

AUDITORIUM

Auditorio de la Ribera
376 766-1697

Located in lower La Floresta, the Auditorio de la Ribera is the venue for dance, music and community events on the Northshore.

Arts and Interest Groups

(Many thanks to Robin Lawrason)

Ajijic Quilt Guild 376 766-0276	Open to the general public. Meets at Laguna B&B, Zaragoza Ote. #29, Ajijic.
Ajijic Society of the Arts (ASA)	Artists working in a variety of mediums who hold exhibitions and sales to the general public. asaprez@hotmail.com
Ajijic Writers Group	Meets at the Lake Chapala Society, 16 de Septiembre #16-A, Ajijic.
Card & Domino Club/Francine 376 766-1658	Club meets at Melanie's Restaurant, Ocampo #30, Ajijic.
Culinary Arts Society of Ajijic/ Donna Carnall 376 766-2520	Cooking enthusiasts who share and compete for best recipes. carnall2@prodigy.net.mx
Lake Chapala Garden Club/ Chris Bublin 376 766-4282	Promotes an interest, appreciation and better understanding of botanical subjects including but not limited to all plant materials, their care and use in the home and garden. Meetings explore the many garden species and practices unique to this area of Mexico. president@lakechapalagardenclub.com; www.lakechapalagardenclub.com
Lake Chapala Society/Charlie Smith 376 766-1140 376 766-3370	Helps non-Mexicans living at Lakeside to have a more enjoyable and worry-free life. Also helps the local Mexican community through a student aid program and classes in art, English, computers, and remedial academics.16 de Septiembre #16-A Ajijic. lcs@laguna.com.mx; chssmith@laguna.com.mx; www.lakechapalasociety.org
Lakeside Little Theatre/ Pat Carroll 376 765-5942	Promotes and produces a season of theatrical entertainment for the English-speaking community including the development of talent in every area of the theatre arts. pcarroll@laguna.com.mx

ANIMAL GROUPS

Animal Shelter
Geoffrey Kaye
376 766-0146

Owned and operated by Geoffrey John Kaye, the shelter provides care and new homes for dogs and cats, sells pet supplies and operates a free bird sanctuary for local children and residents; uglybug@laguna.com.mx

Anita's Animals
Anita Strehlow
387 761-0500

Provides shelter and new homes for abandoned animals. www.anitasanimals.com

Lakeside Spay and Neuter Center
Gudron Jones
376 766-3813

Provides shelter and helps curtail the overpopulation of animals. djonesgzjonex@yahoo.com; www.chapaladogs.com

CONSERVATION GROUPS

Amigos del Lago
376 765-5755

Promotes the improvement in the quality of life around Lake Chapala and spearheaded the adoption of the lake into Living Lakes, the most powerful and best-funded lake-saving group in the world. luis_aguirre@amigosdelago.org or info@amigosdelago.org; www.amigosdelago.org

Lakeside Wildlife Rescue & Rehabilitation/
Vern & Lori Geiger
376 765-4916

Promotes the rescue and rehabilitation of wild animals, trees and plants around Lake Chapala. lgeiger@prodigy.net.mx

EDUCATIONAL GROUPS

ÁCA/*(Asociación Comunitaria de Autosuficienca, A.C.)* Wendee Hill
387 763-1568

Teaches hands-on training in practical organic farming to help communities develop sustainable resource management systems. Their goals are to promote and improve the health of humans and ecosystems and to create co-operative marketing strategies that engender regional solutions. ggs@ggs.com.mx

Biblioteca of San Antonio Tlayacapán/ Lois Cugini 376 766-1790 376 766-0603	Provides Spanish library facilities for children and families in the San Antonio Tlayacapán area. loiscugi@laguna.com.mx
Centro de Desarrollo Jocotepec/ Sylvia Flores 376 766-1679, Diana Wilson 376 766-1152	Jocotepec Center for Development; cedejo@prodigy.net.mx
Centro de Formación Jaltepec/ Linda Buckthorp 376 766-1631	Jaltepéc Training Center; buckthorp@laguna.com.mx
DAR Sponsorship Program/ Flo Michaloski 376 765-2862	Provides scholarships for local students. darmxusa@prodigy.net.mx
E.R.I.C./ Stewart McGowan 376 766-0800	Provides support for the construction and renovation of educational buildings at Lakeside. tsmcc@prodigy.net.mx
Golden Strings/ Roy Forman 387 763-0199	Provides free musical instruments and music lessons to area students. royalmex@yahoo.com
Lake Chapala Society Student Aid Fund/ Coralie White 376 766-0716	Provides financial support to area students to enroll in university, vocational and high school programs. edwincoralie@prodigy.net.mx
Little Blue School/ Robert & Bonnie Kleffel 376 766-1552	Provides financial assistance to a school for disabled students in Chapala. bkleffel@hotmail.com
M.E.C.E.D. (*Minores En Circunstancias Especialmente Difíciles*)/John & Diane McLeroth 376 766-2603	Provides financial assistance for students in area schools. dmcleroth@laguna.com.mx

***Niños de Chapala y Ajijic* (Chapala & Ajijic Children)/** Roman Monroy 376 766-2065, Bill Friend 376 765-5454	Provides financial assistance to enroll in schools for area students. inospres@yahoo.com; bill.friend@help4kids.net
***Niños del Lago y Club del Niños* (Children of the Lake & Children's Club)/** Martha Nussgen 376 766-2549	Provides financial assistance to purchase uniforms and school supplies for area. students. 6595fla@prodigy.net.mx
San Nicolás High School Scholarship Fund/ Marvin Hearthcock 387 763-5093	Provides financial assistance for students at San Nicholás High School (east of Chapala). marvhelaine@hotmail.com
San Nicolás Library/ Robert, Bonnie Kleffel 376 766-1552	After-school resource for San Nicolás children. Reference and reading books in Spanish and lending library. Alberto Reyes #37-A, San Nicolas.
School for the Deaf/Leslie Martin 376 766-2274	Helps to provide meals, hearing aids and medical attention, and pays for room and board for children who come long distances. lesliemartin77@hotmail.com
University & Vocational Assistance/ Lynn Hanson 376 766-2660	Provides financial assistance to enroll in university and vocational programs for area students. dhanson323@yahoo.com

FAMILY SERVICES

Unidad de Atención a la Violencia Intrafamilia Sistema DIF Chapala	Provides assistance to women and children who have suffered from domestic abuse.

MEDICAL GROUPS

Cruz Roja Mexicana Delegacion Chapala J.D. Lydick 376 766-2403	Provides financial support for the local chapter of the Red Cross. dosalmas@prodigy.net.mx
Handicapped Equestrian Learning Program (HELP)/ Jim McCormack 376 766-3984	Provides physical therapy for handicapped Mexican children through the regular riding of horses. aaugie@prodigy.net.mx
Programa pro Niños Incapacitados del Lago/ Robin Lawrason 376 766-3070	Provides financial support for medical treatment of children with disabilities such as cerebral palsy, meningitis, cancer and birth defects. jim2rob@laguna.com.mx; http://programaninos.org
Shriner's Club of Chapala/ Jim Powers 387 761-0017	Provides financial support for medical treatment of children with burns or disabilities requiring prostheses. jimminap@hotmail.com

NATIONAL, GENEALOGICAL, AND HISTORICAL GROUPS

Ajijic Masonic, Lodge #31 376 766-0485	
American Legion Auxiliary 376 765-4342	In charge of Legion fundraising for local charities. Anita Wikum.
American Legion of Chapala Post #7 376 765-2259	Comm. Allyn King, Morelos #114, Chapala.
Amites Francophones 376 766-0149	Roland Van Houdt, rvanhoudt@prodigy.net.mx
British Society 387 761-0257	Meets at Manix restaurant, Ocampo #57, Ajijic. Ceri Dando, cpdando2000@yahoo.com

Canadian Club 376 766-0833	Jack Norman, jacknval@laguna.com.mx
Churchill Rose Museum 376 766-0312	Churchill Maillison, attorney1@juno.com
DAR (Daughters of the American Revolution) Guadalajara Chapter 376 765-2862	Flo Michaloski, darmxusa@prodigy.net.mx
DAR Thomas Paine Chapter 376 762-0834 376 765-2961	Sandra Loridans or Mardel Shamach.
German Speakers 376 765-2442	Thea Petersen.
Historical Society of Lakeside 376 766-1981 or 376 766-4296	Tod Jonson, tod@prodigy.net.mx or todjonson@hotmail.com
Irish Society 376 766-2721	Nancy Creevan, contigo2000@yahoo.com
Navy League of Lake Chapala 376 766-4750	Sandy Bell, larsandbell@laguna.com.mx
Rotary Club of Ajijic 376 766-4869	Meets at Los Telares Restaurant, Morelos #6, Ajijic.
Sons of the Revolution 376 766-3070	Jim Lloyd, jelajijic@yahoo.com

ORPHANAGES AND OTHER CHILDREN'S GROUPS

Mission San Pablo Orphanage/ Loren Reynolds 376 763-5038	Provides financial support for children in this orphanage in Ixtlahuacan de los Membrillos. penlor@prodigy.net.mx

Niños y Jovenes de San Juan Cosalá **(Children & Young People of San Juan Cosalá)/** Rudy Maurin 387 761-0384	Provides food, clothing and cleaning materials for children in this orphanage in San Juan Cosalá. cruderude@msn.com
Niños y Jovenes Caravan/ Reuben Verela 387 761-0606	Delivers food and used clothing to the orphanage in San Juan Cosalá.
Villa Infantil Orphanage/ David Buchen 376 766-3721	Provides financial support for children in this orphanage near San Pedro Testistán. buchend@yahoo.com
Toys for Tots/ Denny Strole 376 766-0485	Provides toys for needy children at Christmas. dendag@laguna.com.mx

SENIORS GROUPS

Casa de Ancianos Marlene Dunham 376 765-2497	Provides support for elderly citizens in Chapala. casadeancianos@asistencia.org

CHARITY SUPPORT GROUPS

Chile Cookoff/ Loren Reynolds 376 763-5038	Provides financial support to selected area charities from proceeds of annual chili competition. penlor@prodigy.net.mx
St. Andrew's Outreach Program/ Betty Prentki 376 766-4292	Provides financial support to selected area charities from church fund-raising activities. bprentki@yahoo.com

SUPPORT GROUPS

(Check local publications for listings.)

Alcoholics Anonymous

CODA
Gamblers Anonymous
Overeaters Anonymous
Womens 16 Step Group

Other organizations you'll find are:

Amigos
Amigos Internacionales
Chess Club
Christian Men's/Women's Fellowship
Computer Clubs
Democrats Abroad-Mexico, Ajijic Chapter
Ham Radio Club
Hash House Harriers Walking Club
Karate Club
Lakeside Fishing Club
Lakeside Garden Guild
LINK-Foreign Community Assistance at Lake Chapala Society
Needlepushers, handwork club
North Shore Auto Enthusiasts
Orchid Club
Republicans Abroad
Red Hat Ladies Society
Storytellers
Tennis Club
Toys for Tots
Volunteer Health Resource (Hospice Group)

Things to See and Do for Kids and Teens of All Ages

BECOME A BALLERINA

Le Petit Ballet Year-round instruction in a bright, airy studio. For children ages 4-14. Open Monday, Wednesday and Friday 5 p.m. to 6 p.m. Plaza Bugambilias 2nd Floor, (next to El Torito grocery) Ajijic. English spoken.

BECOME A JAZZ DANCER, A BALLET STAR OR A GYMNASTICS WHIZ

Estudio Olimpia
01 33 3105-2486

This gym is owed and operated by an athlete who has been practicing for more than 35 years. She offers classes for adults: gymnastics, corrective and reducing exercises, pre- and postnatal, and Golden Age workouts, classic ballet, and low impact aerobics. Open Monday through Friday from 8:10 a.m. to 9:10 am. and 7 p.m. to 8 p.m. and other hours by arrangement. Hidalgo #227, Chapala.

Be careful on the *ciclopista*, the bike path that runs almost continuously from Chapala to Jocotepec. There are walkers, dog walkers and plenty of other bikers riding to and from work in the mornings between 7 a.m. and 10 a.m. and back home again between 6 and 8 p.m. Wear a helmet and carry a card with your name, local address, phone number and the name and phone number of your doctor in case you have an accident. Ring your bicycle bell, whistle or call out to people in front of you who may not hear you coming.

BICYCLE AND 4-WHEELER RENTALS

Bicicletas Rayo

Bicycle and small motorized 4-wheeler rentals for teens. Hand over an I.D. and pay cash. They sell helmets, accessories, and cycling clothes. Open Monday through Saturday 10 a.m. to 8:30 p.m. Carr. Pte. #12, Ajijic.

BIRDWATCH, THE EASY WAY

The Animal Shelter Bird Park
376 765-5514

Opened in 2003, this public bird park houses parrots, English budgies, parakeets, love birds from Africa, cockatiels, several species of pigeons, a Golden Pheasant and a Lady Amerthurst, both from China, and a variety of ornamental ducks. Apply to become a volunteer worker. Open Monday through Friday 10 a.m. to 4 p.m., Saturday 10 a.m. to 3 p.m. Hidalgo #212, Riberas del Pilar, (inside the Animal Shelter, on the *carretera*).

BORROW A PET FOR THE MORNING

The Animal Shelter and Anita's Animals are always looking for dog walkers. Why don't you share a little love, get some exercise and let a dog know he or she is important?

Animal Shelter, A.C.
376 765-5514

Offers healthy, neutered cats and dogs for adoption, a very extensive line of pet foods, products and supplies, free spay and neutering for Mexicans who can't afford the service, and the area's only bird sanctuary. Animal foods are controlled for quality and freshness. It is an affiliated member of WSPA (the World Society for the Protection of Animals) and the RSPCA (the Royal Society for the Prevention of Cruelty to Animals). Open Monday through Friday 10 a.m. to 4 p.m., Saturday 10 a.m. to 3 p.m. Hidalgo #212, Riberas del Pilar (next to Veterinary Doctors Ladron de Guevara). English Spoken.

Anita's Animals
387 761-0500

This private shelter for homeless animals is entirely supported by donations. All support is welcome. In the Raquet Club, San Juan Cosalá. (Please let phone ring a dozen times.)

BUILD A BALLOON/*REGATA DE GLOBOS*

Near the beginning of September watch for a workshop announcing the construction of traditional tissue paper balloons for the colorful Balloon Regatta held later in the month. The workshop and regatta are one of the many activities held during Mexico's month to celebrate their Independence Day, September 16. Participation in the workshop is free. A maximum of 25 balloons are released and each are judged on their "airworthiness." 376 766-1356

BUY A PIÑATA

Candy and Piñatas - In this shop there are three walls of shelves, from floor to ceiling, stacked with candy to fill *piñatas*. *Piñatas* are sold empty, either with the traditional clay pot inside or cardboard. Newer styles feature Spiderman, Batman, Sesame Street characters, the fish from Nemo, mermaids, Barbie, Shrek and more. Morelos #35, (just north of the plaza), Jocotepec.

BUY A CHEAP COPY OF SHREK 2

G & S Cyber
376 766-4233

You can buy DVDs of movies in English, in English with Spanish subtitles, and Spanish for 25 *pesos*, downloaded from the Internet. Plus you can get tapes duplicated and surf the net for the best price in town, 10 *pesos* an hour. They also rent computers. Open Monday through Saturday 10 a.m. to 9 p.m., Sunday 4 p.m. to 8 p.m. Aldama #24, Ajijic. English spoken. graceesquedah@hotmail.com

Dale Hoyt Palfrey

Dale Hoyt Palfrey

***Día del Niño** celebrates children every April 30.*

DIA DEL NIÑO

Every April 30 brings the Day of the Child to Mexico. Look for all kinds of activities and parties designed just for children to commemorate the day. It's like having a birthday party with all of your friends complete with cake, candy, ice cream and plenty of fun things to do.

The Casa de Cultura in Jocotepec initiates the summer vacation season, the beginning of July, with workshops in its new facility on the west side of the plaza. Geared mainly for adults, some classes are just for kids like drawing and painting and are very reasonably priced. Sign up for classes between 10 a.m. to 2 p.m. and 4 p.m. to 7 p.m. Adult classes offered in the 2004 summer season included painting and drawing, yoga and meditation, a literary workshop, English, embroidery, textile painting, balloon decoration, dance, guitar study and other crafts. *Recommended.*

GET A PET

Acuario Chapala
376 765-6633

Best selection of fish and supplies in the area. Saltwater and tropical fish, birds, iguanas, rodents, eels, coral, and supplies including pumps, gravel, filters, food, nets, anti-bacterial drops, aquarium salt, small pet and bird bedding, bird cages, hamster feeders and waterers. Open Monday through Saturday 9 a.m. to 2 p.m., 4 p.m. to 8:30 p.m., Sunday 9 a.m. to 2 p.m. Zaragoza #390-A (across from the Our Lady of Mount Carmel), Chapala.

Mundo Aquatico Ajijic
376 766-4604

Tropical fish, turtles, hamsters, salamanders, manders, fish tanks, accessories and food. Home aquarium set up and maintenance. Open Monday through Saturday 11 a.m. to 2 p.m., 4 p.m. to 8 p.m., closed Wednesday and Sunday. Constitución #41-A, Ajijic.

Veterinaria Chapala
376 765-3718

Check out the pets at the place with the big black and white cow in Chapala. They have turtles, Chihuahua puppies, ferrets, guinea pigs, a few fish, and birds. Open Monday through Saturday 9 a.m. to 2 p.m., 4 p.m. to 7 p.m., Sunday 10 a.m. to 2 p.m. Madero #427-A, Chapala. Some English spoken.

HAM IT UP IN THE PARK

Cristianía Park
376 765-2937

Practice your favorite monologue from Hamlet in front of 300 of your closest friends in the amphitheater at La Cristianía park in

Chapala from 8 a.m. to 8 p.m. for only 5 *pesos* all day. Or swim in their huge swimming pool and slide down the water slides from noon to 5 p.m. (20 *pesos* adults, 10 *pesos* for kids). There are picnic areas with braziers and pavilions, paved bike paths, playgrounds, free bathrooms, tennis courts for 20 *pesos* an hour, soccer fields, and snack bars. But don't bring your dog. She isn't allowed. Do ask your mom to walk around the park with you. She'll love it. Av. La Cristianía #24, Chapala.
www.difchapala.gob.mx
museo_virtual@prodigy.net.mx;

HAVE A PARTY

Quinta Mamá Chuy
376 765-5515
376 765-4126
01 33 3461-3814

This is a one-stop party place. Hire the hall and they'll handle the chairs, tables, glassware, table and chair cloths, the waiters, the flowers, and the musicians. Pepe Guízar #150, Chapala. Goyo2457@prodigy.net.mx

The Magic Carousel/ El Carrusel Mágico
376 766-4410

A fiesta patio, playground and game facility for children, you can rent this indoor/outdoor area for parties. They can provide inflatable bounce houses, a soccer field and volleyball court, kitchen, and bathrooms all in securely-gated grounds. Carr. Ajijic-Jocotepec #530, Ajijic (near La Huerta plaza).

Rainbow

A party place for kids.They rent inflatable playhouses, trampolines, tables, chairs, tablecloths. Juan Alvarez #24, Ajijic (behind El Torito grocery).

HUNT FOR BERRIES

Driscoll's Berries
387 763-2416

Driscoll's is the 500 employee outfit that buys up all the raspberries, strawberries and blackberries from the high-tech farms that surround Jocotepec and ships them to the U.S., Canada, England, Japan, and Australia. Everyone in the Driscoll office speaks fluent English and are happy to greet the curious in search of berries. The farms they buy from are not allowed to sell to local residents but it is possible to buy berries that are too ripe for packing at the farms' sorting tables. The first farms start at the end of Vicente Guerrero, going west, on the right hand side of the road. Then at the crossroads where Vicente Guerrero intersects Highway 15 to Guadalajara, turn left and drive a couple of kilometers. The farms are easy to recognize for their plastic roofs. Raspberry season is from October to February. Driscoll's is open 8 a.m. to 8 p.m. Monday through Friday. Juárez #21-A, Jocotepec. English spoken.

PUMP IT UP!

Arcade
376 765-2080

Try mastering the Pump It Up! dance video game. The arcade at Madero #236 in Chapala (west, across from the plaza on the main street Madero) offers that game and others and sells playstation CDs. Open 10 a.m. to 10 p.m. daily.

Chapala Video

Almost all of the plazas have video arcades suitable for kids.

RIDE HORSES

Horseback riding using the western saddle is available in lower La Floresta at the junction of Camino Real and Paseo del Lago streets not far from the Hotel Real de Chapala. 70 *pesos* an hour, 40 *pesos* a half hour from 11 a.m. to 7:30 to 8:00 p.m. Some English spoken. Ask around, Saturday and Wednesday mornings there are dressage lessons with Chato Flores in the bull ring in Ajijic, next to El Torito grocery. (Horseback riding at the Chapala pier and Cristianía Park in Chapala is *not* recommended.)

ROAST HOT DOGS IN THE PARK

Near the Ajijic pier, from Pedro Moreno to Morelos there are a dozen outdoor grills with picnic tables and benches nearby and playground equipment. There's good shade, good parking and bathrooms nearby as well as a walking path along the lake, unless it's under water! Take grandfather for a stroll and give him a giant hug.

SWIM ALL DAY

Balneario San Juan Cosalá
387 761-0202

A haven for kids and adults with cool wading pools, slides, lap pools, giant hot Jacuzzis, steam rooms, and snack bars galore. Changing rooms and lockers are available. Open 9 a.m. to 6 p.m. 90 *peso* entry fee. Some English is spoken. Expect it to be packed on the weekend and on holidays.

Tobolandia
376 766-2120

Admission 40 *pesos* children, 80 *pesos* adults, parking 10 *pesos*. Go early, get a table in the shade and spend the day riding their giant waterslides. If you're too tiny for the big slides stay in the areas designed especially for little people. Tired of the water? Hang on the monkey bars, shoot hoops on the basketball court, or play volleyball or badminton, kick around a soccer ball on the *fútbol* field, or play video games. Hungry? There are plenty of refreshment stands selling Golden Fried Chicken, ice cream, and all kinds of Mexican snacks. Don't worry, there are plenty of bathrooms everywhere. There's a place to buy a souvenir to remember your day, too. Don't bring in bottles or anything made of glass, bicycles, skates, your iguana or pet dog Ratty, or especially, alcoholic beverages. Expect it to be packed on the weekends and on holidays. Open daily 10 a.m. to 6 p.m. In Ajijic at the junction of the *Libramiento* and the Chapala-Jocotepec *carretera*.

TAKE ART CLASSES

The LCS offers Children's Art Classes from 10 a.m. to 12 p.m. every Saturday. The Lake Chapala Society can be found at 16 de Septiembre #16-A in Ajijic. For more information about their activities visit their website www.lakechapalasociety.org

TAKE A BOAT RIDE

Boat rides from the Chapala pier cruise along the shore of the "Riberas," Spanish for the Riviera, the name once given to Chapala's lovely northshore for 180 *pesos* a boatload, 250 for a 30 minute tour around Scorpion Island, named for its shape, or 310 for an hour's excursion. If you want to stay and walk around the island or sit and have a cold drink, the cost of the boat jumps to 380 for a half hour and 440 for 60 minutes. Buy your tickets at the booth at the foot of the pier and invite up to 10 friends. Treat your *novio* or *novia* to a sunset cruise on Saturday or Sunday. The driver may tell you that last year the Lake Chapala Port Captain put a green light on the Chapala lighthouse, a red one on Ajijic's lighthouse and a white one on Scorpion and Mezcala Islands' *faros*, to guide fishermen lost in the Lake's fog.

TAKE A COMPUTER COURSE

The Virtual Museum
376 765-2937

Curious about the Virtual Museum? Located inside La Cristianía Park in Chapala, the virtual museum has eight computers to teach kids computing skills. It's part of a national program to "democratize" Mexico and can be found in cities and towns throughout the country. Open Monday through Saturday 10 a.m. to 2 p.m., 4 p.m. to 6 p.m. museo_virtual@prodigy.net.mx

WORK IT OUT!

Club Oxygen
376 766-5005

Club Oxygen in the Danza del Sol hotel offers afterschool tae kwon do, pre-ballet, ballet, jazz, tap, tennis and tai chi for children. Find out more by going to their website www.cluboxigen.com. Ocampo #151, Ajijic.

OR VOLUNTEER YOUR TIME WITH THE GOOD PEOPLE AT:

Lakeside Spay and Neuter Center/
Gudron Jones
376 766-3813

Provides shelter and helps curtail the overpopulation of animals.
djonesgzjonex@yahoo.com;
www.chapaladogs.com

Worship

In terms of worship, the Lakeside's international community offers a surprising variety of options. For those seeking out the venerable churches and chapels of the Northshore, some more than 400 years old, you'll find them listed below with the schedule of their services.

AJIJIC

Baha'i Community 376 766-3999	Devotional gatherings, Sundays at noon. bahaiajijic@hotmail.com
***Capilla de la Virgen del Rosario* (Chapel of the Virgin of the Rosary)**	Monday through Saturday 8 a.m. services in Spanish. On Colón, the north side of the plaza.
Eckankar of Mexico 376 766-1230	Tuesday 2 p.m. meeting. Neill James Salon, 16 de Septiembre 16-A, Ajijic. Contact Penny White.
El Lago Community Church	Sunday 11 a.m. services in English. Javier Mina #7, Ajijic.
Lakeside Christian Fellowship 376 766-1407 376 766-0795	Sunday bilingual service 11 a.m. Children and teen ministries. Javier Mina #49, Ajijic.
The Little Chapel by the Lake	Sunday 7:30 a.m. services in English. On the Ajijic-Chapala bypass west of "Birds of Paradise" development.
Open Circle	Sunday 10 a.m. body, mind and spirit meeting in English featuring speakers on a wide variety of subjects, Lake Chapala Society, Neill James Salon, 16 de Septiembre 16-A, Ajijic.
Saint Andrews Apostle	Sunday 9 a.m. and 11 a.m. mass. Marcos Castellanos #14, Ajijic.
San Andrés Roman Catholic Church 376 766-0922	Sunday 9 a.m. mass in English. On the corner of Marcos Castellanos and Guadalupe Victoria, Ajijic.

AJIJIC'S SAN ANDRES PARISH CHURCH

Ajijic's most prominent church began a program of long-term renovation in 2004. The cupolas of the 300-year-old church were repaired as were the gold and oxblood painted embellishments of their ceilings. Restoration was overseen by the parish Curate, a local architect and a restoration specialist of the National Institute of Archaeology and History, as well as the Archdiocese of Guadalajara's Commission on Sacred Art.

P.F.de V.

***San Andres Roman Catholic Church** is a major landmark half a block east of the Ajijic plaza.*

***Santuario de la Virgen de Guadalupe* (Sanctuary of the Virgin of Guadalupe)** — 6 p.m. services daily in Spanish with special events on December 12. On Ocampo near the corner of Fco. Villa in the Seis Esquinas (Six Corners) neighborhood of west Ajijic.

Seventh Day Adventists 376 765-2165 — Saturday 9:15 a.m. service. Madeira #12, Rancho del Oro, Ajijic.

CHAPALA

***Capilla de la Virgen del Carmen* (Chapel of the Virgin of Carmen)** — 6 p.m. services in Spanish, Monday through Friday, 8 p.m. Saturdays, and 9:30 a.m. Sundays. Located at the corner of Zaragoza and Manzanillo in Chapala.

***Capilla de la Virgen de Lourdes* (Chapel of the Virgin of Lourdes)** — Sunday noon services in Spanish. On Av. Lourdes above the Monte Carlo Hotel in Chapala.

***Iglesia del Espiritu Santo* (Church of the Holy Spirit** 376 765-4210	Sunday 10 a.m. and Wednesday 7 p.m. evangelical bilingual services. On Alvaro Obregón #119, in Chapala.
***Templo de San Francisco de Asisi* (Temple of Saint Francis of Assisi)**	8 a.m. and 7 p.m. services Monday through Friday, Saturday 8 a.m., 6 and 8 p.m., Sunday 6, 8 and 11 a.m., noon, and 1, 6, and 8 p.m. in Spanish. On Madero, a half block from the pier.

CHULA VISTA

Lakeside Lutheran Bible Study	Tuesday 2 p.m. at the Little Chapel Nondenominational in Chula Vista.
Little Chapel Nondenominational 376 766-0096	Sunday 11 a.m. service in English. Chula Vista.
New Apostolic Church	Sunday 10 a.m. services. Mirasol.

JOCOTEPEC

Iglesia Apostoica, Bautizados en la Fe de Cristo	Sundays 11 a.m. and 3:30 p.m., Wednesdays 7 p.m. and 9 p.m., Fridays 7 p.m. and 10 p.m. Privada Aldama #54.
Iglesia Centro Cristiano Vida Nueva	Sunday 11 a.m. Miguel Arana #257. Where the Indonesian furniture store used to be.
***Santuario de la Virgen de Guadalupe* (Sanctuary of the Virgin of Guadalupe)**	Tuesday and Sunday 11 a.m. and 7 p.m. services in Spanish. Near the south end of Matamoros.
***Templo del Señor del Monte* (Temple of the Lord of the Mountain)**	Monday through Friday 7:30 a.m. and 7 p.m. services in Spanish, Saturday 7 and 8 a.m. and 7 p.m., Sundays 7 and 8 a.m., noon, and 7 and 8 p.m. On the south side of the plaza.

LA FLORESTA

Las Salvias Lake Chapala Jewish Congregations-Bat Yam 376 766-1652	Temple at Angel Flores #24, corner of 5 de Febrero, Las Salvias.
Lake Chapala Jewish Community 376 766-2960	Weekly Sabbath services at Angel Flores #24-A, Ajijic.

RIBERAS DEL PILAR

The Church of Jesus Christ of Latter Day Saints	Sunday 10 a.m. sacrament meeting. Santa Margarita.
Jehovah's Witnesses 376 766-2663 387 763-1056	Sunday 3 p.m. service in English. Santa Margarita at San Jorge.
Lake Chapala Baptist Church 376 765-2925 376 765-2028	Sunday 10 a.m. bible study and 11 a.m. worship in English. Santa Margarita #147.
St. Andrew's Anglican Church Lakeside 376 765-3926	Sunday 10 a.m. service in English as well as the annual "Blessing of the Animals." Tuesday 10 a.m. and 11 a.m. bible study. San Lucas. www.standrewsparish.org

Church Bells Decoded

For daily church services a single bell rings three times. The first ring comes a half hour before mass, the second one sounds fifteen minutes later, beginning and ending with two rapid clangs to say "get a move on!". The final ring adds another rapid clang on each side of the regular clangs to say "the service is ready to begin!" To announce the death of a community member, knells are sounded, called *clamores*, that are slow and solemn. Multiple bells peal to announce holidays, special masses for Christmas, Easter and the church's patron saint. Bells do not ring on the afternoon of Good Friday to mourn the crucifixion.

SAN ANTONIO TLAYACAPÁN

Abundant Life Assembly of God 376 766-3173 387 763-1498	Sunday 9:30 a.m. service in English, Tuesday 2 p.m. bible study, Jesús García #1.
***Templo San Antonio Tlayacapán* (San Antonio Tlayacapán Temple)**	Monday through Saturday 6:30 and 7:30 p.m. services in Spanish, Sunday 6:30, 8, and 9 a.m., 1 and 7 p.m. On Ramón Corona between Independencia and González Gallo.

Also look for details about study groups for A Course in Miracles and Science of the Mind in the Lakeside Bulletin Board of the weekly Guadalajara Colony Reporter.

Meditation/Fortune Telling/Tarot Readings

MEDITATION

Lake Chapala Society	10:30 a.m. Monday.

(See also Chapter 9, Sports and Fitness, for meditation activities and Special Interest Groups.)

FORTUNE TELLING

387 763-2483	The owner of Viajes Ibañez, Alfonso Ramos Ibañez reads Spanish cards, Tarot, I Ching, interprets dreams, and cleans auras. The aura cleansing is done in 3 sessions of 30 to 45 minutes each on three different days. He also has a naturist orientation. He will guide you to your good luck amulet in Love, Money, Business, Friends and Surroundings, as well as help you find choose crystals for security, health, and harmony. Open Monday through Friday 10 a.m. to 3 p.m., 5 p.m. to 7 p.m., Saturday 9 a.m. to 2 p.m. Call first for an appointment. English spoken. José Santana #29, just east of Hidalgo Sur, Jocotepec.

TAROT READINGS #655-A, Juárez, Chapala.

Dale Hoyt Palfrey

The handsome train station *on Chapala's outskirts was inaugurated with great fanfare in 1920.*

Dale Hoyt Palfrey

"QQ", Quinta Quetzalcoatl, *now a private B&B is where D.H. Lawrence penned his first draft of "The Plumed Serpent.".*

Dale Hoyt Palfrey

Next to the San Francisco *parish church in Chapala (L), is Castillo Braniff, finished by commercial aviation pioneer Alberto Braniff.*

8

Sightseeing and Nearby Excursions

with
DALE HOYT PALFREY

The north shore of Lake Chapala is ideally situated 35 minutes from the Guadalajara airport, Miguel Hidalgo International, with good highway access to Puerto Vallarta, the Costa Alegre (Manzanillo, Barra de Navidad, Melaque), Zacatecas, Morelia, Pátzcuaro, San Miguel de Allende and Mexico City. Nestled in the state of Jalisco, it is three hours from the world's prime *Tequila* growing region, one hour from Guadalajara, Mexico's second largest city, 45 minutes from Tlaquepaque, an outstanding shopping area and Tonalá, an exceptional arts and crafts destination. Major villages on the north shore are Chapala on the east and Jocotepec on the west. Villages on the south shore are engaged primarily in farming, ranching, and craftwork.

Walking Tour of Chapala's Historic Buildings

by DALE HOYT PALFREY

Stunning scenery, a deliciously benign climate and a vein of therapeutic hot springs were the principal natural attributes that turned Lake Chapala's north shore into a prime vacation playground and international travel destination from the tail end of the 1800's through the first decade of the 20th century.

Chapala was "discovered" as a resort destination during the final years of Mexican president Porfirio Díaz's prolonged dictatorship, with the chief executive himself topping the list of distinguished politicians, diplomats and wealthy entrepreneurs who frequented the area.

The era also brought a wave of travelers from abroad, some of whom plunked down roots and substantial investments in the budding tourist haven. Among the major foreign players were Scotsman Duncan Cameron who introduced the first steam-powered boat to Lake Chapala, Englishman Septimus Crowe, original developer of the Villa Montecarlo spa, and Norwegian Christian Schjetznan, the brains and economic brawn behind the Compañía de Fomento de Chapala, S.A. that developed the doomed Guadalajara-Chapala railway line.

Naturally, all these well-heeled travelers required suitable accommodations. In the decades preceding the outbreak of the Mexican Revolution, grand hotels and sprawling estates sprouted up along Chapala's lake front, giving the town a semblance of ritzy enclaves like Newport, Rhode Island and the French Riviera. Many of those stately period structures still stand today, although some have undergone significant transformations over the years. Most remain in private hands and are closed to the public. However, even a look at the exteriors is sufficient to give visitors a sense of Chapala's former grandeur.

A good starting point for a short walking tour through the downtown area is the south end of Avenida Francisco I. Madero where it connects to Paseo Ramón Corona and the lake front tourist zone. Major landmarks are listed under their original names, with current titles or vocations given in parenthesis.

Castillo Braniff (Restaurant Cazadores) Next door to the San Francisco parish church, on the former site of a Franciscan monastery, stands one of Chapala's most distinctive historic homes. Construction was initiated in 1903 by illustrious Jalisco historian and political figure Luis Pérez Verdía and finished several years later by second owner Alberto Braniff, a prominent businessman and pioneer of commercial aviation. Built almost entirely with materials imported from Europe, right down to the brick, most of the original features of the Victorian mansion remain intact today. In 1970 the building was acquired by José Luis Martínez Covarrubias who converted the ground floor and long verandah into a branch of the family's successful Cazadores restaurant chain. Clients are welcome to peak around inside to see the original silk tapestry wall coverings and other decorative appointments along with period antiques and a stern portrait of Porfirio Díaz.

Hotel Arzapalo (OXXO store) Directly across the street, flanking Avenida Madero and facing the water front, is what remains of Chapala's very first hotel. The project was the brainchild of entrepreneur Ignacio Arzapalo, with construction design by renowned architect Guillermo de Alba. Inaugurated in 1898, the 36-room hotel operated for 20 years, providing upscale turn-of-the-century travelers with comfortable lodging and a popular social forum. The front portion was later incorporated into the Beer Garden restaurant, once Chapala's most popular weekend watering hole. The structure was renovated in 2002 as an office and commercial complex, with careful attention to preserve original design details of the building's façade.

Casa Capetillo

Continuing west along Chapala's boardwalk to the corner of the narrow one-block street alternately known as Calle Porfirio Díaz and Aquiles Serdán is one of the earliest lake front vacation homes. It was built at the turn of the century by Manuel Capetillo Villaseñor, scion of wealthy and powerful landowners whose vast properties near Ixtlahuacan de los Membrillos extended through the areas of Buenavista, Cedros, La Caldea, Santa Rosa and the Hacienda Atequiza. Details added to the three-story mansion through various renovations gave it the appearance of a great ship docked at the water's edge. It was owned for many years by Guadalajara's prominent González Luna family. After falling into disrepair towards the end of the 20th century, the house has since been beautifully restored by a U.S. couple who are the current owners.

Villa Aurora (Lake Chapala Inn)

On the opposite corner is Villa Aurora, another early water front mansion which was the home of Christian Schjetznan while he was involved in various unsuccessful commercial schemes to turn Chapala into a resort area of worldwide renown. He brought in various steamboats to ply Chapala's waters and was the force behind the creation of Chapala's first yacht club and short-lived railway service.

Casa de los Mangos (Villa Paz) Halfway between Villa Aurora and the gutted Chapala post office building is the largest of the downtown area's water front estates, Villa Paz, also known as the House of Mangoes. Built by Guadalajara attorney Alberto Arce, the broad structure is distinguished by its tall central tower. Set back deep in the shade of a grove of mango trees and graced with handsome wrought iron work, the house has the aura reminiscent of New Orleans' quirky Latin Quarter.

Mi Pullman Set on Calle Porfirio Díaz a few doors up from Villa Aurora is a tall, narrow townhouse that rates as the most singular structure of Chapala's golden era. Built in 1906 by architect Guillermo de Alba as a cozy vacation home for his own family, the design resembles an upright railway car—hence the name. Though the building is now sadly in need of repairs, passersby may still appreciate the lovely Victorian style details gracing the exterior.

Presidencia Municipal Sitting at the city's main intersection is the former Presidencia Municipal (city hall building), built between 1897 and 1910. The main portion of the building has been closed since 1998 due to severe structural damages caused by a geological fault that the runs along the neighboring mountain range and through the center of town. The building's fate is currently in limbo while local and state officials puzzle over the viability of a costly remodeling job versus the practicality of total demolition. The southern wing, built privately some years later and acquired by the city in 1980, remains sound. It now houses Chapala's historical archives, including an extensive collection of photographic images showing Chapala in its heyday that is well worth viewing. English-speaking Archive Chief Armando Hermosillo is a fountain of information on local history.

Hotel Palmera (Palacio Municipal) Recognizing a burgeoning tourist trade, boosted in part by his own stagecoach service for Guadalajara passengers, Ignacio Arzapalo went on to build Chapala's second major hotel. Setting it off the town's main thoroughfare, just north of his eponymic inn, he and Guillermo de Alba conceived a structure that would be grander in every way—minus the prime lake view. The 96-room Hotel Palmera was inaugurated in 1908. Ownership was divided among Arapalo's descendants in 1925. Spaniard Ramón Nido bought the main portion of the hotel in 1929, rechristening the business with his own name. Subsequent owners Luis Cuevas Pimienta and his wife Natalia Gómez and their offspring maintained the title Hotel Nido until the Ayuntamiento de Chapala purchased the building in 2001. With a modest make-over, the municipal government has preserved an historic landmark as its new home.

Many more stately homes of the past lie strung along the lake front. Those set west of the old post office building are best viewed from tourist boats available for hire at the Chapala pier. Others may be seen on a leisurely stroll along Avenida Ramón Corona and exploration of Chapala's centro.

Of special mention is Quinta Quetzalcoatl, located at Zaragoza #307 between Ramón Corona and Niños Héroes, where English writer D. H. Lawrence resided in 1923 while penning his first draft of "The Plumed Serpent."

And though located well off the beaten track, the handsome Estación de Ferrocarril (railway station) merits a once over. Situated at the north end of Avenida Cristianía near Chapala's outskirts, the massive structure is rated as one of Guillermo de Alba's finest works. Round-trip rail service between Guadalajara and Chapala was inaugurated with great fanfare in 1920, ceasing operation only six years later. The growing popularity of automobile travel, coupled with flood waters that swamped the train station in 1925, contributed to the early demise of the Compañía de Fomento de Chapala. The structure eventually fell into the hands of beloved Jalisco Governor Jesús González Gallo, whose widow donated the property to the state in 1992. Although an ambitious renovation plan for converting the building into a regional museum and cultural center has been plagued by scarce funding and multiple delays, a partial opening of the facility is now projected for some time in 2005.

Chapala and Excursions West

In 1510, the tribal Tecuexe Chief of Poncitlán (63 kilometers east and north of Chapala off Mex15) named "Chapalac" moved into the Chapala area and subjugated the indigenous people and went on to do the same in Ajijic and Jocotepec. Twenty years later under the authority of the Spaniard Nuño de Guzmán, Chapalac was baptized with the name Martín de Chapalac and given the entire area to rule in exchange for embracing the Catholic church. The town of Chapala became a township in 1824 and became a municipality in 1970. Its church honors Saint Francis of Assisi.

SAN ANTONIO TLAYACAPÁN

Five kilometers going west from the municipal seat in Chapala you'll find the village of San Antonio Tlayacapán. This village features the mountainside neighborhood of Chula Vista, the parish of San Antonio de Padua, and the old tower of the Primary School just off the square. (On the Chapala-Jocotepec highway west of Chapala.)

AJIJIC

West an additional kilometer from San Antonio Tlayacapán on the Chapala-Jocotepec *carretera* is Ajijic. Its name comes from the Náhuatl word "Axixic" that suggests "a place where the water spills over." Natives and foreigners interested in the artistic life have lived side by side in this village for years. It is also home to the Lake Chapala Society and the Parish of San Andrés Apóstol where the remains of Father Marcos Castellanos rest. He is famous for his role in maintain-

A walk inside Ajijic's Municipal Panteón provides a unique vista into the history of foreigners living on the Northshore. If you enter the cemetery from its south gate off the west end of Ocampo you'll find side-by-side markers for Nigel Stansbury Millet and Harry S. Stansbury Millett. Nigel Millet wrote two books under two different pen names, Richard Oke and Dane Chandos. Nigel arrived in Ajijic in 1937 at the age of 33, with his father Harry, and friend Peter Lilley. They rented the Hacienda el Tlacuache and opened it as an inn under the name Posada Ajijic, the original Old Posada. Nigel and Peter collaborated on "Journey in the Sun" about Spain, and two books about this area, "Village in the Sun" published in 1946 and "House in the Sun" published in 1949 after Nigel's death from tuberculosis. Nigel's father Harry died in 1947. According to one account Harry died in Mexico City and was first interred in Guadalajara, but later brought to his final rest in the Ajijic cemetery by Sra. Ramirez, wife of then owner of the Posada Ajijic property.

Lakeside resident Binky Chater was a close and long-time friend of Lilley who many years later bequeathed her the San Antonio Tlayacapán property that was the subject of "House in the Sun." Binky Chater arranged for the 1996 re-edition of "Village in the Sun" and later rescued the tattered unpublished manuscript for "Candelaria's Cookbook" which she discovered tucked away in Lilley's desk, to bring it out in print in 1997.

Tombs of many other notable and forgotten expats of yesteryear are found in the Ajijic cemetery, among them Zara Alexyewa, "La Rusa," the legendary semi-retired ballerina and her soulmate Holgar, who, along with Neill James, was a pioneer of the area's expatriate colony. James, a Mississippi-born world traveler and writer, settled in Ajijic in 1942. Although she was not the first foreigner to put down roots in the village, she was a pioneer of the expatriate community who has been credited with putting her adopted home on the map through articles she penned for Life Magazine and other publications and "Dust on My Heart," a book about her Mexico adventures.

by Dale Hoyt Palfrey with Teresa A. Kendrick

ing the independence of Mezcala Island. Yearly events include The Passion of Christ, a live reenactment of Good Friday, the International Chili Cookoff held the first week of February, and village fiestas honoring San Andrés Apóstol held each November 2 to 30. (On the

Chapala-Jocotepec highway, west of Chapala.)

SAN JUAN COSALÁ

13.5 kilometers west of Chapala is San Juan Cosalá where natural thermal pools have been tamed for their therapeutic benefits. Filled with minerals, the waters have a detoxifying effect on the body and hundreds of people flock to the *balnearios*, especially during the holidays. Known originally as Cutzalán by its indigenous people, today it features lakeside seafood restaurants at Piedra Barrenada and an impressive display of devotion to the Virgin of Guadalupe on December 12. (On the Chapala-Jocotepec highway, going west from Chapala.)

JOCOTEPEC

At the extreme west end of the Northshore, Jocotepec was home to the same group of indigenous people as San Juan Cosalá. Its name comes from the Náhuatl language, "Xocotepec" originally meaning "a hill of citrus fruit." The Spanish found it in 1528 but it didn't become a township for another 300 years. The comely, vibrant village is enhanced by its impressive 16th century parish church of the Señor del Monte and its quirky, surreal grounds. *Sarape*-makers continue to produce traditional hand-loomed shawls, rugs, ponchos and table gear. The traditional goat dish, *birria*, is served on terraces overlooking the plaza. (At the western end of the Chapala-Jocotepec highway.)

SAN LUIS SOYATLÁN, JALISCO

At the extreme western end of Jocotepec you'll arrive at a T-junction, highway Mex15. If you turn right it will put you on the old Guadalajara-Morelia highway where you'll pass the villages Zapotitán and Huejotitán and where you can hook up with highways 80, 54, and 15 to Guadalajara, as well as free road 401 and toll road 54D to Colima. If you turn left, you'll be on the portion of Mex15 highway that hugs the south side of Lake Chapala. You'll round the western nub of Lake Chapala and glimpse farm and ranch land. You'll pass through San Pedro Tesistán and San Cristobal Zapotitlan, small towns opposite Jocotepec and San Juan Cosalá.

TUXCUECA, JALISCO

On the south side of Lake Chapala, Tuxcueca is one of the last towns still in the state of Jalisco on the road that follows the lake. Puruagua de Ramón Corona and Tizapán el Alto follow, and then just before Petatán you enter Michocán. Tuxcueca was first inhabited by Chichimeca tribes and later invaded by the Tarascans (also called Purepechas). Their king, Tangaxoan, sought possession of the saltpeter flats of Zacoalco and Sayula to the west, causing what historians describe as the Saltpeter War. This took place before the Spanish conquest. Tuxcueca derives its name from the noise made by huddles of rabbits. This area produces the women's palm hats with wide brims seen in many markets. (On highway Mex15 past San Pedro Tesistán, San Cristobal Zapotitlán, and San Luis Soyatlán.)

TIZAPÁN EL ALTO, JALISCO

This is one of the towns on the south side of the Lake that makes the intricate corn husk dolls seen in markets and shops. Originally inhabited by Toltecas, it fell to the Spanish conquest in 1529. It's name, like many others in this part of Mexico, comes from the Náhuatl, and vaguely means "water over chalk." The ruins of the Ex-Hacienda de San Francisco was the site of intense battles during the war of Independence. Their local delicacy "cajeta" is a candy of quince and peach, not cooked caramel. (On Mex15, south side of Lake Chapala.)

PETATÁN, MICHOACÁN

Just beyond Tizapán el Alto is the tiny fishing community of Petatán. Known to birders, it is the wintering home of the white pelicans, one of the largest and most beautiful birds in North America who enjoy the leavings of the local fish processing plant. Up to 3,000 of the giant birds crowd the shores in the afternoon when workers dump crates of fish heads into the water. The Pelican arrives in early November after flying thousands of miles from western Canada. (On Mex15, just across the Michoacán border.)

Excursions Northeast from Chapala

SANTA CRUZ DE LA SOLEDAD

One kilometer from the municipal seat in Chapala, Santa Cruz sports a small airport. (On Mex23, north of Chapala.) In 2000, a *mariachi* musician, Juan Santos, who was picnicking with his family found mastodon bones near the village. The bones were recovered and sent to

Guadalajara for study. Since then, the discovery has become part of the musical lexicon of area after a song, *a corrido*, was written by Alfredo Arroyo and Gregorio Marin called *Descubrimiento en Chapala*, Discovery in Chapala.

Gentlemen, listen well
to what I'm going to sing
Juan Santos has discovered
a prehistoric animal.

On Wednesday April 12
He couldn't have imagined
What he was to discover
In Lake Chapala.

In this year 2000
Santa Cruz, a son of yours
found in your beaches
something no one was expecting.

Not everyone is so lucky,
this has just been proven:
all the archeologists wish
that they were Juan now.

Everyone has come,
people who investigate
and ask the *mariachi* Juan
many questions.

They say it measures eight meters
from the tail to the tusks
and that there you'll find
cousins, friends and family.

Juan begs of the government
a museum for his town
So the animal doesn't disappear
or get stolen by a bad guy.

They sing it in Santa Cruz,
Mezcala and San Nicolás,
and the musicians of Chapala
Sing the purest truth.

How sad about the Lake
how sad you must feel

even the dead
reclaim the water to live.

SAN NICOLÁS DE IBARRA

In San Nicolás de Ibarra, 3 kilometers north of Santa Cruz de la Soledad, you'll find a lively town with a historic center and the Vista del Lago Golf course and residential area. (On Mex23, north of Chapala.)

Petroglyph and Cave Painting Tours
01 391 921-0839

Guided tours to petroglyph and cave painting sites can be arranged by contacting Francisco Javier Godinez in Poncitlán. He knows the location of 47 and perhaps as many as 80 sites where petroglyphs can be found. Godinez thinks the figures look very similar to rock carvings in New Mexico and that they appear to depict a war between rival tribes or perhaps a natural disaster. He also suspects that they could be extraterrestrials and counts himself among many people who have reported countless UFO sightings around Ocotlán and Poncitlán in recent years.

Courtesy Dale Hoyt Palfrey and Guadalajara Colony Reporter

TLACHICHILCO DEL CARMEN

Fifteen kilometers from Chapala, Tlachichilco del Carmen is a traditional village with a spectacular view of Mezcala Island. (On Mex23, north of Chapala.)

MEZCALA - THE VILLAGE

The village of Mezcala is one of the most insular of all the *pueblos* along the lake. Each August they celebrate the gifts of the *Virgen de la Asunción*, in ceremonies few outsiders see. Festivities last nine days. Every afternoon at 5 p.m. the church bells ring and boys and girls dressed in white carry giant sunflowers and fragrant *nardo*, grown especially for the event, and walk solemnly through the village while musicians play songs praising the Virgin. Their destination is the church where they lay their offerings beneath an elaborate altar bright with candles. Following a mass of thanksgiving, the band strikes up in the plaza, eggs filled with confetti are cracked over the heads of the villagers, and everyone circles the plaza. (Approximately 30 kilometers north of Chapala on Mex23)

MEZCALA - THE ISLAND

Salvador Navarro Sánchez, author of "The Island of Mezcala—La Gesta Olvidada," (Mezcala Island—The Forgotten Exploit) writes that a tiny band of rebels on Mezcala Island played a pivotal role in Mexico's struggle for independence. Written in Spanish, writer Grady Miller interprets, "From 1812 to 1816 a small band of Indian and mestizo rebels defended the island from Spanish General Jose de la Cruz. A massacre of 800 villagers by the Spaniards at Tizapán el Alto (on the south side of the Lake) galvanized support for the rebels and they withdrew to Mezcala Island, where they started building fortifications. From their island fortress, the insurgents raided the mainland with daring, falling upon the enemy and returning to Mezcala loaded with supplies. An all-out attempt by 40 Spanish soldiers to storm the island was fought off. Mezcala's fame spread throughout Mexico and kept alive fading hopes of independence from Spain. But typhoid was the unbeatable enemy, reducing the rebel ranks to half. Those still alive eventually surrendered and, surprisingly, de la Cruz agreed not to punish them and instead gave each man farmland, cattle and seed." An excellent full account of the battle of Mezcala in English can be found in Tony Burton's, "Western Mexico—A Travellers Treasury." (Twenty-five kilometers east of Chapala, about an hour by boat from the Chapala pier.)

ATOTONILQUILLO

At Km. 46 on the Guadalajara-La Barca (Mex35) highway, Atotonilquillo is famous for its quince products and festival, as well as for the 400-year old temple of San Gaspas dedicated to the *Virgen de Guadalupe*. Mid-August brings the Quince Fest, *Feria del Membrillo.* It takes place on a Sunday around mid-August on the town's main plaza and growers compete to bring in the best fruit, *ate* and *ponche. Ate* is solid jam formed in bricks, usually sliced and eaten with *panela*, fresh farmers cheese, or a buttery flavored cheese like edam to bring out its flavor. *Ponche* is a mild liquor. Introduced by Franciscans during Mexico's Colonial era, the quince tree has flourished in the area between

Ixtlahuacán de los Membrillos and Poncitlán since the 1700's.

Local Water Trips

Excursions to Scorpion Island, *Isla de los Alacranes*, and to Mezcala Island, *Isla del Presidio*, in the middle of Lake Chapala can be arranged by boat from the Chapala pier. Scorpion Island is named for its shape, not for the creeping critters of the same name! In 2005 boat rides to Scorpion Island cost 180 *pesos* a boatload, 250 *pesos* for a 30 minute tour by water around the island, or 310 *pesos* for a hour-long excursion. If you want to stay and walk around the island or sit and have a cold drink, the cost of the boat jumps to 380 for a half hour and 440 for 60 minutes. Buy your tickets at the booth at the foot of the pier and invite up to 10 friends. On Mezcala Island enjoy old stone paths, the ruined walls and aged doors of a collapsed prison, and Bull's cave. In the hills above the town of Mezcala you'll find ancient cave paintings. Check current prices at the ticket booth for all water tours.

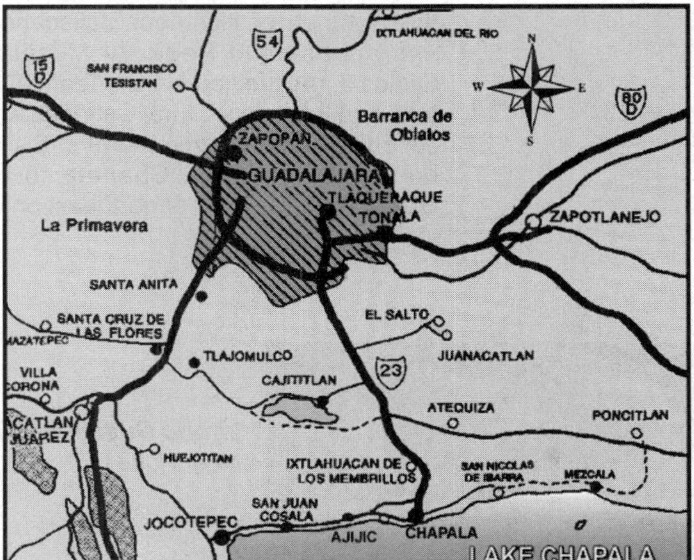

Day Trips (About 1 hour each way)

Guadalajara

At more than 6 million and just over an hour away, Guadalajara is second only to Mexico City for cultural activities. The Guadalajara Colony Reporter weekly newspaper is a good source for listings in English. Subscribe to their website for $30 US a year or pick up a copy at Super Lake grocery in San Antonio Tlayacapán or El Torito grocery store in Ajijic. You'll find excellent Guia Roji street maps of Guadalajara at both stores. www.guadalajarareporter.com

Guadalajara: Centro Histórico

Guadalajara's Historic Center is built around four plazas that form a Latin cross with the Cathedral at its center. From the Plaza de Armas to the Mercado Libertad lies most of the city's historical, cultural and architectural treasures that include the Palacio del Gobierno built in 1774, the gothic and renaissance-style Cathedral begun in 1561, the Rotunda of Illustrious Jaliscans, the *churrigueresque* Regional Museum of Guadalajara, the neo-classic Teatro Degollado and Instituto Cultural Cabañas with its José Clemente Orozco mural in the main dome. (Carretera a Chapala to Calz. González Gallo, right or northeast on Inde-

Pablo Fernandez del Valle

Historic Guadalajara, *City of Roses*

pendencia Sur, left on Avenida La Paz two blocks, right or north on 16 de Septiembre 9 blocks. Park in the area between Avenida Juarez on the south and Avenida Hidalgo on the north.)

***Mercado Libertad/* also called the San Juan de Dios Market**

Located in an area of Guadalajara called San Juan de Dios, the Mercado Libertad is hailed as the largest market in Latin America. Its three levels burst with everything from produce and meat, leather, straw works and birds, to clothing, ceramics, plastics, auto parts, silver jewelry and collectible folk art. Be prepared to experience sensory overload at its profusion of colors, smells, and merchandise. (Carretera a Chapala to Calz. González Gallo, right or northeast on Independencia Sur; find the market between Avenida Juárez and Alfareros. Park on the top level of the market.)

***Casa de las Artesanías/* Parque Agua Azul**

This important collection of Jaliscan folk art by master artists also houses a library of books on the subject available for the public's perusal. Open Monday through Friday 10 a.m. to 6 p.m., Saturday 10 a.m. to 5 p.m., Sunday 10 a.m. to 3 p.m. Gonzalez Gallo #20, Guadalajara. (Carretera a Chapala to Calz. González Gallo, continue to the Parque.)

Expiatorio Church

A few blocks from Plaza Tapatia, one of Guadalajara's most beautiful churches can be found, Templo Expiatorio. Built in 1897, the Gothic style church is even more notable for its rare clock. Everyday at 9 a.m., noon and 6 p.m. a door in the tower opens below the clock and the twelve Apostles march to the carillon. Both inside and out, the church is exceptional. López Cotilla #935. (Carretera a Chapala, east or left on Calz. Lazaro Cardenas, northeast or right on Colón which becomes Washington, four blocks past La Paz turn left on Francisco I.

Madero, right on Enrique Díaz de León, right on López Cotilla.)

Guadalajara Zoo
01 33 3674-4448
01 33 3674-3976
01 33 3674-1699

This world-class zoo and wildlife sanctuary spans more than 40 hectares and houses 360 species of animals. Main attractions include two impressive aviaries and the largest reptile house in Latin America. The visitor facilities are first class. Paseo del Zoólogical #600, Panorámica Huentitán, at the extreme northeast corner of Guadalajara. (Carretera a Chapala to Calz. González Gallo, right or northeast on Independencia Sur which turns into Calz. Independencia Norte, just past Manuel Gómez Morin, on the right.)

Panteón de Bélén

Ultimate place to celebrate Day of the Dead, Nov. 2 (the night before) in Guadalajara. The city's oldest cemetery is eerily beautiful and at one time served as the Rotunda of Illustrious Men. Today it is a popular site for theatrical performances and weddings. Belén and Gral. Eulogio Parra. (Carretera a Chapala to Calz. González Gallo, right or northeast on Independencia Sur, left on Avenida La Paz two blocks, right on 16 de Septiembre past Juárez, Hidalgo, Juan Manuel and then 10 blocks (meanwhile 16 de Septiembre becomes Avenida Alcalde) to Gral. Arteaga, turn right, go three blocks

> If your explorations yield pre-Columbian artifacts, the legal course of action is to register them with the national Anthropology Institute (INAH) in Guadalajara. A minimal fee is required for each piece registered and owners receive a certificate of authenticity describing the piece, its origin and history. The INAH will not appropriate the piece as once feared. Registration insures that the artifact does not leave the country, can be traced if stolen, and free restoration if there is minimal damage. The INAH office is located at Liceo #168, Guadalajara. They are open 8 a.m. to 3 p.m. Monday through Friday. Call them at 01 33 3613-6004.

and park.)

Plaza de Toros To watch the archaic sport of bullfighting, the place to do it is Plaza de Toros. If the sport is too bloody for you, enjoy Portuguese bullfighting in which the bull is not harmed. The Plaza de Toros is just across Calz. Independencia Norte from the new massive Jalisco sports stadium. (Carretera a Chapala to Calz. González Gallo, right or northeast on Independencia Sur which turns into Calz. Independencia Norte, past Circunvalación Dr. Atl three long blocks, right on Puerto Ensenada, bear left into the Plaza.)

Fiestas de Octubre An annual event for more than 35 years, the Fiestas include rodeos, fairs, soccer games, musical concerts and other popular events. Plaza Tapatia is decked out in its finest, filled to the brim with artists and artisans working in every medium possible. It's a great time to spend a weekend in the city in one of the hotels listed at the end of this section. (Plaza Tapatia: Carretera a Chapala to Calz. González Gallo, right or northeast on Independencia Sur, left on Avenida La Paz two blocks, right or north on 16 de Septiembre 9 blocks. Park in the area between Avenida Juárez on the south and Avenida Hidalgo on the north.)

Folk Art Show "Tlaqueparte" at the Expo in Guadalajara Watch for notices for the annual Folk Art, handicrafts, antiques and gift show called "Tlaqueparte" the end of May or in June. The massive show is a must for collectors and aficionados of hand-worked art from Mexico and recently the Caribbean, Central and South America. Check their site www.tlaqueparte.com in English and Spanish. The Expo Guadalajara is at Mariano Otero #1499, corner of Avenida de las Rosas. (Carretera a Chapala, east or left on Calz. Lázaro Cárdenas, take the roundabout three-quarters of the way to make a left on Avenida Mariano Otero, Expo Guadalajara is at Avenida de las Rosas.)

Guadalajara International Book Fair/ *Fería Internacionál de Libros* Held each November, this massive fair is well worth the effort to attend. It is one of the major book fairs in the world with a thousand or more participating publishers and readings by prominent Latin American writers. There's a play area designed just for children. Watch for information about dates and tickets in the Guadalajara Colony Reporter. fil@fil.com.mx; www.fil.com.mx. At Expo Guadalara, Mariano Otero #1499, corner of Avenida de las Rosas. (Carretera a Chapala, east or left on Calz. Lázaro Cárdenas, take the roundabout three-quarters of the way to make a left on Avenida Mariano Otero, Expo Guadalajara is at Avenida de las Rosas.)

Guggenheim in Guadalajara Plans are underway for a Guggenheim art museum and cultural center in far northeast Guadalajara. Watch the Guadalajara Colony Reporter for news about its progress; www.guadalajarareporter.com.

Mariachi Festival in Guadalajara Look for the Mariachi Parade and all kinds of related activities during the first two weeks of September leading up to Mexican Independence Day, September 16. Visit their website www.mariachi-jalisco.com.mx/inicio.htm

Guadalajara Hotels

Camino Real	01 33 3634-1034
Fiesta Americana	01 33 3825-3434 01 33 3825-4848
Presidente Inter-Continental	01 33 3678-1234
Quinta Real	01 33 3615-0000 01 33 3360-1797
Holiday Inn Centro Histórico	01 33 3613-1763
Holiday Inn Select	01 33 3122-2020

Hotel Misión Carlton	01 33 3614-7272
Crowne Plaza	01 33 3634-1034
Del Bosque	01 33 3121-4020
De Mendoza	01 33 3613-7310 01 33 3614-2621
Fénix	01 33 3614-5714
Fiesta Inn	01 33 3669-3200
Francés	01 33 3613-1190
Guadalajara Plaza Expo	01 33 3669-0215
Howard Johnson Plaza las Torres	01 33 3810-3535
Laffayette	01 33 3615-0045
Plaza Génova Best Western	01 33 3613-7500

Half-Day Trips

An excellent source for trips in western Mexico is Tony Burton's *Western Mexico—A Traveller's Treasury.* This delightful, well-written book contains dozens of suggestions for day trips and longer excursions. Burton avoids destinations on the beaten tourist track such as Guadalajara, Puerto Vallarta or Morelia, to concentrate on lesser-known places. Find it locally at the Nueva Posada hotel, Donato Guerra #9, in Ajijic, or at www.sombrerobooks.com. It's also available in Spanish. For current information about hotels in practically every town in Mexico go to the excellent site www.allmexicohotels.com and type in the town you want and press the return key. For help with maps go to www.maps-of-mexico.com.

TLAQUEPAQUE

This southeast area of Guadalajara, once an affluent suburb and now engulfed by the city sprawl, is one of the best destinations in Jalisco for art, *artesanía*, and shopping. San Pedro Tlaquepaque was once a stagecoach stop from Guadalajara to Mexico City. It is recognized as the main handcraft center in Mexico and one of the most important in the world. Fine handmade items, some modest and some elegant, include high temperature ceramics, blown and spun glass, *papiér mâche*, iron work, scrap metal sculptures, silver, brass, textiles and hand carved wooden furniture. The larger stores can help arrange with shipping. You'll find an ATM machine opposite the Parián (where you can have your fill of Mariachi music over a cold drink), money changing houses, and three good restaurants on Independencia: Casa

Fuerte, Los Patios and the restaurant inside Adobe Designs. (North from Chapala on the Carretera a Chapala, go east on the Calz. Niños Heroes exit, turn right on Juárez. Park in the next four blocks. The street parallel and north alongside Juárez, Independencia, is a pedestrian street. Both Juárez and Independencia constitute the main shopping area.)

Hotels

Casa de las Flores B&B 01 33 3659-3186	This very nice B&B is located at Santos Degollado #175, San Pedro Tlaquepaque. www.casadelasflores.com

TONALÁ

Superb for wholesale *artesanía*, this pre-hispanic market town whose name means "place in the sun" is the birthplace of nine different kinds of pottery. Its prolific craftspeople produce wood and metal furniture, hand-blown glass, sculpture, *papiér mâche*, clothing, tinwork, pottery, paintings, and above all, ceramics. Master artists working in ancient techniques, *petatillo* and *bruñido*, are keeping traditions alive. Every Thursday and Sunday mornings are market days. (North from Chapala on the Carretera a Chapala, east on Calz. Lázaro Cárdenas, southeast on Autopista a Zapotlanejo, north on Tonaltecos, past Benito Juárez three long blocks. That will place you in the middle of the huge artesanía market that lines both sides of Tonaltecos.)

ZAPOPAN

Located on the northwest side of Guadalajara, Zapopan is known for its Basilica built in 1690 by Franciscan Missionaries. The Basilica houses a powerful Virgin, the Virgin of Zapopan, made from corn husk paste in the 16th Century and brought to the area by Christian monks. Called the Peace Maker and the Queen of Jalisco, the Virgin is credited with many miracles. Every year for six months she tours 130 parishes and returns to the Basilica on October 12. Whole villages stop when the Virgin tours; her visit is a deeply-felt religious event. Next to the Basilica is the Huichol Museum where you can buy their sacred art and that of the Cora Indians. (Plaza de las Américas y Eva Briseño #152.) Zapopan is also popular for Colomos Park, its restaurants, and lively student atmosphere. (North from Chapala on the Carretera a Chapala, to the Nogales-Tepic periférico, take the Guadalupe exit east to Avenida Patria north.)

SAYULA

Just an hour and a half away, Sayula is a charming town with some wonderful attractions. The town's name, Zaulán, comes from the Náhuatl language which means "place of flies." Despite this dubious distinction, you'll find this lovely town a pleasing weekend getaway. Sayula is the (not undisputed) birthplace of Juan Rulfo, one of Mexico's most illustrious literary sons. Author of the "Burning Plain" and other works, a display about his life can be found in the Casa de Cultura on the main plaza. Also found inside is an archaeological museum with artifacts of pre-Spanish inhabitants: statues of Colima dogs and fragments of mastodon bones. While in Sayula, try some of the local favorites: *ponche Sayula*, a punch made from pomegranates, guavas, and myrtle; *tatemado*, a casserole baked in clay of pork, chicken or beef with *chile de árbol*, oregano, and served with hand-made *tortillas*; and the local sausage, *salchichón.* At the T-junction of Mex15 at the western end of Jocotepec, turn right toward Guadalajara. At the end of the highway where 401, 54 and 80 meet, take the free road 54 (*libre*) or the toll road 54D (*cuota*) towards Colima, take Sayula exit.

Ojeda Knife Factory
342 422-0227

Thirteen generations of the Ojeda family have been making exceptional kitchen, sport and working knives, cutlery, walking cane stilettos, and other bladed instruments of high-quality German stainless steel. Internationally famous for their work, they fashion handles made from high-end woods, buffalo and impala horn, and inlay them with ivory, mother of pearl, and shell. Daniel Larios #23, Sayula. almao@prodigy.net.mx.

Cajeta Lugo
342 422-1998

In 1915, the Lugo family of Sayula rediscovered a candy-making recipe that produced a superior caramel candy from this region. Called *cajeta* and made by boiling goat milk, sugar and flavorings over a long period, this candy, ice cream topping, crepe and pastry filling is an authentic gastronomical treasure. Visit them at Ocampo #60, in Sayula or watch them make it in their new workshop at Alameda #166 (next to the *Santuario de Nuesta Señora de Guadalupe*), Sayula. (Workshop phone is 342 421-1660.) These candies and syrups make welcome and traditional Christmas gifts.

Figueroa Hermanos
342 422-1066

Visit the workshop of carpenter Noe Figeroa who exports his furniture made of fine wood all over the world. Figueroa Hermanos, Dr. Celso Vizcaíno #99, Sayula.

Casa de los Patios
342 422-0112

Spend the night at La Casa de los Patios, a superb small hotel just a half block from the Ojeda Knife Factory. Their friendly staff will serve you meals in their restaurant and provide you with a memorable moment in their bar. One of the town's enduring legends is the ghost of Sayula (*Anima de Sayula*). Inside the bar is a life-sized figure of a ghost spiriting away a bag of money. Try to reclaim the bag of money and see what happens. You're bound to blush. Email them for reservations. *Recommended.*
lacasadelospatios@hotmail.com,
www.lacasadelospatios.zzn.com.

COCULA, JALISCO

Located two and a half hours from Lakeside, this is the original *Mariachi* town where visitors can hear live musicians play nearly 24 hours a day. Although some scholars have argued over the origin of the term *mariachi* and some even claim that the musical style originated in other areas of Jalisco, Nayarit or even Veracruz, foremost scholars agree that the music and the name came from Cocula. (At the T-junction of Mex15 at the western end of Jocotepec, turn right toward Guadalajara. At the end of the highway where 401, 54 and 80 meet, choose highway 80. Go past Villa Corona to Cocula.)

MAZAMITLA, MICHOACAN

Located one and a half hours around Lake Chapala heading west just across the border into Michoacán, you'll climb to 7300 feet and find yourself in an alpine village where shops sell fresh cream, cheeses, preserves, woolen sweaters and ponchos. (Take highway 15 on the south side of the lake, just after Tuxcueca turn right and follow the signs to Mazamitla.)

Restaurante La Troje
382 538-0070

This large, well-run restaurant's specialty is *trifajitas*, sizzling strips of chicken, beef and

shrimp with all the fixings. Located four blocks from the square across from a Pemex station on Galeana #53, it's a perfect place to cap your day. Open every day 9 a.m. to 6:30 p.m.
la_troje_de_mazamitla@hotmail.com

Las Piedrotas, the Tapalpa rocks *entice many photographers.*

Pablo Fernandez del Valle

TAPALPA, MICHOACÁN

Two hours west of Lakeside, this lovely alpine village bears an uncanny resemblance to the Italian alps. The vista provides a dramatic backdrop to the parish church. Its wildflowers and the starkly beautiful Tapalpa Rocks (*Las Piedrotas*) lure many visitors, as do its cozy inns. (At the T-junction of Mex15 at the western end of Jocotepec, turn right toward Guadalajara. At the end of the highway where 401, 54 and 80 meet, take free road 54 or 401 past Zacoalco, Techaluta, Amacueca, Tepec to Tapalpa.)

TEQUILA, JALISCO

About two and a half hours north of Lakeside against the backdrop of blue *agave* fields, the town of Tequila is the original source of *tequila*. Now five states produce this national drink identified so completely with Mexico. For tours, go to the main plaza in front of the church and look for tour guides who will sell tickets to various distilleries.

(Take the Carretera a Chapala north toward Guadalajara, pick up the Nogales-Tepic portion of the *periferico* just past the airport, drive through the city to its northern boundary near the Primavera Forest, and pick up the toll road to Tepic, 15D.)

P.F.de V.

The Tequila Train This 12-hour tour to the historic Herradura Hacienda and distillery near Tequila includes transportation to Guadalajara from Lakeside, rail transportation to the Hacienda, a tour of the facilities, a large lunch buffet and show, as well as all the *mariachi* music you can listen to and all the *tequila* you can drink. Tickets are available through most local travel agencies.

Two- to Four-Day Excursions

For more information about these areas, an Internet search will yield plenty of information. Don't forget to do a hotel search at www.allmexicohotels.com. Type in the town you want and hit the return key on your keyboard.

BARRA DE NAVIDAD AND MELAQUE

About 5 hours southwest of the Lakeside area, the road to this pair of beach villages twists through miles and miles of spectacular coconut and banana plantations.

MANZANILLO

About three and a half hours southwest of Lakeside, Manzanillo's laid-back beach ambiance belies its status as Mexico's foremost Pacific coast port. Good for sport fishing, bird watching, and sunset cruises.

PUERTO VALLARTA

About five and a half hours northwest, Vallarta remains a popular tourist destination for partying, shopping, sightseeing, and beach excursions. December 15 marks the beginning of the whale season in Banderas Bay when humpback whales arrive from their summer home in Arctic waters to reproduce before heading back toward the North Pole in

February and March. Watch for tours from Lakeside or hook up with tours once you get to Vallarta.

MORELIA

About five and a half hours southeast, this colonial city is a jumping-off point for excursions to Pátzcuaro and the Monarch Butterfly Sanctuary near Zitácuaro where some one hundred million wintering butterflies fly into Mexico. Sadly, the sanctuary has been overused and there are rumors that the habitat is in serious trouble. See "Western Mexico—A Travellers Treasury" by Tony Burton for full details of this annual event. www.sombrerobooks.com.

PÁTZCUARO

Pátzcuaro offers up many charms including the nearby ruins of Tzintzunzan, the Day of the Dead destination, Janitzio, and excellent markets and craftspeople. Be sure to wander through the town's center and shop in the *Once Patios* or Eleven Patios, where you'll find all kinds of handmade wares.

"El Jorongo"
434 342-0924

One of many notable enterprises in Pátzcuaro is El Jorongo, the workshop of Ruth and Sabino Aguilar, master weavers and knitters of rugs, sweaters, ponchos, jackets and caps. Ruth revived this traditional work by controlling the entire process from using criollo wool from local, mixed-breed sheep and merino, to the hand dyeing and weaving components. Av. Lázaro Cárdenas #521, Pátzcuaro, Michoacán 61600
eljorongo@mail.ml.com.mx

La Casa Encantada B&B
434 342-5237

Beautifully restored suites in this colonial mansion in the historic center give visitors a glimpse of the past.
www.lacasaencantada.com

SAN MIGUEL DE ALLENDE

Some three and half hours northeast of Lakeside, San Miguel is a colonial silver mining town filled with 16th and 17th century churches. It bustles with galleries, schools, and sophisticated restaurants and nightspots.

ZACATECAS

Four and a half hours north of Lakeside, Zacatecas is another one of Mexico's colonial Silver Cities. At 8,000 feet it is breathtaking (literally!) for its excellent museums, churches and mine tours.

Tourist Information, Travel and Guides

Chapala Secretary of Tourism Office
376 765-3141
Information in Spanish, Sr. Hugo Pequeros, Madero #407, upstairs, Chapala. www.jalisco.com

TOUR AGENCIES

Adventure Charter Club Tours
Ajijic: 376 766-1777
Guadalajara: fax 01 33 3122-1214
Tours with bilingual, federally certified guides, first-class bus and car rentals, airport transportation. Tours include shopping trips to Guadalajara, the Ballet Folklorico, Mexico City at Christmas, coastal trips, and more. Tailor-made tours and group discounts are also available. Open Monday through Saturday, 9 a.m. to 5 p.m. Carretera Ote. #1, in the Plaza Montaña opposite the traffic light at Colón, Ajijic. *Recommended.* info@charterclubtours.com.mx.

Amigo Tours
376 766-3811
01 33 3141-6398
Shopping, sightseeing and adventure. Destinations throughout Mexico.

Amigos Tours and Travel
376 766-2157
376 766-1035
fax 376 766-2157
Reservation and ticketing for domestic and international airlines, tours, cruises, hotel reservations. Tours to Copper Canyon, Tequila Express, and more. Inside Plaza Bugambilias next to El Torito grocery store. Carretera Ote. #54-3, Ajijic. sylviaatr@yahoo.com; www.amigotours.com

Chevy's Custom Tours
376 766-0179
01 33 3460-4783
Official, licensed tour guide for Guadalajara, Tlaquepaque, Tequila Express, Tonalá, Mazamitla, Ocean/Beach, and around Lake Chapala. Will also drive you to the airport, bus depot, Ballet Folklorico or for shopping in Guadalajara. Other services include Fa-

cilitation for FM3 renewals, translations, interpretation. Will also rent cars and drive vehicles to the U.S. border. tourswithus@msn.com

Mexjourneys with Isabel Fuente
376 766-0822

A bonded official Jalisco tour guide, Isabel Fuente leads cultural journeys for small and large groups through western Mexico in English, Spanish and French. Ask about her journeys to *haciendas*, to the workshops of master artists, and her cooking and music tours. She's available for custom day tours and more. mexjourneys@prodigy.net.mx. *Recommended.*

Ray Travel Resources
376 766-2795
fax 376 766-4402

Individual and group travel, customized itineraries, and cruises throughout the world. South America a specialty. Discounts on cruises, car rentals and rail. 18 years experience. *Recommended.*
raytravel@mexico-wireless.com; www.raytravelresources.com.

***Turismo Sonrisa/* Sonrisa Tours**
376 766-5317
376 766-3032

Domestic and international airline tickets, bus tickets, beach packages. Open Monday through Friday 9 a.m. to 6 p.m., Saturday 9 a.m. to 2 p.m. Carretera Chapala-Ajijic #60-4, (inside Plaza San Andres, across from Telmex) Ajijic.

***Viajes Ajijic* (Ajijic Travel)**
376 766-0575
376 766-0695
fax 376 766-0203

Reservation and ticketing for domestic and international airlines, tours, cruises, hotel reservations, car rentals. English spoken. Open Monday through Friday, 9 a.m. to 6 p.m., Saturday 9 a.m. to 2 p.m. Carretera Aji-jic #9, Ajijic. (Across the highway and east from El Sarape restaurant.)

***Viajes Ibañez* (Ibañez Travel)**
387 763-0214

Alfonso Ramos Ibañez has 20 years in the travel business. He offers travel packages, bus trips to U.S., and other tours. Open Monday through Friday 10 a.m. to 3 p.m., 5 p.m. to 7 p.m., Saturday 9 a.m. to 2 p.m. José Santana #29, just east of Hidalgo Sur, Jocotepec. English spoken in the mornings.

PRIVATE GUIDES

Carlos Alfaro
Ajijic: 376 766-1777
Guadalajara:
01 33 3122-1214

Professional, certified, bilingual tour guide for regional or colonial tours. Private, air-conditioned vans are available for local or tailor-made tours.
carlosealfaro@prodigy.net.mx.

René Castañeda
376 762-0127

Bilingual, bonded, insured tour guide since 1986 for tours to Guadalajara, Tonalá, Tlaquepaque, Tequila, Tala and other destinations. Your car or his large van.

Rosa Elia Cepeda
Ajijic: 376 766-1777
Guadalajara:
01 33 3122-1214

Certified, bilingual tour guide offers custom tours and transportation anywhere in Mexico. Vans are equipped with air-conditioning.
rosye@prodigy.net.mx

Isabel Fuente
376 766-0822

Tri-lingual, bonded, fully-insured Jalisco tour guide based at Lakeside. Offers tours to Mexican master artists, cooking, music and art tours, custom source tours in Guadalajara for art and furniture, and beach tours for large groups or small.
mexjourneys@prodigy.net.mx

Justus Hauser
376 763-5333
fax 376 763-5335

Personal assistance, interpretation services for visits to notary, doctor, IMSS, etc.
justushauser@hotmail.com;
www.deutscheweltweit.de/all-in-1.html

Ilse Hoffman
01 33 3647-3912

Certified bilingual tour guide Ilse Hoffman offers personal and professional services for sightseeing; guidance about retiring in Mexico including information on housing, banking, medical services, and immigration; English-Spanish interpreting; assistance with business negotiations; factory tours of Mexican handicrafts and furnishings. Ilse40@megared.net.me;
Ilsehoffman@iedsa.com;
www.mexicoadventure.com/chapala/guadalajara.htm

José
01 33 3121-2385

Bilingual, university-degreed guide with private car who can pick you up at your home or hotel for tours of Guadalajara and Tlaquepaque and help with rentals.
joseinterpreter50@yahoo.com

Ricardo Mendoza

This bonded, official guide offers tours to Guadalajara, Tlaquepaque, Mazamitla, Tonalá, and Tequila (6 to 8 hour tours) that cost approx. 700 *pesos*. Normal tour charges are 200 *pesos* an hour. Suburban with driver costs 180 *pesos* each hour. Transportation to airport is 250 *pesos*, bus depot in Tonalá is 300 *pesos*. Can also arrange shopping days in Tonalá, Sunday Ballet Folklorico in Guadalajara, and reservations for the Tequila Express. Carr. Chapala-Jocotepec #139, San Antonio Tlayacapán (near Super Lake). Arcos98@hotmail.com

Car Rentals

Lakeside Car Rental
376 766-3732
24 hr 01 33 3157-1891

Car rentals by the hour, day, week, or month. Rental of Ford Kas, Nissan Platina, Focus Sedan, Focus wagon, and Ford Freestar 7-Passenger van. Plaza Bugambilias #10, next to El Torito grocery.
ffrancesi@hotmail.com ;
www.ajijiccarrental.com

Linea Professional
376 766-2555
fax 376 766-0066

Car rentals by the day, week or month. Daily rates include 300 kilometers free mileage. Unlimited mileage on weekly rentals. Prompt pick up and delivery service. Advance reservations suggested. Open Monday through Friday 9 a.m. to 5 p.m., Saturday 9 a.m. to 1 p.m. Carretera Ote. 33-C (Next to Multivalores Ajijic.)
letivera@laguna.com.mx

S&S Auto
376 765-4800

Daily rentals, discounted weekly and monthly rates. In case of collision, renter pays deductible. Open Monday through Friday 9 a.m. to 5 p.m. Carretera Chapala-Ajijic #101, Riberas del Pilar. (Next to Chicken Lick'n Deli.) ssauto@laguna.com.mx

Sunset Tours
376 766-4771

Car rentals include insurance and free mileage. Ka, economy sedan 500 *pesos* per day; Nissan Sentra 500 *pesos* per day; Volkwagon Pointer 500 *pesos* per day. Also can rent a Dodge Ram.

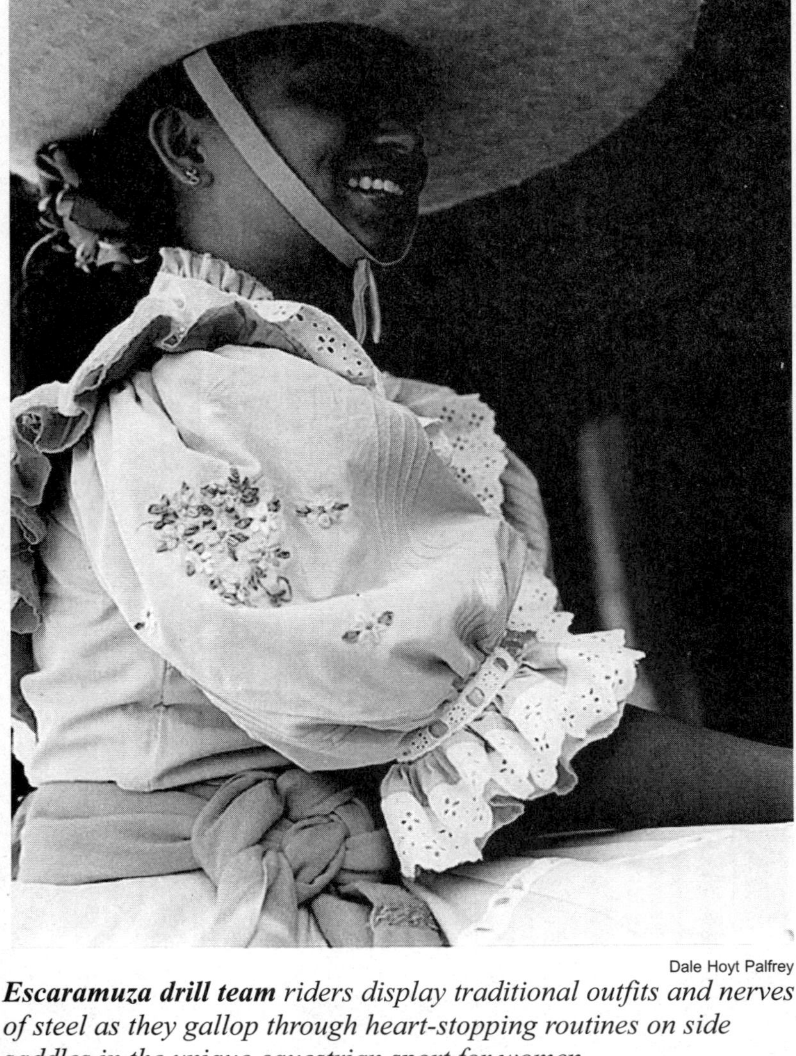

Dale Hoyt Palfrey

Escaramuza drill team *riders display traditional outfits and nerves of steel as they gallop through heart-stopping routines on side saddles in the unique equestrian sport for women.*

9

Sports and Fitness

with
DANIEL JACKSON GARCIA

The Northshore of Lake Chapala offers plenty of activities for an active holiday. Its best feature is, of course, its superb climate. You'll be able to golf, ride horses, enjoy public thermal pools, swim, play tennis, walk, hike and bike. The area has good parks and several good gyms. Some of the activities you'll find listed below do not meet year-round, but rather during the high season, from October through March when many in the foreign community are in residence.

The most reliable place to check for ongoing sports and fitness activities is in the Bulletin Board section of the Guadalajara Colony Reporter, the Listings Section of El Ojo del Lago, or in a similar section of the Lake Chapala Review. New activities are announced via flyers on the Lake Chapala Society, El Torito grocery, Super Lake and the Ajijic Post Office bulletin boards.

Thermal Baths & Water Activities

BALNEARIOS

Balnearios, or thermal baths, are one of the Lakeside's most relaxing and therapeutic attractions. Underground thermal springs are numerous, and can be found in remote mountain areas and occasionally still in private homes. The largest and most well known public *balneario* is the Balneario San Juan Cosalá.

Balneario San Juan Cosalá

Balneario San Juan Cosalá
387 761-0302
387 761-0222

Just south of the Carretera Chapala-Jocotepec on La Paz #5, San Juan Cosalá, is the Balneario San Juan Cosalá, open 9 a.m. to 6 p.m. Some English is spoken. 90 *pesos* per person for the day. The Balneario is closed Mondays to change and clean the pools. This three-part complex offers natural, odorless, thermal water in a number of swimming pools, three hotels, and a restaurant. Part one, the largest area best suited to family outings, features five pools, a very large hot tub, two Jacuzzis, and an underground steam room. There are water slides, snack bars, changing booths, poolside tables and chairs, and hotel rooms that overlook the pools and can be rented for the day. On weekends this area is packed with children and families who bring picnic lunches and stay throughout the day and afternoon. Expect it to be mobbed during *Semana Santa* and *Semana de Pascua*, the weeks before and after Easter. The facilities overlook the Lake and you'll find mixing with people of all ages endearing.

For visitors looking for a more sedate experience, seek out the second part of the complex Villa Bordeaux, marked by Ruben's Grill. Here you can spend the day in a country club-style setting, ordering food and drink from the restaurant, swimming in the pool, sunning on their grounds, taking massages from their staff, all of which are located just west of the big family complex described above. They also offer rooms for rent. See the Hotel and Accommodations chapter, San Juan Cosalá section, for rates.

In part three of the complex, behind the pool area and situated between the main Carretera Chapala-Jocotepec and the gravel access road to the pools, is a larger block of hotel rooms offering phones, showers, bathrooms, and an indoor thermal pool in each room. The Hotel Monte Carlo in Chapala also offers a small thermal pool.

Villas Buena Ventura
387 761-0202
387 761-0303

Opposite the Raquet Club, this hotel offers 1 and 2 bedroom apartments with natural thermal water Jacuzzis or hydromassage tubs. A small private thermal swimming pool can be rented by the hour. Garden areas are decorated with Sergio Cuevas ceramics and sculpture. Open Monday through Sunday 9 a.m. to 9 p.m. Carretera Ajijic-Jocotepec Km. 13.5, San Juan Cosalá. Some English spoken.

SWIMMING

Cristianía Park
376 765-2937

Swim in their huge swimming pool and slide down the water slides from noon to 5 p.m. (20 *pesos* adults, 10 *pesos* for kids). There are also picnic areas with braziers and pavilions, paved bike paths, playgrounds, free bathrooms, tennis courts for 20 *pesos* an hour, soccer fields, and snack bars. The pool is periodically closed for cleaning and filling. Av. La Cristianía #24, Chapala.

Tobolandia
376 766-2120

Admission 40 *pesos* children, 80 *pesos* adults, parking 10 *pesos*. Go early, get a table in the shade and spend the day riding their giant waterslides. If you're too tiny for the big slides stay in the areas designed especially for little people. Tired of the water? Hang on the monkey bars, shoot hoops on the basket ball court, or play volleyball or badminton, kick around a soccer ball on the *fútbol* field, or play video games. Hungry? There are plenty of refreshment stands selling Golden Fried Chicken, ice cream, and all kinds of Mexican snacks. Don't worry, there are plenty of bathrooms everywhere.

Don't bring in bottles or anything made of glass, bicycles, skates, pets, or alcoholic beverages. Expect it to be packed on the weekends and on holidays. Open daily 10 a.m. to 6 p.m. In Ajijic at the junction of the *Libramiento* and the Chapala-Jocotepec Carretera.

The following hotels may allow you the use of their pool for the day in the slow season, approximately April through September, for a small fee of about 20 *pesos* per person.

Hotel Real de Chapala 376 766-0014 376 766-0021 — Paseo del Prado #20, La Floresta, Ajijic.

Hotel Monte Carlo 376 765-2120 376 765-3366 — Hidalgo #296, Chapala.

Mama Chuy's 387 761-0022 — La Puerta #100, San Juan Cosalá.

Boating

There are two yacht clubs on the Northshore. Both have dry boat storage and dining facilities but foreign membership is allowed only at Club Nautico. To cruise Lake Chapala for an hour, you'd have to rent one of the colorful launches from the Lake Chapala pier. Boats cruise along the shore of the "Riberas", Spanish for the Riviera, the name once given to Chapala's lovely north shore for 180 *pesos* a boatload, 250 *pesos* for a 30-minute tour around Scorpion Island, or 310 *pesos* for an hour's excursion. If you want to stay and walk around the island or sit and have a cold drink, the cost of the boat jumps to 380 *pesos* for a half hour and 440 *pesos* for 60 minutes. Buy your tickets at the booth at the foot of the pier and invite up to 8 friends.

Club Nautico 376 766-0164 — Club Nautico opened its door to foreign members in late 2003. Open Tuesday through Saturday 9 a.m. to 5 p.m., Sunday 9 a.m. to 8 p.m. For 20 *pesos*, non-members can gain access to the grounds and use a limited number of facilities including its restaurant. Membership in the club requires a 2,000 *peso* initial fee and a 2,000 *peso* installment every two months and allows members the use of club facilities including a pool and sauna, dock access and dry boat storage. Paseo de la Huerta #57, La Floresta, just west of the Real de Chapala Hotel.

Chapala Yacht Club/ *Club de Yates de Chapala*
376 765-2276
Exclusively Mexican membership; sponsorship by two senior members is required. Open daily 9 a.m. to 5 p.m. Ramón Corona #22-A, Chapala.

***Capitanía de Puerto-* Lake Chapala Harbor Master**
376 765-2230
The Harbor Master's duties include enforcing all laws, approving boating licenses for the state of Jalisco, and providing all services related to the use of Lake Chapala. If you bring a boat be sure to check with this office for regulations. Among other duties, the Harbor Master organizes search and rescue missions. In case of a boating mishap contact this office for help.

Sport and Recreational Activities

BALLET

Le Petit Ballet Company
376 766-0075
Year-round instruction in a bright, airy studio. For children ages 4-14. Open Monday, Wedneday and Friday 5 p.m. to 6 p.m. Plaza Bugambilias 2nd Floor, (next to El Torito grocery) Ajijic.

BALLROOM DANCING

Lake Chapala Society
Noon Saturday. Free to members.Check for listings. 16 de Septiembre #16-A, Ajijic.

Club Oxygen
376 766-5005
Classes for members. Call for dates and times. Hotel Danza del Sol, Ocampo #151, Ajijic.

BICYCLING

In late 1999 the major portion of the Chapala-Jocotepec *carretera* that runs along the northshore of Lake Chapala was reconstructed to include a *ciclopista* or protected bicycle lane. Since then the lane has become a major artery for walkers, dog walkers, runners and bicycle commuters. Traffic in this lane moves in both directions and peak hours are from 8 a.m. to 10:30 a.m. and again in the afternoon from 6 p.m. to 8 p.m. Care should be taken to listen for bicyclists approaching from behind.

LONG DISTANCE CYCLING has become a serious sport in Guadalajara. On many weekends throughout the year huge packs of cyclists ride from Guadalajara to Lake Chapala and back, clogging the *carretera*, the *Libramiento,* and creating traffic jams from slow-moving pace cars. You'll note that these cyclists do not usually use the *ciclopista*, much to the dismay of locals who view their imperious habits as dangerous and maddening. *Use extreme care around cyclists.* They are not trained to integrate into traffic and cannot be ticketed by police for breaking the simplest of laws. If you hit a rider you are at fault.

Bicycle Sales and Repair

Bicicletas Rayo Ajijic Repairs, parts, and rentals of bicycles and small motorized 4-wheelers. Hand over an I.D. and pay cash. Sales of helmets, accessories, cycling clothes. Open Monday through Saturday 10 a.m. to 8:30 p.m. Carr. Pte. #12, Ajijic.

Bicicletas Rayo Chapala Reputable bicycle sales, tune-ups and repairs operated by a former Mexican bicycling champion. Open Monday through Saturday 10 a.m. to 2 p.m., 4 p.m. to 7 p.m. Juárez #256, Chapala.

Bicicletas Refacciones "Nelles" New bikes for sale, repair and maintenance, service for old bikes. Open Monday through Saturday 9 a.m. to 6 p.m. Miguel Arana #280-A, on the main road into town on the lake side, Jocotepec. Some English is spoken.

BILLIARDS

Must be 18 or older to enter and this one is for guys only. On the west side of the plaza in San Antonio Tlayacapán. Open Monday through

Thursday 9 a.m. to midnight, Friday, Saturday and Sunday 9 a.m. to 2 a.m. Independencia #131-C, San Antonio Tlayacapán.

EXERCISE

Mild unisex exercises are held at the *Auditorio de la Ribera* (Lakeside Auditorium) in Lower La Floresta Monday and Thursday at 9:30 a.m. Check the Lakeside Bulletin Board section of the Guadalajara Colony Reporter for details.

Exercise Group at the LCS — An exercise group meets at the Lake Chapala Society in Ajijic, Monday, Wednesday and Friday at 9 a.m. 16 de Septiembre #16-A, Ajijic.

GOLF

Chapala Country Club at Vista del Lago #1
376 763-5136 — Located 7 kms from Chapala on the Chapala-Mezcala *carretera*, this 18-hole course with double tees 3 and 12, allows non-members special rates for play on weekends and holidays after 2 p.m. and Junior memberships for players less than 35 years of age. cccgolf@prodigy.net.mx

Chula Vista Golf Club
376 766-2515 — This well-placed club offers a 9-hole, par 31 course. Rental equipment is available by the hour. Minimum two rounds with caddy. No carts, full bar, separate shower facilities with saunas for men and women. Ask about annual family memberships. Paseo del Golf #5, Chula Vista, Ajijic.

Nearby Golfing

Isla de Navidad
01 315 355-3556 — Barra de Navidad, Jalisco. 27-hole course in a grand setting.

El Tamarindo
01 315 351-5032 — 18-hole course 20 miles north of Melaque on the highway to Puerto Vallarta (Mex 200).

Club Las Hadas
01 314 334-1968 — Considered to be a tricky 18-hole course close to the Hotel Las Hadas and Karmina Palace in Manzanillo.

Club Santiago
01 314 335-0410 — Nine and 18-hole courses in the huge Club Santiago development on the northern end

of Manzanillo.

GYMS

Club Oxygen
376 766-5005

Fitness center offers Pilates, yoga, tai chi, tae bo, step training, free weights, weight machines, pool, and tennis courts. Afternoon classes for children include tennis, tae kwon do, pre-ballet, ballet, jazz, tap and tai chi. Full, partial, snowbird, tennis only, and other memberships available. Club is open Monday through Friday, 7:30 a.m. to 8 p.m., Saturday and Sunday 9 a.m. to 3 p.m. Hotel Danza del Sol, Ocampo #151, Ajijic.

Graves Gym

In Chapala, 2 blocks behind the bus station.

Kelly's Aerobics

At La Huerta gated community. Monday, Wednesday, Friday 7:45 a.m. Look for newspaper listings.

Liga de Fisico-Constructive y Fitness
387 763-2598

Weights, stationary bicycles, and instructors. No sign. Open Monday through Friday 6 a.m. to 11 a.m., 4 p.m. to 10 p.m., Saturday 7 a.m. to 11 a.m. Pedro Moreno Sur #75, Jocotepec.

Spinning & Pilates Gym
Stand Bike/
Ciclismo Bajo Techo
376 765-6271

Aerobic and cardiovascular exercise that helps eliminate stress, reverse overweight, burn fat, tone muscle. One hour group classes with music and trained instructors. Carr. Pte. No. 11-C, Ajijic. (Behind Pemex on the *Libramiento*.)

Status Gym
376 765-4774

One of Lakeside's biggest gyms, Status offers nautilus and free weights, lockers, showers, dressing rooms, a sauna/steam room, and aerobics. Open Monday through Friday 7 a.m. to 2 p.m., 4 p.m. to 9:30 p.m., Saturday 8 a.m. to 2 p.m. Miguel Martínez #441, Chapala.

Structure Gym

Nautilus equipment with very helpful instruction. Personal trainer Enrico Rosselli is on staff from 7 a.m. to 1 p.m. Open 6 a.m. to 2 p.m., 4 p.m. to 10 p.m. Monthly dues. Carr.

Ote. #33-B, Ajijic (near Ajijic clinic). English spoken.

HIKING

with Daniel Jackson Garcia

North above Ajijic, San Antonio Tlayacapán, and Chapala looms the Sierra Travesaño. Behind Jocotepec, Cerro Los Agraciados is the prominent hill. North of it, beyond a small interior valley, is the highest peak in the Lakeside area, Cerro Viejo, part of a ridge known as the Sierra el Madroño. Tony Burton, author of the Companion Map to this guide, tells us that Cerro Viejo's summit is 2,960 meters (9,711 feet) above sea level. Behind San Juan Cosalá is Sierra Las Vigas, sometimes called Sierra Tecuán. There is a network of trails throughout these mountains that can be hiked if you are experienced and in very good condition. Not maintained in any way, the trails offer exciting hiking, fairly good footing, shade, spectacular views, and especially in the rainy season, June through September, waterfalls and small pools. Always hike with one or more companions and carry a cellular phone, water, and first aid gear. It is not always possible to get a clear cellular signal, though, so be extra careful to avoid accidents. A new book by Gerry Green, "Walks and Trails Around Ajijic," published in 2005 is an excellent resource. Look for it at Libros y Revistas in the Bugambilias Plaza.

Trail Heads

Lomas del Manglar

On the east side of Riberas del Pilar in the neighborhood of the same name, you'll find a trailhead at the north end of San Jorge. This 15-minute uphill walk takes you to the *"Presa de Coco"* where you may see large numbers of hummingbirds. From there you're about a hundred meters from a large field of blue *agave.*

Dale Hoyt Palfrey

Hikers cool off *in the Tepalo Falls.*

Tepalo

Follow J. Encarnación Rosas north of the *carretera*, bear right so that you're on the Callejon de Tepalo, until you've reached the Tepalo trailhead. A novice hiker can get to the first waterfall, about 10 minutes up the trail. Two others follow and at the third waterfall you'll see a sign that says *Bienvenidos a Tepalo*, "Welcome to Tepalo." From there the trail leads to an open field of prickly pear cactus. From there the trail splits. If you go straight and follow the *arroyo* up, you'll find the going difficult after about an hour. A *machete* is required to pass, especially if you're hiking during the rainy season. If at the field of prickly pear you take the left hand trail it'll take you to the ridge of Chupinaya, a hike of about an hour, that allows you views north toward Guadalajara and of the lake in Cajititlán. On extremely clear days you may even see the *Volcán del Fuego*, the active volcano in the state of Colima to the west. During this hike you're likely to see flowers and insects found only on the upper slopes, herbs for tea, wild anise and *camotes del cerro*, white tubers similar to yams. You will also see fox and bobcat scat although sightings of the bobcat are very rare.

Tempisque

The Tempisque hike is the most rugged and interesting hike of those above Ajijic. Follow *calle* Tempisque on the north side of the *carretera* (above Aquiles Serdán) as far up as you can drive and park your car. It's a good idea to place a good-sized rock behind one of your wheels before you set out. About 50 yards up the trail you'll come upon a bathing pool and are likely to see people splashing in the cold water. Above the pool the trail splits. To the left is a very challenging climb to Chupinaya ridge mentioned in the Tepalo hike. You'll know you're on the trail if you pass a huddle of *chozas* or shacks. If you don't take the trail left to Chupinaya and continue straight up from the bathing pool, you'll be rewarded with an incredibly wild hike where you may see as many as thirty waterfalls. The trail is for serious hikers as you'll scale huge mossy rocks, climb through chutes, pass earth slides and walk over plenty of loose rocks. Tunnels from two abandoned gold mines pocket this *arroyo* so be aware of this hazard. At the top of the *arroyo*, a hike of more than four hours, you'll find a high *mesa* with incredible views of the area. A sturdy walking stick or *bastón* is suggested.

HORSEBACK RIDING

Horseback riding using the western saddle is available in lower La Floresta at the junction of Camino Real and Paseo del Lago streets not far from the Hotel Real de Chapala. Riding costs 70 *pesos* an hour, 40 *pesos* per half hour from 11 a.m. to 7:30 to 8:00 p.m. Wranglers can be hired for guided excursions. Some English is spoken.

El Caballo Rojo
01 33 3459-9300

Guided horseback and trail riding on horses trained in the United States. Private lessons available. Hourly rides, lunch, dinner and sunset rides as well as day and overnight camping rides available. Stables are in La Cristina, west of Ajijic. riding@caballorojo.com

***Horseback riding** is a great way to enjoy the area's natural beauty.*

Dale Hoyt Palfrey

MARATHON RUNNING

Race Only for the Wild/*Carrera solo para salvajes*
376 766-1356

Formerly called the Chupinaya Sky Race, runners compete in a grueling 20-kilometer marathon through the mountains overlooking Ajijic. The run draws athletes from all over the world who hope to qualify for the International Sky marathon. Held in November, registration is handled by area runner and current mayor of Ajijic, Ricardo Gonzalez who can be found at his Glass and Frame shop, Guadalupe Victoria #38, in Ajijic.

MARTIAL ARTS

Club Oxygen
376 766-5005

The club schedules martial arts classes for kids. Check for days and times. Hotel Danza del Sol, Ocampo #151, Ajijic.

MEDITATION

Grupo Sidha Yoga
376 766-0176

Meets Wednesday 7 to 9 p.m. for chanting and meditation. English spoken. Paseo de las Brisas, La Floresta, Ajijic.

Lake Chapala Society At the Lake Chapala Society. Look for listings. 16 de Septiembre #16-A, Ajijic.

PARKS

Cristianía Park
376 765-2937

Large, well-maintained park in Chapala has lovely gardens, picnic tables, braziers, paved bike paths, eight tennis courts, public pool, basketball court, soccer fields, amphitheater, strolling trails, and snack bars. Park is open 8 a.m. to 8 p.m. for only 5 *pesos* all day. Swim from noon to 5 p.m. for 20 *pesos* for adults and 10 *pesos* for kids. Play tennis for 20 *pesos* an hour. No dogs allowed. Av. La Cristianía #24, Chapala. www.difchapala.gob.mx; museo_virtual@prodigy.net.mx

SHOOTING CLUB

Club Cinegetico Not yet open, this club owner is waiting for a permit to be issued out of Guadalajara. Independencia #42 Norte, Jocotepec.

SOFTBALL

376 766-3671 Co-ed, Friday, 9:30 a.m. Call Charlie for locations.

SPORT SUPPLIES

Polo Sport
387 763-0815

Sales of sport shoes, shirts, barbells, weights, gear bags, gloves, soccer balls, flags, trophies and other items. Will make sport uniforms to specifications. Open daily 9 a.m. to 8 p.m. Hidalgo Sur #119, main street going south from plaza, Jocotepec.

Rescue Numbers

Red Cross *(Cruz Roja)* (376) 765-2308, (376) 765-2553

Civil Rescue for Ajijic and Chapala (376) 766-3615

Civil Rescue for San Juan Cosalá and Jocotepec (387) 763-1804

TAI CHI

With Lonny Riddle Monday and Friday 10:30 a.m. at the upper park in La Villita, next to Tobolandia.

ULTRALIGHT FLYING

It's possible to arrange for charter flights on ultralight planes with Aeroclub Chapala. There is a fee to cover fuel and maintenance costs. Aeroclub Chapala meets on weekends at the Santa Cruz de la Soledad airport,1 km from the municipal seat in Chapala on the Chapala-Mezcala highway (follow signs to Vista del Lago).

Dale Hoyt Palfrey

VIDEO ARCADES

Video Juegos Itzel Arcade for kids. Snacks and soft drinks. Open daily noon to 9 p.m. Independencia #13-A, on the west side of the plaza, San Antonio Tlayacapán.

"No Name" Arcade Deep, cavernous arcade with 32-game machines—dancing, driving, shooting, and flying. Sell soft ice cream, soft drinks, nachos. Safe place for kids. Open daily 10 a.m. to 10 p.m., Saturday and Sunday until 11 p.m. On the west side of the plaza, Hidalgo #32, Jocotepec.

VOLLEYBALL

La Cristianía Park Co-ed in Chapala, 9:30 a.m. Tuesday, Thursday and Saturday. Check newspaper listings. Av. La Cristianía #24, Chapala.

WALKING

Hash House Harriers Meet at the Old Posada on the Ajijic pier. Saturday 8:30 a.m.

WATER RESISTANCE EXERCISES

La Joya del Lago At the hotel pool, Rio Zula #7, Ajijic. 1:30 p.m. to 2:30 p.m. Tuesday, Thursday and Saturday. Rio Zula #7, Ajijic.

YOGA

Lake Chapala Society	2 p.m. Thursday. Watch for schedule changes. 16 de Septiembre #16-A, Ajijic.
Prasad Health Food Store 376 766-0006 376 766-5154	This store offers classes in experimental dance, Kundalini yoga, hatha yoga as well as conferences, workshops, Japanese massage. Classes are held at Constitución #38, Ajijic. Find the store at Carr. Ote. #117-B, Ajijic.
Yoga Motion 376 766-0523 01 33 3190-0100	Advanced and beginners yoga in a beautiful property in lower La Floresta east of the Real de Chapala Hotel. Tuesday, Thursday and Saturday classes 9 a.m. to 10:15 a.m. Paseo de las Brisas #45, La Floresta.
Yoga in Mexico with Barbara Luboff	For serious yoga training and retreats in Mexico. More than 30 years of practice and teaching. www.yogainmexico.com *Recommended.*

Pablo Fernandez del Valle

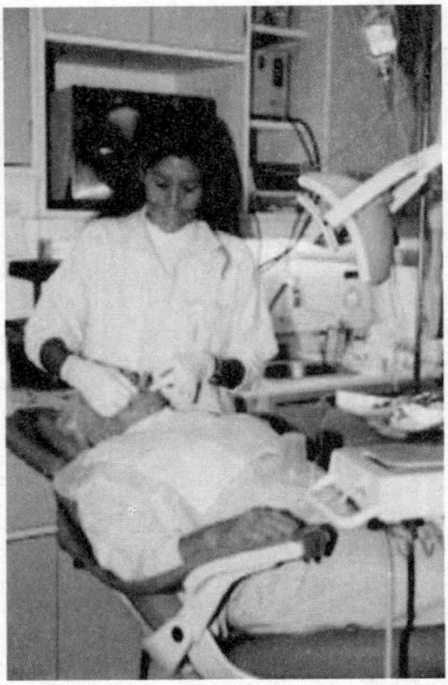

Pablo Fernandez del Valle

Health and grooming services are available at Lakeside.

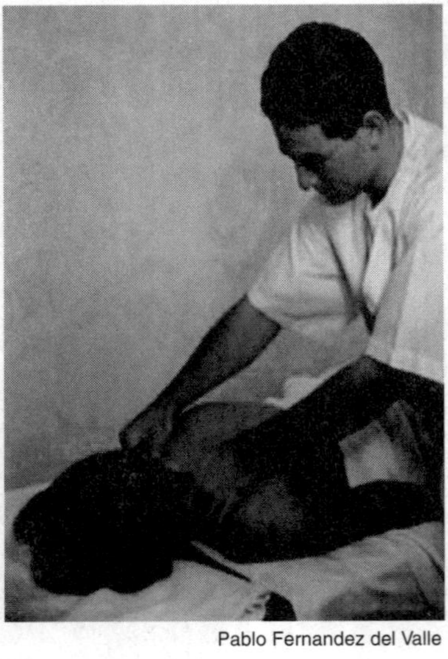

Pablo Fernandez del Valle

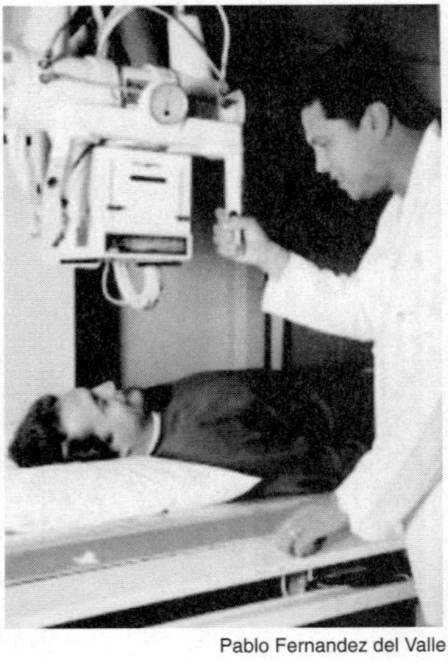

Pablo Fernandez del Valle

10

Health and Personal Services

Medical and Alternative Care, Pharmacies, Veterinarians, and Personal Services

with
DON ADAMS and ZOFIA BARISAS

If you should be unlucky enough to suffer an illness or an accident while on holiday in the Lakeside area, don't worry. Lakeside practitioners can address most problems the traveler is likely to experience. If your problem is *serious*, Lakeside practitioners, clinics, and ambulance services can stabilize you and then direct you to specialists and hospitals in Guadalajara. Remember, taxis can get you to a doctor's office or clinic, but don't wait until the middle of the night to seek medical attention if you can help it—it's much easier to be treated during regular working hours.

Until recently, you had to bring cash to pay for services at the Lake, but now many clinics will accept U.S. insurance. Most likely you'll pay first and be reimbursed later.

TURISTA

Traveler's diarrhea, often called *turista* and not to be confused with dysentery, salmonella or e-coli infections, is a normal byproduct of travel. The worst thing you can do is dose yourself with a drug such as Lomotil to trap the unfamiliar bacteria inside your body and stop the body's normal flushing process. An excellent way to prevent a reaction from new foods is to dose yourself with live acidophilus bifidus before and during your stay. The better the product, the better the results. Another strategy is to begin taking Pepto Bismol tablets or liquid before you come. If you do end up with normal diarrhea a product called Pedialyte® works to restore the body's lost electrolytes from the dehydration that

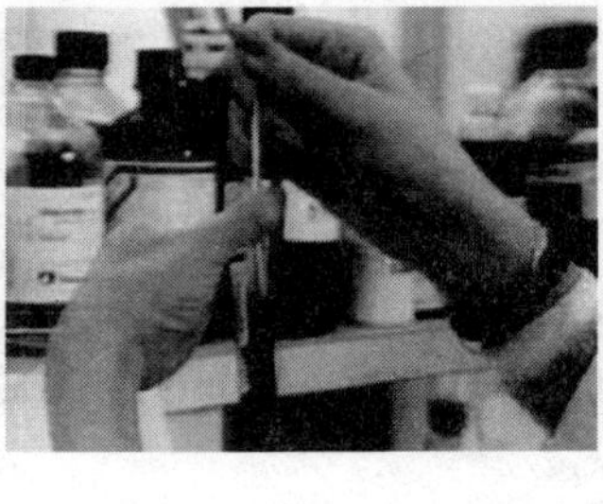

AMBULANCE VOCABULARY

My name is ...	*Yo soy ...*
My address is ...	*Mi domicilio es ...*
My phone number is ...	*Mi teléfono es ...*
Send an ambulance...	*Mandar ambulancia ...*
I fell and I am hurt.	*Me caí y estoy herido.*
I am very sick.	*Estoy muy enfermo.*
Bring oxygen for a heart attack.	*Traiga oxígeno por ataque cardiaco.*
Bring oxygen for an asthmatic attack.	*Traiga oxígeno por ataque asmático.*
There is an auto accident at ...	*Hay un accidente de autos en ...*
I have allergies to..	*Tengo alergias a...*
My blood type is...	*El tipo de sangre es...*
I am diabetic.	*Soy diabético.*

Courtesy of the Chapala Red Cross

results from diarrhea. Several liters a day will be wonderfully restorative. Strawberry flavor is probably the most palatable. How many days is normal for a bout of diarrhea? As many as three days of sweating, vomiting, and fevers up to 103 degrees, according to the CDC, Center for Disease Control in Atlanta, Georgia, U.S.A.

In April, when the mercury climbs into the 80's, 90's F., 30º to 40º C., *taco* stand food and especially the *salsas* they serve can easily spoil. Why not carry your own *salsa*? Salmonella from spoiled foods and *salsas* can lay you low for many days. It's better to eat fast food at night from vendors who set up early in the evening than those who have been out all day. Diarrhea can also be prompted from sun exhaustion, especially at this altitude. If you're out sightseeing, be sure to drink plenty of water throughout the day, in addition to other beverages.

www.medtogo.com

The website for this book "MedToGo, Mexico: Health & Safety Travel Guide" offers more useful information than many we've found. Look for Guadalajara and Lake Chapala information by clicking the "About

Mexico" link on the home page and then by clicking the "Central Pacific" link from there. The site lists useful medications and suggests immunizations for travelers.

Emergency Care

If your malady or mishap allows you to get yourself to a clinic, practitioner, or the Red Cross (Cruz Roja) in Chapala, it is unlikely that you'll need the services of an ambulance. However, ambulance service is readily available.

24-HOUR AMBULANCE SERVICE

Chapala	
Red Cross	376 765-2553, 765-2308
IMSS	376 765-2240
Clínica Ibarra	376 765-4805
Clínica Municipal	376 765-5421
Ajijic	
Ajijic Hospital Center	376 766-0500, 766-0662
Riberas del Pilar	
Clínica Máscaras	376 765-4805
Jocotepec	
Clínica Municipal	387 763-1920

AIR AMBULANCE SERVICE

Global Life Flight
01 33 3615-2471
01 33 3615-9547

This emergency carrier works with clients who already have coverage through their insurance policies. If a patient does not have coverage in this way, Global Life operators will arrange for a flight once you guarantee payment. For more information, globallifeflight@infosel.com.mx. If a Spanish speaker answers, ask for someone who can help you in English.

Skymed International
Toll Free from Mexico
001 866 805-9624

An annual fee is required to engage this service that airlifts patients to the U.S. for treatment. For individuals the fee is $300 US per year + $180 (for the NATO option that is necessary for residents in Mexico) + a one-time application fee of $30. For couples or families the fee is $420 + $360 + $40. Renewal rates do not include the application fees. How it works: the patient is taken to the nearest local clinic, he or she presents a Skymed card and the attending physician calls the Skymed number above. If the patient has a preference of hospital, he tells the physician. If he or she is unable to, the attending physician will make that decision with the Skymed team. info@skymed.com; www.skymed.com.

Mexican Manners

When entering a waiting room for doctors or dentists it is polite to address the room with a *Buenos Días* or *Buenas Tardes* before making your way to your seat.

Clinics, Insurance, Hospitals, Doctors, Labs and Pharmacies

Plans are underway for a complete Medical Center that will specialize in service to the entire community. It will have complete trauma, surgical, delivery, and diagnostic services (MRI, CT, X-ray, etc.), with the possibility of a heart wing. It is planned to include a free clinic for prenatal and diabetic care and possibly a rehabilitation center and assisted living center. Construction is planned for as early as 2005. Until then, local clinics and the Red Cross in Chapala serve to stabilize seriously ill or injured patients before they are transported to excellent hospitals in Guadalajara, one hour away. If you need to be hospitalized expect to have a fam-

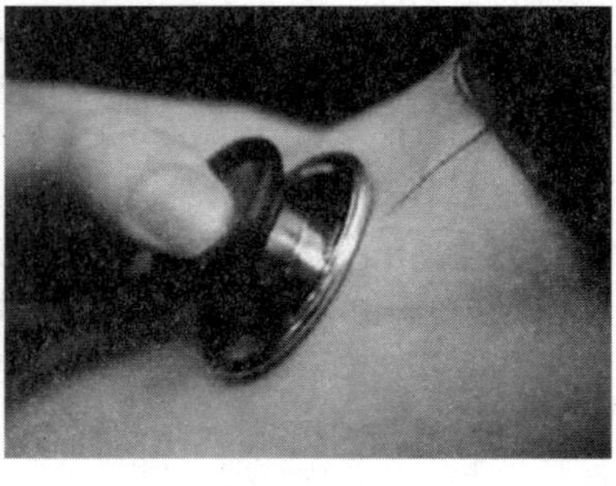

ily member or friend at the hospital to help attend you until you're discharged.

LAKESIDE CLINICS

Ajijic Hospital Center 376 766-0500	Twenty-four hour emergency and ambulance service, X-ray, EKG, laboratory, emergency, operating and private rooms, rehabilitation clinic, house calls. Visiting specialists come weekly from Guadalajara. U.S. insurance accepted. Carretera Chapala-Ajijic Ote. #33 in Ajijic.
Ajijic Telemedicine Center 376 766-4989	This center connects patients with doctors, medical centers, research facilities and the UAG Angel Leaño Hospital in Guadalajara by computers, video cameras and the latest electronic diagnostic tools. This center is affiliated with Johns Hopkins, Baltimore, Maryland; Creighton University Medical Center in Omaha, Nebraska; Washington University Medical in St. Louis, Missouri; University of Iowa Health Care, Iowa City, Iowa; Midwest Health Partners of Norfolk, Nebraska; and the Colorado Center of Reproductive Medicine, Denver, Colorado. Open daily, noon to 8 p.m. Zaragoza #165, inside the Danza del Sol hotel, Ajijic.
Clínica Ibarra 376 765-3396 01 33 3150-9937 01 33 3203-5973	Dr. Sergio Ibarra Soltero. Paravertebral myotherapy, pediatrics, x-rays, childbirth. Monday, Wednesday, and Friday 10 a.m. to 2 p.m., 5 p.m. to 9 p.m.; Tuesday, Thursday and Saturday 10 a.m. to 2 p.m. Madero #230, Chapala.
Clínica María Auxiliadora 387 763-1088	Twenty-four-hour emergency service and consultations by appointment. Family practitioner Dr. Teresa Morales; Clinical pathologist Dr. Joaquin Ramos. X-ray, ultrasound, pharmacy with consultations by specialists. Morelos Ote. #149, Jocotepec.

Clínica Nueva Galicia
376 765-2400

Open Monday through Friday 10 a.m. to 2 p.m., 4 p.m. to 8 p.m., until 2 on Saturday. 24-hour emergency service. Juárez #563-A, Chapala.

Clínica Nuñez
387 763-0770
376 763-0836

Twenty-four-hour-emergency clinic with ten-bed capacity. Pharmacy and lab on premises. General surgery, deliveries, other specialties. Vicente Guerrero #25, Jocotepec.

Grupo Médico Lago
376 765-5006

General medicine, EKG testing, laboratory, daytime emergencies, inhalation therapy, dialysis and other treatments. Open 10 a.m. to 8 p.m. Monday through Saturday. Av. Hidalgo #219, Chapala.

Máscaras Clinic
376 765-4805

Twenty-four-hour emergency and ambulance service, X-ray, laboratory next door, operating and private rooms, house calls, mammograms and X-rays. Visiting specialists come weekly from Guadalajara. U.S. insurance accepted and the clinic offers their own "insurance" program. Their advertising may lead you to believe that they also offer ultrasounds, CT scans, and MRI in Chapala, but those services are available in Guadalajara at Justo Sierra #2350. Clinic address is Hidalgo 79-G. Riberas del Pilar, between Ajijic and Chapala.

Red Cross/*Cruz Roja*
376 765-2308

The Red Cross takes walk-in clients at their Chapala location and sends their mobile units, equipped for cardiac emergencies, to the scene of accidents twenty-four hours a day, 365 days a year. The clinic is open to everyone, including travelers and visitors and is staffed by three doctors, eight paramedics, and four nurses. Their clinic lacks X-ray facilities, though. They teach first aid and CPR in local schools and conduct training sessions for a youth group. To maintain neutrality, International Red Cross rules dictate that no government funds can be used

Scorpion Alerts

In Jalisco there are eight different species of scorpions and although their bite is rarely fatal, people who have heart and respiratory diseases, children weighing less that 30 pounds, and the very elderly are mostly at risk. Scorpions appear during their reproductive period and tend to make themselves a nuisance in the months between April and September. If you are stung you're likely to feel stinging pain, numbness and inflammation from one day up to several weeks. Doctors advise putting ice on the bite and remaining calm. Benadryl or aspirin can be taken for mild cases. For serious symptoms, anti-venom serum is available at nearly every clinic or pharmacy. Difficulty breathing or speaking, tightening in the throat, pain that travels from the bite to the chest for several days, fever, headache and up and down blood pressure and heartbeat are symptoms of a severe reaction and anti-venom serum is in order. The serum is administered via a syringe and the patient should be watched for about an hour in case of a severe allergic reaction to the serum.

Courtesy Guadalajara Colony Reporter

for their support. They are entirely supported by donations. Always give generously, especially during their fundraising drives. When you donate, get a card to put in your wallet that shows your blood type and keep a handy emergency vocabulary card by your telephone. They are the only facility sanctioned by Mexican law to attend to accident victims. Open daily around the clock. González Gallo #1, Chapala.

Sanatorio Santa Teresita
387 763-0008

Twenty-four-hour emergency service and consultations by appointment. Full time staff includes lung, trauma, and bone specialists, as well as a gynecologist and internist. Facilities include a pharmacy. Miguel Arana #253, Jocotopec.

INSURANCE

Medical Coverage for U.S. Veterans Living in Mexico For complete information on this subject email author Don Adams who wrote "Head for Mexico—The Renegade Guide" at dondelmundo@ yahoo.com. He has written the definitive article on this program that treats veterans with at least a 10% service connected disability rating from the V.A.

IMSS OR MILITARY HOSPITALS

Military and IMSS (Mexico's social medicine system) hospitals, located in Guadalajara provide bare-bones care. If your hospitalization plan is with these facilities it would be smart to have a packed kit on hand. Include a pillow, light blanket, robe, slippers, towels, toothbrush, toothpaste, comb, soap, toilet paper and hand lotion. Books, ear plugs, and a sleep mask might also make your stay easier. You are also expected to have a friend or relative with you to help with your care. Make sure you have someone lined up who is willing to help.

GUADALAJARA HOSPITALS

Hospital Angeles Del Carmen
01 33 3813-0042
Tarascos #3435, Monraz section of Guadalajara. Dial the room number or extension of the patient or party you wish to reach; 0 for a live operator or simply stay on the line.

Hospital Angel Leaño Av. Dr. Angel Leaño #500, Guadalajara.

Nurses: How Do They Compare?

There are at least three levels of professional nursing in Mexico. There may be others on a more informal level as there are in U.S. The equivalent to an RN or Registered Nurse finishes Prepa, which is approximately equivalent to a U.S. high school, and then attends a professional school of nursing, followed by a year of clinical training, to become a general nurse. S/he may undertake further clinical training and specialize in a particular area, such as operating room nursing. The "*auxiliar*" finishes Secundaria, roughly U.S. grade 9, followed by two years of further training; the "*cuidadora*" may have finished only Primaria, U.S. grade 6, followed by three months of training.

01 33 3648-8484	
Hospital Militar 01 33 3617-7171	Belisaro Domínguez y Medrano.
Hospital Santa Maria Chapalita 01 33 3678-1400	Av. Niño Obrero #1666. Their voice message asks you to dial the room number of the patient, the extension number of the person you're calling, or 0 to talk to a live operator.
Hospital San Javier 01 33 669-0222	Av. Pablo Casals #640, Providencia section of Guadalajara. Dial the room number or extension of the party you wish to reach.
Mexico Americano 01 33 3641-3141	Colomos #2110, Villas del Country section of Guadalajara. Dial the room number or extension of the party you want to reach or stay on the line.
Sanatorio San Francisco de Assis 01 33 3817-5013	Av. de las Americas #1946.

Typhoid is a disease that can be commonly diagnosed during the dry season. Old typhoid and paratyphoid tests have given patients false positives and relegated them to long courses of antibiotics that ended up being expensive and debilitating. If you are being tested, be sure that the lab you've selected uses a six panel test that looks for typhoid O, H; paratyphoid A and B; brucella 2 mercapto etanol and the proteus bacteria.

DOCTORS

Clinics are the first place to go in search of a general practitioner or specialist. The second place to go to get referrals is probably the Lake Chapala Society, friends and acquaintances who have lived here for quite a few years. You're likely to encounter two stories for each doctor you mention, one negative and one positive. Keep asking around. Eventually a pattern will emerge revealing which doctors, dentists, clinics, and nurses are the most reliable, professional, and informed. Visit the Lake Chapala Society website at www.lakechapalasociety.org and click the Medical link for helpful information. A few doctors are listed below.

Dr. Raul Cuauhtémoc Reyes Rayas, M.S. 376 766-1198 376 765-2400 (Chapala)	Dermotology, treatment and prevention of skin cancer, hair and nail disorders, mole removal, skin surgery, botox. Appointments every Monday 3:30 to 6 p.m. at Clínica San Andres at the Hotel Danza del Sol, Ajijic; and 6:30 to 9 p.m. at the Clínica Nueva Galicia, Juárez #563-A, Chapala.
Dra. Monica Garzón Diaz 01 33 3667-7881	Plastic and reconstructive surgery.
Dr. Ricardo Heredia 376 765-2233	Surgery, general and alternative medicine. Av. Flavio Romero #453, Chapala.
Dr. Juan Lastra Berriozábal 376 766-1740 01 33 3676-3515	Permanent Medical Attention System, surgeon, and births. Ocampo #149-C, Ajijic.
Dr. José Orozco Beltrán 376 765-2030	Specialist in the treatment of diabetes.
Dr. Iliana Ramos 387 763-0291 01 33 3156-5344	Gynecology, obstetrics. Josefa Ortiz #29B, Jocotepec.

Is a *podólogo* the same as a Podiatrist?

A *podólogo* is a *"técnico,"* a technician, who works under the supervision of a physician. She or he treats various foot and nail diseases and disorders, may do some minor surgeries for which a doctor is present, makes orthotics and does pedicures.

Education and training do not have the length, breadth and depth of US training in Podiatry. In the U.S. you are a graduate of one of seven, four-year schools of Podiatric Medicine, followed by internship and residency. The scope of practice is not as extensive or independent as for U.S.-trained and licensed podiatrists. In short, a *podologo* is not a podiatrist, though there is a fair amount of overlap in practice. The advantage is that an on-site physician is nearby for consultation.

Dr. Carlos Rivera Mendoza 376 765-2400 376 765-3073	Pediatrics and Infectious diseases.

PODIATRIST

La Casita del Pie Feliz 376 765-2320 376 765-2424	Dra. Fely González de G., R.N. Excellent custom orthotics, removal of ingrown toenails, examinations, professional pedicures, diabetic foot care. Open Monday through Friday 10 a.m. to 1 p.m., 4 p.m. to 7 p.m. Morelos #154, Chapala.
Z Boing Boing Shoe Store 376 766-0422	Pain-relief footwear for men and women: leather, sport shoes, sandals and clogs. Shop also sells foot care products and the owner, Gloria G. Garcia, RN, MSN, will check customer's blood pressure for free. Open Monday through Saturday 10 a.m. to 4 p.m. English spoken. U.S. 800 number: 1-800-268-6239, 01 33 3158-0720 ggzboing@prodigy.net.mx;www.zcoil.com.

LABS

Labs can be found across the street from many doctors who will direct you to them for tests. Several are listed below.

Laboratorio Clínica de la Ribera 387 763-1067	10% discount given on all tests. Will go to your home to collect samples. No results given by phone. Open Monday through Friday 8 a.m. to 7 p.m., Saturday 8 a.m. to 7 p.m. Juárez #120, Jocotepec. English spoken.
Laboratory for-Chemical & Bacteriological Analysis 376 766-1086	Open Monday through Friday 8 a.m. to 2 p.m., Saturday 8 a.m. to noon. Home service with 24-hour notice. Colón #4-B,Ajijic.
Laboratorio de Patología Clínica "Chapala" 376 765-4527	Open Monday through Friday 8 a.m. to 3 p.m., Saturday 8 a.m. to 2 p.m. Flavio Romero #448-A, Chapala.

Laboratorio de Patologia Clinica "Chapala" 376 766-0615 — (Seis Esquinas Location) Open Monday through Friday 8 a.m. to 3 p.m., Saturday 8 a.m. to 2 p.m. Ocampo #148, Ajijic.

PHARMACIES

Pablo Fernandez del Valle

Most medications, with the exception of controlled substances, are available over the counter without a prescription. Some drugs are less expensive than at home, but if the drug you need is imported or under a fresh patent it is likely to cost more. For refills, take the empty box. You'll find that generic drugs are available but note that they may not be the exact replicas you thought they were. Be careful that you don't let a pharmacy worker prescribe a medicine "as a favor" to you in order to bypass a doctor's visit.

Farmacias Cristina 376 766-1501 — Well-stocked pharmacy with an across-the-board 20% discount on all prescription and over-the-counter drugs. Efficient and courteous service. They also carry a good selection of cosmetics, baby supplies, toiletries, office supplies, film and will make xerox copies. Open daily 8 a.m. to 9 p.m. Plaza Bugambilias (next to El Torito grocery), Carr. Ote. #54, Interior 11, Ajijic. English spoken. *Recommended.* farmcris@laguna.com.mx

Farmacias Guadalajara — 24-hour mega drug and sundries store. Drugs can be purchased with credit cards. Open daily, 24 hours. Carretera Chapala-Jocotepec #42, Ajijic.

Farmacia Máscaras 376 765-5827 — Next to the Máscaras clinic; small selection of drugs and supplies, some with a 40% discount. Fax or call in prescriptions (may get answering machine with messages in English and Spanish.) Will deliver. Hidalgo #79-C, Riberas del Pilar. English spoken.

Farmacia San Francisco
376 765-4316
Sells patented and generic drugs. Open Monday through Sunday 9 a.m. to 3 p.m. Hidalgo #236-A, Chapala. English spoken.

Farmacia Similares-Ajijic
See above for same hours and days. Carr. Ote. #1, (in Plaza La Montaña, near the stop light at Colón), Ajijic. English spoken at this location.

Farmacia Similares-Chapala
1 800 911-6666
This national chain of pharmacies sells generic drugs available in Mexico at a discount up to 75%. Not all drugs are available and not all compounds are exact replicas of name-brand drugs. They can be useeful for veterinary medicines. Open Monday through Saturday 9 a.m. to 9 p.m., Sunday 9 a.m. to 3 p.m. Morelos #425-B,Chapala. www.farmaciasdesimilares.com.mx

Hector's Farmacia Morelos
376 765-4002
Av. Madero #435-A, Chapala.

Dentists

Ajijic Dental Clinic
376 766-3682
Oral rehabilitation, surgery, implants, root canals, crowns, cleaning. Open Monday through Saturday 9 a.m. to 2 p.m. Carr. Ote. #58, second floor, across the highway from Telmex. English spoken.

Consultorio Dental
387 763-0708
Dr. Antonio Flores Espinoza. General Dentistry. Degollado Pte. #30, Jocotepec. Inside Nutri-Salud building, north of Morelos, just east of Josefa Ortiz.

Dr. Alberto Don Olivera, DDS
376 765-4805
Oral rehabilitation, endodontics, teeth whitening. At Máscaras Clinic, Hidalgo 79-G, Riberas del Pilar. English spoken.

Dr. Hector Haro
376 765-3193
376 765-6410
Cosmetic dentistry, crowns, bridges, and dental implants. Calle San Luis #83, Riberas del Pilar. English spoken.

Odontologia Integral 376 762-0378	Maria Guadalupe Aquilar, Dental Surgeon. Orthodontics, endodontics, porcelain veneers, bleaching, bonding, and other services. Obregon #103, Ixtlahuacan de los Membrillos.
Hilda Tavizón de C. 01 33 3642-1871	Oral surgery, rehabilitation and implants; 35 years experience. Av. Manuel M. Dieguez #903, Guadalajara.
Abraham Waxstein, DDS 01 33 3615-1041	Cosmetic dentistry, bleaching, oral rehabilitation, general and preventive dentistry. Av. Mexico #2309-1, Guadalajara. English spoken. bumiw@hotmail.com

DENTAL LAB/DENTURE REPAIR

Laboratorio Dental, Dr. Gustavo Reyes Carreton 01 33 3170-8416	Same-day service on denture repairs, dentures, and porcelain veneers. Juárez #571-A, Chapala.

Handicapped and Care Services

Business and government agencies have become more aware of the needs of the handicapped, especially in Guadalajara. However, for people using wheelchairs or carts in the 400-year old villages along the Northshore, the cobblestone streets with high curbs and narrow sidewalks are especially treacherous, as are tiny restrooms, doorways and circulation paths inside buildings. There is access on the Chapala, Ajijic and Jocotepec plazas.

BLOOD PRESSURE EVALUATIONS

Blood pressure check-ups at the Lake Chapala Society are free. Check the monthly newsletter or the LCS bulletin board for days and times. LCS is open Monday through Friday 10 a.m. to 1 p.m. 16 de Septiembre #16-A, Ajijic.

BOOKS FOR THE BLIND

Talking Books Service at the Lake Chapala Society is available to members. Open Monday through Friday 10 a.m. to 1 p.m. 16 de Septiembre #16-A.

DRUG REHAB

Hacienda del Lago
376 766-1514
376 766-2220
01 800 713-7144

Alcoholism and Addiction Treatment Center. Callejón del Arroyo #160, Ajijic (in Villa Nova).

HEARING AIDS

Starkey Digital Hearing Aids
01 33 3813-0700

Available in Mexico through a direct distributor. Custom-manufactured in the U.S. to fit at less than north-of-the-border prices. One year warranty and accident, loss or robbery insurance. They offer consultation with physicians who are specialists. Open Monday through Friday 10 a.m. to 3 p.m. by previous appointment. Tarascos #3514, Guadalajara. Hilda Aquirre Alejo, M.D.
haguirre@mail.medinet.net.mx;
www.starkey.com

MEDICAL EQUIPMENT

Lake Med Center
376 766-2088

Rental and sales of medical equipment: wheelchairs, crutches, canes, walkers, hospital beds, raised toilet seats; portable oxygen tanks, liquid oxygen, blood pressure machines, ostomy and diabetec equipment; disposable medical supplies, gloves, bandages and other items. Open Monday through Friday 10 a.m. to 1 p.m., 4 p.m. to 7 p.m. Constitución #64, Ajijic. English spoken.

Oxireyes
376 765-5040

Supplier of Medigas, oxygen, direct distributor of Proxair (U.S. company). 24 hour service. They also provide acetylene, helium, nitrogen, and other gases. 24 hour ambulance service. Acupuncturist available. For sale or rent: portable oxygen tanks, hospital beds, hydraulic moving slings, oximeters, nebulizers, crutches, walkers, De

Vilbess-brand oxygen concentrators, and Millenium Responics and Americair wheelchairs. They repair all equipment. Registered and approved by La Sociedad Medica de la Ribera de Chapala, A.C. y el Colegio de Medicos de la Ribera de Chapala, Jalisco, A.C. oxireyes._@prodigy.net.mx

NURSING SERVICES/HOME HEALTH CARE

Lake Med Center
376 766-2088
Emergency:
01 33 3159-9080

Offers general to specialized care with medically-trained attendants, general nurses (*enfermeras generales*) and specialized nurses (*enfermeras especialistas*). Care from 150 to 350 *pesos* an hour and up. Can be hired for short visits or for 6-, 8-, and 12-hour shifts. Some English spoken.

OPTOMETRISTS

Marco Antonio Martín Santana
Optometrista
387 763-0499

This optometrist has been making glasses for 15 years. Lenses are made in the lab on the second floor. If you are in a hurry, ask if the materials are available. If not, they are ordered from Mexico City and it takes longer. Lab technician speaks English and can translate. Open Monday through Saturday 10 a.m. to 8 p.m. Hidalgo Sur #187, Jocotepec.

Dr. Jorge Padilla, MD
Opthamologist
01 33 3157-4984

Open 11 a.m. to 2 p.m. Monday, Wednesday and Friday. On the Carr. Chapala-Jocotepec, corner of Juárez, Ajijic. English spoken.

Optica Cardona
376 765-2260

Optometrist J. Gariel Cardona gives a free eye exam and sells glasses. Open Monday through Friday 9 a.m. to 2 p.m., Saturday 9 a.m. to 1 p.m., Hidalgo #222-B, Chapala.

Optica Suyapa,
Dr. José Padilla,
Opthamologist
387 763-1000

Examinations, prescriptions, lenses, frames, glass or plastic progressive lenses, hard, soft and cosmetic contact lenses, general repairs. Office hours 4 p.m. to 6 p.m.

Allende Norte #27, Jocotepec. English spoken.

PHYSICAL REHABILITATION

Dra. Beatriz Medina
376 766-1596

Physical therapist. Makes house calls. English spoken. *Recommended.*

Physical Rehabilitation
376 766-0500
376 766-0662

Part of the Ajijic Clinic's complex, this facility offers post-surgical and trauma rehabilitation. They specialize in spinal cord and disc problems, Parkinson's, Multiple Sclerosis, stroke and arthritis patients, fractures, sprains, and muscle injuries. Therapists are currently scheduled Wednesdays 10:30 a.m. to 3 p.m. Carretera Ote. #33, Ajijic. English spoken.

Physiotherapy and Spinal-Muscular Rehabilitation/*Unidad de Fisioterapia y Rehabilitacion Músculo-Esqueletica*
387 763-1989
01 33 3469-6430

Treatment of sports injuries, spine and muscle problems, shoulder and knee problems, vertebral column disorders, sciatic nerve, etc. Treatment may include ultrasound, electrostimulation, laser, infrared and heated paraffin under the guidance of Juan Calleros Aldrete. Specialist Dr. Miguel Angel Olmedo will come by appointment to Jocotepec for consultation for more serious injuries. Open Monday through Friday 9 a.m. to 2 p.m., 5 p.m. to 7 p.m., Saturday 9 a.m. to 2 p.m. Traumatology and orthopedics Wednesday 9:30 a.m. to 1:30 p.m. Morelos Pte. 88-A, past the main market going west, Jocotepec. Some English spoken.

RETIREMENT AND ASSISTED LIVING HOMES

Alicia's Convalescent
376 766-0721
376 766-3152
376 766-3087

Full-care nursing, English spoken. Calle del Lago, La Canacinta (just west of Ajijic).

La Casa Nostra
376 765-4187
fax 376 765-5142

24-hour nursing staff. Weekly doctor visits, free local transportation. Santa Mónica #22, Riberas del Pilar.

SUPPORT GROUPS

Alcoholics Anonymous, Al-Anon, Gamblers Anonymous: Check the Bulletin Board section of the Guadalajara Colony Reporter for meetings in English.

THERAPY

Speech, Swallowing, Stroke, & Neurological Therapy

Michele Boudreau, M.A., CCC-SLP
376 765-4085

U.S.-trained therapist treats adults for swallowing, voice, stroke and neurological disorders and children for language and articulation problems due to cleft palate and lip malformation. Offers services in the Puerto Vallarta area; inquire via email. Home and nursing home visits or by appointment at Clinica Máscaras, Hidalgo #79-C, Riberas del Pilar. bdr201@aol.com

Alternative Care

ALTERNATIVE CLINICS

Clinika El Chante
387 763-2608

Holistic clinic and spa designed to Feng Shui specifications. Healing programs include hydro and steam therapies, mud, colonics, nutrition, compresses, massages, reflexology, meditation, yoga, iv serums, and homeopathic remedies for all degrees of illness. M.D.s on staff. State of the art noninvasive diagnostic testing. Day, weekend, week and multiple week packages available. Av. Paseo Rivera del Lago #170-1, El Chante, (between San Juan Cosalá and Jocotepec).

NATUROPATHIC, HOMEOPATHIC, CHIROPRACTIC, HERBS, MASSAGE

Chiropractic

Dr. Robert Fischel
376 766-4128

Many years of experience and care. Excellent and reasonably priced. By previous appointment. *Recommended.*

Health Food Store

Prasad
376 766-0006

The proprietor of this store has been in the health food business in Brazil, England and Guadalajara for 30 years. His shop carries vegetarian "meats", various health breads baked in Guadalajara, brown rice, linseed, ginseng, German KH3, fresh yogurt, vitamins and other products. Every Tuesday Dr. Rafael Urrieta, a naturopath, iridologist, and chiropractor comes to offer treatments and nutritional advice. Carretera Ote. #117-B, Ajijic. tiendaprasad@hotmail.com

Homeopathic

Barbara Rotthaler
376 766-1987

Expert homeotherapist. Calle La Bandera #209, San Antonio Tlayacapán. b_rotthaler@yahoo.com.mx

Homeopathic Pharmacies

Farmacia Homeopática y Naturista-Vida y Salud II-Chapala
376 765-4030

Open Monday through Wednesday and Friday 9 a.m. to 2 p.m., 4 p.m. to 7 p.m., Thursday, Saturday and Sunday 9 a.m. to 2 p.m. Morelos #170, Chapala.

Farmacia Homeopática Vida y Salud
387 763-0490

Well stocked with homeopathic compounds. Practicioner Marta Avila Gallo de Gomez is available every Monday, Tuesday and Thursday 1 p.m. to 3 p.m. Farmacia hours are Monday through Saturday 10 a.m. to 3 p.m., 4 p.m. to 8 p.m., Sunday 10 a.m. to 3 p.m. Hidalgo Sur #140-A, Jocotepec. Some English spoken.

Homeopathic Treatment

Dr. Felipe de J Mendoza L.
01 33 3479-0847
By appointment.

Naturopathic

Dr. Victor Garcia Díaz
376 765-2320
376 765-2424
Allopathic and integral medicine; acupuncture, laser treatment, peelings, collagen injections, amino acid products, general medicine. Morelos #154, Chapala. English spoken.

Dr. Jose Ricardo Herredia G.
376 765-2233
Allopathic, naturopathic, and chiropractic medicine. Trained as an acupuncturist in China. Meganutrition. Av. Flavio Romero #453, Chapala. English spoken.

Nutritionist

Nutri Salud
387 763-0448
Nutritionist Olga Barreal Arias focuses on natural medicine, medicinal plants, vitamins, fibers, teas. Massage, anti-aging, and other cleansings available. Degollado Pte. #30, Jocotepec.

Vitamins and Herbs

Health Quest Vitamin and Herb Store
This mail order company sells Solary products including enzymatic therapies.
www.healthquestusa.com

Herbal Store
376 765-2646
Open Tuesday through Friday 9:30 a.m. to 3 p.m., Saturday 9:30 a.m. to 1 p.m. López Cotilla #333-B, Chapala.

Health and Beauty

First-time visitors will be pleased by the low cost of barbering, salons and spa services. Barbers generally take walk-ins, but appointments are needed for most hairdressers, salons, and massage therapists.

ARTIFICIAL NAILS

Uñas
376 766-5155

Acrylic and crystal nails. French style, your style, manicures and pedicures. Ocampo #168, Ajijic. Call for an appointment.

BARBERS

Barbershop Manuel Cuevas Pérez
(not marked)

No sign indicates this shop. At Hidalgo Norte #76 look through an old metal open door and see one chair for cuts and one for waiting. Owner Sr. Cuevas has been cutting hair for 30 years, 20 in Nayarit, 10 in Jalisco. He gives shaves and the price for a man's haircut is a mere 10 *pesos*, less than a dollar. Open Saturday through Thursday 10 a.m. to 3:30 p.m., 5 p.m. to 8:30 p.m. Closed Fridays. Hidalgo Norte #76, Jocotepec.

Peluqueria Aguayo
376 766-1094

Barbering for men and women, 25 years in the same location. Open Monday through Saturday 10 a.m. to 2 p.m., 4 p.m. to 7:30 p.m. Colón #22, Ajijic.

Pancho's
376 766-1094

Walk-in services mostly for men, but good hairdressing for women with short hair. Open Monday through Saturday 9:30 a.m. to 2 p.m., 4 to 8 p.m. Colón #22, Ajijic.

BEAUTY SALONS

Edith's Salon International
376 766-1510

Hair styling, perms and coloring, massages, manicures, pedicures, acrylic nails and silk wraps, waxing and makeup. Bridal and special occasions, gift packages and hair products. Open Monday through Friday 9 a.m. to 6 p.m., Saturday 9 a.m. to 3 p.m. Ocampo #15A, Ajijic.

Estetica Unisex D'rosy
376 765-6250

Cuts, color, permanents, styling and other services. Open Monday through Friday 4 a.m. to 8 p.m., Saturday 10 a.m. to 8 p.m. Flavio Romero #462-F, Chapala.

Estetica Xochilt
387 763-0136

Hair cuts for women, men, children; highlights and other color treatments; hair removal, pedicures, acrylic nails. Open Monday through Saturday 10 a.m. to 2 p.m., 4:30 p.m. to 7 p.m., Sunday 10 a.m. to 2 p.m. Matamoros #87, Jocotepec. English spoken.

Estética Yoly's
376 766-2260

Full-service salon for hair, skin, and nails. Color, cuts, tints, styling, manicures, pedicures, permanents and facials. Carr. Chapala-Ajijic #56-A, Ajijic (next to El Torito grocery). English spoken.

Mary Tere Estética

Cuts, perms, color. Open Monday through Saturday 10:30 a.m. to 2 p.m., 4:30 p.m. to 8 p.m., Sunday 11 a.m. to 3 p.m. Closed Wednesday. Hidalgo Sur 174-B, Jocotepec.

Professional Makeup
376 766-5024

With Leticia Chavez. Hair and makeup for photographs, *quinceañeras*, weddings, and special events; makeup classes. Ajijic.

Sofia Unisex Estética
376 766-3079

Hair cutting, very good coloring techniques including foil and highlighting, deep conditioning, make-up, facials; non-surgical facelifts; anti-cellulite, firming, hot stone, and relaxation therapies; waxing, exfoliation, massage. Ask about permanent eye makeup for eyebrows, lips and eyelids. Acrylic and gel nails. Carr. Ote. #46, (across from Telmex) Ajijic.

Weekend Beauty Studio of Pedro Dario Marquez
376 766-4908
01 33 3405-001

All kinds of skin and beauty treatments, hair styling, manicures, and pedicures, beauty spa treatment. Monthly specials. Open daily from 10:30 a.m. to 2 p.m., 4 p.m. to 7 p.m. Ocampo #185, Ajijic.

SPAS

Baños de Vapor de Erick's

Steam baths and showers for men and women. Large communal steam room, two small private rooms with showers and changing areas. Family-run operation, very hygienic, with waiting room, TV and music. Open Monday through Saturday 8 a.m. to 8 p.m., Sunday 8:30 a.m. to 3 p.m. Priv. De Degollado #402, Chapala. (Behind the laundry.) English spoken. (Left on Zaragoza, left on Flavio Romero, left on Privado de Degollado.)

Corpus Novus
376 766-2849

Rejuvenating treatments including facials, massage, hand and feet treatments, hair and makeup for special occasions. Open Monday through Friday 9 a.m. to 2 p.m., 3 p.m. to 6 p.m., Saturday 9 a.m. to 2 p.m. Carr. Pte. #63-6, Plaza Hacienda, Ajijic (near the Waffle House) on the west side of Ajijic.

El Naranjo Aromatherapy and Reiki
376 766-4568

Make an appointment for a Reiki energy or aromatherapy session to correct psychological upsets, traumas and stress with a therapist on Saturday. Shop sells a large selection of a German line of Primavera oils, grown with pesticide-free plants. Also bath salts, bubble bath and mats, handmade Mexican soaps, soap trays, natural bristle brushes, European, Mexican and German teas, tea strainers, wax bowls and lamps, aromatic oils, 100% cotton towels and robes, comforter sets, and relaxation CDs. Open daily 1 a.m. to 6 p.m. Constitución #33-A, Ajijic. English spoken.

Esencias Spas
376 766-0383

Massages, aromatherapy, Reiki, shiatsu, facials, manicures and pedicures, reflexology, chiropractic adjustments. Colón #33 in Hotel Ajijic Plaza Suites, Ajijic.

Herbal Massages/ *Herbolaria Masajes*
376 765-2646

Massages using herbs. Open Tuesday through Friday 9:30 a.m. to 3 p.m., Saturday 9:30 a.m. to 1 p.m. Juárez #551, Chapala.

Massage with Charlie
376 766-1510

By appointment Monday through Friday 9 a.m. to 6 p.m., Saturday 9 a.m. to 3 p.m. Ocampo #15A, Ajijic.

Rio Caliente Spa In the Primavera Forest in Guadalajara, this European-style resting spa features thermal waters, hiking, and an alternative clinic, as well as massages, facials, mud wraps and other health treatments. They don't take walk-ins. Make arrangements through their California office via their website, www.riocalientespa.com.

The Spa at Danza del Sol
376 766-4505
Formerly at Riveria Alta, The Spa at Danza del Sol offers massages, body wraps, exfoliations, aromatherapy, scalp massages, pedi treatments and facials by a U.S. Nationally-Certified Massage Therapist with experience at 5-star spas. Ask about their spa packages and series discounts. Open Monday through Friday 9 a.m. to 6 p.m., Saturday and Sunday 9 a.m. to 3 p.m. or by appointment. Danza del Sol, Ocampo #151, Ajijic. relax@SpaAtDanzaDelSol; www.SpaAtDanzaDelSol.com

Total Body Care
376 766-3379
Specialized facials, body waxing, a variety of massages, manicures, pedicures, acupressure, body scrubs, reflexology, paraffin treatments, firming wraps and other services. Monthly promotions and home service available. Open Monday through Saturday from 10 a.m. to 3 p.m., 4 p.m. to 6 p.m. Ocampo #33, Ajijic.
www.rtkenterprise.com/tbc

Veterinary and Animal Care

If you are traveling with a pet that becomes injured or ill, you'll be able to find care in the Ajijic area with veterinarians who speak English. Be sure to pay close attention to instructions the vet gives you regarding drug dosages. If you don't understand, ask again before you leave. You'll purchase your pet's medicine either from the veterinarian or at a local pharmacy.

El Rodeo
387 763-1588
Dr. Jesús Cuevas Torres. Eight-year-old small and large animal practice for dogs,

cats, horses, cows and other farm animals. Does clinical analysis, dog training and grooming. Sells some accessories, dog houses, dog food. Office hours daily 9 a.m. to 9 p.m., on call 24 hours. English spoken. José Santana #113, just west of Hidalgo Sur, Jocotepec.

Drs. Ladrón de Guevara
376 765-5940

Excellent small animal veterinary care: surgery, physical therapy, chemotherapy, nutrition, vaccinations, I.D. chip implants, x-ray, grooming, cremation service. Emergency care and house calls. Open Monday through Saturday 9:30 a.m. to 2 p.m. Hidalgo #210, Riberas del Pilar. English spoken.

Memo's Veterinary Service, Grooming and Supplies
376 766-0885
Emer. 376 766-1352

Vaccinations, surgery, worming and other care. They sell a wide variety of imported and national dry and canned dog and cat foods; bulk foods for dogs, cats, fish and birds; collars, leashes, beds, toys, pet carriers, I.D. tags; Advantage® and Frontline® flea and tick control; and grooming by appointment. Open Monday through Saturday 9 a.m. to 2 p.m. and 4 p.m. to 7 p.m. Constitución #15, Ajijic. English spoken.

Pet's Food
376 766-2982

Purina Eukanuba, Diamond, Hill's Science Diet, Nutro's Natural Choice, Pedigree foods for dogs and cats, goldfish food, and flea remedies. Open Monday through Friday 9 a.m. to 6 p.m., Saturday 9 .m. to 2 p.m. Carr. Pte. #213, Ajijic. English spoken.

Every year, Rev. Iris Slocum of St. Andres Anglican Church performed a Blessing of the Animals on or near the date of St. Francis Day, Oct. 4. Church members brought their pets to the church grounds where a service was held to bless their presence in the our lives. Newly retired, we hope Iris' successor will continue this inspired tradition.

Salud Animal
376 766-1009
fax 376 766-3862

Jesús Medeles, MVZ. Small animal practice and grooming. Monday through Saturday 10 a.m. to 7 p.m. and after-hours for emergencies. Guadalupe Victoria #73, Ajijic. English spoken.
jesusmedeles@prodigy.net.mx.

Veterinaria Ajijic
376 766-1662

This well-stocked store is distinguished by its full-sized black and white plastic cows that stand out front. The store carries medicines, supplies, and a full line of pet foods including Alpo, Eukanuba, Friskies, Pedigree, Diamond, Hill's Science Diet, Nupec, Purina, Sportsman's Choice, Whiskas. Ask for Frontline flea and tick medicine, bird seed, dog and cat beds and carriers, and toys. Look for its sister store in Chapala. Open Monday through Saturday 9 a.m. to 6 p.m., Saturday 9 a.m. Carr. Pte. #3C, Ajijic. English spoken.

Veterinaria Chapala
376 765-3718

The area's best-stocked pet store. They sell Hi Dog, Purina, Pedigree, Hill's Science Diet, Diamond, Eukanuba, Nupec, Nutro's Kasco pet foods; metal, leather and nylon collars and leashes, large wire cages, muzzles, halters, pet carriers, food and supplies for birds and fish, aquariums, horse halters,

Scorpion and Black Widow Spider Bites

The primary symptoms for bites from these two insects can be similar. Your pet might show pain around the bite wound, swelling, hyperactivity or nervousness, discharge from the nose and watery eyes and dilated pupils. The heartbeat will be either very slow or very fast, there may be trouble breathing, swelling in the abdomen, trembling or shaking, and without treatment, especially for the smaller breeds of dogs and cat, the bite could be fatal. A vet will give your pet antihistamines, analgesics and advise that you keep him or her very quiet. Ice wrapped in a facecloth over the bite or sting can be beneficial.

mineral blocks, kitty scratching posts, Victorinox knives, lottery tickets, spurs, and full line veterinary medicines and vaccines, flea and tick sprays and dips, horse grooming tools, metal engraved dog tags, horseshoes, stock bedding forks, kitty litter, and small pet bedding. Pets include turtles, chihuahuas, ferrets, guinea pigs, a few fish, birds. Open Monday through Saturday 9 a.m. to 2 p.m., 4 p.m. to 7 p.m., Sunday 10 a.m. to 2 p.m. Madero #427-A, Chapala. Some English spoken.

Veterinary Clinic Pepe Magaña
376 765-2717
Emergencies:
044 376 769-3959

Large and small animals. Hidalgo (highway) #92, Riberas del Pilar (next to Telecable).

Dr. Carlos Zavala
376 766-1604
Emergencies
01 33 3480-6686

Veterinary service for large and small animals, including surgery. Grooming. Open Monday through Friday 9 a.m. to 1 p.m., Saturday 9 a.m. to noon. Javier Mina #38, Ajijic. English spoken.

ANIMAL SHELTERS

Animal Shelter, A.C.
376 765-5514

Offers healthy, neutered cats and dogs for adoption, a very extensive line of pet foods, products and supplies, free spay and neutering for Mexicans who can't afford the service, and the area's only bird sanctuary. Animal foods are controlled for quality and freshness. It is an affiliated member of WSPA (the World Society for the Protection of Animals) and the RSPCA (the Royal Society for the Prevention of Cruelty to Animals). Open Monday through Friday 10 a.m. to 4 p.m., Saturday 10 a.m. to 3 p.m. Hidalgo #212, Riberas del Pilar (next to Veterinary Doctors Ladron de Guevara) English Spoken.

Anita's Animals
387 761-0500

Private shelter for homeless animals supported by donations. All support is welcome. In the Raquet Club, San Juan Cosalá. (Please let phone ring a dozen times.)

Bird Sanctuary
376 765-5514

Opened in 2002, this public bird park houses parrots, English budgies, parakeets, love birds from Africa, cockatiels, several species of pigeons, a Golden Pheasant and a Lady Amerthurst, both from China, and a range of ornamental ducks. Open Monday through Friday 10 a.m. to 4 p.m., Saturday 10 a.m. to 3 p.m. Hidalgo #212, Riberas del Pilar, (inside the Animal Shelter, on the *carretera*).

FEED STORES

Alimentos Balanceados
376 766-1017

This store sells feed for birds, pigs, cattle, and dogs, including bulk grains, alfalfa hay, and hay. Occasionally they sell live puppies, cats, chicks, quail, and goats. You'll also find dried shrimp, peanuts and *chilis.* Full-sized, unadorned saddles cost about 2500 *pesos.* Open Monday through Saturday 8:30 a.m. to 6:30 p.m. On the Ajijic *carretera* across from Plaza La Montaña near the traffic light on Colón.

Nutrimentos Purina
387 763-0003

In business for 30 years, this store sells feed for cows, pigs, horses, rabbits, Cornish hens, ostriches, pheasants. Brand name dog and cat food is available as are accessories for dogs. Also for sale are live canaries. Open Monday through Saturday 9 a.m. to 7 p.m., Sunday 9 a.m. to 2 p.m. Hidalgo Sur #100, Jocotepec. *Recommended.*

***Pasturería Perales/* Perales Feed Store**
376 765-5402

This very well stocked feed store has rolled oats (hard to find in Mexico), alfalfa hay, cracked corn and a huge selection of feed for chickens, horses, cattle, and rabbits.

Feed is either bagged or in bins. They also carry some Mexican-brand vegetable seeds. Open Monday through Saturday 8 a.m. to 8 p.m., Sunday 8 a.m. to 7 p.m. Hidalgo #94, Riberas del Pilar. English spoken.

HORSESHOEING

Martín
376 766-2258

Also known by the nickname, "Camarón", Martín can be found Saturday, Sunday and during school vacations in Lower La Floresta at the junction of Camino Real and Paseo del Lago streets where horses are hired for riding. Home: San Jose #223, San Antonio Tlayacapán.

PETS

Pet Grooming

Dee's Pet Care
376 766-3062

Dee Leatherman, U.S. Certified Groomer. Professional Grooming, flea and tick dipping.

Seigrid Pet Grooming
376 765-2717

San Luis #17, Riberas del Pilar (behind Telecable).

Pet Boarding

Doglandia
376 766-4170

Three different types of accommodations. Homemade meals, personal attention and exercise. Across from the closed Flor de Cordoba restaurant, near OXXO, San Antonio Tlayacapán.

Pet Stores/Aquarium Supplies

Acuario Chapala
376 765-6633

Best selection of fish and supplies in the area. Saltwater and tropical fish, birds, iguanas, rodents, eels, coral, and supplies including pumps, gravel, filters, food, nets, anti-bacterial drops, aquarium salt, small pet and bird bedding, bird cages, hamster feeders and waterers. Open Monday through Saturday 9 a.m. to 2 p.m., 4 p.m. to 8:30 p.m., Sunday 9 a.m. to 2 p.m. Zaragoza #390-A, Chapala.

Mundo Aquatico Ajijic
376 766-4604

Tropical fish, turtles, hamsters, salamanders, fish tanks, accessories and food. Home aquarium set-up and maintenance. Open Monday through Saturday 11 a.m. to 2 p.m., 4 p.m. to 8 p.m., closed Wednesday and Sunday. Constitución #41-A, Ajijic.

Acuario Yukko

Two walls of various aquariums stocked with about 20 different species of fish. Sales of pumps, colored pebbles, fish food and other supplies. Open Monday through Saturday 9 a.m. to 1 p.m., 5 p.m. to 8 p.m. Ramón Corona Pte. #90-A, Jocotepec.

SADDLES

Talabartería Durán
387 763-0658

The Durán family has been making saddles for four generations, for over 150 years. The present owner, Onorio Durán, started learning the craft as a child and has been in business for 28 years. His saddles are works of art and range in price from $130 US to $2300 US. He also makes all kinds of leather tack. Open 9 a.m. to 7 p.m., Monday through Saturday. Independencia Nte #25, just north of Morelos, Jocotepec. Look for sign above the door.

Talabartería "Nico"
01 33 3628-9811

Beautifully ornate silver saddles by Zapopan craftsman Nicolás Pacheco Pérez. Playa Tenacatita #1368-21, Colonía Nueva Primavera, (Zapopan) Guadalajara.

Ajijic's weekly **tianguis**, *or outdoor market.* Dale Hoyt Palfrey

Pablo Fernandez del Valle

Pablo Fernandez del Valle

A typical take-out *is shown in the photo - almost* everything *here is packaged in plastic bags, or* bolsas.

11

Managing While You're Here

Groceries, Cooking, Household, Automotive and Construction

with
DON ADAMS and ZOFIA BARISAS

Groceries, Sundries, and Cooking Terms

INDOOR MARKETS-CHAPALA AND JOCOTEPEC

Chapala and Jocotepec boast permanent indoor markets that are open every day. The Chapala market is a two story rectangular building on the east side of the plaza, bordered on the north by López Cotilla, on the west by Madero, on the east by Juárez, and on the south by Hidalgo. In the market, you'll find three butchers, three vegetable stands, a flower vendor, a sundries stall where you can get the batteries in your watch replaced and two lunch counters, all downstairs. Upstairs you'll find four separate fish vendors and a place to purchase *birria*. Fish vendors sell fish trucked in from Nayarit and hauled from the Abastos market in Guadalajara. Shop early, their selection is small. They open every day at 8:30 a.m. and close at 3:30 p.m. Downstairs, the earliest market stalls open at 7 a.m. and the latest close at 6 p.m. Outside the market you'll find a shop selling rotisserie-cooked chickens, a butcher, a fruit vendor, several *taco* stands, and restrooms on the Juárez (east) side.

Bananas, whether they are *plátanos machos*, the big plantains used for cooking, or the ones you eat by hand, ripen naturally by developing small black dots over the surface of the skin. Bananas that have been picked green and gassed to make them ripen artificially, darken in big blotches while the rest of the banana stays green.

The Jocotepec market is located at the northeast corner of Morelos and Josefa Ortiz, one short block north and west of the police station on the plaza. Morelos is the main street in Jocotepec for food shopping with a concentration of butcher shops, *cremerías*, candy stores, fruit and vegetable vendors and the main market at its west end. Inside the market there are butcher shops along both sides, a bakery in the corner, three fish stalls that sell freshwater *tilapia* and carp, two stalls that sell fresh chicken and eggs, a row of juice stands, fruit and vegetable stalls, a naturist drugstore, several grocery outlets, and last but not least, a counter selling cellular telephones. To the left of the market entrance there is a small restaurant that serves shrimp, oyster or squid *cocteles*, and spicy shrimp *a la diabla* or with garlic. On the Josefa Ortiz side at #18A, you'll find a dry goods shop that faces outward toward the street selling brown rice, lentils, all kinds of beans, corn, hominy, pumpkin and sunflower seeds, garlic, dried peppers, tamarind, *piloncillo* or brown sugar cones, brand name dog food and birdseed. At #22A you can buy saltwater fish, baby shark, red snapper, bass and others. Just west of the market on Morales #54 you can purchase raw milk cheeses such as *panela*, cottage and farmer's cheese and *jocoque*, a type of yogurt.

> Prepare yourself for a morning at the *tianguis* by carrying plenty of change, small bills, and sturdy shopping bags for purchases.

OUTDOOR MARKETS

Outdoor markets can be found in nearly all of the villages, one designated day a week. Called in this part of Mexico, "*tianguis*" (tee-AWN-geese), you can find a large variety of items including fruit and vegetables; fish, shrimp, and other seafood; yogurts and cheeses; jewelry, clothes, shoes; toys; pottery; small appliances, recorded and blank CDs, DVDs, and videos; watch batteries; household and kitchen supplies; cut and potted flowers, herbs and shrubs; native medicines; and "fast food" *tacos* and pizzas. *Tianguis* are open from 8 a.m. to 3 p.m.

Monday *Tianguis* in Chapala

Along the north end of Madero on the west side of the avenue across from the Pemex.

Tuesday *Tianguis* in San Juan Cosalá

On Porfirio Díaz on the plaza, one block west of the church.

Wednesday *Tianguis* in Ajijic

On Revolución, the south side of the Carretera, alongside Salvador's Restaurant (next to El Torito grocery) and the Charro Ring.

Thursday *Tianguis* in Jocotepec

Starts at Morelos and Independencia

Sunday *Tianguis* in Jocotepec

Hidalgo Norte between Morelos and Degollado just north of the plaza. You'll find normal *tianguis* fare but also check the plaza for handwoven *sarapes (English spelling is serapes), ponchos* and rugs. Open morning to mid-afternoon.

PET FOOD AND ANIMAL FEEDS

For pet foods and animal feeds, go to the Veterinary section in Chapter 10.

GROCERY STORES

Ajijic

El Torito 376 766-2202	Groceries, fruits, vegetables including organic greens from ÁCA, breads, cold cuts, meat counter, refrigerated and frozen foods, coffee, tobacco, dry goods, cleaning supplies, toiletries, pet food and sundries. Newspapers. Wines and liquors next door. Delivery available. Open 8 a.m. to 10 p.m. Carretera Ote. #56 (Plaza Bugambilias).
La Despensa	Dry goods, meat counter advertising American-style cuts, cheeses, liquor, beer, and sundries. Open daily 8 a.m. to 9 p.m., Sunday 8 a.m. to 4 p.m. Carretera Ote. #14-A (across from Bruno's restaurant).
Surtidor de la Ribera 376 766-0076	Groceries, deli and dairy case, dry goods, cleaning products, diapers, canned, bottled and boxed foods, shampoo and other sundries. Open Monday through Friday 8 a.m. to 8 p.m., 8 a.m. to 3 p.m. Saturday and Sunday. Carretera Ajijic-Chapala #7.

Chapala

Dulcería la Abeja (Bulk stores) Side-by-side bulk stores across the street on the north side of the market offer staples, sweets and party items. Store A sells bulk grains, beans, cereals, spices, and teas like *jamaica*. Store B sells bulk candies, party favors and supplies, and *piñatas*. Select the items you want in either store, receive a ticket with the amount, pay at the cashier in store A and return to pick up your goods. Open Monday through Saturday 8 a.m. to 7 p.m., Friday 8 a.m. to 3 p.m., Sunday 8 a.m. to 3 p.m. López Cotilla #343 A & B, Chapala.

La Despensa 376 765-4433 Dry goods, liquor, meat counter with "American cuts," and fresh rotissiserie-cooked lamb (*cordero* or *borrego*), pork shank (*chamorro),* and chicken. Open Monday through Friday 8 a.m. to 9 p.m., Saturday 8 a.m. to 10 p.m., Sunday 8 a.m. to 4 p.m. Madero #453.

VEGETABLE VOCABULARY

VERDURAS/LEGUMBRES (POD VEGETABLES)

Asparagus	*espárragos*	**Lime**	*limón* (Mexican variety)
Avocado	*aguacate*	**Mushrooms**	*champiñones*
Beans	*frijoles*	**Olives**	*aceitunas*
Beet	*betabel*	**Onions**	*cebollas*
Bell pepper	*chile morrón*	**Parsley**	*parejil*
Broccoli	*brócoli*	**Peas**	*chícharros*
Cabbage	*col*	**Potato**	*papa*
Carrot	*zanahoria*	**Pumpkin**	*calabaza*
Cauliflower	*coliflor*	**Radish**	*rábano*
Celery	*apio*	**Spinach**	*espinacas*
Corn	*elote*	**Squash**	*calabaza*
Cucumber	*pepino*	**Sweet potatoes**	*camotes*
Eggplant	*berenjena*	**Tomato**	*tomate* or *jitomate*
Garlic	*ajo*	**Turnip**	*nabo*
Green beans	*ejotes*	**Watercress**	*berro*
Leek	*poro*		
Lettuce	*lechuga*		

GROCERY VOCABULARY

SPICE/*ESPECIAS*

Allspice	*pimienta dulce*	**Marjoram**	*mejorana*
Anise	*anís*	**Mint**	*hierbabuena*
Basil	*albahaca*	**Mustard**	*mostaza*
Bay leaves	*hojas de laurel*	**Nutmeg**	*nuez moscada*
Cayenne Pepper	*pimienta*	**Oregano**	*orégano*
Celery Seed	*semillas de apio*	**Paprika**	*pimentón*
Cloves	*clavo de olor*	**Pepper**	*pimienta*
Coriander seed	*cilantro*	**Rosemary**	*romero*
Cream of tartar	*crémor tártaro*	**Sage**	*salvia*
Cumin	*cómino*	**Saffron**	*azafrán*
Dill	*eneldo*	**Thyme**	*tomillo*
Cinnamon	*canela*	**Tumeric**	*cúrcuma*
Ginger	*enjibre*	**Vanilla**	*vainilla*
Mace	*macis*		

Soriana Launched in 2004, Soriana is the first Mexican mega-market to come to Lakeside. The giant store offers a fresh produce section, a fresh and frozen seafood counter, a meat counter with "American cuts", deli and dairy cases, frozen foods, prepared foods to go, a sit-down snack bar, and a bulk section with cleaning products, beans, rice, and dry dog food. Products packaged under the Soriana brand are better than average bargains. Besides food, you'll find housewares, cosmetics, sewing supplies, men's, women's and children's clothing, baby supplies, small and large appliances, sporting goods, toys, greeting cards, office supplies, hardware, automotive supplies and electronics.Wheelchair carts are available. Under Soriana's roof are restrooms, two ATM machines at either entrance, public phones that require calling cards, a video arcade and specialty shops selling everything from cellular phones to Bluebell ice cream. Outside you'll find several other shops selling shoes. Open daily 8 a.m. to 10 p.m. Francisco Madero #699, north of the Pemex station, Chapala.

Super Guba Grocery Store 376 765-3895	Excellent neighborhood market with a small meat counter and a surprising number of US products. They buy empty soda bottles for 3.50 *pesos* and stock a large selection of cigarettes. Open Monday through Saturday 7:30 a.m. to 9 p.m., Sunday 7:30 a.m. to 3 p.m. On the corner of Flavio Romero y Juárez.
Surtidor de la Ribera 376 765-4340	Dry goods, some dairy, small meat counter with cold cuts and cheeses, baby food, boxed drinks, disposable picnic supplies, cleaning fluids, diapers. Some imported food items. Open daily 7:30 a.m. to 8:30 p.m. López Cotilla #351 (street that runs along the north side of the plaza).

Jocotepec

Abarrotes y Perfumeria Aldrete	Groceries, cleaning supplies, toiletries (no refrigerated goods). Open Monday through Saturday 8 a.m. to 3:30 p.m., Sunday 7:30 a.m. to 3:30 p.m. José Ortiz #5 (across from indoor market on Morelos)
Cremería Osos	Dairy products, cold meats, cold drinks and some groceries. Open Monday through Friday 8 a.m. to 3 p.m., Saturday and Sunday 8 a.m. to 3 p.m. and 6 p.m. to 9 p.m. Morales #21 (across from the indoor market).

GROCERY VOCABULARY

FRUITS/*FRUTAS*

Apple	*manzana*	**Lemon or lime**	*limón*
Apricot	*chavacano*	**Melon**	*melón*
Banana	*plátano*	**Orange**	*naranja*
Plantain	*plátano macho*	**Papaya**	*papaya*
Cantaloupe	*melón de chino*	**Peach**	*durazno*
Cherry	*cereza*	**Pear**	*pera*
Coconut	*coco*	**Pineapple**	*piña*
Fig	*higo*	**Plum**	*ciruela*
Grape	*uva*	**Prune**	*ciruela de pasa*
Grapefruit	*toronja*	**Strawberry**	*fresa*
Guava	*guayaba*	**Watermelon**	*sandía*

Cremería Martinez
387 763-0696

Groceries, wide variety of cold cuts, cheeses, eggs, butter in bulk, homemade beans, *salsas*, pickled peppers and pork skin. Home delivery in Jocotepec. Open daily 8 a.m. to 3 p.m., 6 p.m. to 10 p.m. Morelos #55 (just north of the plaza).

Frutería La Colmena
387 763-1584

Fresh fruits and vegetables, dried fruits, nuts. Home delivery in Jocotepec. Open daily 8 a.m. to 10 p.m. Corner Hidalgo Norte and Morelos (the short block from the plaza).

Super Osos
Carnicería Osos
Cremería Osos
387 763-0147

Three side-by-side shops offer groceries, meats and dairy products. Super Osos carries dry foods, canned products and a variety of household goods. Home delivery in Jocotepec. Open Monday through Friday 7 a.m. to 4 p.m., 6 p.m. to 9 p.m., Saturday and Sunday 7 a.m. to 4 p.m. Morales #21 (across from the indoor market).

La Floresta

Super La Playa
376 766-3817

Some groceries and picnic supplies, some refrigerated foods and drinks. Large selection of beer, wine and liquor. Also tobacco. Open 9 a.m. to 8:30 p.m. daily, until 8:30 p.m. on Saturday. Carretera Chapala-Ajijic #48, La Floresta (at the light at the junction of the *Libramiento* and the Carretera).

San Antonio Tlayacapán

Super Lake
376 766-0174

Provides the largest variety and selection of imported goods in the area. Groceries, fruits, vegetables, dairy, breads, deli counter, refrigerated and frozen foods, coffee, tobacco, teas, dry goods, cleaning supplies, toiletries and sundries. Also gardening supplies, kitchen ware, and some hardware items. Pet food. Newspapers and books in English. Open daily 8 a.m. to 9 p.m. Carretera Pte. #145 (across from Corona Beer Distributorship). superlake@hotmail.com

Super Laura Grocery On the west side of the plaza, this grocery store has dairy, meat, and cold meat counters, all kinds of dry goods and sundries, fresh fruits and vegetables and a good selection of spices. Open 6:30 a.m. to 10 p.m. Independencia #137, San Antonio Tlayacapán. Some English spoken. *Recommended.*

FISH VOCABULARY

Red snapper	*Huachinango*
Baby shark	*Cazón*
Sea bass	*Robalo*
Flounder	*Flounder* (or sometimes *pescado blanco)*
Crab	*Cangrejo* or *jaiba*
Shrimp	*Camarón*
Lobster	*Langosta*
Clams	*Pata de mula*
Oysters	*Ostiones*

MEAT/POULTRY/FISH VENDORS

Fresh fish is trucked in daily from San Blas, Nayarit and other points west and brought from the *Abastos* market in Guadalajara or the *Mercado del Mar* Seafood Market in Zapopan. Fish from the lake is sold to locals from a vendor working from a wheelbarrow on Colón in Ajijic. You'll notice that Mexican beef is extremely lean. You might ask your butcher to add some fat or *grasa* to be ground into your *carne molida* (ground beef) if you want to fry it for hamburgers. This is an unusual request, so don't be surprised if he or she gives you a long look before doing so. One of the most tender cuts of pork is the *lomo*. Taken from either side of the spine, it can measure up to 6 inches around. When sliced it produces medallions; a nice pork roast when left whole and baked. As a general rule, chickens tend to be smaller and tougher.

Ajijic

Carnes Viba
376 766-4673
Authorized distributors of fine cuts of Angus beef: filet mignon, top sirloin, New York strip, T-Bone, hamburger patties, *fajitas*, *carne asada*, rib eye, short rib, skirt steak or *arrachera*. Carr. Chapala-Jocotepec

	Pte. #29-A, Corner of Juárez, Ajijic.
Carnicería La Fuente	On the extreme west side of the Ajijic plaza by the fountain, this well-scrubbed butcher shop offers a small selection of sausages and fresh meat cut to order. Go early, it's popular with the neighborhood ladies. Open 7 a.m. to 2 p.m., closed Wednesday. Marcos Castellano #17.
La Despensa	Offers American-style cuts, deli meats and cheeses at their meat counter. Open daily 8 a.m. to 9 p.m., Sunday 8 a.m. to 4 p.m. Carretera Ote. #14-A (across from Bruno's restaurant).
Pescadería Las Playas 376 766-3985	Fresh fish including farm-raised catfish. Open 7 a.m. to 3 p.m. Monday through Saturday. Closed Sunday. Parroquia #20 (on the south side of the plaza).
Pescadería Las Playas 376 766-3628	Fresh fish daily from San Blas including farm-raised catfish and Tilapia from Michoacán, and fresh trout on Fridays after 11 a.m. Open daily 7 a.m. to 3:30 p.m. Carr. Pte. #2, on the *carretera* near the traffic light at Colón.
Polleria Gutierrez	Fresh chicken cut up or whole; ground chicken, *fajita*-cut chicken, and pounded

MEAT VOCABULARY

Pork	*Puerco*
Pork chops	*Chuletas*
Chicken	*Pollo*
Whole chicken	*Pollo entero*
Sausage	*Salchicha*
Ground beef	*Molida de res*
Ham	*Jamón*
Ribs	*Costillas*

Many American cuts of beef (*res*) keep the same name. For example, ribeye, New York, T-bone, etc.

and breaded chicken "Milanesa". Open daily 8 a.m. to 2 p.m. Parroquia #14-A on the south side of the plaza.

Tony's Meat Market
376 766-1614
Large selection of fresh and frozen meats including "American cut" beef, pork, poultry, lamb, sausage, cold cuts and slab bacon. Open Monday through Friday 9 a.m. to 5 p.m., Saturday 9 a.m. to 2 p.m. Carretera Chapala-Jocotepec #147, next to Super Lake grocery in San Antonio Tlayacapán.

Chapala

Chapala Indoor Market

Carnicería de La Torre
376 765-2817
First butcher shop on the left as you enter the plaza side of the market, the west side, this shop sells "American-cut beef," commercial *chorizo* (Mexican sausage), ready-made *salsas*, Tlajomulco brand cooked beans, and slab bacon cut to order. Open daily, 7 a.m. to 6 p.m.

Carnicería La Popular
376 765-3287
On the NW corner of the market facing outwards, this butcher sells a variety of meats including goat (*chiva)* for *birria* and *menudo*. Open daily 7 a.m. to 3 p.m.

Carnicería La Chapalence
376 765-5023
This meat and dairy counter takes up most of the north wall of the market. It offers the largest selection of beef, pork, chicken, eggs, cheese, butter, yogurt, cold cuts, *salsas*, packaged *tortillas*, and cooked beans to go. Open daily 8 a.m. to 4:30 p.m.

Carnicería López
376 765-4767
Small meat counter on the NE corner of the market that sells, among other things, *longaniza (*sausage*)*, *chicharrón*, and *carnitas*. *Chicharrón* is pork skin that has been deep-fried twice, once in 325°F. oil, then again in 375°F. oil, making it balloon into a honeycombed puff. *Carnitas* means "little meats", small bits or shreds of inexpensive cuts of pork or beef first simmered

GROCERY VOCABULARY
CHEESES/*QUESOS*

Panela	Mild, soft fresh cheese, molded in 4 inch rounds and often sliced as an appetizer.
Queso añejo	Dried hard cheese grated and used like parmesan.
Queso Asadero	A roasting cheese closely resembling mozzarella.
Queso de Oaxaca	White cooking cheese not unlike monterrey jack.
Queso fresco	Generic name for a number of unripened cheeses such as *requesón* and *panela.*
Queso Manchego	Very popular white cheese used for melting and cooking. Made from sheep or cow's milk.
Requesón	Soft, unformed fresh cheese used like ricotta.

in a small amount of water until tender, then fried until browned. *Carnitas* are usually eaten with *salsa* and are sometimes used as the filling in *tacos* and *burritos.* Open daily 8 a.m. to 3:30 p.m.

In the Village

Carnicería Chapala Fresh cuts of lean meats and poultry. Open Monday through Saturday 9 a.m. to 5 p.m., Sunday 11 a.m. to 2 p.m. Madero #451-B.

Jocotepec

Carnicería La Fortuna
387 763-1141
Mexican beef and pork; *carnitas* (fried prok skin and meat) every morning at 9 a.m. Home delivery in Jocotepec available. Open Monday through Sunday, 7 a.m. to 4 p.m. Corner of Morelos and Hidalgo Norte.

Carnicería Osos Mexican meats. Open daily 7:30 a.m. to 3 p.m. Morelos #21 (across from the indoor market).

GROCERY VOCABULARY

NUTS/*NUECES*

Almond	*almendra*	**Peanut**	*cacahuate*
Cashew	*anacardo*	**Pecan**	*castillo*
Hazel	*avellana*	**Pistachio**	*pistacho*
Hickory	*nogal americano*	**Walnut**	*nogal*

Riberas del Pilar

Puritan Poultry
376 765-4399
Fresh poultry, eggs, some groceries, and deli. Open Monday through Saturday 10 a.m. to 5 p.m. Carretera Ote. #101.

San Pedro Tesistan

Granja Los Faisanes/ Exotic Bird Breeders
387 763-2188
387 763-2014
Pheasants and other fowl for eating. English spoken. Carr. a Jiquilpan-Guadalajara Km. 90, San Pedro Tesistan. faisanes@laguna.com.mx

SUPERMARKETS IN GUADALAJARA

Fortunately for Lakeside residents an extensive commercial market in the southwest area of Guadalajara, called the *Abastos*, offers a huge selection of produce, fruit, meat, seafood, paper products, spices and sundries, including pet foods. In business now for more than 35 years, it is west-central Mexico's agricultural reception and distribution hub. It is the largest supplier to the city's restaurants and non-chain grocery stores and open to individuals. Off Lázaro Cárdenas and the Mariano Otero traffic circle, the market sprawls 15 city blocks and is open 24 hours a day.

Sam's Cub, Costco, Wal-Mart, Megamercado, Gigante, Commercial Mexicana, Soriana, and Aurerra are also Guadalajara options.

Seafood Market
More than 30 stalls carry quality fresh fish and seafood at good prices. On J. M. Pino Suárez in Zapopan.

SUNDRIES

Cleaning Supplies in Bulk

Limpieza Total
Bulk cleaning supplies rebottled to save you money, including furniture oil, Clorox, floor and

window cleaners, kitchen degreasers and dish detergent, shampoo, body cremes, hair gel, pet shampoos, vinyl polishers for cars. Open Monday through Friday 9 a.m. to 3 p.m., 4:30 p.m. to 6:30 p.m. Guadalupe Victoria #45, Ajijic.

Limpiosos 376 765-4118 — Bulk cleaning products. Open Monday through Friday 9:30 a.m. to 1 p.m., 2:30 .m. to 7 p.m., Saturday 9:30 a.m. to 1 p.m. Zaragoza at the corner of Miguel Martínez, Chapala.

DELI SHOPPING

The deli person may ask you this:

What are you going to take?	*¿Qué va a llevar?*
Give me a half kilo.	*Deme un medio kilo.*
Give me a quarter kilo.	*Deme un quarto kilo.*
Give it to me in one piece.	*Deme lo entero.*
Give it to me in slices.	*Demelo en rebanadas.*

Variety Stores/Plastic Stores

Accesorios Para Cocina 376 766-3094 — All kinds of kitchen items, hand towels and small electric appliances. Open Monday through Saturday 10 a.m. to 2 p.m. Ocampo #67, Ajijic.

Importaciones El Gallo — Our favorite "cheap shop" notable for the variety of useful items they stock: small kitchen appliances, pots and pans, dish sets, small electronics, towels, bed linens, comforters and pillows, umbrellas, toiletries, cleaning products, some foods, plastic goods, including outdoor chairs, men's socks and T-shirts, luggage. Open 9 a.m. to 9 p.m.; Thursdays and Saturday 9 a.m. to 3 p.m., closed Sunday. Madero #425, Chapala. Some English spoken.

La Cumbre 01 33 3199-9993 — Plastic shop with small- and large-budget appliances, cookware, bedding, mattresses. In Ajijic on Marcos Castellanos #27. In San Juan Cosalá on Porfirio Díaz #91.

"No Name" Kitchen and household items including pots and pans, dishes, kitchen utensils, silverware, small appliances, plastic chairs and small tables, garbage cans, laundry baskets, ironing boards. Open daily 9 a.m. to 3 p.m. Morelos #59, just west of the main market, Jocotepec. Some English spoken.

Sources for Organic, Health and Native Foods

ÁCA - Asociación Comunitaria de Autosuficiencia
387 763-1850
This organic farming and educational association sells fresh organic produce at their country store in Jaltepec, 3.5 Km west of San Juan Cosalá. Their country store is worth the drive for organic produce and other handmade goods. Look for their bagged organic greens, "Great Greens", herbs and other veggies sold in the refrigerated produce case at El Torito grocery in Ajijic. Look for fresh stock on Wednesdays and Saturdays. In Jaltepec on the north side of the *carretera*. www.peoplesguide.com/1pages/chapts/nonprofit/aca/aacaindex.html

RAW MILK AND RAW MILK CHEESES

Caritina Cuevas This vendor sells milk and cheeses made from raw milk: *panela*, cottage cheese, *requesón* (similar to ricotta), and *jocoque*, a type of yogurt. West of the market on Morales #54, Jocotepec. If her small table is not out front, ring the bell.

El Torito
376 766-2202
Besides offering "Great Greens", El Torito sometimes offers organic eggs that you can find in the refrigerated case. The chickens are fed only vegetarian foods without hormones or other additives. Carretera Ote. # 56, Ajijic.

Prasad
376 766-0006
The proprietor of this store has been in the health food business in Brazil, England and Guadalajara for 30 years. His shop carries vegetarian "meats", various breads baked in Guadalajara, brown rice, linseed, ginseng,

German KH3, fresh yogurt, vitamins and other products. Every Tuesday Dr. Rafael Urrieta, a naturopath, iridologist, and chiropractor comes to offer treatments and nutritional advice. Carretera Ote. #117-B, Ajijic. tiendaprasad@hotmail.com

Señor Sushi 376 766-4606 — This restaurant, while not being macrobiotic, comes closer than any other one in town. You can order miso soups, green tea, sushi rolls, and other rice dishes. Carretera Pte., Chapala-Ajiijc #429-A, Ajijic. You can also order out and the outgoing owner will help you stock your own kitchen by allowing you to order from his supplier at no extra cost.

Super Lake — The Japanese-Chinese food section of Super Lake doesn't have everything for the macrobiotic kitchen, but it stocks many staples: short grain brown rice, tamari, nori, tofu, rice vinegar, somen noodles, black sesame seeds, sesame oil and packages of chopsticks. Carretera Chapala-Ajijic Pte. #145, San Antonio Tlayacapán.

FRESH *TOSTADAS*

The folks at Juárez #588, in Chapala have been doing this very thing for about half a century. They make the all-*maíz tortillas* for *tacos dorados* and *tostadas* fried in oil.

TORTILLAS

Fresh tortillas are available in neighborhoods throughout the villages on the Northshore. Many close by 2:30 or 3 p.m. so go early. Prices vary somewhat. Prices in 2004 in San Antonio Tlayacapán for a kilo was 6 pesos. You can buy them by the kilo, half kilo or quarter kilo or by simply saying, "Cuatro pesos, por favor."

Bakeries and Pastries

Pastelería América 376 765-2301 — Cakes, including Tres Leches, for 100 *pesos* and up; pies, *flan*, and other sweets. Whole or by the slice. Open Monday through Saturday 9 a.m. to 9 p.m., Sunday 9 a.m. to 6 p.m. Morelos #186-A, Chapala.

Pastelería Emporio
376 765-3452
Bakery specializing in very large, and multi-tier specialty cakes for weddings and other occasions. Open Monday through Saturday 9 a.m. to 9 p.m., Sunday 9 a.m. to 6 p.m. Madero #459-A, Chapala.

Pastelería Ilse
376 765-2050
044 33 3809-2207
Cakes and pies for all occasions: communions, wedding, *quinceañeras*, baptisms, for children. They also make cheesecake and chocolate cheesecakes; chocolate, vanilla, pineapple, peach, *limón*, pecan, opera, and three kings' cakes; and cheese, *salados*, *atún*, *pollo*, spinach and corn pies. Open Monday through Saturday 10 a.m. to 8 p.m., Zaragoza #362, Chapala.

Pastelería K&K
Next to Super Lake grocery, this small bakery sells burger buns, pies, cakes, cookies, donuts, granola and bags of croutons. Open daily 9 a.m. to 9 p.m. Carretera Pte. #145, San Antonio Tlayacapán.

Pastelería Miky's
Very high-quality cakes and pies to eat in or take out. Open Tuesday through Sunday 8 a.m. to 8 p.m. Boulevard Ajijic #62, La Floresta (across from Tobolandia on the "Avenue of Trees" as you enter Ajijic from the bypass, Ajijic.

Pasteles Enciso Cárdenas
376 766-1405
Quality pastries, canapés, cookies, pies, *bocadillos* (appetizers) and chocolates by Alicia Cardeas D'Enciso, the wife of Mario Paz, owner of *Restaurante Mario's* in San Antonio Tlayacapán. Paseo Del Conejo #18, San Antonio Tlayacapán.

Rochata's
387 763-0295
Run by three Garcia Barba sisters, this shop bakes cakes and pies to order, from your recipe or theirs. Gifts, party supplies, *piñatas*, American coffee, teas. Home

delivery in Jocotepec. Open Monday through Sunday 10 a.m. to 7 p.m. Vicente Guerrero #10, Local 3, Corner Hidalgo Sur, Jocotepec.

High Altitude Cooking

Because the altitude at Lakeside is over 5,000 feet, adjustments need to be made in cookie, cake, yeast bread, quick bread, pudding and cream pie filling recipes as well as those for candies, syrups, and jellies. At high altitude there is lower air pressure which decreases water's boiling temperature. This affects the cooking of vegetables, eggs, candies, and the internal structure of baked products because water and liquids evaporate faster and leavening gases in breads and cakes expand more. Even deep fat frying is affected. An excellent small booklet called High Altitude Cooking in Mexico by Libby Colterjohn is available at St. Andrew's Anglican Church, Calle San Lucas in Riberas del Pilar. Their number is 376 765-3926. It's also available at Smokee's La Sala in Bugambilias Plaza or by calling the author 376 766-0867. All proceeds from the booklet go to the Outreach Program of St. Andrew's Anglican Church. Also a web search for "high altitude cooking" will yield plenty of information.

Mexican ovens can vary considerably from the temperature you set when you're ready to bake. Buy an oven thermometer that you can hang from the inside grill and check it often to make sure your temperature is stable.

OVEN TEMPERATURE CONVERSION

F.	C.
225	108
250	120
275	133
300	148
325	160
350	175
400	202
425	218
450	230

Household Furnishings, Appliances, Electronics, and Cleaning Services; Jewelry, Watch and Clock Repair; Shoe and Leather Repair

If an address is on the Carretera Chapala-Jocotepec it means that it's located on the main highway that runs from Chapala to Jocotepec. If the address specifies Carretera Chapala-Jocotepec Oriente #123, often abbreviated to read Carr. Ote. #123, it means that it's east of the stop light at Colón, toward Chapala. If it reads Carretera Poniente #123, abbreviated, Carr. Pte. #123, it means it's west of Colón toward Jocotepec.

CLAY BARBECUE COOKERS

Asadores de Barro Don Lindon
Attractive barbecue cookers and accessories, including slab cutting boards. Open daily 10 a.m. to 6 p.m. Carr. Ajijic-Jocotepec #424-2, Ajijic (near Sr. Sushi restaurant).

CLEANING SERVICES

Janitorial Services
376 766-0089
044 376 769-3549
Polishing and refinishing for floors; cleaning, shampooing and maintenance of carpets and furniture. Hidalgo #69, Ajijic. English spoken.

Professional Window Washing
376 765-4507
01 33 3443-8588
Hard water stain removal from windows and shower doors, paint, stucco, cement removal from glass, mini-blind cleaning, pressure wash exterior walls and driveways, bird nest removal, construction cleanup and move in-move out cleaning. Ten years experience. Satisfaction guaranteed. La Palma #8, Chapala. English spoken.

Spring Clean
376 766-4469
376 766-2425
Upholstery, carpet, windows, drapery, car wash and detailing, floor polishing and waxing, whole house cleaning. Free estimates. Open Monday through Friday 9 a.m. to 6 p.m., Saturday 9 a.m. to 2 p.m. Carretera Chapala-Jocotepec #152-C, San Antonio Tlayacapán. English spoken.

CLOCK REPAIR

Tic-Toc Clock Shop
376 765-5565
Mechanical antique clock repair by Rudy Oggier. This long-time professional makes house calls, gives estimates and guarantees. *Recommended.* rocop@laguna.com.mx

CURTAINS

Beatriz Rojas Campos
01 33 3154-8059
Curtains, blinds, re-upholstery, valances and carpets.

Diseños Magnolia
376 766-0225
Curtains, curtain rods, pillows, bedspreads, tablecloths and other fabric treatments for the home. Open 9 a.m. to 5 p.m. Monday through Friday, Saturday 10:30 a.m. to 2 p.m. 16 de Septiembre #15, Ajijic.

Rosaura Velázquez
376 766-0576
Constitución #83, Ajijic.

ELECTRONICS SALES AND REPAIR

AD Audio
376 766-4168
Sales of TVs, stereos, microwaves, refrigerators, gas ranges, small appliances, bicycles, and sales and installation of car stereos, equalizers, speakers: Sony, Panasonic, Pioneer. Open Monday through Saturday 9 a.m. to 8 p.m. Carretera #26-C, Ajijic. audio-gigital@hotmail.com; www.lakeside.com.mx/audioyvideomendoza.htm

Centro Pionero
Stereo, TV, sound equipment, VCR and other electronics repair. Open Monday through Friday 9 a.m. to 2 p.m., 4 p.m. to 8 p.m., Saturday until 2 p.m. Flavio Romero #444, Chapala. English spoken.

Mendoza Audio and Video Sales
376 765-5927
Lakeside's own "RadioShack". This friendly store is a Panasonic distributor and offers a wide selection of well-priced TVs, car, personal and home stereos, headphones, remotes, telephones, plugs, jacks, adapters, refrigerators, fans, Wahl brand hair clippers,

small kitchen appliances: blenders, mixers, toasters, shake machines. They rent sound systems for parties and are a partner store to AD Audio in Ajijic. Open Monday through Saturday 9 a.m. to 9 p.m., Sunday 9 a.m. to 3 p.m. Madero #459-A, Chapala. English spoken.

Pioneer - Sound, Vision, Soul Sound systems, TVs, blenders, microwaves, VCRs, stoves, washing machines. Home delivery at Lakeside. Open Monday through Saturday 10 a.m. to 6 p.m., Sunday 10 a.m. to 3 p.m. Morelos #54, just west of the main market, Jocotepec.

Reliability TV Repair Repair of TVs, video and audio tape recorders, and CD players. Reasonable prices. Hidalgo #50, Ajijic (one and a half blocks west of the plaza).

Servi-Todo
376 765-6419 Repair of VCRs and TVs. Good prices. Obregón #92, Chapala.

FILM/FILM DEVELOPING

Farmacias Guadalajara This 24-hour megastore normally has one-hour developing for color prints. Black and white and other special film and prints are sent to Guadalajara. Open daily. Carr. Chapala-Jocotepec #42, Ajijic.

Kodak Jocotepec One hour developing service, color and black and white film, enlargements, selection of cameras for sale, as well as VCRs, speakers, walkmans, photo albums. Open Monday through Friday 9 a.m. to 2 p.m., 4 p.m. to 8 p.m., Saturday 10 a.m. to 2 p.m., 4 p.m. to 8 p.m., Sunday 10 a.m. to 2 p.m. Allende #27, on the east side of the plaza, Jocotepec. Some English spoken.

FIREWOOD/LEÑA

Firewood Sales and Delivery
376 766-2159 Mesquite 1000 *pesos* a cubic meter, other wood 800 a cubic meter or 400 a half. Shout a greeting at the gate to let them know you're

there. From 7 a.m. to 9 p.m., more or less. Carr. Pte. #150, Ajijic.

Adolfo Ramírez Flores
01 33 1107 9631
044 33 1107 9631
Sale of firewood that is guaranteed to burn. He also cleans chimneys. *Recommended.*

José Tavares
376 765-4531
01 33 3138-6606
Sale of firewood: *guamuchil* and *encino* (oak).

James Le Wilson
376 765-4803
English spoken. *Recommended.*

FLOWER VENDORS

There are fresh flower vendors at the weekly markets. Look to them for the best deals on cut flowers. You can also order flowers online with a credit card at www.floramex.com

Florería
387 763-1517
Small flower shop in the center of Jocotepec. Page through a book of flower arrangements or bring your own photo; they'll make it. Baskets, vases, choice of fresh flowers. Will deliver to Ajijic and Chapala. Open Monday through Saturday 10 a.m. to 2:30 p.m., 5 p.m. to 9 p.m., Sunday 10 a.m. to 2:30 p.m. Allende #5, short block north of the plaza, Jocotepec.

Florería Belen
01 33 3407-1621
Flower arrangements for weddings including church, reception hall, cars, bride. Estimate given without obligation. Good selection of flowers for simple arrangements, vases or baskets. Home delivery in Jocotepec. Open 8 a.m. to 2 p.m., 4 p.m. to 8 p.m. Monday through Saturday, Sunday 8 a.m. to 2 p.m. Allende #45, turn right at the plaza, on the east side of the street, Jocotepec. Some English spoken.

Florería Colibrí
376 766-3609
Fresh flowers, artistic floral arrangements and gifts. Only official Lakeside member of the Floramex network for worldwide and local delivery with minimum purchase. Easy

parking. Open Monday through Friday 9 a.m. to 6 p.m., Saturday 9 a.m. to 3 p.m. Constitución #13, Ajijic. *Recommended.* gbco@prodigy.net.mx

Florería Cristy
Fresh flowers and arrangements. Open daily 8 a.m. to 4 p.m. At Ocampo #105, west Ajijic, near the *Seis Esquinas* (Six Corners) neighborhood.

Florería Natali
376 765-4475
Fresh flowers and arrangements. Home delivery. Open Monday through Saturday 9 a.m. to 2 p.m., 4 p.m. to 8 p.m., Sunday 9 a.m. to 2 p.m. Av. Madero #230, Chapala.

Florería Orquídeas
Small store with cut flowers, glass vases, bouquets, bark and basket containers. Lakeside delivery. Open Monday through Sunday 10 a.m. to 2:30 p.m., 5 p.m. to 8:30 p.m. Miguel Arana #182, Jocotepec.

FURNITURE

Arden Furniture and Importers
376 765-3540
High-end antiques and new furniture from Belgium, India, Thailand, Indonesia, England, Scotland, and the U.S. as well as custom work by independent furniture makers. Open daily. Visa and Mastercard accepted. Hidalgo 81-A, Riberas del Pilar. English spoken. *Recommended.* arden@laguna.com.mx

Arte Amanecer
01 33 3721-5486
Manufacturers of rustic, painted iron and wood furniture, with a large variety of accessory pieces. Good place for custom painting on furniture. Open Monday through Friday 9.m. to 6 p.m., Saturday 9 a.m. to 4 p.m. Hidalgo #116-A, Riberas del Pilar (across from Telecable). English spoken.

C & D's Furniture and Accessories
376 766-4972
The exclusive Lakeside dealer for Ther-A-Pedic mattresses and Betty's Lamps of Zapopan, they carry imported Devane brand French furniture, art work by Jorge Mendez and Audrey Lizaola, custom iron furniture, unique tree trunk jewelry boxes, "fine rustic"

furniture with snug wooden drawer guides, and other dried pine furniture with wax finishes. Can do custom designs from photos. Open Monday through Friday 9:30 p.m. to 4:30 p.m., Saturday 9:30 a.m. to 2 p.m. Carr. Chapala-Ajijic #119 Local A, San Antonio Tlayacapán. Fluent English spoken. *Recommended.*

Casa Mora
376 766-0413
Mexican, Korean, US brands of washers, dryers, refrigerators, stoves, kitchen items, TVs, VCRs, electronics, mattresses, bicycles, shoes, fabric, etc. Delivery available. Parroquia #12-A, in Ajijic (south side of the plaza). casamora@terra.com.mx

Casa Mora Department Store
376 765-4324
Mexican, Korean, US brands of washers, dryers, refrigerators, stoves, kitchen items, TVs, VCRs, electronics, mattresses, bicycles, shoes, fabric, etc. Delivery available. Morelos #158, Chapala, and. Madero #258-13, Chapala.

Duke
376 765-3358
Hand-forged iron furniture and accessories, hand-painted *tule* furniture, paintings, pottery, arbors, seasonal items; custom and catalog work available. Delivery service. Open Monday through Friday 10 a.m. to 6 p.m., Saturday 10 a.m. to 4 p.m. Hidalgo #64, Riberas del Pilar (across from the Animal Shelter). jdimmitt@dukeusa.com

Fabricantes de Equipales
01 33 3691-0154
José Gómez Salcedo makes the traditional Mexican equipal furniture—leather and wood. Calle Mango #171, Colonia Lomas del Chamichin, Tonalá.

Furniture Connection
376 766-1916
Imported, custom, high-end and mid-range furniture, fine art, accessories, drapes, upholstery, rugs, and economical interior design services with Ricky. Open Monday through Friday, 9 a.m. to 6 p.m., Saturday 9 a.m. to 2 p.m. Carretera Ajijic-Jocotepec #111, Ajijic. English spoken. *Recommended.*

México Rústico
376 765-4103

Manufacture and sales of rustic pine furniture. Free delivery. Open Monday through Friday 2 a.m. to 4 p.m., 4 p.m. to 6:30 p.m., Saturday 9 a.m. to 2 p.m. Avenida Hidalgo #86, Riberas del Pilar.

Mueblería Anaya

Large store stacked with furniture, mattresses, large and small appliances. Open daily 9 a.m. to 2 p.m. Josefa Ortiz #26, (near the market) Jocotepec. Some English spoken.

Mueblería del Lago
376 765-2019
fax 376 765-2122

Good selection of mid-range Mexican furniture, sofas, recliners, dining sets, large and small appliances, electronics, fans, heaters, linens, kitchen ware, vacuum cleaners, mattresses, box springs and lamps. Master Card, Visa and American Express accepted. Free delivery in Lakeside area. Open Monday through Friday 9 a.m. to 2 p.m., 4 p.m. to 7 p.m. Saturday 9 a.m. to 3 p.m. Madero #443. Chapala. English spoken.
www.muebleradellago.com

Mueblería Navarro

Rustic solid wood furniture, mattresses, TVs. Open Monday through Saturday 10 a.m. to 8 p.m., Sunday 9 a.m. to 2 p.m. Miguel Arana #328B-C, to your left on the main street into Jocotepec.

Muebles San Francisco
376 765-5771

Mexican brand furniture, washers, stoves, refrigerators, TVs and small appliances for the budget minded. Cash or layaway. Open Monday through Friday 10 a.m. to 7 p.m., Saturday 10 a.m. to 5 p.m., corner of Hidalgo and Madero at the traffic light in Chapala.

Ramírez Rábago
387 763-0543

Part of a chain of stores in Jalisco, Ramírez Rábago sells large and small appliances, electronic equipment, mattresses, bicycles, motorbikes, furniture. There is a wide choice of goods, all with warranties; delivery free or for a small fee. Prices typically lower than in Chapala and Ajijic. Open Monday through Saturday 9 a.m. to 2 p.m., 4 p.m. to 7 p.m., Sundays from 9 a.m. to 2 p.m. Miguel Arana #171, Jocotepec. Some English spoken.

David Robles and Sons Master Carvers
387 763-2548
Frames, door panels, headboards, tables, and benches. Will work from your design or from photographs. Look for them at the Ajijic Wednesday *tianguis*, the outdoor market, or visit them in their workshop. Aldama Ote. #143, Jocotepec.

Rústicos El Angel
Rustic pine furniture, can be made to order. Hidalgo #96-A (next to Telecable) in Riberas del Pilar.

FURNITURE UPHOLSTERY

Arturo Garcia
Corner of Degollado y 5 de Mayo in Chapala.

Teflon for Furniture
376 765-1964
Sprayed-on Teflon coating for furniture, Everclean brand. Three year guarantee.

Upholstery Oscar Tapicería
376 765-2366
Upholstery of furniture, chairs, cushions and pillows. Good selection of fabric samples. Open Monday through Friday 9:30 a.m. to 2 p.m. and 4 p.m. to 6 p.m., Saturday 9:30 a.m. to 2 p.m. González Gallo #16, Chapala (between the old train station and the Red Cross near La Cristianía park) English spoken. *Recommended.*

Upholstery Tapicería
Rafael Morales. Forty-three years experience. Open Monday through Friday 9 a.m. to 6 p.m. He's in an unmarked shop with the green and white awning at Carr. Pte. Ajijic-Jocotepec #9-A, Ajijic (a few doors west of the cow, just west of Colón).

GAS LOGS

Tecno Aqua
376 766-3730
376 766-3731
Sells Peterson Real Fyre gas logs installed in woodburning fireplaces. Carr. Pte. #250, Plaza La Huerta, Ajijic.

INTERIOR DESIGN AND DECORATION

Furniture Connection
376 766-1916
Imported, custom, high-end and mid-range furniture, fine art, accessories, drapes, upholstery, rugs, interior design services, well-priced with Ricardo Hernandez. Open Monday through Friday, 9 a.m. to 6 p.m., Satur-

day 9 a.m. to 2 p.m. Carretera Ajijic-Jocotepec #111, Ajijic. English spoken. *Recommended.*

Rommy Custom Designs
376 766-2033
376 766-3437
Texas: 956 624-1445

Original and reproduction fine art finishes, trompe l'oeil, gold leafing, pergamino paper; oil, acrylic and watercolor paintings; decorative painting around fireplaces, domes and murals; planning, construction and remodeling of rooms and homes. Trained as an engineer, Roman Guevara can provide perspective drawings and blueprints to scale. One minute past La Cristina (toward Jocotepec) on the north side of the highway. romyart@prodigy.net.mx; www.romycustomdesign.com

Tapicolor
376 766-3022
376 766-3063

Antonio Sánchez ASID. Wide range of custom furniture built to your specifications, custom fabrics, coordinated draperies and bedspreads, blinds, carpets, and accessories. Open Monday through Friday 10 a.m. to 6 p.m., Saturday 10 a.m. to 2 p.m. Carr. Pte. #264 #18 & 19, Ajijic (in Plaza La Huerta). English spoken. *Recommended.*

JEWELRY REPAIR

Jeweler Daniel Jackson Garcia
376 766-2223

Reputable master jeweler with 20 years experience. Designs, remakes, and repairs gold and silver jewelry; re-sets stones, sizes rings; has excellent stone suppliers. Ask about watch and clock repairs. Call for an appointment. Hidalgo #29-A, Ajijic. Fluent English spoken. *Recommended.*

El Mexicano Gift Shop
376 765-2349
376 766-3147

Jewelry repair and sale of silver jewelry, watch battery replacement. Open Monday through Saturday 10 a.m. to 2 p.m. and 4 p.m. to 6 p.m. 16 de Septiembre #2, Ajijic (close to the Ajijic pier). English spoken.

LAUNDRY AND DRY CLEANING

Canada Tintorería y Lavanderías 376 766-0321	Pricey dry cleaning and laundry service with long (3-day) turn-around time. Open Monday through Friday 10 a.m. to 5 p.m., Saturday 10 a.m. to 2 p.m. Juárez #29 Local 3, Ajijic.
Cecy's Laundry	Drop-off service only. Open Monday through Friday 9 a.m. to 6 p.m. Guadalupe Victoria #118-A, Ajijic (behind El Torito grocery store).
Del Mar Laundry	Laundry, dry cleaning and ironing service. Open Monday through Friday 9 a.m. to 7 p.m., Saturday 9 a.m. to 4 p.m. Plaza La Floresta #46 (next to Domino's Pizza) at the traffic light at the junction of the *carretera* and the bypass.
Lakeside 2 Hour Dry Cleaning/Tintoreria 376 765-2347	Highly recommended for dry cleaning, self or full-service laundry by the kilo. Can dry-clean rugs, curtains comforters. Clothing repair and ironing service. Open Monday through Saturday 9 a.m. to 8 p.m., Sunday 9 a.m. to 2 p.m. Zaragoza #341-A,Chapala. *Recommended.*
Lakeside 2 Hour Dry Cleaning and Laundromat 376 766-4677	Dry cleaning on premises, ironing service. Self- or full-service laundromat. Open 9 a.m. to 6 p.m. Monday through Saturday. Carr. Ajijic-Jocotepec #61, Ajijic (near Waffle House).
Lavandería	Drop-off service, and ironing by request. Open Monday through Saturday 8:30 a.m. to 7 p.m. At Colón 24-A, Ajijic.
Lavandería La Rivera	Wash and fold and dry cleaning services. Big machines for large items such as quilts and rugs. Open Monday through Saturday 10 a.m. to 6 p.m. Guadalupe Victoria #96-A, Jocotepec. Some English spoken.
Lavandería Patty 376 765-3160	Full-service laundry, with ironing and dry cleaning services. Open Monday through Friday 9 a.m. to 7 p.m., Saturday 9 a.m. to 3 p.m. Hidalgo #79-A, Riberas del Pilar

(across from the Animal Shelter).

Lavandería Real
376 766-1044
Self-service and drop-off service with three-hour minimum. Open Monday through Friday 9 a.m. to 6 p.m. and Saturday 9 a.m. to 3:30 p.m. Constitución 13-A (around the corner from the Ajijic Post Office).

Lavandería Riberas del Pilar
376 765-4266
Laundry and dry cleaning. Open Monday through Friday 9 a.m. to 2 p.m., Saturday 9 a.m. to 3 p.m. Hidalgo #79-A, Riberas del Pilar.

Tintorería 3 Servicios
376 765-2121
Dry cleaning (including drapes and bedspreads) and clothing repair, hat blocking and cleaning, leather dyeing and repair. 10 years in same location. Open Monday through Saturday 9 a.m. to 2:30 p.m. Hidalgo #226-B, Chapala. Some English spoken.

LOCKSMITHS/CERRAJERIA

Accesorios para Carros Morales (Locksmith)
01 33 3448-8253
Locksmith services and key duplication. The shop also sells all kinds of car accessories and snack items.Open daily 8 a.m. to 10 p.m. Josefa Ortiz Norte #45, near the market, Jocotepec.

Aragón Locksmith
376 765-3252
24-hour emergency service. Will open cars with keys inside, can copy ignition keys for Ford, GM, VW, Dodge, Chrysler, Toyota, Nissan, Saab, Honda, Mazda, and for '90 and older Mercedes. Open Monday through Friday 9 a.m. to 2 p.m. and 3 to 7 p.m. Heriberto Aragón, Morelos #172, Chapala. *Recommended.*

Cerrajería Cardenas
376 766-3003 for housecalls
Lock service and key duplicating for all kinds of locks, motorcycles and cars including Volkswagen, Ford, Nissan, Chrysler, Dodge, Jeep, Mercury, Honda, and Mercedes after 1998. Will open cars with keys inside. Open 9:30 a.m to 6 p.m., Sunday 9:30 a.m. to 3 p.m. Look for the yellow booth on Revolución next to Salvador's Restaurant in the El Torito/Plaza Bugambilias area of

Ajijic.

Cerrajería Casillas
376 766-1074
Key duplication, lock repair for home or car, and can change lock combinations. Open Monday through Saturday 9 a.m. to 5 p.m. Small booth in front of the Coca Cola distributing plant on the Carretera Chapala-Jocotepec #227, San Antonio Tlayacapán and on Calle La Bandera #71, San Antonio Tlayacapán.

MUSICIANS

Feminil Tecalitlán
0133 3825-8592
Dynamic female *mariachi* troupe. Guadalajara.

Los Bohemios
376 766-1094
376 766-0960
376 766-0600
376 766-1160
Romantic acoustic quartet for parties, birthday, and other events. Colón #22, Ajijic.

Los Flamingos
376 766-1343
376 766-1270
376 766-0635
Romantic acoustic quartet for parties, birthdays, and other events. Hidalgo #43, Ajijic.

OUTDOOR AWNINGS

Carmen and Octavio Robles
376 766-0045
Exterior awnings, crank out awnings, and sunbrellas. Some English spoken. *Recommended.*

OUTDOOR FURNITURE

Muebles Fundidos Artisticos
01 33 3681-4480
01 33 3681-8290
01 33 3691-1065
01 33 3681-8766
Cast aluminum and iron outdoor furniture and spiral staircases. Over 200 models. Open 9 a.m. to 6 p.m. Carr. A Tonalá 1.749 (old highway to Tonalá), Tonalá. English spoken. ventas@mueblesfundidos,com.mx; www.mueblesfundidos.com.mx

PARTY SUPPLIES AND STAFF

Bartender
376 766-1338
Gustavo Marquez finds bartenders for your gathering or party.

Cerveza Corona de Chapala	Corona retail shop that sells brand name novelties, beer, kegs and will rent party tents, tables, chairs and coolers. Open daily 8 a.m. to 8 p.m. Carretera Chapala-Ajijic #136, San Antonio Tlayacapán (opposite Super Lake).

SECONDHAND FURNITURE

Barbara's Bazaar 376 766-3636	Large selection of furniture, household accessories and antiques. Consignment sales, outright purchase and estate sales. Open daily 10 a.m. to 2 p.m., 3 p.m. to 5 p.m., Saturday 10 a.m. to 4 p.m. Closed Thursday and Sunday. Independencia #7, Ajijic.
Bazaar Ajijic 376 766-4628	Small assortment of collectibles, antiques, estate sale items and kitsch. Open Monday through Saturday 10 a.m. to 4 p.m. Javier Mina #33, Ajijic. bazarajijic@hotmail.com
Bazaar de Carlos 376 766-3939	Furniture, appliances, household items on consignment. Estate sales. Open Monday through Saturday 10 a.m. to 4 p.m. Marcos Castellanos #22, Ajijic.

SHOE AND LEATHER REPAIR

Pionero La Piel 376 766-3768	Sale of ready- or custom-made leather shoes, purses wallets, leather repair and dyeing services; sale of crocheted purses, wallets and hats. Open Monday through Friday 10 a.m. to 2 p.m., 4 p.m. to 6 p.m., Saturday 10 a.m. to 3 p.m., Sunday 11 a.m. to 3 p.m. 16 de Septiembre, #1-C, Ajijic.
"No Name"	Repair of leather bags, belts; replacement of soles and heels and other general shoe repairs. Open Monday through Saturday 10 a.m. to 2 p.m., 5 p.m. to 7 p.m. Allende #1, corner of Morelos, just north of the plaza, Jocotepec. Fluent English spoken.
Shoe Repair Shop	Half soles, rubber soles, stitching, dyeing, fast service! Also threads and key duplication. Open Monday through Friday 9 a.m. to 8 p.m. Felipe Angeles #1B, upper Ajijic.

Tintorería 3 Servicios 376 765-2121 — Leather dyeing and repair. Ten years in same location. Open Monday through Saturday 9 a.m. to 2:30 p.m. Hidalgo #226-B, Chapala. Some English spoken.

SHOE REPAIR VOCABULARY

Repair	*Reparar*	**Reinforce**	*Reenforsar*
Glue	*Pegar*	**Polish**	*Pulir*
Sew	*Coser*	**Paint or dye**	*Pintar*
Heel	*Tacón*	**Shine**	*Bolear*
Sole	*Suela*		
Leather	*Cuero*		

SILK FLOWER CENTERPIECES

Centros de Mesa (Table Centerpieces) — Tasteful silk flower centerpieces for weddings, baptisms, graduations and other formal occasions. Also gifts for wedding, communions, *quinceañeras*; Bibles, candles, candleholders, etc. Will do onsite decoration. Open Monday through Friday 9 a.m. to 2 p.m., 4 p.m. to 7 p.m., Saturday 9 a.m. to 2 p.m. Miguel Arana #222-A, on the main street going into Jocotepec from points east.

SMALL AND LARGE APPLIANCE REPAIR/AC CHARGING

Electrodomesticos Camarena Jocotepec: 387 763-0093 — Repair and parts for blenders and other small appliances, refrigerators, washers and dryers. Auto AC charging. Open Monday through Friday 10 a.m. to 7 p.m., Saturday 10 a.m. to 4 p.m. Three locations: Colón #38-A (on the mountain side of the *carretera),* Ajijic, 766-2256; López Cotilla #299, Chapala; and Matamoros Sur #24, Jocotepec.

Sekarto-Audio — Repair of televisions, DVD, CD, MP3 and VCR players, car stereos, computers, wash-

	ing machines, and microwave ovens. Open daily 10 a.m. to 8 p.m. Guadalupe Victoria #195-B, Jocotepec.
Teleservicio Calvario 387 761-0379	Reliable repair of televisions, VCRs, CD players and video cameras. Open daily 9 a.m. to 2 p.m., 3:30 p.m. to 6 p.m. Madero #40-A, San Juan Cosalá. Past the second speed bump, look to the right for a small street that vees off to the right where you see a sign saying "*Taller Mecánico Los Compas.*"

WASHER/DRYER/REFRIGERATOR SALES AND SERVICE

Técnicos Unidos Refrigeration and Appliance Repair 376 765-4266	Sales, service, delivery, installation and parts for washers, dryers, refrigerators. Home repair service. They also charge car air conditioners. Open Monday through Saturday 10 a.m. to 6 p.m. Hidalgo #79, Riberas del Pilar.

WATCHBAND REPAIRS OR REPLACEMENTS, WATCH BATTERIES

Look for a gentleman at the weekly *tianguis* who can replace watch batteries (*pilas*) and watchbands (*extensibles*); he has a large selection of both.

Tailoring/Alterations/Mending/Fabrics/Notions/Embroidery

TAILOR SHOPS/SUIT RENTALS

Leopoldo Brisaño	40 years experience making suits and slacks for men and women, and blazers for men, with or without patterns. Fabric samples available. Takes about 2 weeks for suits. Open Monday through Saturday 9 a.m. to 6 p.m. Juárez #592, Chapala.
Taller de Sastreria Carreño	Small tailor shop for repairs and alterations. They also sell bedspreads and some ready-

made clothing. Open Monday through Friday 9 a.m. to 2 p.m., 4 p.m. to 8 p.m. Saturday and Sunday 9 a.m. to 2 p.m. José Santana, just west of Guadalupe Victoria, on the right hand side, Jocotepec.

Trajes Hernández (Hernandez Suits)
01 33 3152-6562
Highly-skilled professional tailors in business since 1945. Suits made to order in a variety of styles. The shop offers a wide choice of evening wear for men and boys. Dress suits for rent. Will do repairs of women's clothing. Open Monday through Friday 9 a.m. to 2 p.m., 4 p.m. to 7 p.m., Saturday and Sunday 9 a.m. to 2 p.m. Miguel Arana #248, on the main street going into Jocotepec from points east. English spoken.

Embroidery/*Bordados*
376 765-3004
Will personalize single-piece custom orders or larger projects. Bring your own items: shirts, T-shirts, Polo shirts; leather or canvas bags. Or bring your own design. Charged by 1,000 stitches. Open 9 a.m. to whenever. Hidalgo #92-A (on the *carretera*), Riberas del Pilar.

Papelería Hidalgo
In the back of this paper goods store is a good selection of threads, buttons, ribbons and other notions. Hidalgo #29, Ajijic.

Mercería
Small store on the outside of the Jocotepec market sells embroidery thread, ribbon, sewing thread, buttons, knitting material and some fabrics. Open daily 10 a.m. to 2 p.m. Josefa Ortiz #27, Jocotepec.

Heidi's Fashions/Bear with Me
376 766-4721
Custom clothing. Open Monday through Saturday 10 a.m. to 2 p.m., 4 p.m. to 6 p.m. Hidalgo #10, Ajijic. rhfischer@hotmail.com

El Durazno
376 766-4178
376 766-1481
Sewing and alterations, her material or yours. Maria Elena Mendoza. Expect up to four weeks wait in busy season. Open Monday through Friday 11 a.m. to 3 p.m., 4:30 p.m. to 7:30 p.m., Saturday 11 a.m. to 3 p.m., Sunday noon to 3 p.m. 16 de Septiembre #8-B, Ajijic.

Enedia González Alterations. Paseo del Conejo #21, San Antonio Tlayacapán.

Tintorería 3 Servicios
376 765-2121
Dry cleaning (including drapes and bedspreads) and clothing repair; hat blocking and cleaning; leather dyeing and repair. 10 years in same location. Open Monday through Saturday 9 a.m. to 2:30 p.m. Hidalgo #226-B, Chapala. Some English spoken.

FABRICS

Decortinas Lyon
01 33 3630-2185
Professional interior design fabric source open to designers and the public. Several floors of all levels of fabrics for upholstery, bedding and curtains. They will construct your window or bedding projects to professional specifications or to your custom specs. Av. Mariano Otero #280, near the Niños Heroes monument and a Pemex station, Guadalajara.

Fabrics & Threads/ *Telas y Mercería*
376 765-3174
Dressmaking, drapery and upholstery fabrics, notions, threads, and sewing machine supplies. Fabric dyes, patches, buttons, fasteners, lace, ribbon, interfacing, embroidery thread and patterns, craft supplies. Wedding and *quinceañera* gifts. Ask them for their list of people who do alterations. Open Monday through Friday 9 a.m. to 2 p.m., 4 p.m. to 8 p.m., Saturday 11 a.m. to 2 p.m. and 4 to 7 p.m. Juárez #573-A, Chapala (behind the indoor market).

Retacería Hernández
01 33 3161-5709
Huge selection of mill ends, imported fabrics, including slightly imperfect towels and toweling, purchased by the kilo. Open 8 a.m. to 6 p.m., Saturday 8 a.m. to 2 p.m. Carr. a Chapala Sendero La Capilla #1, Fraccionamiento San Mateo. Some English spoken.

Fumigation/House and Garden Insecticides

Fertilizantes y Agroquimicos SAON	This owner has 30 years in the business and is an Asgrow authorized distributor. Sale of pesticides, fertilizers, seeds, feed for livestock, milk cans, spraying apparatus, dog food, dog accessories, horse accessories, spurs. Miguel Arana #71, half block from the plaza on the main street, Jocotepec. Some English spoken.
Fumi-Tech 376 766-1946	Commercial and residential pest control service, including birds. Free estimates.
FumiXTerminator 376 766-4733 376 766-0383	Safe for humans and pets, odorless. Bilingual, and fully registered service. Free estimates. hfumix@hotmail.com
Matabichos Fumigation Service and Pest Control 376 765-2763	Jorge Pavón.
Pest Control 376 766-4411 376 766-3805 01 33 3181-7765	Treats cockroaches, flies, rats, fleas, scorpions and other creepy crawlies. Oscar Reyes Camarena and/or Francisco Reyes P. Carr. Ote. #3, Ajijic.
***Venta de Agroquimios y Aspersores*/House and Garden Chemicals** 01 33 3363-6068	Biological and organic insecticides, fungicides, chemical sprayers, grass seed, fertilizers; free estimates. Open Monday through Friday 9:30 a.m. to 5 p.m., Saturday 9:30 a.m. to 2 p.m. Libramiento #135, San Antonio Tlayacapán (across from Pemex on the *Libramiento*). *Recommended.*

Automotive and Motorcycle Repair, Parts, Sales and Services

AUTOMATIC CAR WASH

Car Wash Chapala	Automatic car wash and detailing offers interior vacuuming, dash cleaning, upholstery and carpet shampoo, motor steam cleaning,

liquid wax. Watch from their waiting room. Open Monday through Saturday 9 a.m. to 7 p.m., Sunday 9 a.m. to 2 p.m. Venustiano Carranza #6, Chapala (across the street, east and south of the Pemex station). English spoken.

Multiservicio La Calabaza
387 763-2394
Car wash, interior cleaning and motor wash. Niños Héroes Sur #151-A, just north of Vicente Guerrero, Jocotepec.

AUTO SALES

S&S Auto
376 765-4800
New and used auto sales, Honda motorcycles, and insurance. Open Monday through Friday 9 a.m. to 5 p.m. Hidalgo #101, Riberas del Pilar (on the main *carretera*). ssauto@laguna.com.mx

"No Name" - Cars and Pick-up Trucks for Sale
These three places have mostly used pick-ups for sale, sometimes, vans, and cars. Look for orange triangles on the roofs of the vehicles. Sellers are there most days between 11 a.m. and 5 p.m. First place: Just before entering Jocotepec on the main road, on the north side of the street just before the Pemex gas station. No English spoken. Cellphone 01 33 3457-1835. Second place: Across the road from the Pemex station (see above). Some English spoken. Arturo Perez (387) 763-1260. Third place: Just further along the road from the second place (see above). Gerardo Tello (387) 763-1730. Look for him on Thursday, Friday and Saturday.

CAR REPAIR AND PARTS

Riberas del Pilar, San Antonio Tlayacapán, and Chapala are home to many car repair garages. Particularly in Riberas and Chapala, you'll find specialists able to work on brakes, transmissions, air conditioners, and electrical systems, who can do machine work, and other services, and who have up-to-date diagnostic equipment. Several guarantee that they can get parts for any car.

Auto Repair

Auto Bip
387 763-1234

Owner Ricardo Cervera Garcia has more than 20 years in the business of general auto mechanics. Auto Bip can repair power steering, suspension, shocks, balance tires and align. Open Monday through Friday 9 a.m. to 2:30 p.m., 4:15 p.m. to 8 p.m. Vicente Guerrero #72, half a block east of the traffic light at Hidalgo Sur, Jocotepec. Look for the Chevron sign. English spoken.

Francisco's
376 765-5807

This very secure, big clean shop does general mechanical repair and specializes in fuel injection and electrical repairs. Open Monday through Friday 9 a.m. to 2 p.m., 4 p.m. to 6 p.m., Saturday 9 a.m. to 2 p.m. Hidalgo #70, Riberas del Pilar (on the highway). English spoken.

Llantera Hernández
376 766-0612

The Hernández brothers own this well-established garage next to Tony's meat market and Super Lake grocery in San Antonio Tlayacapán. They sell, repair and balance tires; do alignments, oil changes and lubes; work on suspensions and repair electrical problems. Friendly, fast service. Open Monday through Friday 8 a.m to 7 p.m., Saturday 8 a.m. to 3 p.m. Carr. Chapala-Jocotepec #130-A, San Antonio Tlayacapán. English spoken. *Recommended.*

Ochoa's Garage
387 763-0861

Following twenty-years experience in California, Jesús Ochoa now repairs American, Asian and European cars, diesel and heavy equipment. He has the latest tools and equipment. Open Monday through Friday 9 a.m. to 6 p.m. English spoken. Carretera Chapala-Jocotepec #8, just east of Jocotepec on the south side.
ochoasgarage@hotmail.com.

Refaccionaria Zuñiga
387 763-0411

Huge selection of automotive parts. Open Monday through Friday 8 a.m. to 8 p.m., Saturday 8 a.m. to 4 p.m. Juárez Ote. #78, Jocotepec.

Rivas Auto Repair
01 33 3197-3748

Trained in US dealerships, Al Rivas can get any part for any car, guaranteed, including performance parts, speed parts and after market parts. In the business for 18 years, he consults from a full library of shop manuals. In addition to general repairs, he rebuilds air conditioners, services heaters, repairs transmissions, and works on electrical systems. He can arrange for machine work. Open Monday through Friday 9 a.m. to 7 p.m., Saturday 9 a.m. to 2 p.m. Hidalgo #78, Riberas del Pilar. English spoken. *Recommended.*

S&S Auto
376 765-4800

Car repair using computer diagnostic equipment; car rentals, new and used auto sales, sales of Honda motorcycles, and insurance. Open Monday through Friday 9 a.m. to 5 p.m. Hidalgo #101, Riberas del Pilar (on the main *carretera*). ssauto@laguna.com.mx

Tito's Auto Shop
376 765-4178

Twenty years at the same location, Tito's offers a well stocked auto parts store on the premises. You'll find Quaker State, Chevron, Havoline, Castrol and Mobil oil; batteries; rebuilt generators and alternators, fuel and air filters, and other items for many makes of cars including BMW, Honda, Nissan, Renault and Peugeot. His garage is clean and well ordered, and he doesn't work on more than three vehicles at a time. He'll do general repairs as well as transaxels, brakes, transmissions. Work is guaranteed. Open Monday through Friday 9 a.m. to 2 p.m. and 4 p.m. to 7 p.m., Saturday 9 a.m. to 3 p.m. Hidalgo #90, Riberas del Pilar. English spoken.

Ron Young
By appointment
376 765-3361

Master mechanic certified in Canada. Repair, design and fabrication of performance vehicles. Madero #602, Chapala. English spoken.

Car Body and Paint

DuPont Chapala
376 765-4570

Body repair and painting. DuPont authorized distributor; Centari, Lucite, Chroma One, Imron paints. This is a gold mine of finishes. Open Monday through Friday 10:30 a.m. to 7 p.m., Saturday 10:30 a.m. to 2 p.m. Pepe Guízar #14, Chapala. *Recommended.* davidrenato@yahoo.com.mx .

Gonzales Auto Body (Junior's)
376 765-4477

Body repair and paint for all cars. Open Monday through Friday 9 a.m. to 8 p.m., Saturday 9 a.m. to 4 p.m. Carr. Chapala-Ajijic #74, Riberas del Pilar. English spoken.

Laminado y Pintura

Body repair and paint shop. Will replace windshields, locks and mufflers. Open Monday through Saturday 9 a.m. to 2 p.m., 3 p.m. to 6 p.m. Niños Héroes Sur #156, just north of Vicente Guerrero, Jocotepec.

Robert's Paint and Body
376 765-4185
Parts 376 766-0330

Paint and body shop with waiting area. Open 9 a.m. to 1 p.m., 2 p.m. to 6 p.m., Saturday 9 a.m. to 1 p.m. Hidalgo #68, Riberas del Pilar (on the main highway). English spoken.

Car Window Tinting

Kaley
01 33 3634-2397

Car window tinting (polarization). Cruz del Sur 3273, Zapopan.

Motorcycle and Motorbike Sales

Alfa Motos
387 763-2962

New vendor of motorbikes and four wheelers. Has authorized repair person on staff. Open Monday through Friday 10 a.m. to 7 p.m., Saturday 10 a.m. to 1 p.m. Hidalgo Nte. #22B, Jocotepec.

Electro Libros (MB Motos)
387 763-1332

Motorcycle and motorbike sales, easy credit and layaway options. Open Monday through Saturday 9:30 a.m. to 2:30 p.m., 4 p.m. to 7:30 p.m., Sundays 9 a.m. to 4 p.m. Miguel Arana #181, Jocotepec. (The most prominent sign says Electro Libros, not MB Motos but that is the official name of the business.)

Ruben's Sells used motorbikes and four wheelers from his grocery store but can bring you new Honda motorbikes and four wheelers from the Honda dealership in Ocotlán. Open Monday through Friday 9 a.m. to 3 p.m., 6 p.m. to 9 p.m. Morelos #184-A, Jocotepec. Look for the big gray door with old Tia Rosa Pan Dulce and La Villita billboard stickers, across the street from a Quaker State oil dealer.

S&S Auto
376 765-4800
Sales of Honda motorcycles, and insurance. Open Monday through Friday 9 a.m. to 5 p.m. Hidalgo #101, Riberas del Pilar (on the main *carretera*). ssauto@laguna.com.mx

Mufflers and Radiators

Mofles y Radiadores
376 765-5183
Repair of mufflers, radiators, and gas tanks. Open Monday through Friday 8 a.m. to 9 p.m. Madero #713,Chapala (drive to the north end of Madero toward Guadalajara and turn right at the gray overhead pedestrian bridge just past the Goodyear Store). English spoken. *Recommended.*

Power Windows, Power Locks, Car Alarms

Nacho's
044 33 3138-1560
Repair and installation of power windows, doorlocks, gaskets, and car alarms. Open Monday through Friday 9:30 a.m. to 2 p.m., 4 p.m. to 7 p.m., Saturday 9:30 a.m. to 2 p.m. 24 years experience in Guadalajara. Av. Pepe Guízar #70, Chapala.

RV Repair and Maintenance

Scott Wolf
376 766-3940
Call for details.

TIRES

Agroquimicos y Llantas
376 765-3975
387 763-1466
This shop on the main drag in Chapala sells tires and fertilizers, seeds and farm chemicals. Strange marriage. Tire lines include BF Goodrich, Pirelli, Goodyear, Dean, Toyo, Michelin, Bridgestone, Euzkadi. They stock tires for wheelbarrows, carts, wagons and motor-

cycles, inner tubes, hubcaps and custom alloy wheels. Open Monday through Friday 8 a.m. to 7 p.m., Saturday 8 a.m. to 2 p.m. Madero #483-B, Chapala. In Jocotepec, Allende #37.

Fuentes Peña (Goodyear Store)
376 765-3915
Goodyear, Pirelli, Michelin, Kumho, and special order tires. They sell and replace shocks (including Monroe shocks), brakes, do front-end alignment, tune-ups, computer tire balancing, and general mechanic work. Visa and Mastercard accepted. Open Monday through Friday 9 a.m. to 6 p.m., Saturday 9 a.m., to 3 p.m. Madero #578, Chapala.

Llantas y Lubricantes
376 765-2398
Tire lines include Yokohama, Goodyear, Firestone, Michelin, BF Goodrich, Cooper, Euzkadi, Uniroyal, Toyo, Multi-mile, Bridgestone. Oils for sale include Pennzoil, Chevron, Quaker State, Castrol GTX & Syntec, Motorcroft. They repair and install mufflers, batteries, transmission, air conditioners, shock absorbers, do front-end alignments, tire balancing, oil changes and general mechanics. Look for Moog auto and suspension parts. Open Monday through Friday 9 a.m. to 6 p.m., Saturday 9 a.m. to 2 p.m. Hidalgo #50, Riberas del Pilar (on the main *carretera*). Some English spoken.

Multiservicio La Calabaza
387 763-2394
Oil changes and tire sales with computer balancing. Tire brands include Michelin, Riken, Uniroyal, Euzkadi, and others for cars, pickups, tractors, buses. Niños Héroes Sur #151-A, just north of Vicente Guerrero, Jocotepec.

UPHOLSTERY FOR CARS

Tapicería Daniel's Upholstery
01 33 3466-0890
01 33 3466-3121
Reasonably priced upholstery for cars including carpets. Also does furniture, awnings, and pleated curtains. Open Monday through Friday 9 a.m. to 6 p.m. Hidalgo #1, San Nicolás de Ibarra (on the highway). Some English spoken.

Building, Remodeling, Pools, Etc.

AUTOMATIC GARAGE DOORS

Reynaldo Herrera González
01 33 3400-9715
Herreria Puertas y Ventanas (Iron Doors and Windows), and the installation and maintenance of automatic garage doors. Carretera Ote. #26, Ajijic.

Antonio Leal
376 766-4973
01 33 3157-6536
Sales, installation and replacement of automatic garage door openers, remote controls, secure electric door knobs, intercom phones. Ocampo 15-B, Ajijic.

Herrería Saucedo
044 376 769-3530
Sells and installs garage door openers. See also ironworking. Carretera Pte. #23-A, Ajijic (across from El Sarape restaurant).

BUILDING AND HARDWARE SUPPLIES

Concretos de Pacífico
01 33 3670-4225
Decorative moldings, fireplace hearths and surrounds, naves and balusters; bricks, blocks, pavers and stepping stones; roof tiles and wall brick panels. Periferico Sur #4276, Toluqilla. Ask at Puertas y Ventanas (Doors and Windows) how to get to this distributor's house. Carr. a Chapala #228-A, Ixtlahuacan de los Membrillos (on the Highway near the new OXXO).

Distribuidora del Lago
376 766-1668
The area's best selection of kitchen and bath cabinets, quality plumbing fixtures, water pressure systems, painted, porcelain and stainless steel sinks. They offer a huge selection of ceramic floor and wall tiles, including handmade floor tiles, slate flooring, and clear and colored glass blocks. They'll arrange installation. Open Monday through Friday 9 a.m. to 2 p.m., 3 p.m. to 6 p.m., Saturday 9 a.m. to 1:30 p.m. Blvd. Ajijic #105, La Floresta, Ajijic. English Spoken. *Recommended.*

Ferretería Celia Cuevas E.
Chapala's Handy*person's* Heaven with friendly, knowledgeable, bilingual service.

Recently expanded hardware store stocks a large selection of woodworking, plumbing, and electrical supplies. They carry traditional lighting fixtures, chicken wire, and vegetable seeds. Open Monday through Friday 8 a.m. to 6:30 p.m., Saturday 8 a.m. to 3 p.m. On the corner of Morelos and Juárez in Chapala. *Recommended.*

Ferretería Economica, Azulejos y Sanitarias Chapala
376 765-3902
Good selection of tools, hardware, roofing supplies, electrical and plumbing supplies, including wire, electrical boxes and connectors, outdoor lighting, gas water heaters. Open Monday through Friday 8 a.m. to 7 p.m., Saturday 8 a.m. to 4 p.m. Madero #270-B, Chapala.

Ferretería El Venado
01387 763-0125
Store popular with construction contractors. Well-stocked with steel for doors and windows, metal beams, corrugated plastic sheets, bricks, etc. Open Monday through Friday 8:15 a.m. to 3 p.m., 4 p.m. to 8 p.m., Saturday 8:15 a.m. to 3 p.m., 4 p.m. to 6 p.m., Sunday 8:30 a.m. to 2 p.m. Vicente Guerrero #170, left at the traffic light at Hidalgo Sur and Vicente Guerrero, Jocotepec.

Grupo Ferretero Milenio (Amutio)
376 766-3522
Large hardware and building supply store conveniently located next to Farmacia Guadalajara in Ajijic. Some items on display, others need to be asked for. Can be pricey. Open Monday through Saturday 8:30 a.m. to 7 p.m.

Materiales Jara
The ultimate hardware and supply store, Ajijic's Handy*person's* Heaven, with excellent bilingual service and discounts. Sole direct distributors of Apasco cement. You can find Caster and Prisa paints, Poly-form of Mexico, Fester of Mexico, Supremo Gesso, Eureka, G.E. light bulbs (including colored bulbs), Black & Decker, Stanley, and De Walt tools, lengths of rope, chain, screening and a million other things. They also sell a rat poison that isn't harmful to pets called C Reel-B in paraffin

cubes or pellets. Open Monday through Friday 8:30 a.m. to 6 p.m., Saturday 8:30 a.m. to 2 p.m. Carretera Chapala-Ajijic #39, Ajijic (near Pemex). *Recommended.*

CARPENTRY

Carpintería Sebastián Espíritu
376 766-1441

Doors, closets, kitchens, cabinets, shelves. English spoken. Guadalupe Victoria #32, Ajijic.

Carpintería Hernández
387 763-0241

Two brothers make kitchen cabinets, tables, bed frames, headboards, chairs and custom furniture. Open Monday through Saturday 8 a.m. to 6p.m. Jose Santana #60-A, Jocotepec. English spoken.

Carpintería Medina
387 763-2251

Forty years in the business, the Medina family do finish carpentry as well as build shelves, furniture, kitchen and bathroom cabinets, wooden window frames and other installations. Can provide an English speaking translator. Open Monday through Saturday 9 a.m. to 2 p.m., 3 p.m. to 6 p.m. Guadalupe Victoria Sur #190, Jocotepec.

Pablo Luvian
376 766-0600

Good finish carpentry; drawers, cabinets, entertainment centers, bookcases, etc. Open Monday through Friday 8 a.m. to 8 p.m. or until the light gives out, Saturday 8 a.m. to 6 p.m. Guadalupe Victoria #68, Ajijic.

Maderería y Carpintería Ramos
387 763-0097

The Ramos family has been in the carpentry business for 55 years. They make kitchen cabinets, closets, doors, etc. They sell lumber, mostly planks 3 meters long or less. Open Monday through Friday 9 a.m to 2 p.m., 4 p.m. to 6 p.m., Saturday 9 a.m. to 2 p.m. Independencia Norte #26, Jocotepec. Some English spoken.

"Manuel"

All manner of carpentry work. Open Monday through Friday 9 a.m. to 2 p.m., 4 p.m. to 7 p.m., Saturday 9 a.m. to 2 p.m. Carr. Pte. #7, Ajijic (not far from the black and white cow, west of the light at Colón and the *carretera.*)

Arnulfo Nuñez & Sons
376 766-1339
Premium-quality plywood, painted, lacquered, and varnished finishes, louvered door and windows. 50-years experience. Aldama #19, Ajijic.

Taller de Carpintería
376 766-4837
376 766-0260
José María Ramos. Fabrication of closets, doors, cabinets, tables, chairs, stairs, handrails, case pieces, book shelves. Repair of all classes of furniture. Open daily 8 a.m. to 7 p.m. Constitución #42, Ajijic.

Home construction *is booming along Lake Chapala.*

Dale Hoyt Palfrey

CHAIN SAW SHARPENING/WATER PUMP REPAIR/ LAWN MOWER REPAIR AND SHARPENING

Bombas y Motores
All small-engine repair including generator motors and water pumps, can get all parts including those for Briggs & Stratton and Kohler. Sells weedeater cord and machine sharpens chainsaw blades. Open Monday through Friday 9 a.m. to 8 p.m., Saturday 9 a.m. to 2 p.m. Madero #558B, Chapala (on access road across from Goodyear by statue of Pepe Guízar).

CIVIL ENGINEERING AND LAND EVALUATIONS

Construvida, S.A. de C.V.
387 763-0705
Civil engineering, project evaluations for buildings, urban planning, topographic plot plans and elevations, for the purchase and sales of houses and buildings. Open Monday through Friday 9 a.m to 3 p.m., 5 p.m. to 7

p.m., Saturday 9 a.m. to 2 p.m. Juárez #101, Jocotepec.

ELECTRIC FENCES

Optimus
01 33 3603-0544
High-tension electric fences, 10,000 volts, with battery backup and alarm.10-year warranty offered. Volcán Villarica #4448, Huentitán El Bajo, Guadalajara.

Security Systems
01 33 5305-3029
Intec sells home and business security systems including intercom telephones, closed-circuit TV systems, wireless intercoms, electric locks, etc. Carr. Chapala-Jocotepec #133-A, San Antonio Tlayacapán.

ELECTRICAL SUPPLIES

Super Eléctrica
387 763-0845
Repair of electrical items in shop. Sells fuse boxes, high and low voltage lighting fixtures, all sizes of light bulbs, outdoor lamps, and electrical parts. Open Monday through Friday 9:30 a.m. to 2 p.m., 4 p.m. to 7 p.m., Saturday 8:30 a.m. to 2 p.m., 4 p.m. to 6 p.m. Vicente Guerrero #10, Local 2, (in the small mall across from CFE, the electricity office) Jocotopec. Fluent English spoken.

ELECTRICIANS AND PLUMBERS

Hector Gaytan
01 33 3117-8548
376 766-0894 msg.
Good plumbing and electrical repairs. Reliable. English spoken. *Recommended.*

La Casa de Plomero
376 766-1546
01 33 3453-9030
Héctor Martínez Zuñiga. Carr. Poniente #29 y 29A, Ajijic.

Mantenimiento Zaragoza
376 766-1480
376 766-3054
General contractor, plumbing and electrical work, drain clearing. Open 9 a.m. to 2 p.m. Marcos Castellanos #12, Ajijic. English spoken.

José Martínez
376 765-3297
01 33 3174-1282
Excellent, dependable, expert service. Besides plumbing and electricity, he also has a service to clean septic tanks. His rates can

be higher than your neighbor who "sort of knows" how to do things, but his professionalism is well worth paying for. Some English spoken. *Recommended.*

Carlos Pineda
376 766-0468
01 33 3451-0836
24-service, electrician, plumbing, construction. Privada Emiliano Zapata #2-A, Ajijic.

FENCING

Chain link-Alambrados
01 33 33823-3131
In Guadalajara

GENERAL CONTRACTORS

Chema
044 376 769-3886
Call for appointment.

Comtor Company/ Comparan Salazar Urbano
376 766-0165
01 33 3150-8622
Fine wash finishing, surface cracking, imitation marble, surface washing, *mapiados*, general painting, impermeability, *palapas*, XVI century style furniture. Hidalgo #35, Interior 4-A, Ajijic.

Francisco Gómez Barba
376 766-1668
Building, remodeling, design, carpentry, restoration, iron work, plumbing, painting. Distribuidora del Lago. Blvd. Ajijic #105, La Floresta, Ajijic. English spoken.

Jose Luis Gonzalez
387 763-0934
New construction, renovations, additions. Family business for 25 years. Can provide English-speaking translator. Hidalgo Sur #383, Jocotepec.

Gustavo Marquez
376 766-1338
Well-managed construction and remodeling projects of all sizes with more than 170 workers on staff. Zaragoza #60-B, Ajijic. English spoken. *Recommended.*

Home Services
376 766-1569
376 766-2936
General contracting, septic tank cleaning, pool maintenance, chemicals, filters and solar equipment, fountain pumps, UV water purifiers, and local moving. Open Monday through Friday 8 a.m. to 6 p.m., Saturday 8 a.m. to 3 p.m. Carretera Chapala-Jocotepec

	#159-C, San Antonio Tlayacapán. English spoken. jpgiovas@hotmail.com.
Juan Gutiérrez 044 376 769-0689	Dependable, well-priced contractor sought after for brick and tile work, plumbing, electricity, painting. Specializes in cupolas. Felipe Angeles #2, Ajijic. English spoken.
The Little Company-TLC 376 766-4008	Remodeling, new construction, pools, fountains, carpentry, painting, plumbing, ironwork. Home inspections. Zaragoza #5, Ajijic. English spoken. tlcjg@prodigy.net.mx
Miguel Ramirez of Muebles Rústicos San Andrés 376 766-1278 376 766-0861	General construction, pools, all services. Also ironworking, iron and wood furniture-making. Carr. Ote. #10, Ajijic.
John Worthington 387 763-2687	New construction and remodeling, landscaping, design, plans, house inspections. English spoken. Carretera Ajijic-Jocotepec #67, just before Jocotepec at Lucy's Deli.

GLASS, MIRRORS, ALUMINUM WINDOWS, DOORS

Aluminio y Cristales 376 765-5326	Custom mirrors, aluminum doors, windows, shower and tub doors, window screens. All custom work in this tidy shop. Open Monday through Friday 8:30 a.m. to 2 p.m., 3:30 p.m. to 7 p.m., Saturday 9 a.m. to 2 p.m. Madero #475-A, Chapala. English spoken.
Los Canceles 387 761-0621 01 33 3459-2453 Fax 387 761-0247	Aluminum, ironwork and glass, screening, doors, windows, garage doors, grates, dividers, sheet rock, molding, burglar bars, mirrors, beveling, crystal finishes. Carr. Chapala-Jocotepec #46, San Juan Cosalá.
Puertas y Ventanas (Doors & Windows) 376 762-0009	Fabricators of elaborate, decorative, designed gates and doors; screen doors, aluminum doors, cast aluminum decorative trim and other items; makes and installs automatic garage door openers; and fountains. Extensive experience in Ajijic and Mirasol. Open Monday through Friday 9 a.m. to 2 p.m., 3 p.m. to 6 p.m., Saturday 9 a.m., to 2 p.m. Carr. a

Chapala #228-A, Ixtlahuacan de los Membrillos (on the Highway near the new OXXO).

Vidriería Sales and installation of glass in frames, mirrors, sliding shower doors made to order, beveling. Framing made to size. Open Monday through Friday 9 a.m. to 6:30 p.m., Saturday 9 a.m. to 5 p.m. Miguel Arana #298, Jocotepec. Some English spoken.

ViLuMa
376 766-0064
They claim to beat anyone's prices. Sales and service of glass, mirrors, aluminum windows, door and window framing, tub and shower enclosures, etching and beveling services. Open Monday through Friday 8:30 a.m. to 1 p.m., 2 p.m. to 6:00 p.m., Saturday 9:30 a.m. to 2 p.m. Carr. Pte. #5, Ajijic. jaimeviluma@prodigy.net.mx

Unzueta Iron and Aluminum
376 766-0041
Carr Ote. #37, Ajijic.

HANDYMAN SERVICES

James Le Wilson
376 765-4803
This young man has 17-years experience at Lakeside and can be hired for all kinds of tasks. Responsible and reliable. He also sells firewood. Excellent English. *Recommended.*

HARDWARE, CONSTRUCTION MATERIALS AND MACHINERY

Construction Equipment/ Andamios Resendiz
376 765-5993
Sales and rental of construction equipment: bobcats, portable and cable scaffolding, cement mixers and carts, concrete cutters, floor jacks, earth tampers, hydraulic rollers, generators, chain saws,and submersible pumps. Also metal structures and sheet aluminum sales. Equipment maintenance repair person on premises. Open Monday through Friday 8:30 a.m. to 6 p.m., Saturday 8:30 a.m. to 1 p.m. Av. Hidalgo #228, Riberas del Pilar, fax 376 765-5954

Ferretería y Tlapalería Galvez Ajijic: 376 766-0880 Jocotepec: 387 763-0341 387 763-1305	Sand, gravel, cal, paint, rebar, cement, plumbing and electrical supplies, hardware, hand tools, garden and soil deliveries, rental of dump trucks, backhoes and other heavy machinery. Carretera Ote. 35-A, Ajijic, Hidalgo Sur #152, Jocotepec.
Malaco's 376 766-2833	Cement, stone, sand, fill dirt; paving stones, bricks, decorative tiles, and roof tiles (*telas*); rental of dump trucks, rollers and other construction equipment. Brick trucks park here or on the other side of the highway. Open Monday through Friday 9 a.m. to 6 p.m., Saturday 9 a.m. to 2 p.m. Carretera Pte. #510, Ajijic (west of Ajijic toward La Canacinta).
Materiales San Juan 376 763-5361	Construction materials, concrete, and heavy equipment contracting. Open Monday through Friday 8 a.m. to 6 p.m., Saturday 8 a.m. to 3 p.m. Carretera Chapala-Mezcala #1, San Juan Tecomatlán (past the Vista del Lago golf and country club before Tlachichilco). English spoken. *Recommended.*

HOME ALARMS AND SECURITY SYSTEMS

DAL Alarms 01 33 3826-2238 01 33 3124-3205	In Guadalajara.

HOUSE PAINTING

Joel Guzmán 376 766-4889	General painting inside and out. Also plumbing. Calle Cuitzeo #24, Ajijic.

IRONWORKING

Herrería Artística "Tecoluta" 376 766-3465	Custom metal work. Security bars, windows, doors with artistic flair. They'll work from your design or a photo. Zaragoza #113, Ajijic.
Herrería Manuel Naranjo 387 763-2653	Artistic metal work for gates, headboards, coffee tables, chandeliers; from photos or your own designs. Wide experience with design-

ers. Also makes doors, windows and car gates. Has translator when needed. Open Monday through Saturday 8 a.m. to 8 p.m. Jose Santana #40-A, half block west from main street Hidalgo Sur, going south, Jocotepec.

Herrería Ruben Reynoso
387 763-0879
In the metal working business for 25 years, Ruben makes artistic, custom doors, gates, windows, furniture decorations, wall sconces, and anything from photographs. He has been a stalwart mentor for young metalworkers. Open Monday through Saturday 9 a.m. to 6 p.m. José Santana #29, Jocotepec. One worker speaks English.

Herrería Saucedo
044 376 769-3530
Custom metal working, garage doors, etc. and furniture to your specifications. Also sales and installation of garage door openers, electrical work, painting, construction and plumbing. Ask for John. Carretera Pte. #23-A, Ajijic. *Recommended.*

Núñez Artistic Ironwork
376 766-3777
Custom and traditional work of all kinds: lamps, candelabras, mirrors, windows, chests of drawers, screened doors, tables, chairs and benches, staircases, beds and headboards, gates. Open Monday through Friday 10 a.m. to 6 p.m., Saturday 10 a.m. to 3 p.m. Carr. Chapala-Jocotepec #143, San Antonio Tlayacapán.

LANDSCAPING, FORKLIFT, LEVELING, EXCAVATION, CANTERA

***EspacioVerde/* Green Space**
387 763-1178
387 763-0975
Landscaping, sprinklers, maintenance, fumigation, nursery, *cantera* stone. Matamoros Sur #125, Jocotepec.
espacioverde@prodigy.net.mx

LANDSCAPE DESIGN AND WATERING SYSTEMS

Albercas del Lago
376 766-2121
Design and installation of Rain Bird and Toro sprinkler systems. Open Monday through Friday 9:30 a.m. to 6 p.m., Saturday 9:30 a.m.

to 2 p.m. Carretera Chapala-Jocotepec #139-B, San Antonio Tlayacapán (across from Corona Beer). English spoken. hechtpools@hotmail.com

Los Zalates
376 765-5068
Landscape Design and installation, Rainbird sprinkler systems, drip systems, chemical and natural pest control. Open Monday through Friday 9 a.m. to 5 p.m. Hidalgo #69, Riberas del Pilar. English spoken. loszalates@yahoo.com.mx

José Tavares
376 765-4531
01 33 3138-6606
Garden design and decoration. Sales of ready turf, and firewood: *guamuchil* and *encino* (oak).

***Todo para su Jardín/* Everything for your Garden**
387 763-1389
Arturo Gonzalez and Teresa. Decorative rock for gardens and pathways, volcanic rock for grills, top soil, manure. Home delivery. Iturbide Pte. #168, Jocotepec.

LAWN MOWER REPAIR

Equipos Insumos Agricolas de Jocotepec
387 763-2581
Sales and service of lawn mowers, chain saws, weedeaters, backpack insecticide sprayers (*mochilas)*, all gas engines. Service for Husqvarna, Murray, Echo, Arimitzu, Cifarelli, Honda, Maruyama, Pouland brands. Open Monday through Friday 9 a.m. to 2 p.m., 4 p.m. to 7 p.m. Vicente Guerrero Pte. #222, Jocotepec.

Mecánico en Jardinería, Ricardo Sanchez
376 765-3007
Sales and service of used push mowers, gasoline mowers, weedeaters and other tools for the garden. Open Monday through Friday 9 a.m. to 6 p.m., Saturday 9 a.m. to 2 p.m., closed Sunday. Zaragoza #415, Chapala (on the south side of the bridge). *Recommended.*

LIGHTING

Ilumina y Decora
376 765-5067
Lighting and decoration. Sales and installations of lighting fixtures, laminated floors, blinds, fans and curtains, sales of oil lamps and low energy bulbs. Open Monday through Saturday, 9 a.m. to 2:30 p.m., 4 p.m. to 7

p.m. Madero #427, Chapala.

Lighting and Design Center
376 766-3506
Large selection of sophisticated architectural lighting fixtures and lamps. They carry hard-to-find bulbs, including halogen. Open Monday through Friday 9 a.m. to 6 p.m., Saturday 10 a.m. to 2 p.m. Carr. Chapala-Ajijic #54, Plaza Bugambilias #12 & 20 upstairs, Ajijic. Some English spoken. l_dcenter@yahoo.com

LUMBER YARDS

Maderas-Atlas
376 765-6387
Very small lumber yard carrying plywood, dimension lumber, hollow-core doors, and some hardware. Open Monday through Friday 8:30 a.m. to 6:30 p.m., Saturday 8:30 a.m. to 2 p.m. Madero #598-A, Chapala. Some English spoken.

Madereria y Carpentería "Real Ortega"
376 765-2404
Largest and best-stocked lumber yard in the area. Dimension lumber, interior and exterior plywood, treated woods, beams for terraces, decorative moldings, hinges, heavy sliding door parts, Sayer-Lack paints, Stanley tools, more. Open Monday through Friday 8:30 a.m. to 1:30 p.m., 3 p.m. to 6:30 p.m., Saturday 8:30 p.m. to 1:30 p.m. Madero #571 (on the access road to the west side of Madero near the Statue of Pepe Guizar, traveling out of Chapala toward Guadalajara). English spoken. *Recommended.*

MARBLE AND GRANITE

EXMAR Fábrica de Marmol, Exportadores Mármoles Jocotepec
387 763-0679
Mexican marble from Puebla and Torreon for table tops, counters, floors and walls. For large orders (to the states) they pack and ship. Will sell to individuals locally as well as various furniture store clients in the U.S. Open Monday through Friday 8 a.m. to 6 p.m. At the northeast corner of Miguel Arana (main street into Jocotepec) and González Ortega at the traffic light, Jocotepec. Some English spoken. jocomarmol961121@yahoo.com

Marble & Granite Ajijic
376 766-1306
Free estimates on marble and granite for all kinds of installations. Open Monday through Friday 9 a.m. to 1 p.m., 3 p.m. to 5 p.m. Carr. Chapala-Jocotepec #232, Villa Nova. (Across from Sr. Sushi.)

MARBLE/STONE/TILES

Distribuidora del Lago
376 766-1668
The area's best selection of kitchen and bath cabinets, quality plumbing fixtures, water pressure systems, painted, porcelain and stainless steel sinks. They offer a huge selection of ceramic floor and wall tiles, including handmade floor tiles, slate flooring, and clear and colored glass blocks. They'll arrange installation. Open Monday through Friday 9 a.m. to 2 p.m., 3 p.m. to 6 p.m., Saturday 9 a.m. to 1:30 p.m. Blvd. Ajijic #105, La Floresta. English Spoken. *Recommended.*

La Casa de los Azulejos
376 765-6081
Wide selection of hand-painted tiles, "Mi Casa es Su Casa" and other custom plaques, sophisticated tile murals, colored glass blocks, faux brick panels, outside decorative pavers, sinks and commodes. Open Monday through Friday 8:30 a.m. to 7 p.m., Saturday 8:30 a.m. to 2 p.m. Call after hours in an emergency! Madero #270-A, Chapala.

Mexstone
376 765-3209
01 33 3469-4155
Marble floors, columns, furniture, sinks, granite, onyx sales and installation. Av. Hidalgo #77-3, Riberas del Pilar, one block east of Máscaras clinic. www.mexstone.com

ProCasa Interceramic
Complete line of plumbing fixtures for bathrooms: floor, wall, decorative tiles; sinks, toilets, vanity cabinets, glue and grouts. No in-house contractors. Open Monday through Friday 9 a.m. to 2 p.m., 3 p.m. to 6:30 p.m., Saturday 9 a.m. to 2 p.m. Carretera Ote. #3-A, Ajijic.

PAINT

The Color Shop Full selection of paints, brands and colors made perfect by color equalizing. Rollers, brushes and other paint equipment for sale. Open Monday through Friday 8:30 a.m. to 2 p.m., 4 p.m. to 7 p.m., Saturday 9 a.m. to 3 p.m. Miguel Arana #217, Jocotepec. English spoken in the afternoon when the manager is there.

Comex Paint
387 766-2090
National paints in the Mexican palette, including metal paints. Computer color matching, spray guns, tape, tack rags, brushes, rollers; masonry brushes, putty, and sandpaper. Open Monday through Friday 8:30 a.m. to 7 p.m., Saturday 8:30 a.m. to 2 p.m. Carretera Pte. #4-C, Ajijic.

Prisa Paints
376 766-1314
Best stocked paint store in the area. Interior and exterior paints including waterproof paints with computer matching, spray, automotive, and anti-corrosive paints; brushes including those for artists, rollers, masonry brushes, putty, tape, solvents, plastic sheets, spray guns, spray foam, sandpaper and sanding belts, Elmers wood filler and carpenter's Wood Glue, contact cement, silicone sealant, cabinet pulls and latches, hinges, drawer slides, wood screws and finishing nails. Open Monday through Friday 9 a.m. to 6 p.m., Saturday 9 a.m. to 3 p.m. Carretera Pte. #17, Interior 1, Ajijic. info@prisa.com.mx www.prisa.com.mx

Prisa Paints
376 765-2093
Smaller selection of paints and supplies than the store in Ajijic. Miguel Martínez #548, Chapala. info@prisa.com.mx www.prisa.com.mx

Sherwin-Williams
376 766-3935
376 766-3936
Small selection of paints all lead-free, including custom mixes, name brand acrylics, oil and water based enamels, varnishes, stains, lacquers, pool paints, floor paints, waterproofing; and brushes. Will deliver. Can recom-

mend painters. Open Monday through Friday 9 a.m. to 6 p.m., Saturday 9 a.m. to 2 p.m. Carretera Ote. 37-F, Ajijic.

PLUMBING SUPPLIES

La Casa del Plomero
376 766-1546

Very good selection of PVC and copper plumbing pipe and fixtures, good selection of tools and hardware; cement, large selection of tile, barbed wire, lighting fixtures, vent-a-hoods, garbage disposals. Open Monday through Friday 8:30 a.m. to 6 p.m., Saturday 8:30 a.m. to 3:30 p.m., Sundays 10 a.m. to 1 p.m. Carretera Pte. #29 & 29-A, Ajijic.

POOLS AND WATER PRODUCTS

Albercas del Lago
376 766-2121

Chemicals, water filters, pumps, reverse osmosis and UV water purification systems, water softeners, pressure systems, fountains, pool construction and maintenance, solar and gas heating systems, *tinaco* and *aljibe* cleaning. Open Monday through Friday 9:30 a.m. to 6 p.m., Saturday 9:30 a.m. to 2 p.m. Carretera Chapala-Jocotepec #139-B, San Antonio Tlayacapán (across from Corona Beer). English spoken.
hechtpools@hotmail.com

Crystal Water
376 766-0768
376 766-0784

Equipment and supplies for pools, in-house purification systems, water pressure systems and accessories, centrifugal, jet and submersible pumps. He gives a 1-year guarantee on motors and pumps, a 5-year guarantee on pressure tanks. Open Monday through Friday 10 a.m. to 5 p.m., Saturday 10 a.m. Plaza Bugambilias #7 Upstairs, Ajijic.

Handy Man Services
376 766-1569
376 766-2936

Offers the *best* prices on pool equipment and supplies. Open Monday through Friday 8 a.m. to 6 p.m., Saturday 8 a.m. to 3 p.m. Carretera Chapala-Jocotepec #159-C, San Antonio Tlayacapán. English spoken. *Recommended.* jpgiovas@hotmail.com

Tecno Aqua
376 766-3730
376 766-3731
Sales of purified drinking water, water purifiers, filters softeners, pressure systems, submersible and jet pumps; pool and jacuzzi design; solar and gas heaters, filters, pumps, ladders, covers and other pool accessories, and chemicals. Carr. Pte #250, Plaza la Huerta (west Ajijic near La Playa).
tecnoa@prodigy.net.mx
www.tecnoaqua.8m.com

Ultra Pure
376 766-4765
Pool equipment, supplies and maintenance. Filters, pumps, bagged chlorine and maintenance service. Open 10 a.m. to 5 p.m. Monday through Friday, Saturday 10 a.m. to 2 p.m. Carretera Ote. Km 39 C, Ajijic (near Telmex). ultrapureline@hotmail.com

SEPTIC TANK CLEANING

Escumovil
01 33 3834-2829
Emergencies:
01 33 3944-2176
01 800 713-9353
Professional cleaning of septic tanks (*fosas*), storm drains, grease traps, drains and drainage ditches using the latest equipment. Treatment in their state-of-the-art treatment plant.

José Martinez
376 765-3297
Chapala. *Recommended.*

SHEET ROCK

Muro Ligero
Sales and installation of Sheetrock Drywall Systems and ceilings, styrofoam wall systems, suspended ceiling tiles and grid and floating mud and tools. Also decorative styrofoam moldings and fiberglass insulated panels. Open Monday through Friday 9 a.m. to 2 p.m. and 3 p.m. to 6 p.m. Saturday 9 a.m. to 1 p.m. Carretera Chapala-Ajijic #119B, San Antonio Tlayacapán.
muroligero@hotmail.com

STEEL

Aceros y Materiales Ajijic
All types of hardware and construction materials at discount prices. Open Monday

376 766-0172 through Friday 8 a.m. to 8 p.m., Saturday 8 a.m. to 4 p.m. Carr. Ote. #50, Ajijic.

De Acero Distribuciones
376 765-3557
376 766-4304
Well-run, well-stocked yard selling screen wire, galvanized flat panels and sheet steel welding supplies, metal shears, round and square iron T-posts, round and square tubing; metal roofing, tin, flat bar, rebar, angle iron, square stock channel iron, decorative finials, decorative iron panels and rods, concrete reinforcement wire, metal latches, grind stones and cutting wheels, welding machines, construction cages, copper tubing, iron pipe, expanded metal rolls, steel fence posts. Open Monday through Friday 9 a.m. to 5:45 p.m., Saturday 9 a.m. to 12:45 p.m. Hidalgo #58, Riberas del Pilar. *Recommnded.*

TREE CUTTING

Chapala Tree Service
376 762-0602
Trimming, pruning, removal, hauling and clean-up. Free estimates. English spoken.

James Le Wilson
376 765-4803
English spoken. *Recommended.*

WALL AND FLOOR TILES

Hogar Cerámico
387 763-0946
Good prices on Daltile, Orion, Perdurastone, and Hydromagic and more. Everything in stock and ready to send, without charge. Also sinks, faucets, bathtubs, bathroom cabinets. Will recommend an installer upon request. Open Monday through Saturday 8:30 a.m. to 2:30 p.m., 4 p.m. to 7:30 p.m., Sunday 9 a.m. to 2 p.m. Miguel Arana #329, Jocotepec. English spoken.

Materiales de Barro López
387 763-0981
New store that delivers free to Jocotepec, Ajijic and Chapala. Claims to beat any quoted price. Quality floor and roof tiles, painted tiles for kitchen, bathrooms, borders. Open Monday through Friday 8 a.m. to 2:30 p.m., 3:30 p.m. to 7:30 p.m. Saturday 8 a.m. to 3 p.m. Some English spoken. Miguel Arana

#336, on main street into Jocotepec on south side.

Mosaico Vazquez
387 763-1239

Tiles constructed with black sand and cement and hand painted. Many sizes, colors and designs including non-skid tiles for patios and garages. Good place to look for broken or missing tiles in your home. Open Monday through Friday 9 a.m. to 2 p.m., 4 p.m. to 6 p.m. Guadalupe Victoria #110, Jocotepec.

Pablo Fernandez del Valle

English language *books and magazines are available at several bookstores.*

Pablo Fernandez del Valle

Bulletin Boards *are an important source of information for foreigners.*

Pablo Fernandez del Valle

Local, national *and international publications can be found in the Lakeside area.*

12

Communications

with

ZOFIA BARISAS and LAURA LEMING

On the Northshore, it won't take you long to discover that written materials in English, or even Spanish, are scarce compared to European and northern North American standards. There are just a few places to purchase new reading material; those bookstores and newsstands are listed below. However, if you're a member of the Lake Chapala Society you may borrow from their library, the largest repository of English-language materials south of the U.S. border and a few books are for sale there by area writers. Visit the Society at 16 de Septiembre #16-A in Ajijic. For more information about their activities visit their website www.lakechapalasociety.org.

Some newsstands do carry some of your favorite magazines and newspapers, but the selection is small and expect to pay premium prices for them. To stay current, why not subscribe to your favorite newspapers online? A google search of "newspapers magazines online" will yield more than two million sites including www.world-newspapers.com; newslink.org; newsdirectory.com and www.metagrid.com.

Need to understand something written in Spanish? Go to www.freetranslation.com for help.

English Language Publications and Sources

ENGLISH LANGUAGE BOOKSTORES/ NEWSTANDS/SOURCES

Libros y Revistas de Chapala This is the most complete bookstore at Lakeside. It has two locations: Downstairs in Bugambilias Plaza (near El Torito grocery) in Ajijic and on the main street near Lloyd Investment house in Chapala.

***Libros y Revistas Ajijic/*Books and Magazines**
376 766-4319
Ajijic store is open Monday through Saturday 9 a.m. to 5 p.m. Carr . Ote #54, Plaza Bugambilias downstairs, Ajijic.

***Libros y Revistas Chapala/*Books and Magazines**
376 765-2534
Open daily 9 a.m. to 5 p.m. Madero #230, Chapala, near Lloyd investment house.

Galeria Di Paola
376 766-1010
fax 376 766-2401
This gallery and book store has a very large selection of books about Mexico in English, as well as books on other subjects. Visa & MC accepted. Open Monday through Saturday, 10 a.m. to 2 p.m., 4 p.m. to 6 p.m. Colon # 11, Ajijic. English, Italian and French spoken. dipaolablum@yahoo.com www.lakeside.com.mx/business/galeriadipaola.htm

Publicaciónes O'Shea
Daily Mexican newspapers, Guadalajara Colony Reporter (weekly English paper), Ojo del Lago (free monthly magazine in English). Spanish language magazines including Cosmopolitan, Seventeen, Marie-Claire, cooking magazines. Open Monday through Friday 8 a.m. to 2 p.m., 4 p.m. to 8 p.m., Saturday and Sunday 8 a.m. to 2 p.m. The owner Juan O'Shea speaks English and can be found at the *papelería* next door. Miguel Arana #65, near the plaza, Jocotepec. Look for a branch office in Ajijic.

El Torito
This grocery store sells the Guadalajara Colony Reporter, USA Today, the Miami Herald International Edition, Guia Roji maps and a small selection of magazines. Open 8 a.m. to 10 p.m. Carretera Ote. #56 next to Plaza Bugambilias, in Ajijic.

Super Lake
This grocery store sells the Guadalajara Colony Reporter, USA Today, the Miami Herald International Edition, Guia Roji maps and a selection of magazines and new paperbacks in English, including this guide to the

area. Open daily 8 a.m. to 9 p.m. Carretera Pte. #145 (across from Corona Beer Distributorship), Chapala. superlake@hotmail.com

Mom's Deli and Restaurant Mom's has a free trading library of paperbacks that operates on the honor system. Take one to read and bring it back so others can. Open 9 a.m. to 4 p.m. Monday through Friday, Saturday until 3. Closed Sundays. Hidalgo #79-I, Riberas del Pilar.

ENGLISH LANGUAGE PUBLICATIONS

Newspapers

Guadalajara Colony Reporter
376 766-3338
01 33 3615-2177
01 33 3615-0606

40-year-old weekly newspaper in English out of Guadalajara with sections covering news from Manzanillo, Lake Chapala, Ajijic, and Puerto Vallarta. Look for a new edition every Friday. Ajijic office to place advertising and conduct other business is open Monday through Friday 9 a.m. to 2 p.m. in the Plaza Bugambilias. Subscribe online at www.guadalajarareporter.com

El Ojo del Lago
376 765-3676
fax 376 765-3528

Free monthly magazine in English out on the first of each month. Advertisers get a free webpage on www.chapala.com. Hidalgo #223, upstairs, Chapala.

Lake Chapala Review
376 766-4200

Free monthly magazine in English out on the 15th of each month. Carr. Ote. #17-3, Ajijic. review@laguna.com.mx ; www.chapalareview.com

The Miami Herald, Mexico Edition
376 766-4319

To subscribe call 9:30 a.m. to noon. After the demise of The News, it is now the only English language paper out of Mexico City.

Spanish Language or Bilingual Publications

El Antiquario Superb bilingual quarterly magazine devoted to art, music, antiques, art-related attractions and other cultural events. One of the best sources for cross-cultural education,

	history and collecting. www.elantiquario.com
el Charal 376 766-3340	Local, partially bilingual weekly newspaper. Ocampo #200-B, Ajijic. elcharaldelaribera@hotmail.com
La Guía del Lago 01 33 3966-6172	Free advertising circular that comes out every two weeks.
Palabra 01 33 3465-4364 01 33 3131-9853 01 33 3811-1149	Free Spanish-language weekly covering the Lake Chapala region. Miguel Martínez #544-B, Chapala.

Spanish Language newspapers

El Informador	Daily, conservative out of Guadalajara, good classified ads.
El Occidental	Daily out of Guadalajara.
Ocho Columnos	Daily liberal out of Guadalajara.
El Publico	Daily out of Guadalajara.
Siglo XXI	Daily liberal out of Guadalajara.

Newsletters about Mexico

AIM	A newsletter about retirement and travel in Mexico. www.Mexico-Newsletter.com or write AI, POB 434, New Boston, NH 03070

Online Sources in English About Mexico

Mexico Connect	The Internet's largest subscription site about Mexico in English. Check out their free site, too. www.mexconnect.com. *Recommended.*
Mexico-Insights	Monthly online subscription magazine devoted to the Lake Chapala area. www.mexico-insights.com. *Recommended.*
Mexico News Interpreted	Go to www.planeta.com and ask when they'll schedule their next Mexico News Seminar that examines the evolution of the Mexican press and how topical issues are covered in the national and foreign press

today. If you want to get the real story on Mexican news, these seminars are excellent.

Telephones, Cellular Phones and Internet Access

If you're worried that you won't be able to communicate with your office, your family or your broker, or keep up with your favorite online newspapers or sites, don't be. In the past five years the Lakeside area has taken an enormous leap into the world of consumer telecommunications. Mexico's telephone company, Telmex, offers home telephone service with a number of options like call waiting, caller identification, and *buzón*, mailbox. Telmex also sells computers, fax machines, palm pilots and other electronics in their office in Ajijic, has in-country long distance plans, dial up and DSL Internet service, and Telcel brand cellular phones. The Telmex office for the Lakeside area is located in Ajijic, on the mountain side of the *carretera* roughly across from El Torito grocery store. It is there that you will contract for services, pay bills, purchase telephone equipment, computers and other electronics, and buy calling cards for pay phones, cellphones, and Multiphones. The office is open between the hours of 9:30 a.m. to 3:30 p.m., Monday through Friday and located at Carretera Chapala-Jocotepec #113, Ajijic.

Telmex Help through LINK If you need help with Telmex contact Ed White via email or look for him at the Lake Chapala Society every Monday from 10 a.m. to noon at 16 de Septiembre #16-A, in Ajijic. edwinncoralie@prodigy.net.mx

If your problem is poor reception or noise on the line, check to see if you aren't causing the problem with the equipment you're using. Reconditioned or cheap "Made in China" phones bought at the market are often not up to standard. It's best to use good quality equipment, or equipment provided or purchased from Telmex.

When the electricity goes out and your cordless phone will not work. You'll need to have at least one fixed-wire phone plugged in to a receptacle to make or receive calls. The Telmex network is designed to operate with one main phone and two extensions that ring for incoming calls. Turn off the ringers on any additional extensions to help with noise on the line or poor reception.

How to Dial

Telmex Phone Primer

Time of Day	030
Information	040
Repair	050
Operator Assistance for Mexican numbers	020
Operator Assistance for International numbers	090

Area Codes

Ajijic	376
Barra de Navidad	315
Bucerias	329
Chapala	376
Colima	312
Guadalajara	33*
Jocotepec	387
Manzanillo	314
Mexico City	55*
Monterrey	81*
Puerto Vallarta	322
San Antonio Tlay., Chula Vista, La Floresta	376
San Blas	323
San Juan Cosalá	387
San Nicolas, Tlachichilco	376
Tepic	311

*In Nov. 2001 Mexico's 3 largest cities received two digit area codes: Mexico City 55; Guadalajara 33; Monterrey 81, followed by eight-digit numbers. All other cities have 3-digit area codes followed by 7-digit numbers.

To call San Juan Cosalá or Jocotepec from Ajijic, Chapala	dial 01 387 + #
To call Guadalajara from Lakeside	dial 01 33 + #
To call other parts of Mexico	dial 01 + area code + local #
To call Canada or the US	dial 011 + area code + local #
To call other parts of the world	dial 00 + country code + area code + local #
To call person to person to a number in Mexico	dial 02 + area code + local #
To call person to person to a number in Canada or the U.S.	dial 09 + 1 + area code + local
To call person to person to a number in the rest of the world	dial 09 + country code + area code + local #
To dial Mexican 800 numbers	dial 01 800 + #
To dial 800 numbers in the U. S. or Canada from Mexico	dial 001 + 880 (change 800 to 880) + the 7 digit #. The charge to call from Mexico is not free, but is a reduced rate.

To Place Calls from the U.S. or Canada to Mexico	
To call Mexico from Canada or the U.S.	dial 011 52 + area code + #
To call Ajijic, Chula Vista, La Floresta, San Antonio Tlay., Chapala, San Nicolás, Tlachichilco from the U.S. or Canada	dial 011 52 376 + #
To call San Juan Cosalá, Raquet Club, and Jocotepec from the U.S. or Canada	dial 011 52 387 + #.
To call Guadalajara from Canada and the U.S.	dial 011 52 33 + 8 digit #
To buy Mexico phone books	go to www.Mexicophonebooks.com

If you're thinking of having a friend rig your telephone line it might turn out to be a big mistake. It's better to contract Telmex to connect your new phone line all the way from the pole to the telephone apparatus, instead of a cross-connecting box on the exterior of your home.

Multifon at Telmex
01 800 123-0101

If you don't use your phone much, are a landlord, or want to keep teenagers or workers from running up bills on your line, you can buy prepaid amounts of air time for your home hardline telephone. It can be used for long distance calls and Internet time, too. Multifone cards come in 30, 50 and 100 *peso* denominations. Each card provides a PIN number to activate your account from any phone line, including public phones. There is no monthly service fee with the Multifone plan. If you already have a phone line and wish to switch there is a charge for the change. You can sign up for it at Telmex or go to www.telmex.com

PUBLIC TELEPHONES FOR LOCAL, LONG DISTANCE, AND INTERNATIONAL CALLS

All public telephones bearing the Ladatel logo use prepaid phone cards that you can buy in many places including the grocery store, in stationers' shops, or at Telmex, Carr. Chapala-Jocotepec #113, Ajijic, between the hours of 9:30 a.m. to 3:30 p.m., Monday through Friday.

Pablo Fernandez del Valle

Public phone service in the form of public kiosks staffed by a live attendant is available where you see a *Servicio de Larga Distancia* sign. The attendant will dial your number and when it answers, will direct you to a booth where you'll pick up the phone and talk. If you don't speak Spanish it will be helpful to use the following vocabulary:

Collect call	*por cobrar*
I'll pay here.	*pago aqui*
Station to station	*a quien conteste*
Person to person	*persona a persona*
City	*cuidad*
State	*estado*
Country	*país*
Area code and number	*área y número*
from (your name)	*de*
Hang up	*cuelga*
Don't hang up	*no cuelge*
Dial your number	*marque su número*

If you want to pay with a credit card the question in Spanish is *"Acepta usted tarjeta de crédito?"*

PUBLIC FAX

Mailboxes, Etc.
376 766-0647
fax 376 766-0775

This business can send faxes or receive them for a fee. Open Monday through Friday 9 a.m. to 6 p.m., Saturday 9 a.m. to 3 p.m. In San Antonio Tlayacapán, Carretera Chapala Jocotepec #144. English spoken.

LONG DISTANCE AND PUBLIC FAX

You can place long distance and local telephone calls and faxes. Open daily 9 a.m. to 9 p.m. Morelos #37, one short block north of the plaza, Jocotepec.

CELLULAR PHONE SERVICE

As of this writing, Telcel, the cellular phone division of Telmex, is the

As of August 1, 2004 it is illegal to talk on your cell phone while driving a car in Jalisco. Your cell phone dealer can sell you a hands-free apparatus that'll keep you from getting a ticket but the safest way to use a cellphone is to pull over out of traffic.

strongest cellular presence in Mexico. Their distributors sell Motorola, Siemens, Sony Ericsson, Nokia and PalmOne brand "smartphones."

Mexico is divided into 9 cellular regions. Even though Telcel and Iusacell, another cellular provider, claim to offer coverage in all of the regions, Iusacell services don't work here. Telcel and Movistar are the best choices for Lakeside residents.

Cellular providers offer two plans: a fixed monthly fee appropriate for executives who use many options such as email conferencing, Internet surfing and emailing; and Prepaid Cards, sometimes called Recharge cards. In this option, clients buy cards with pre-determined amounts of airtime and program the code scratched off the back of the card into their phone. If you don't use up all the airtime during a 60 day period, (30 days for Movistar) the balance of airtime will be forfeited, at least until you activate it with another recharge card. Dial *333 to check your existing balance.

At present, leading technology in cellular phones worldwide is GSM (a type of technology) which uses a chip. In Mexico only Telcel, (www.telcel.com and www.telcel.com/gsm) and Telefonica Movistar (www.telefo-nicamovistar.com.mx) offer this service. Coverage is fairly good for both of them in large cities and on highways, but Telcel is slightly better. Iusacell, Unefon, and Nextel brand cellphone services don't work for visitors either bringing phones or for residents of the Northshore.

Reprogramming a North of the Border Cellphone to Work at Lakeside

If you have an older TDMA (type of technology) phone, it will have to be permanently reprogrammed to work with Telcel plans. Newer GSM phones work with a chip. If you have one of these you can buy a Telcel or Movistar chip, switch it into your phone and use it during your stay. Some GSM phones are locked for one chip only, though. If you travel between these countries regularly it would be a good investment to buy a new-technology GSM cellphone that allows you to install either Mexican chips or chips suitable for service in Canada or the U.S. The newest GSM cellphones allow you to check email, send photos and

To convert a north-of-the-border phone to service in Mexico call Samuel Kovac. His number is 376 765-4439; email samykovac@gmail.com. He speaks perfect English and provides you with a handy reference sheet that explains dialing procedure and airtime costs. He offers two services: one that reprograms your phone permanently depending on the type of phone you have, the other temporarily inserts a chip "card" into the phone with a local phone number. When you go home, you have the chip card removed, give up the local phone number and return with the same telephone and number you came with. Ask Samuel for current rates. *Recommended.*

The all-Spanish Help Line Number for cell phones is *264. To check how much credit you have on a prepaid card dial *333. The cost is 1.15 *pesos.*

send short text messages (SMS) using the pre-paid, pay-as-you-go recharge cards.

The Lake Chapala area falls within the Guadalajara Region; all other areas are roaming for phones based here. That means that calls between a land line in Ajijic or Chapala and a cellphone is long distance. Calling in the city of Guadalajara is a local call.

To Make Calls to and from Cellular Phones

Cell. to Guadalajara-based cellular phone:	33 + eight digit number (Local Call)
Cell. to hard-line phones in Chapala:	376 + 765 + four digits (Long distance)
Cell. to hard-line phones in Ajijic:	376 + 766 + four digits (Long distance)
Cell. to hard-line phones in San Juan Cosalá/Jocotepec:	387 + 763 + four digits (Long distance)
Cell. to hard-line phones from Guadalajara to Guadalajara:	Eight digit number (Local call)
Cell. to phones in USA & Canada:	001 + area code + number (Long distance)
Hard-line phone to Guadalajara-based cellular phone:	01 + 33 + eight digit number

To Make Calls to a Cellular from a Land Line

If you want to tell someone at Lakeside to call you on your cellular, tell them to dial 01 + 33 + your cell number. If they're calling from Guadalajara from a land line they must dial 044 + 33 + your cell phone number. If you want someone abroad to call you on your cellular tell them to dial 011 + 52 + 33 + your cell number.

Buying More Airtime

Both Telcel and Movistar sell recharge cards. The higher the recharge, the better the prices for calling. Movistar requires you to recharge every 30 days, Telcel every 60 days or you will lose or suspend unused credit. Prices for airtime are approximately 5 *pesos* per minute, charged in minutes. For example, 2 minutes 5 seconds are charged as 3 minutes. If you are calling in a region other than Guadalajara, you'll pay an additional 3 to 4 *pesos* more. You don't pay to receive calls from Guadalajara-based phones (both land line and cellular), if you are in the Guadalajara region which includes Chapala and Ajijic. In all other cases, you pay airtime and possibly long distance surcharges if you are in a roaming area to receive a call.

Telcel
376 766-5500

This Telmex cellphone distributor offers various models, prepaid air time cards, and activation of U.S. cellphones. Their cell phones claim to reach anywhere in Mexico; realistically the signal will be weak or nonexistant in very rural areas. Carr. Chapala-Ajijic #32, across from Tobolandia at the junction of the *carretera* and the Libramiento. English spoken.

Comunicarte
376 766-4151

Official distribuidor of Movistar cellular phones and service. Open Monday through Friday 9 a.m. to 2 p.m., 4 p.m. to 6 p.m. In Plaza Bugambilias (near El Torito grocery in Ajijic), Carretera Ote. #54-1, Ajijic.

Telcel Cellular Phone Rates (Current as of 2005.)

To call another cellular phone from your cellular phone in Ajijic or Chapala the rate per minute is 4.30 *pesos*. To call from your cellular to a hard line in Ajijic or Chapala the rate is 7 *pesos* per minute. Long distance calls are 4 *pesos* a minute plus 7 to 9 *pesos* a minute depending on the area you are calling.

To find out the rate you will be charged calling long distance from your cellular, dial *264 and ask to speak to someone in English. You may have to wait a moment until an English speaker comes on the line. If you are paying to receive a call the cost is 2.90 a minute.

How the Telcel Amigo Plan Works

Choose five cellular numbers that you call frequently from your cell phone, write them down on a piece of paper (they have to be Telcel phones) and then dial *264 and say you want to activate *"Amigos Frequentes"* plan. Cost per minute to talk to these five numbers is a cheap 1 *peso* per minute.

CREDIT CARD CALLING

To charge a long distance call to your Visa, Mastercard, American Express, Discover, and ATT calling cards, dial the access number 01 800 288-2872 and then key in the number you want to call, key in your calling card number or your credit card number and the four-digit expiration code. If you're calling from a pay phone you'll have to use a Ladatel prepaid card to make the call. Insert the prepaid card, dial the access number above, and follow directions from the automated operator. If the call does not complete, dial this access number 001 800 462-4240 and follow instructions. For more information and rates go to their website: www.att.com/traveler

TELEPHONE CALL BACK SERVICES

Global Instant
376 766-0149

Callback service to USA and Canada 11 cents a minute, to Europe 13 cents a minute (from Guadalajara or Mexico City). Monthly bills can be paid in cash or by credit card. Billed in 6-second increments. Rvanoudt@prodigy.net.mx. To sign up go to www.1134.Total-Talknet

Call for Less
376 766-0054

Callback service to USA and Canada for 22 cents a minute. Excellent service since 1997. Cash, credit card, U.S. check, calling card for traveling, six-second billing increment. Open Monday through Friday 9:30 a.m. to 5:30 p.m., Saturday 10 a.m. to 12:30 p.m. Vivianne Reynier. *Recommended.* call4less@prodigy.net.mx.

Call USA & Canada
376 766-3040

Callback service to USA and Canada for 17 cents a minute. One hour activation, cash or credit card, no monthly minimums, no fees, six-second billing and calling card. You can monitor your account online. Ongoing 5% discount for referrals.

INTERNET AND BROADBAND TELEPHONE SERVICE

A Broadband Internet connection is a high-speed connection, typically known as 'Cable Internet' or 'DSL'. It is supplied by an Internet service provider through a cable modem, the phone company, or via a wireless system. This service allows you to make international calls using your home telephone equipment or with headphones plugged into your computer. Rates are very low, and most companies charge a monthly fee to a credit card for the service. A google search of "Internet broadband telephone service" will yield many companies offering this service such as www.vonage.com; www.dialpad.com and others.

INTERNET PROVIDERS

Lagunanet
376 766-0297
376 766-2877

This local provider offers web hosting, high-speed wireless, and dial-up Internet access. Carr. Ote. #58, Ajijic (across from Telmex in Plaza San Andres). English spoken. rodc@laguna.com.mx, www.lagunanet.net.mx

Telmex Prodigy
01 800 123-2222

Dial up and DSL service (in some areas). At Telmex, open 9:30 a.m. to 3:30 p.m., Monday through Friday. Carr. Chapala-Jocotepec #113, Ajijic, www.prodigy.com.mx

Mexico-Wireless
376 766-0413

Wireless high-speed DSL Internet service. Open Monday through Friday 9:30 a.m., to 4:30 p.m., Saturday 10 a.m. to 2 p.m. Just east of Telmex on the mountain side of the *carretera* in Ajijic. support@mexico-wireless.com; www.mexico-wireless.com

TELMEX DSL

DSL lines are, at this writing, available in central Ajijic, from Villa Nova on the west to San Antonio Tlayacapán on the east. New lines are being installed all the time. Called Infinitum, the service allows you to be on-line via your home telephone line and receive calls at the same time. The basic service for a 256 Kbps connection speed is approximately 350 *pesos* a month. They offer 512 Kbps, 1 and 2 Mb speed for increased rates. If you contract for 24 months the special modem is free. If not, the modem costs 999 *pesos*. If you break your 24-month contract you will pay a penalty of approximately 599 *pesos*. To find out if DSL is in your area, visit the Telmex office in Ajijic at Carr. Chapala-Jocotepec #113 between the hours of 9:30 a.m. to 3:30 p.m., Monday through Friday.

You can check your email from either Prodigy or Lagunanet anywhere in the world by going to the following Internet sites:

Lagunanet	www.lagunanet.com.mx
Prodigy	http://mail.prodigy.net.mx/cgi-bin/webmail.cgi

INTERNET CAFES & COMPUTER STORES

The CIA
Café Internet Ajijic
376 766-3626

This well-located Internet café offers classes, quickie business card and brochure design, scanning, photo printing, printing and copying, long distance phone calling and fax service as well as Internet access. Their snack bar serves sandwiches, hamburgers, soups and beverages. Open Monday through Friday, 8:30 a.m. to 5 p.m., Saturday 8:30 a.m. to 2 p.m. Carr. Ajijic #58C, (across from Telmex) Ajijic. English spoken.

Casablanca Hotel and Cybercafe
376 766-4440

Internet and cafe across from the Lake Chapala Society. Open daily 7 a.m. to 8 p.m. 16 de Septiembre #29, Ajijic.

Copy Top
376 766-4464

High-speed Internet service, black and white and color copying, enlargements, laminating, binding. Open Monday through Saturday 10 a.m. to 7 p.m. Guadalupe Victoria 2-A, Ajijic (at the plaza).

San Cristobal Internet & Papelería
376 766-3879

Three Internet stations for surfing, email and printing. The *papelería* sells all kinds of paper goods, pens, pencils, gift bags, stickers, and other office supplies. Open Monday through Friday, 7:45 a.m. to 8 p.m., Saturday 10 a.m. to 8 p.m. Marcos Castellanos #15B, near the Ajijic square. Some English spo-ken. normagus@prodigy.com.

G & S Cyber
376 766-4233

You can buy DVDs of movies in English, in English with Spanish subtitles, and Spanish for 25 *pesos*, downloaded from the Internet. Plus you can get tapes duplicated and surf the net for the best price in town, 10 *pesos* an hour. They also rent computers. Open Monday through Saturday 10 a.m. to 9 p.m., Sunday 4 p.m. to 8 p.m. Aldama #24, Ajijic. graceesquedah@hotmail.com. English spoken.

Cyber Centro

Internet service in an air conditioned environment, sales of Epson-compatible printer ink cartridges. Computer help available in the afternoons. Open Monday through Saturday 10 a.m. to 2 p.m., 4 p.m. to 8 p.m., Sunday 10 a.m. to 3 p.m. Morelos #77, one short block north of the plaza, Jocotepec. Cybercentro_jocotepec@hotmail.com

Cyber Joco

Internet service, computer repairs. Open Monday through Friday 9 a.m. to 10 p.m. On the west side of the plaza, #26-3, Jocotepec. English spoken.

COMPUTER SALES, SERVICE, INSTRUCTION

Computer Supplies

L.M.@com Computer Store
376 766-1788

Best local prices on repairs, parts and supplies. Owned and operated by Martín Leal Perez. Open 10 a.m. to 2 p.m., 4 p.m. to 6 p.m., Monday through Friday, 10 a.m. to 2 p.m., Saturday. Ocampo #32, Ajijic. lma@prodigy.net.mx. *Recommended.*

Tiendas Telmex
01 800 123-1110

Telmex offers payment plans that allow you to purchase desktop and laptop computers and palm pilots in the Tiendas Telmex program. (Spanish speaking).

Computer Repair

Jose Alberto Márquez
376 766-2823

Both cybercafe and PC repair shop, Jose Alberto Márquez makes house calls to help customers configure networking and wireless cards, Internet connections to Prodigy, Lagunanet hardline and wireless service, and other hardware and software problems. House calls are scheduled from 8 a.m. to 2 p.m. by previous appointment, Monday through Saturday. Fast, courteous, knowledgeable service. House call fees per hour start at 100 *pesos*, a real bargain. Carr. Pte. #9-A, Ajijic. English spoken. *Recommended.*

Martín Leal Perez
376 766-1788

Owner of L.M.@com Computer offers reliable, knowledgeable computer repair. Open 10 a.m. to 2 p.m., 4 p.m. to 6 p.m., Monday through Friday, 10 a.m. to 2 p.m., Saturday. Ocampo #32, Ajijic. lma@prodigy.net.mx. *Recommended.*

New World Technology
376 766-4343
376 766-4395

Sales of new computers, accessories and other office equipment; repairs, installation and upgrading service; video email and websurfing at their internet kiosks all are offered in this conveniently located store. Open Monday through Friday 9 a.m. to 3 p.m., 4 p.m. to 6 p.m., Saturday 10 a.m. to 2 p.m. Plaza Bugambilias next to El Torito grocery, Ajijic. English spoken. www.computersinthelake.com.

Tecno Soluciones
387 763-2774

Service and maintenance of computers, computer accessories, cell phones, cell phone prepaid cards, computers for sale with previous order. Open Monday through Friday 10 a.m. to 2 p.m., 4:30 p.m. to 8:30 p.m., Saturday 10 a.m. to 2 p.m., 4 p.m. to 7 p.m. Hidalgo Sur #130, Jocotepec. English speaking staff on weekends. tecnosoluciones@prodigy.net.mx

HOW TO MAKE SURE YOUR OUTLETS ARE GROUNDED

Grounded receptacles should have two slots and one circular hole. Take the cover off and check that the wire wrapped in black (sometimes red) carrying 127 Volts is attached to the smallest rectangular slot in your outlet. The neutral wire, usually white, attaches to the larger parallel slot. The third wire is the ground. It is often green or copper and leads to the circular hole. If any of the wires are crossed, you are in danger of being shocked or having your equipment, particularly your electronics, fried during the rainy season when lightening strikes. An AC-Outlet Analyzer, about $7 US from Radio Shack, will tell you if the wires are properly connected. It won't show how good your grounding is, however. So surge protectors are a must all during the year. If you don't have a surge protector, always unplug electronic equipment when you're not using it.

Courtesy Peter Johanson and the Guadalajara Colony Reporter.
(Look for his weekly column.)

Computer Help
376 765-4156

Software, hardware tutoring and general help with Mike. Will make house calls. 250 *pesos* an hour. English speaking. *Recommended.*

Computer Help by Samuel Kovac
376 765-4439
01 33 1163-6196

Internet setup, virus cleaning, software installation and other services. Will make house calls. 130 *pesos* an hour.
Samykovac@gmail.com

Mac Users Club

The Lake Chapala Society in Ajijic hosts a Mac users group (MUGS) for members the second Tuesday of each month from 10 a.m. to 2 p.m. LCS is located at 16 de Septiembre #16-A in Ajijic. For more information about their activities visit their website www.lakechapalasociety.org

Computer Repair MacIntosh

MacSys Hayakawa, S.A. de C.V.
01 33 3810-6870
01 33 3810-6871
01 33 3810-6872

Very knowledgeable sales and repairs of MacIntosh systems. Make an appointment. Hayakawa visits Lakeside clients once a week from Guadalajara. Guamuchil #1548, corner of Pelican, 1 block from Av. Lázaro Cárdenas, Colonia del Fresno, Guadalajara.English, Spanish and Japanese spoken. Macsys@megared.net.mx

Consultation

Zacar Technology
376 766-4986
01 33 3104-1852

Grounding and surge protection for all types of electrical appliances and electronics. Also phone repair Jerry Hathaway, 25 years experience. Home inspection for electrical systems. zacar22@hotmail.com

Computer/Video and Photography Services

Foto Galería
387 763-2783

Photography and video services, digital services, scanning, photos from videos, photos onto CD, photo retouching, enlargements and posters, restoration of old photos, montages. Open Monday through Saturday 9 a.m. to 2 p.m., 4 p.m. to 7 p.m., Sunday 9 a.m. to noon. Be sure to call first. At Juárez, corner of Matamoros, Jocotepec.

Foto Estudio Zaragoza
376 765-5452

All kinds of services. Open Monday through Saturday 10 a.m. to 2 p.m., 4 p.m. to 8 p.m. Thursday only until 2 p.m. Miguel Mártinez #534, Chapala.

Video Filmación Camarena
387 763-1497

Miguel Camarena makes videos of weddings, birthdays, family reunions and other events. He also does photography and enlargements. Available by appointment. Vicente Guerrero #62, west of Hidalgo Sur, Jocotepec.

Digital Camera and Gaming Repair

Digital PC
376 765-6494

Professional service for digital cameras, video cameras, discman, Net MD, DVD, X-box, Playstation 1, II, Dream Cast, Game Cube, audio equipment, laptops, scanners, CPU. Cybercafe 10 *pesos* an hour. 5 de Mayo at the corner of Morelos in Chapala.

TELEGRAM SERVICE

Sending telegrams, *telégrafos*, from post offices within Mexico is very inexpensive. Before long this service will become a quaint memory as messaging will come via the Internet and email. In Ajijic the telegraph office is found inside the post office. You may pick up money (show your passport) or wire money to other locations in Mexico at the post office by asking for a postal money order. Money can also be wired from outside Mexico and converted to local currency, and you only need a passport or current driver's license to collect it. Wiring money as a deposit for room reservations is useful when hotels do not accept credit cards, especially in rural areas.

You may send three kinds of telegrams:

Urgente	Urgent; will be sent immediately
Ordinario	Regular; will be sent the same day
Carta nocturna or carta de noche	Night letter; will be sent that day or the next.

If you are receiving a telegram you can specify how it will be delivered:

To the telegraph office in Chapala or Jocotepec

To the post office in Ajijic, Chapala or Jocotepec

To your hotel (Be sure to supply an address)

To a private home (If there is no clear street address, try to supply a succinct description of where the house is located, such as the last house after Km 16, Carretera Chapala-Jocotepec. In this case it may be better to collect the telegram at the telegraph office if it is possible.)

If you collect a telegram at the local post office it must be addressed as:

Lista de Correos
Your Name
Ajijic (or Chapala or Jocotepec)

If you collect a telegram elsewhere at a telegraph office it has to be addressed as:

Lista de Correos
Your Name
Town or City

Telegrams

Telecomm Telegramas
376 765-2181

National and international telegrams. Open Monday through Friday 10 a.m. to 3 p.m. Paseo del Arte y la Cultura #1 (formerly Encarnación Rosas) on the south side of the plaza, Chapala.

Telegrams/Western Union

Telecom/*Telégrafos*
387 763-0239

Telegram office, Western Union, and the place to pay phone bills in Jocotepec. Open Monday through Friday 9 a.m. to 2 p.m. Guadalupe Victoria #71, just south of the main street Miguel Arana, in the Auditorio Municipal, main floor, Jocotepec. No English spoken.

Mail, Shipping and Delivery

Postal Service/*Correo*

Regular Mexican postal service is slow but reliable, helped by postal workers who have widespread ties to village citizens. Ajijic and Jocotepec have post offices near the central plazas. Chapala's post office is four and a half blocks from the plaza on Degollado, in a temporary space, following the demise of its former building. Items that the postal service will not accept are food, drugs, guns, liquids, glass, and live animals. Commercial postal service is available through Mailboxes, Etc., and Packaging and Shipping.

Ajijic Post Office
376 766-1888

You can send telegrams, receive or wire money (show your passport), buy stamps, send packages, send registered, express,

MAILING AND SHIPPING VOCABULARY

Customs	***Aduana***
Post office box	***Apartado***
Zip Code	***Código***
Airmail	***Correo Aéreo*** or ***Por avión***
Post Office	***Correos***
Special Delivery, Express	***Entrega Inmediata***
Money Orders	***Giros Postales***
General Delivery	***Lista de Correos*** or ***Posta Restante***
Post Office	***Oficina de Correos***
Parcels	***Paquetes***
Registered Mail	***Registrado***
Certified (insured mail)	***Certificada***
Stamps (sometimes rubber stamps)	***Sello***
Postage Stamps	***Timbres***

and certified mail, pick up General Delivery mail, and rent post office boxes. Post office box rental is currently 150 *pesos* a year and is due in January. Open 8:30 a.m. to 3 p.m. Monday through Friday. Colón #2, Ajijic. On the corner of Colón, the same street that changes to Morelos going towards the lake, and where Ocampo to the west becomes Constitución to the east.

Chapala Post Office
376 766-1888

In this temporary location, you'll notice that the phone number for the Ajijic and Chapala post offices are the same, even though they are in different villages. You can send telegrams, receive or wire money (show your passport), buy stamps, send packages, send registered, express, and certified mail, pick up General Delivery mail and rent post office boxes. Open 8:30 a.m. to 3 p.m. Monday through Friday. Degollado #323-B, four and a half blocks east on Degollado from the main street of Madero, past DIF, Chapala.

ZIP CODE (Código Postal)	
Ajijic	45920
Chapala	45900
Jocotepec	45800
San Juan Cosalá	45820
San Antonio Tlay.	45900
Ixtlahuacán de los M.	45850
San Nicolás de Ibarra	45940
San Pedro Tesistán	45830
Nextipac	45800
Chantepac	45825

Pablo Fernandez del Valle

Jocotepec Post Office
387 763-0322

You can buy stamps, send packages, send registered, express delivery, and certified mail, and pick up General Delivery mail. Post office is around the back of the building. Very little English spoken. Open 8 a.m. to 3 p.m. Monday through Friday. Hidalgo #40, Jocotepec.

GENERAL DELIVERY

If you don't have a post office box, you may have your mail sent to *Poste Restante* (General Delivery) in care of:

Lista de Correos
(Your Name)
(Town), Jalisco, Mexico
C.P. (See Zip code chart)

To claim your letter or parcel, ask for the *Lista de Correos* and show your passport or current driver's license.

PRIVATE MAIL SERVICES

Mail Boxes Etc.
376 766-0647
fax 376 766-0775

MBE offers a U.S. address in Laredo, Texas, private mail boxes, faxing and copying service, office supplies, as well as packing and shipping services. Customs levies heavy duties on packages, so many customers learn not to have packages sent to their MBE postal address. Fed Ex, DHL, UPS, Estafeta will deliver to this address, just be sure to include the zip code, 45900 on the waybill and your telephone number with the area code included. When the package arrives you can pick it up. Call first, it may save you a trip. Carr. Chapala-Jocotepec #144, San Antonio Tlayacapán 45900 mbechapala@laguna.com.mx

Mailboxes Etc.
01 387 761-0363
fax 376 761-0364

There is no courier service from this location in San Juan Cosalá, but packages can be left here with the San Antonio Tlayacapán return address and it will be shuttled over to San Antonio Tlay. for pick-up. Add another day, though. Carr. Chapala-Jocotepec #400, San Juan Cosalá, 45820.

Handy Mail
376 766-3813

Weekly mail forwarding service from Laredo, Texas to San Antonio Tlayacapán. Rates start at $20 US per month for a larger-than-standard post office box and the service includes a U.S. address. Mail leaves Laredo, Texas every Tuesday and arrives one to three days later. One kilo of letters, newspapers, magazines, and large envelopes are allowed without surcharge; no packages can be received through this service. Handy Mail is located inside the Mr. Handyman store, Carr. Chapala-Ajijic #159C, San Antonio Tlayacapán, near Café Due.
Handymail@prodigy.net.mx

Packaging and Shipping International Mailbox
376 765-2875

They offer private mail boxes, packaging and shipping, a U.S. address in Laredo, as well as first class mail to the U.S., UPS and FedEx service. Open Monday through Friday 9 a.m. to 6 p.m. Hidalgo #236-A, Chapala.

Barbara's Bazaar Mail
376 766-3636

Offers mail service to the U.S. for a yearly rate of 380 *pesos*. Letters only; ask about small packets. Mail goes out every Tuesday. Leave mail at the Bazaar Monday, Tuesday, Wednesday, Friday and Saturday, 10 a.m. to 2 p.m., 3 p.m. to 5 p.m., Saturday 10 a.m. to 4. Closed Thursday and Sunday. Independencia #7, Ajijic.

Lake Chapala Society

As an important perk of membership, LCS members receive free mail service for letters. Volunteers transport U.S.-stamped letters to the United States two or three times each week and mail them there. They will also weigh them and sell you the correct postage. The Society office is open Monday through Friday 10 a.m. to 2 p.m. 16 de Septiembre #16-A, Ajijic.

Express Mail, Packaging and Shipping Services

Mailboxes, Etc.
376 766-0647
fax 376 766-0775

Offers the following express mail service:
Fed Ex www.fedex.com
DHL 800-CALL-DHL www.dhl.com
Estafeta (Shipping within Mexico only). www.estafeta.com (look for the English link). Open Monday through Friday 9 a.m. to 6 p.m., Saturday 9 a.m. to 3 p.m., Carr. Chapala-Jocotepec #144, San Antonio Tlayacapán, 45900.

Fed Ex at Ajijic Real Estate
376 766-2077

Morelos #4, Ajijic. Open 9 a.m. to 5 p.m., Monday through Saturday.

Mexico Express at Viajes Vikingo
376 766-0936

Open Monday through Friday 9 a.m. to 6 p.m., Saturday 9 a.m. to 1 p.m. Carr. Chapala-Ajijic #133-A, San Antonio Tlayacapán. This travel agency offers Mexico Express service, 01 800 322-8872; www.mexicoexpress.com.mx.

Estafeta
376 765-3309

Courier service and shipping within Mexico for letters and boxes. Open Monday through

Thursday 9:30 a.m. to 5 p.m., Friday and Saturday 9:30 a.m. to 2 p.m. Hidalgo #69-D, Riberas del Pilar. Fax can be used next door at Intermex Corporate Services (376) 765-2090. www.estafeta.com.mx

UPS at Coldwell Banker Real Estate
376 765-3676
Office is open 9 a.m. to 5 p.m. Monday through Friday, 9 a.m. to 1 p.m. Saturday. Hidalgo #223,Chapala. www.ups.com

WHICH ONE HAS THE BEST RATE?

In August 2004 we compared the price of shipping a 3.5 lb. manuscript to a Canadian address. We found:

Mexican Post Office-MexPost	Cost 356 *pesos* plus 30 *pesos* to register it. Arrival: 2 to 3 weeks
DHL Worldwide Express	Cost: 401 *pesos* Arrival: next day
UPS Worldwide Service	Cost: 401 *pesos* Arrival: next day
Federal Express	Cost: 411 *pesos* Arrival: next day
Mexico Express	Cost 360 *pesos* Arrival time: 48 hours

Office Supplies/Stationers

Papelería de Colores
School supplies, backpacks for children, some artist supplies, gifts, photocopying, laminating, binding. Open Monday through Friday 8 a.m. to 2 p.m., 4 p.m. to 8 p.m., Saturday and Sunday 8:30 a.m. to 2 p.m. Miguel Arana #63, Jocotepec. English spoken.

Papelería Marthita
In business for 22 years, small store full of school supplies, art materials, colored and

decorated printing paper, greeting cards in Spanish. Two photo copiers, reductions and enlargements made. Fast and efficient service. Also gift boxes, ribbons, lace ribbons, colorful cards, wrapping paper, buttons (not on display, must ask for them). Will do a beautiful job of gift wrapping. Open Monday through Saturday 8 a.m. to 2 p.m., 4 p.m. to 8 p.m., Sunday 8 a.m. to 2 p.m. Allende #31, on east side of plaza, Jocotepec. English spoken. *Recommended.*

Papelería del Lago
Copies, lamination, large selection of school and office supplies, craft supplies. Will fill special orders quickly. Open Monday through Friday 8 a.m. to 9 p.m., Saturday 9 a.m. to 7 p.m., Sunday 9 a.m. to 4 p.m. Degollado #392, Chapala.

PRINT SHOP

Ediciones de la Noche
01 33 3825-1301
Books and magazines and print on demand. Emmanuel Carballo, English spoken.Madero #687, Guadalajara.
noche@megared.net.mx;
emmcarballo@hotmail.com.

Edigrafik
01 33 3811-0444 x228
Press 4 for English and then ext. 228
fax 01 33 3811-0444 ext. 211
Print on demand and conventional printing. Calle 14 #2430, Guadalajara (Zona Industrial).

Imprenta Jocotepec
387 763-0746 & fax
Greeting cards, business cards, wedding invitations, bills, posters, pamphlets, flyers, envelopes. Will print books but only in large quantities to warrant the cost. Owner Jorge Trujillo speaks fluent English. Open Monday through Saturday 9 a.m. to 2 p.m., 4 p.m. to 7 p.m. Miguel Arana #190, on the main street into Jocotepec from points east.

GREEN ANGELS

Green Angels national number 01 800 903-9200; Guadalajara area 01 33 3668-1800 Ext. 1+31489; use your best Spanish to communicate.)

One of the best reasons to have a cellphone is for road assistance. The Green Angels (*Los Angeles Verdes*) operates a fleet of trucks all over Mexico supported by the Ministry of Tourism who provide mechanical help, first aid, radio-telephone communication, basic supplies and small parts, towing, tourist information, and protection. The service is free and spare parts, fuel and lubricants are provided at cost. Some mechanics are bi-lingual and can really help you out of a jam. If you break down between Lakeside and the Guadalajara area use the Guadalajara number 3668-1800, wait for the recording, then dial 1+31489 (if you are calling from a non-cellular phone dial 01 33 3668-1800 and then the extension 1+31489); if you break down elsewhere dial their toll free number on your cellular 800 903-9200 (don't dial the 01) and tell them what highway you are on or what city you are near. They'll provide you with a local number to call. If you need to speak in English for the 800 number ask "*Me permite hablar en Inglés?*" and an English-speaking person will come on the line.

Quadrimag Printers
01 33 3618-8975
Tabloids, books, flyers, other printing jobs. Guillermo Zapeda. English spoken. Silva Romero #92, Guadalajara.

World Digital
Printing
01 33 3183-0913
Business cards, flyers, banners and signs. Rubén Galindo. Fermin Riestra #1496-10, Guadalajara (Colonia Moderna).

Getting around *can be somewhat daunting when faced with a language barrier in a foreign country.*

Pablo Fernandez del Valle

Pablo Fernandez del Valle

Public transportation *services in Mexico are prolific, efficient and economical, but late-night transportation is limited. Should you wish to travel at night, make arrangements in advance with a friend or off-hours taxi driver.*

Pablo Fernandez del Valle

Pablo Fernandez del Valle

13

Getting Around

with
DALE HOYT PALFREY

Taxis and Buses

Lakeside rates are standardized so don't expect to see meters in taxis. Before departing be sure to agree on a price. It isn't customary to tip taxi drivers in Mexico, although special service can always be rewarded.

TAXI STANDS

You'll find taxi stands or *sitios* on town plazas, sometimes near a kiosk with a phone. Don't make the mistake of parking in the taxi area marked by a yellow-painted curb and the word *Sitio* painted in black. You'll be hastily chased off and urged to park elsewhere or towed. *Se usará grua* means you'll be towed!

You'll find taxi stands or *sitios* near the Chapala and Ajijic plazas, and also near the church in Jocotepec. In Chapala and Ajijic you can phone for taxis. Drivers pick up calls from the phone in plaza taxi kiosks during the hours listed below.

There are two taxi stands in Jocotepec: one in front of the main church on Hidalgo Sur and the other across from the plaza, next to the first

Taxi Phone Numbers & Hours

Taxi Stands

Taxi Stand at the Chapala Bus Station: 376 765-4697

Chapala Taxi Stand: 376 765-3511, 376 765-4697, 6 a.m. to 9 p.m.

Ajijic Taxi Stand: 376 766-0674, 376 766-1663, 7 a.m. to 8 p.m.

Jocotepec: No phone, 7 a.m. to 9 p.m. Benjamin Zuñiga 0133 3498-8901.

Taxi Fares from Ajijic

To Go to or From	Cost in *Pesos*
Ajijic - Jocotepec	100 Plaza to Plaza
Chapala - Ajijic	50 Plaza to Plaza
Ajijic -Riberas	40
Ajijic - Chula Vista	40
Ajijic - Danza del Sol Hotel	30
Ajijic - San Juan Cosalá	50
Ajijic - El Chante	90
Airport - Lakeside (Days)	250
Airport - Lakeside (Nights)	280
Fares as of April 2005	

birriería on Miguel Arana. Two drivers speak English at the *sitio* on Miguel Arana.

Airport Taxi Pickup

Taxi drivers in Mexico are controlled by the government and their union at the airport is strong. At this writing, local taxi drivers say they can't offer airport pickup, so travelers must engage one of the airport taxis by buying a ticket at the taxi booths.

After-Hours Taxi Service

Be sure to make arrangements at least 24 hours in advance.

Francisco Miramontes (Pancho)
376 766-1142
English Spoken.

Carlos Soto
376 766-0784
Cell. 01 33 1144-8736

Samuel Reyes
376 766-3662
01 33 3482-0167
044 376-769-3835
24 hour taxi service by appointment.

Juan Ibarra López
376 765-2329
01 33 3102-9443
Pino Suárez #39, Chapala. By appointment.

Joaqun 0133 3947-4952	24 hours, Jocotepec.

Major Taxi *Sitios* in Guadalajara

Taxi Express	01 33 3637-4525
Acuña y Terranova	01 33 3642-6946
Álvaro Obregón	01 33 3617-5503
Américas	01 33 3817-2363
Chapalita	01 33 3122-2393
Colomos	01 33 3817-2249
Colón-Industrial	01 33 3645-6780
Colón Sur	01 33 3645-6780
Hilton	01 33 3614-7075
Independencia	01 33 3617-2077
Las Águilas	01 33 3632-7401

Taxi Vocabulary

How much to (Chapala)?	*Cuánto a (Chapala)?*
Here	*Aqui*
At the corner	*En la esquina*
Right	*Derecha*
Left	*Izquierda*
Straight ahead	*Derecho*
Keep going ahead	*Mas adelante*
Behind	*Atrás*
Will you wait?	*Me espera?*
Will you pick me up at 6 p.m. or 18:00	*Me recoje a las seis p.m.* or *diez y ocho?*
Pick me up at (Hidalgo #11.)	*Recojeme a (Hidalgo once.)*
What are your fares?	*Las tarifas?*
Do you have change?	*Tiene cambio?*
Is it close to___?	*Está cerca de ___?*

LAKESIDE BUS SERVICE

Shuttle Buses

Small, thirty-passenger shuttle buses that serve the area between Chapala

P.ablo Fernandez del Valle

Shuttle buses *bearing either a red, yellow or blue stripe serve the Lakeside villages of Ajijic, Chapala, San Antonio Tlayacapán, and San Juan Cosalá.*

and Ajijic begin their route from the bus stop on Madero near Lloyd in Chapala. This is the bus stop in front of Checo's Bar on the west side of Madero between Degollado and Flavio Romero. It shouldn't be confused with the Chapala bus terminal that's located on the east side of Madero. At noon the drivers take short breaks before continuing their route.

The shuttles leave Chapala along the main Chapala-Ajijic *carretera*, turn south on Jesús García in San Antonio Tlayacapán, past the plaza before turning right on Colón to head back to the main *carretera*.

The shuttles follow along the *carretera* in La Floresta, turn south on Aldama in Ajijic to follow a 14-block route west along Guadalupe Victoria and Zaragoza before retracing their route east through Seis Esquinas and Ajijic along Ocampo and Constitución.

There is no local bus service in Chapala, Lomas del Manglar, Chula Vista, Riberas del Pilar, upper La Floresta, upper Ajijic, Villa Nova or Rancho del Oro.

Shuttle buses run from approximately 7 a.m. to 8:30 p.m. and are painted with either a red, yellow or blue stripe over a white background. The exact time of the first and last bus is determined by the hours of sunrise and sunset. The drivers will travel the main Chapala-Jocotepec highway (*carretera*) before full morning light, but will not begin their route along the village lanes until they can clearly see to drive them. The buses run every 15 minutes or so. See the companion map for routes.

When you board the bus tell the driver where you're going and he'll tell you the fare. Be sure to carry coins or bills of 20 *pesos* or less. To get off, press the red button on the pole at the rear of the bus to let the driver know you want to get off at the next stop or say "*Pare* (spoken par-aye, the second syllable "e" sounded with a long aaa sound) *aqui, por favor.*" There is no smoking on any bus.

First Class Bus Service/*Primera or Chapala Plus*

First class Chapala Plus buses run from Guadalajara to Chapala to Ajijic and back. Premier buses begin in Jocotepec and make regular stops along the *carretera* to Ajijic and then carry on to Guadalajara via the *Libramiento*. Buses operate from 5 a.m. to approx. 11 p.m., passing through Ajijic on the half hour. Chapala Plus buses leave the Chapala bus station at the top of the hour. First-class buses which feature televisions, VCRs, air conditioning and bathrooms, are very comfortable and have space for luggage above the seats inside or below, under the bus.

Second Class Bus Service/*Segundas*

These older, full-sized buses run from Jocotepec to Chapala along the *carretera;* some Segundas provide service through Ajijic but no further, taking the *Libramiento* or bypass from Ajijic to Guadalajara, stopping wherever passengers request. Buses operate from 5 a.m. to approx. 11 p.m. Second class buses are older first class buses with or without air conditioning and bathrooms.

First and Second Class Tickets

You may buy your ticket from the bus driver or at the terminals listed below. Be sure to hold on to your ticket. Bus inspectors board from time to time and will ask you to get off the bus if you cannot produce a ticket. A ticket also covers your medical expenses if, through the fault of the driver, you are injured. For long distance travel to other parts of Mexico buy tickets at travel agencies in advance.

Bus Service from Chapala, Ajijic, San Juan Cosalá, Jocotepec to Guadalajara

Primera, Chapala Plus and *Segunda* buses have service to Guadalajara from the stations in Chapala and Jocotepec, as well as from the ticket "booths" in Ajijic and San Juan Cosalá. All buses take you to the old bus station in Guadalajara, *La Camionera Central Vieja*. **But if you ask the driver to stop at the Valencia exit, he'll drop you where you can get a quick taxi to the new bus station, *La Nueva Central***

Tell the Bus Driver:

Pare por la salida Valencia, por favor.	Stop at the Valencia exit, please.

Tell the Taxi Driver:

Voy a La Nueva Central Camionera.	I'm going to the New Bus Station.

***Camionera* in Tonalá.** For long distance travel throughout Mexico or to the border you need to transfer to the new bus station in Tonalá, a suburb on the southeast side of Guadalajara. Arrangements and ticketing for long distance travel can be done at the terminal or in advance at travel agencies.

Chapala Bus Station/ *Central Camionera Chapala*
376 765-2212

Three blocks from the plaza, at the intersection of Madero and Miguel Martínez you'll find the Chapala bus terminal with lanes for 6 buses and waiting room chairs for 50 passengers. The terminal houses a ticket booth, snack bars, a barber shop, newsstand and restrooms. **Please note that fewer buses run on Sundays and holidays and follow unpublished schedules.**

SCHEDULE:

Bus Service from Chapala to the Old Bus Station in Guadalajara

Chapala-Plus Direct*

Buses leave from 5:30 a.m. to 9:15 p.m. nearly every 30 minutes.

Segunda Class Buses from Chapala to Old Bus Station in Guadalajara*

Buses leave from 5:30 a.m. to 9:15 p.m., every 20 or 30 minutes.

**Segunda* buses get to the old bus station in Guadalajara but stop at every town along the way. Travel time is greatly increased.

Second Class Service from Chapala to Lakeside Villages

Segunda Class Buses from Chapala to Jocotepec

Buses leave from 6:30 a.m. to 9:40 p.m., every 20 or 30 minutes.

Segunda Class Buses from Chapala to Mezcala	Buses leave regularly from 7:20 a.m. to 9:20 p.m.
Segunda Class Buses from Chapala to San Juan Tecomatlán	Buses leave regularly from 8:15 a.m. to 8 p.m.

First Class Service from Chapala to Mexico City and Puerto Vallarta

Primera Plus from Chapala to Mexico City	Leaves at 10:30 p.m. 456 *pesos.*
Primera Plus from Chapala to Vallarta	Leaves 9:45 p.m. 375 *pesos.*

Ajijic Ticket Booth

At the traffic light at the intersection of Colón and the *carretera* there is a small ticketing office and waiting area with chairs for about 5 passengers. The ticket agent wears a white shirt with a red circular logo on the pocket and is often next door if he's not behind the desk. **Please note that fewer buses run on Sundays and holidays and leave follow unpublished schedules.**

SCHEDULE:

Bus Service from Ajijic to the Old Bus Station in Guadalajara

Directions Primer

Privada or Privado, abbreviated Priv. means cul de sac, or a street that has no exit. It isn't always a private road. You'll also notice that street names are listed first and then followed by the address. This is because nearly all cities and towns have several streets that commemorate important dates in Mexican history, such as 16 de Septiembre, 5 de Mayo, 8 de Julio, that start with a number. To avoid confusion, the address is always listed after the name of the street. In Guadalajara you'll find streets marked *Prolongación*, abbreviated Prol., which means an extension of a street, and *Circunvalación*, abbreviated Circun. that indicates a ring road or bypass. The *Periférico* road circling Guadalajara literally means peripheral or outlying road.

According to INEGI, Mexico's statistics bureau, Jalisco drivers are the worst in the nation. An average of 718 people die on Jalisco roads every year; more than 10% of them are killed by city bus drivers.

Premier Direct via the Libramiento	Buses leave from 5:30 a.m. to 7:25 p.m. After 7:45 a.m. all buses leave 25 minutes after the hour.
Chapala Plus	Buses leave from 7:10 a.m. to 8:45 p.m., every 20 or 30 minutes.
Segunda Bus Service to Guadalajara*	Buses leave from 5:30 a.m. to 9:10 p.m., on the hour, on the half hour, and ten past the hour. **Segunda* buses get to the old bus station in Guadalajara but stop at every town along the way. Travel time is greatly increased.

Jocotepec Bus Station

One block south and one block west from the plaza, the bus station is at the intersection of Miguel Arana and Matamoros.

SCHEDULE:

Bus Service from Jocotepec to Guadalajara

Primera*

Jocotepec to Guadalajara via Chapala	Buses leave from 5 a.m. to 8:40 p.m. *All buses going to Ajijic and Chapala pick up and drop off passengers along the Northshore.

Directo

Jocotepec to Guadalajara via the Libramiento Directo	Buses leave from 5 a.m. to 7 p.m.

Via Mex15

Jocotepec to Guadalajara via old Highway Mex15	Buses leave from 5 a.m. to 6 p.m. and stop at the Plaza del Sol shopping center in Guadalajara, before continuing on to the old bus station.

San Juan Cosalá Bus Stop

Just past the overhead sign that announces *"San Juan Cosalá, Aguas Termales"* there is an informal bus stop where you can buy tickets from the drivers on the bus or at a nearby table under a Pepsi tent. Look for a sign that says *"Boletos."*

Bus stops for Chapala Plus, Premier and Segunda Class	Look for international bus stop signs, benches and shelters on either side of the *carretera* or where people are gathered.

A WORD ABOUT BUS TRAVEL

Long distance bus travel during *Semana Santa,* the week before Easter, and *Semana de Pascua,* the week after Easter, can be very hectic. Be sure you've made arrangements well in advance. As a major holiday, the bus lines are packed with people on their way to the beach or other holiday destinations. Even hardy locals find other means of transportation during that time. Local shuttle bus traffic is always crowded on market days (Monday for Chapala, Wednesday for Ajijic), and between 2 and 3 p.m. during the school week.

Village Driving

The most important thing to remember about driving in the villages around Lake Chapala is that the streets were originally designed for pedestrian and equestrian traffic. Large cars, trucks, SUVs and vans have a hard time circulating on narrow streets. Medium-sized to small cars with high clearance fare the best.

YELLOW ZONES

Don't park along yellow painted curbs especially those at the end of the street. This free area allows cars to make tight right-angle turns onto narrow perpendicular streets. Parking in yellow zones is a common, maddening fault of out-of-town drivers accustomed to wider roads.

NO PARKING/BLOCKED GARAGE ACCESS

Since virtually all private garages in the villages open onto the streets, be extremely conscious to not block a garage door that displays an "E" inside a circle with a slash through it. It is the symbol for No Parking (*No Estacionarse*). In other circumstances, you may not be able to park on the opposite side of the street from the garage door as well, since the car must use the entire width of the lane to swing into the garage opening. In that case, the No Parking symbol will be displayed on an exterior wall across the street from the garage.

Pablo Fernandez del Valle

***Don't park** here!*

IMPERIAL DRIVING AND PARKING

Visitors from Guadalajara, Mexico City and other places in Mexico, as well as international visitors often adopt an imperial, uncooperative attitude when driving in this area. Perhaps the excitement of being on vacation blinds drivers to the constraints of village traffic, but large service trucks must use the narrow village lanes for their deliveries. Precision parking and courteous behind-the-wheel behavior are essential. Other unsavory practices include excessively fast or slow driving, the almost universal failure to signal, and blocking parked cars.

EXCESSIVE SPEED

Cobbled lanes are unsuitable for excessive speed, especially since cars must share them with pedestrians and horses. Cautious drivers show respect by watching for and yielding to them. Be especially careful; the person behind the wheel is responsible until proven otherwise.

SINGLE LANE SHARING

When streets are further narrowed by parked cars, circulating vehicles traveling in opposite directions cannot pass one another at the same time. One of the cars will have to pull over into the parking lane while the other passes. It is courteous to watch for oncoming cars and to make the conciliatory gesture of pulling over and waiting first. You will often be rewarded with a wave of thanks by the passing driver.

TOPES

Speed bumps, sleeping policemen, or traffic calming devices. Whatever you call them they're out there to slow traffic. Some drivers sail

Pablo Fernandez del Valle

***Stop** if you see one of these!*

***Slow down** for* topes.

over them as if they weren't there, others stop before rolling over one. Be careful not to collide with the car in front of you whose driver decides to take a *tope* ultra slow.

GLORIETAS

The driver in a *glorieta*, or roundabout, has the right of way. If a driver leaving a *glorieta* is struck by another entering the circle, the car entering the *glorieta* is blamed for the accident.

BICYCLISTS

Bicyclists cannot be ticketed—be careful around them.

WHAT DOES THE YELLOW LIGHT MEAN?

It means either slow or go—same as north of the border. If a traffic officer tells you otherwise and gives you a ticket, it will be invalidated, if you can prove it.

CAN YOU DRIVE USING YOUR OWN LICENSE?

Mexico accepts foreign drivers's licenses for the term of the person's residency so long as it isn't expired.

CELL PHONES

It is illegal to talk on your cellphone while driving in Jalisco.

Pemex Gas Stations

Pemex gas stations are found in the following locations. They offer two choices of fuel: Magna, octane 87, or Premium, octane 92. Most stations also offer diesel.

On the Ajijic Bypass or Libramiento 376 766-3393	Open 24 hours.
In Ajijic: Across from Plaza San Andrés 376 766-0633	Open 6 a.m. to midnight.
In Chapala: On the *carretera* going north to Guadalajara 376 765-2454	Open 5 a.m. to midnight.
In Jocotepec: On Miguel Arana, just before entering Jocotepec on the *carretera* from Ajijic	Open 6 a.m. to 10 p.m.
In Ixtlahuacan de los Membrillos, 7 k. from Chapala going toward Guadalajara	Open 6 a.m. to 10 p.m.

Towing

Aguirre Towing 387 763-2767	Jocotepec.
Aguirre Towing 376 765-4280	Chapala-Ajijic area.
Grúas Asturias 01 33 1055-6235 01 33 1055-6236 01 33 1055-6237	They tow disabled, abandoned and wrecked cars and will haul *chatarra*, large refuse. They'll buy your junker. Ask them. Open daily 9 a.m. to 6 p.m. Hidalgo #54-A, Riberas del Pilar (on the main *carretera*).

Grúas Casillas South and southeast areas of Guadalajara.
Guadalajara:
01 33 3605-5086
Tonalá:
01 33 3602-0458
Toluquilla (Base):
01 33 3606-3445

Motorcycle cops perform stunts *for local events.*

Dale Hoyt Palfrey

Lakeside Law

by Dale Hoyt Palfrey

MEXICAN POLICE

Visitors from abroad often find Mexico's police structure confusing. This simplified overview will clue you in to who's who and corresponding jurisdictions.

The primary tasks of the local *Dirección de Seguridad Pública* (Public Security Division) are preventing crime and enforcing municipal ordinances that cover minor infractions such as drunkenness and disorderly conduct. Local police do not have the authority to investigate or prosecute more serious criminal matters. Officers are uniformed and generally patrol the community in pick-up trucks bearing police department insignia. Some Chapala officers have an adequate command of English.

Jalisco traffic police, called *agentes de tránsito*, have jurisdiction on state highways and local thoroughfares. They are uniformed in blue pants and white shirts and may be seen driving motorcycles, white patrol cars and pick-up trucks as well as standing duty to direct traffic or check for parking violations. Agents of the *Policía Federal Preventiva* (PFP-Federal Preventative Police) have authority over all federal highways. They can be recognized by their black and white patrol cars.

Pablo Fernandez de Valle

State and Federal Police—commonly referred to as *judiciales*—enforce higher criminal codes. They may be uniformed (usually black pants, tee-shirts and jackets with corresponding emblems) or dressed in plain clothes. They occasionally turn up in the Chapala area to set up temporary road blocks, called *volantines*, while on the look-out for stolen vehicles, unauthorized weapons and drugs. Unless there is a motive for suspicion these officers generally display extreme courtesy when dealing with foreigners. Although few speak English, they invariably carry proper identification.

Officers of the *Ejército Mexicano* (Mexican Army), dressed in olive drab fatigues, are likewise authorized to set up inspection points to search for arms and drugs. Foreigners are often flagged through these roadblocks, but may be pulled over and asked to get out of their vehicles to allow a search for contraband.

When you find yourself dealing with a Mexican authority, whether it's a policeman, military officer, immigration official or other government employee, the first rule is to remain cheerful, friendly and courteous. Belligerency and any aggressive behavior that may be deemed to threaten the official's realm of power tends to be counter-productive. Never forget that you are a guest in Mexico and must abide by its laws and customs, however much they may clash with those of your native land.

CRIME

Though still a relatively safe place by most standards, the Lake Chapala area has experienced an upswing in the local crime rate in recent years. Observers cite economic hardship, the emergence of youth

To report crimes and other emergencies dial 066 to contact Jalisco's El Palomar hotline center where operators forward dispatches to pertinent first response agencies. To contact local police directly call 376 765-4444 in Chapala; 376 766-1760 in Ajijic; and 387 763-0074 in Jocotepec.

street gangs, a surge in illegal drug use and the evident wealth disparity between native and expatriate inhabitants among caustive factors.

Foreigners are most commonly the victims of non-violent criminal acts such as pick-pocketing, break-ins to their cars or homes, auto theft and ploys by con artists (see Familiar Scams). Muggings, rapes and murders are rare.

While all serious crimes merit filing a report with local police and the *Ministerio Público* (Public Prosecutor's Office), the requisite paperwork can be time-consuming and tedious. The wheels of justice move slowly, with criminal investigations and judicial procedures that can draw out over many weeks, months or even years.

Stolen vehicles must be reported to collect insurance claims and to avoid problems with immigration and customs officials upon departure from Mexico. Replacing lost credit cards, traveler's checks, passports and immigration papers can be a protracted hassle that wreaks havoc on your vacation or tranquil retirement life. Pilfered possessions are rarely recuperated. Common-sense precautions will help you avoid becoming a victim.

Don't wear flashy jewelry and expensive wristwatches or display large amounts of cash in public. Discreetly put your money away before walking out of a bank, ATM module or money exchange. Don't carry around a lot of cash, your credit cards or valuable documents unless you need to. Otherwise, they should be kept stashed away in a safe spot. Photostatic copies of hard-to-replace documents and a back-up list of your card and check numbers can be a godsend in case of loss or theft.

Pick-pockets generally work in crowded, busy public places, particularly street markets and buses. Take extra precautions in bus stations and airports. Keep your luggage close at hand. Thieves prey on tourists who seem confused or distracted and sometimes create diversionary tactics by working in teams. Intoxication is an invitation to disaster, so it's best to measure your consumption of alcohol.

Dale Hoyt Palfrey

Always close windows, lock doors and activate alarms and other anti-theft devices when you park your car. Make sure valuables are secured well out of sight. Study points of vulnerability and talk with neighbors to determine appropriate security measures to protect your home or rental property.

EMERGENCY NUMBERS

Jalisco Emergency Hotline	066
Red Cross Hotline	065
Chapala Red Cross	376 765-2308, 765-2553
Chapala Police	376 765-4444
Ajijic Police	376 766-1760
Jocotepec Police	387 763-0074, 763-0784
Chapala Fire Department-Search & Rescue	376 766-3615

PERSONAL LEGAL TROUBLES

Prudent foreigners don't often experience serious personal run-ins with Mexican law. Carrying unlicensed weapons and drug possession are serious federal offenses that can land you in a Mexican jail. Consular officials have little authority to help you in such cases. Gun permits, issued by the Mexican Army, are very difficult to procure. If you're inclined to use intoxicating substances, stick to *margaritas* and other legal liquid drugs—but don't blame us for the morning after! Public drunkenness and disorderly conduct may land you overnight in the local slammer and result in a moderate fine.

If you do happen to run seriously afoul of the law you will need the services of a Mexican lawyer to help straighten things out. There are many English-speaking lawyers in the Chapala area and nearby Guadalajara. Your situation may be more complicated if you don't have a traveling companion or friend to help with the footwork.

Mexican jails are extremely austere, so you will probably need someone on the outside to provide you with decent meals and basic creature comforts such as a pillow and blanket. Local authorities, who are used to dealing with foreigners in all contexts, may help put you in contact with a representative from your Consulate. Obviously your best bet is to stay out of trouble altogether.

According to Mexican law, a person may be arrested and held up to 72 hours without being charged. Because there is no jury system, all legal cases are resolved by judges. In general Mexican law is arcane. In making statements to legal authorities your words will be paraphrased by the presiding official rather than recorded verbatim. All legal documents and testimony must be filed in Spanish. Any bilingual person you trust can act as an interpreter, but you may need to hire an authorized professional translator to provide certified translations of written legal documents.

We advise avoiding civil lawsuits at all costs. The process is long, the results uncertain, even if you're convinced you're right, and lawyers are usually the only ones who come out ahead. Take heed of the Mexican proverb: *"Mejor un mal arreglo que un buen pleito."* (Better a bad arrangement than a good dispute.)

TRAFFIC LAWS AND ACCIDENTS

Most legal problems involving foreigners are related to traffic violations and automobile accidents. Traffic regulations, established by individual state codes, are on the whole similar to those of other nations.

Road signs, classified as preventative, restrictive and informative, are generally self-explanatory and conform to internationally recognized symbols. Warning signs are diamond-shaped and colored yellow or orange. Most restrictions are posted on white, rectangular signs with indications enclosed in a red circle. Speed limits are posted in kilometers per hour (km/h). A diagonal slash over an arrow means do not drive in the indicated direction. A slashed "E" or a yellow line painted along the curb marks a no-parking zone. Highway directions appear on green signs with white letters. Blue rectangles marked with illustrative icons lead you to nearby services and points of interest.

For complete information on current rules of the road, visit the lakeside office of Jalisco's *Secretaría de Vialidad y Transporte* (SVT Traffic and Motor Vehicles department), located on the Chapala-Ajijic highway in Riberas del Pilar. Foreigners holding immigration papers for permanent or temporary residence (FM-2 and FM-3) are eligible to apply for Jalisco driver's permits. Inquire at the local office for a list of prerequisites and the latest license issuance schedule.

Dale Hoyt Palfrey

Should you become involved in or witness a traffic accident *in the Chapala area, contact local traffic police at 376 766-4747.*

The widespread practice of settling minor traffic violations with an on-the-spot gratuity, known as a *mordida,* makes most foreigners uncomfort-

Jalisco Traffic Cop Whistles Decoded

One long blast	Pay Attention
One short blast	Stop
One long and one short blast	Pay attention and stop
Two short blasts	Keep driving
Three short blasts	Hurry Up
Three long blasts	Everybody stop

able. Some, however, overcome ingrained squeamishness and opt for this expedient tactic. We recommend taking the high road. Avoid arguing with the officer and politely accept the traffic ticket, called a *folio*. Fines should be paid at the nearest *Recaudadora* (state tax office). The established charge is usually less than what you would shell out for a *mordida* and a substantial discount is applied if you pay within five working days.

Should you become involved in or witness a traffic accident in the Chapala area, someone should immediately contact local traffic police at 376 765-4747. The telephone is normally manned 24 hours a day, with an English-speaking officer often on duty. If there are injuries, first call the Chapala *Cruz Roja* (Red Cross) at 376 765-2308 or 376 765-2553. The Jalisco Red Cross also operates a central emergency hotline you can reach by dialing 065. The operator will request the type and location of the accident, name and telephone number of the caller and whatever details can be offered regarding the injured. Do not move the vehicles or injured persons involved until officers or rescue personnel reach the scene.

In traveling Mexico's highways and by-ways you will soon discover whole new meanings to the terms "defensive driving" and "road kill." While courtesy, friendliness and a relaxed attitude towards time are among the most winning characteristics of Mexican people, these traits seem to instantly evaporate once they get behind the steering wheel. Many motorists tend to be oblivious to others or aggressive in the extreme.

Worse still are the hazards presented by free-roaming livestock (cattle, horses and burros) that may bolt suddenly or meander across the roadway. Other latent dangers range from potholes provoked by heavy traffic and summer rains to less than optimum placement of directional signs. While the usual caveat to avoid traveling after sundown applies elsewhere, it is relatively safe to drive around most lakeshore communities where streetlights illuminate the main throughfares. Between the towns, however, roadways can be dark and dangerous. In any case, staying fully alert at all times is imperative for your safety.

AUTO INSURANCE

Mexican auto insurance is a must for all foreign visitors. Be sure that legal insurance is included. This provides a bond to keep you from being incarcerated if you are in an accident where someone is injured or killed. Your policy should include emergency telephone numbers to contact the nearest adjuster who will help handle the details.

Rachel's Insurance 376 765-4316	Insurance on foreign-plated and Mexican vehicles. Open Monday through Friday 9 a.m. to 3 p.m. Av. Hidalgo #236-9, Chapala. rachelin@prodigy.net.mx
Lloyd 376 766-3110 376 766-3598 fax 376 766-3115	Ask for Ma. Teresa Pinedo. Carr. Chapala-Jocotepec #40, Ajijic. seguros@lloyd.com.mx; www.lloyd.com.mx
Parker Agency 376 765-4666 376 765-4070	Hidalgo #52, Riberas del Pilar. sanbornprkr@prodigy.net.mx

FAMILIAR SCAMS

Wily con artists occasionally prey on unsuspecting foreign travelers and residents. Here's a run-down on some common scams that have been detected in the Chapala-Guadalajara region.

Bird-do Cleanup: A friendly person appears suddenly pointing to a fresh splatter of bird poop on your back or shoulder. In the confusion of helping you wipe up the mess—which turns out to be a squirt of yellow mustard—the "aide" or an accomplice lifts your wallet.

Tire Slashing: This rip-off tactic often targets foreign-plated cars parked at the Guadalajara airport and the city's popular shopping complexes (notably outside Walmart, Sam's and Costco). Soon after driving away, you notice you have a flat tire. (You will later discover it has been deliberately punctured or slashed.) As soon as you pull over you are approached by a couple of "Good Samaritans" who jump into the task of changing the damaged tire. While you're distracted with that activity one of the helpers helps himself to belongings left unattended inside your car, leaving you stripped of cash, blank checks and other valuables you were carrying in a purse, brief case or luggage.

ATM and Card Cloning Scams: Be wary of making withdrawals from automatic teller machines after dark and in deserted locations where thieves may be lurking for prey. If your card becomes stuck in the ATM apparatus you may have been set up by swindlers who have installed a fake device that will allow them to retrieve the card and clean out your account after they have detected your PIN number by spying or offering assistance during the problem. Turn down help from strangers and immediately report the loss of the card to the issuer. Some cases of debit and credit card cloning at stores and restaurants have been reported in the past, although most issuing companies nowadays are more efficient at tracking charges and alerting clients to unusual spending patterns.

Investment Ploys: Over the years the Chapala area has attracted some shrewd English-speaking white collar criminals who have taken advantage of expatriate retirees anxious to stretch their finances. More than a few have lost hard-earned savings and real estate properties through cunning investment schemes. Be wary of stratagems involving off-shore accounts, especially those that promise tax evasion. The promoter isn't necessarily trustworthy by virtue of sharing your native language or nationality. If a deal sounds too good to be true, it probably is. It's worth your while to seek independent legal counsel before signing any kind of contract or power of attorney that could put your assets in jeopardy. Likewise, it's wise to get a translation from a reliable outside source before affixing your signature to binding legal documents in Spanish.

JALISCO TRAFFIC COPS

According to the Jalisco Secretariat of Transportation (SVT), 30% of traffic violation fines challenged by motorists are cancelled. They are cancelled if the motorist can prove he did not commit the infraction, or if the SVT has the fine in their database but can't put their hands on the original paperwork or if the ticket was incorrectly filled out by the traffic officer.

To make a complaint about police pulling you over for the *mordida*, or if you witness behavior that might be illicit, write a letter in Spanish, or have a friend help you. Be sure to get the policeman's full name, badge number and a good physical description, note the time and date, the street and cross streets, and accept the ticket. (Pay the ticket within 24 hours and 50% of the fine is removed.) Fax your complaint to El Consejo Cuidadano de Seguridad Pública, Prevención y Readaptación Social at 01 33 3819-2499 or by email to denuncia@jalisco.gob.mx

T.Kendrick

Whether entering Mexico *by air or car, be sure to make photocopies of all your documents, and keep the originals in a safe place. Obtaining relacements can be both time-consuming and expensive.*

T. Kendrick

14

Getting Here and Getting Home

by
DON ADAMS

Mexico is the number one foreign retirement destination for other North Americans; between 15 and 16 million U.S. citizens visit the country every year. Depending on which source you believe, anywhere from 650,000 to 800,000 live here year round. Over 750,000 U.S. Treasury checks are sent to Mexico each year.

Permanent resident figures are not available for Canadian citizens but over 900,000 visit each year and many of them are either full-time residents or live here for six months of the year.

This chapter contains a great deal of information to help make your visit easier and more enjoyable but for those of you who want to spend more time in Mexico, or perhaps move here permanently, you are encouraged to take a look at my website www.headformexico.com. You'll find information about my book, "Head for Mexico—The Renegade Guide", as well as numerous columns I've written for other publications.

Immigration

If you are a U.S. or Canadian citizen and your visit is to a border town, you do not have to acquire a visa or a tourist card if your stay is for 72 hours or less. You must stay within the "border zone", which is the area within 20 to 30 kilometers of the U.S. border, depending upon where you are. Ask the authorities for clarification before you wander too far afield.

TOURIST VISA, TOURIST CARD, FM-T

Although a true visa is not required for entry into Mexico the terms *tourist visa* and *tourist card* both refer to the FM-T or *Forma Migratoria de Turista* issued to visitors by the *Instituto Nacional de Migración.*

U.S. and Canadian citizens traveling as tourists beyond the border zone or entering Mexico by air must have an FM-T or other official documentation. They are available from Mexican consulates, Mexican border crossing points, Mexican tourism offices, airports within the border zone and most airlines serving Mexico. The fee for the tourist card is generally included in the price of a plane ticket for travelers arriving by air. Flight attendants will distribute blank forms for FM-T applications and Customs (*Aduana*) declarations. Instructions are in both English and Spanish. When you arrive at the airport in Guadalajara you'll present your documents to be stamped by the *Migración* officer, or in the case of Customs, retained by them. If you enter by car or on foot stop first at the office of *Migración* to get your FM-T. Don't treat your FM-T casually; you have to surrender it to Mexican authorities when you leave the country.

NECESSARY DOCUMENTATION FOR FM-T

Show your passport (or a notarized birth certificate) and a photo ID such as a driver's license. By December 31, 2006 all visitors from the U.S. who come to Mexico by air and sea will be required to have a passport. By December 31, 2007 a passport will be required for all methods of entry. Until then, U.S. citizens who carry a certified copy of a U.S. birth certificate, a Naturalization Certificate, a Consular Report of Birth Abroad, or Certificate of Citizenship instead of a passport could be subjected to delays or misunderstandings. Driver's permits, voter registration cards, affidavits and similar documents are not sufficient to prove U.S. citizenship when returning home. You can apply for a passport at most post offices, and I suggest you do so. This is also an excellent idea for Canadian citizens. Online information can be found at:
www.ppt.gc.ca/passport_office/contact_us_e.asp for Canadians.
www.travel.state.gov/passport/et/first/first_829.html for Americans.

FM-T's are issued for up to 90 days with a single entry or, as some sources say, for 180 days with multiple entries if you present proof of sufficient funds. However, I've never been asked about my financial status during any entry. If you are driving deep into Mexico the *Migración* official may authorize the full 180 days if you ask for it. If not, any tourist card for less than 180 days may be extended in Mexico by the Mexican immigration service at all international airports, other ports of entry, and in major cities. You must leave Mexico before your tourist card expires or you'll be fined.

BUSINESS TRAVELERS FM-N 30 DAYS

After business travelers arrive in Mexico they must complete and submit Form FM-N 30 days, authorizing them to conduct business for a 30-day period. This doesn't authorize them to be employed in Mexico by a Mexican business, though. That must be arranged through the Mexican employer.

TRAVELERS ON A MISSION

Visitors intending to participate in humanitarian aid missions, human rights advocacy groups or international observer delegations should contact the nearest Mexican consulate or Embassy for guidance on how to obtain the appropriate visa before traveling to Mexico.

If you want to stay longer than 180 days, or plan to conduct business or religious work, special permission is required. Contact the Mexican Embassy or the nearest Mexican Consulate for a visa or permit. Persons conducting religious work on a tourist card are subject to arrest and deportation as are any non-Mexican citizens who engage in internal political activity in Mexico.

REPLACING YOUR FM-T

If you lose your FM-T or any other permit allowing entry into the country you'll have to replace it. In this area the *Migración* office in Chapala is your closest option. While it isn't necessary to hire *gestores*, facilitators or intermediaries to process your immigration paperwork, it can be helpful for newcomers who have little or no grasp of the language. If you are up to the task you can do it yourself at the INM, National Immigration Institute, office in the Chapala City Hall. The process is divided into three parts. One staff member takes information, one delivers documents and the other receives documents. Breaking it down into three sections makes the process must faster. You'll find the office on the second floor.

Chapala City Hall/
Municipio de Chapala
376 765-5600

Visa applications and renewals. Open Wednesdays 10 a.m. to 2 p.m. Madero #202, Chapala.

Or you may want to engage one of the professionals listed below:

Ajijic Legal and Immigration Services
376 766-4777
376 766-4888
Adriana Perez and Kevin Paulini. This Mexican-Canadian team can handle most legal and immigration issues. They can also arrange for U.S. notary services. English spoken. Carretera Ote. #58-G, upstairs, Ajijic. info@ajijiclaw.com www.ajijiclaw.com

Lake Chapala Immigration Services
376 766-4856
Open Monday through Saturday 9 a.m. to 3 p.m. Closed Wednesday. English spoken. 16 de Septiembre #25-B, Ajijic (across from the Lake Chapala Society).

Legal & Immigration Services
376 766-4249
They are willing to make house calls. English spoken. Open Monday through Friday 9 a.m. to 2 p.m. Colón #41-A, Ajijic. Eli4130@prodigy.net.mx

Mago's Office
376 765-3640
fax 376 765-4199
English spoken. Madero #230-1 (upstairs), Chapala. mago@theoffice.net

Notaries

Notarío #5
Sergio Macias
376 765-2740
376 765-4510
or fax after hours.
Litigation, official real estate closings, wills, powers of attorney, certification of documents, bank trust cancellations. English spoken. Hidalgo 245-D, Chapala. notaria5@prodigy.net.mx

Notario #1
Antonio Basulto Ruiz
376 765-2111
376 765-3211
Madero #3266, Chapala.

I recommend that you make copies of your FM-T and all other documents (passport, driver's license, birth certificate) and stash the originals along with your airline tickets and valuables in your hotel safe or other place you deem secure and carry the copies on your person. If you lose your wallet or handbag, you won't have to replace your original documents. At the Ajijic Legal and Immigration Services office listed above you can also get a color copy of pertinent passport pages verified by *Migración* and returned to you with a holographic stamp. This will allow you to travel freely throughout Mexico without your original passport as long as you have your tourist or immigration documents with you.

Entering Mexico by Car

Tourists wishing to drive into Mexico beyond the border zone (*la frontera*) must get a temporary importation permit, the *solicitud de importación temporal de vehículos* or risk having their car confiscated by Mexican customs officials. Offices at the border, many right beside immigration offices at ports of entry, will issue it. The permit will be indexed to your FM-T and as long as your FM-T is valid your permit is valid. A Banjercito branch located at a Mexican Customs office at the port of entry will accept the processing fee which is currently about $30.00 US. Vehicle permits cannot be obtained at checkpoints in the interior of Mexico. Ignore anyone outside any vehicle permit office who offers to get permits without waiting in line. Getting the permit is relatively easy. It's the same whether you're from Canada or the U.S.

To get the car permit you must present originals and copies of:

- evidence of citizenship
- vehicle title
- a registration certificate
- a driver's license issued outside of Mexico—it will be valid in Mexico if it is not expired
- a notarized letter from your lien holder if you do not have clear title, authorizing you to drive the car into Mexico
- a notarized letter from the leasing company if you have a rented or leased vehicle, authorizing you to drive the vehicle into Mexico
- if you are driving a company-owned vehicle, a notarized letter from your employer stating both your connection to the company as well as authorizing you to drive the vehicle into Mexico

Depending on where you cross, you'll need either two or three copies of all of these documents. There will likely be a copy service close to where you apply for the permit, but it never hurts to be prepared. Sometimes they refuse your copies and insist on their own.

You may also apply online for the permit. Go to www.banjercito.com.mx/site/tramiteitv_ing.jsp. Instructions are in English. You can complete the registration process and download the form so that you can present it when you cross. It should hurry things along.

All documents, including credit or debit cards, must be in the name of the person applying for the permit. Be sure to contact your credit card company or bank to let them know you're planning to use your card(s) in Mexico. Each tourist is allowed one vehicle per visit. That may sound strange, but if you're driving down in an RV for example, and towing a smaller vehicle as many do, you need to insure that each vehicle registration shows both names, or each shows a single name so that each of you can apply separately for vehicle permits.

To pay for the permit(s) you need an American Express, Visa, or MasterCard credit card. Although some sources say you can't, I've also used debit cards displaying the Visa or Mastercard logos and had no problems. Those who do not wish to use credit cards will need to post a cash bond of between $200 and $400, depending on the age of the car. The bond guarantees that you remove your vehicle from Mexico. In order to recover this bond or avoid credit card charges, travelers must return to any Banjercito facility just before leaving Mexico. When your permit is issued, a representative will either accompany you to your vehicle and place the sticker on the windshield above the VIN plate on the dashboard, or instruct you to place it yourself. When you leave Mexico ask the official if you should remove the sticker. Some will want to scrape it off themselves.

You must carry all of the original paperwork you receive at the border in the vehicle while you are operating it. When you stop for the night, or if you break down on the road and have to leave the car, take the papers with you. Failure to comply with all Mexican laws can result in vehicle confiscation and a fine of $200 to $500US. Incidentally, only *Aduana* (Mexican Customs) or *Administración Local de Auditoria Fiscal Federal* (Mexican IRS), have the authority to legally confiscate your vehicle.

At www.ajijiclaw.com use the navigation bar button "Forms and Laws" to get to the entry "Police Identification Form". *Licenciada* Adriana Pérez gives you permission to download the bilingual form and suggests you use it any time you feel you have been stopped unfairly or illegally or if anyone attempts to take your vehicle. Keep a few copies in your vehicle and one in your purse or wallet. You might also download both English and Spanish language copies of the documents "Vehicle Importation (Article 106)".

WHO CAN AND CANNOT DRIVE YOUR CAR

Once in Mexico only you, your spouse, your children who have a driver's license, or another non-Mexican with tourist or immigration status at the same or a higher level are authorized to drive your car if you're not in it. A Mexican citizen may drive your vehicle if you are in it. The exception is that a mechanic making repairs may test drive your vehicle during normal business hours without you aboard.

BORDER CROSSING HOURS

The Banjercito facility operating times at each of these ports of entry are 24 hours a day, seven days a week unless otherwise noted. Double check the times at smaller crossings as they may change occasionally.

Arizona

Bisbee/Naco
Douglas/Agua Prieta
Lukeville/Sonoyta - 6 a.m. to midnight, daily
Nogales/Nogales - Deconcini
Nogales/Nogales - Mariposa
San Luis/San Luis Rio Colorado
Sasabee/El Sasabee - 8 a.m. to 8 p.m., daily

California

Calexico/Mexicali
Otay Mesa - 4 a.m. to midnight, daily
San Diego-San Ysidro/Tijuana - (This is the world's busiest port of entry)
San Diego/Tecate - 6 a.m. to midnight, daily

New Mexico

Antelope Wells/El Berrendo - 8 a.m. to 4 p.m., daily - no tourist services available
Columbus/Palomas
Santa Teresa/Jeronimo - 6 a.m. to 10 p.m., daily

Texas

Brownsville/Matamoros - South Padre Island International Bridge - 8 a.m. to midnight, daily
Brownsville/Matamoros - Gateway International Bridge
Roma/Miguel Aleman Brownsville/Matamoros - Los Indios Free Bridge - 6 a.m. to midnight, daily
Brownsville/Matamoros - Veterans International Bridge - 6 a.m. to midnight, daily
Del Rio/Amistad Dam - 10 a.m. to 6 p.m., daily

Del Rio/Ciudad Acuna - International Bridge
Eagle Pass - Bridge I
Eagle Pass - Bridge II
Eagle Pass/Piedras Negras - 7 a.m. to 11 p.m., daily - located in Allende, Coahuila, MX
El Paso/Ciudad Juarez - Bridge of the Americas - largest International Crossing area in the U.S.
El Paso/Ciudad Juarez - Paso del Norte
El Paso/Ciudad Juarez - Ysleta
Fabens - 6 a.m. to 10 p.m., daily
Fort Hancock (for Shawshank Redemption fans) - 6 a.m. to 10 p.m., daily
Harlingen/General. Rodrigo M. Guevedo
Harlingen (Between Harlingen and San Benito - Free Trade Bridge
Laredo/Colombia - 8 a.m. to midnight, daily
Laredo/Nuevo Laredo - Gateway to the Americas
Laredo/Nuevo Laredo - Lincoln Juarez Bridge
McAllen/Reynosa
Pharr/Reynosa - 6 a.m. to midnight, daily - 3.2 miles (This is the longest border crossing in the world.)
Presidio/Ojinaga
Progresso/Nuevo Progresso
Progresso/Los Indios International Bridge - 6 a.m. to 12 a.m.
Rio Grande City/Los Ebanos - Rio Grande City Bridge - 7 a.m. to 12 a.m., daily
Rio Grande City/Los Ebanos Ferry Crossing - 8 a.m. to 4 p.m., daily
Roma/Miguel Aleman - Falcon Heights Internacional Bridge - a.m. to 9 p.m.
Roma/Miguel Aleman - Rio Grande Internacional Bridge - 7 a.m. to 12 a.m.
Roma/Miguel Aleman - Roma International Bridge

To see how long you might expect to wait to cross at these locations go to http://apps.cbp.gov/bwt.

AUTOMOBILE INSURANCE

Your U.S. or Canadian insurance isn't valid in Mexico. In many places in Mexico insurance is not required. But in the state of Jalisco, in which Lake Chapala is located, it is required. You have several options for buying insurance for your south of the border trip.

AAA (www.aaa.com) or **CAA** (www.caa.ca), if you're a member.

Carmen Garcia AIG Insurance 376 766-3974	Colón #1, Ajijic. E-mail Garcia_615@hotmail.com
Lloyd	www.lloyd.com.mx or e-mail seguros@lloyd.com.mx
International Insurance Group, Inc.	Flagstaff, AZ, www.internationalpro.com or e-mail jim.labelle@mexpro.com
Parker Insurance Brokers 376 765-4666	Hidalgo #52, Riberas del Pilar. E-mail sanbornprkr@prodigy.net.mx
Sanborn's Insurance	www.sanbornsinsurance.com, or e-mail info@sanbornsinsurance.com

These agents and companies can issue policies and send your new policy via e-mail, fax, or surface mail before you leave home. If you decide to wait until you get to the border to purchase insurance, there will be plenty of agencies in the bigger border towns advertising their services.

As a former adjuster I'm betting that you've never read your auto insurance policy. When you receive your Mexican policy I suggest that you do so. There will be a "Statutory Disclosure For Insurance Coverage In Mexico" included with policies purchased from U.S.-based companies. Here are things you need to know:

- Loss or damage to the under-parts of the vehicle as a result of overloading or rough roads is not covered.
- Pilferage or partial theft of parts and/or accessories isn't covered. Theft coverage is provided only if the entire vehicle is stolen. Vandalism is also excluded. Contact International Insurance Group about a policy providing coverage.
- Trailers or boats that are towed must be listed on the policy in order to be covered. If the trailers or boats are not listed, there is no coverage for either the unlisted trailers, boats nor the towing vehicle, even if listed.
- If you return to the U.S. without an adjuster's report, coverage is void.

HOW MUCH DOES IT COST TO DRIVE FROM LAREDO TO GUADALAJARA?

Prices change so often that this one is almost impossible to answer. It's approximately 1,700 kilometers so you may be able to figure your gasoline cost if you know the MPG rating of your vehicle. Gas prices change frequently but in April 2005 regular, 87 octane gasoline (Pemex's Magna) cost approximately $2.60 US a gallon.

Tolls will be about $125 to $150 US. I suggest you use Mexico's excellent *"cuota"* or toll road system. If you're driving from anywhere in Texas take what may look like a longer route to Lake Chapala. Get to highway 57 south of Saltillo as soon as you can and take toll roads through San Luis Potosí, Aguascaliente, and Guadalajara. Highway 54 through Zacatecas looks much shorter but it's very mountainous and winding, as well as two-lane much of the way. I avoid it.

You'll need *pesos* to pay your tolls. Change several hundred dollars before you leave the border. If needed, you can use your debit card or credit card to withdraw cash at an ATM along your route.

There are a number of hotels and motels near most border crossings so you're on your own with this choice. And the cost of a place to spend the night en route will likewise be dependent upon your choice of roads and where you enter into the country. For hotels on the north side of the border visit www.hotels.com and book on-line. For hotels south of the border go to www.allmexicohotels.com. Type in the town you want and press the return key.

I suggest that you carry a cooler with both food and water. If you break down on the road they'll be very useful and comforting. I especially recommend lots of sodas iced down in a cooler—read on to discover why.

FUEL AND OTHER AUTOMOTIVE NECESSITIES

At this time Pemex is your only choice for gasoline and diesel fuel in Mexico. In many isolated areas you may find someone selling gas from a 55 gallon drum but it all comes from one source, Pemex. They sell 87 octane Magna sin, regular unleaded at the green pumps, and 92 octane Premium unleaded. Diesel pumps will be located away from the gas pumps so trucks can get to them easier.

You'll find auto products in the cages beside the gas pumps. Injector cleaner, windshield washer fluid, anti-freeze (coolant), oil, octane booster, and brake fluid are available at most stations.

Someone, and not always the uniformed attendant, might offer to wash your windshield. It's rare that anyone will volunteer to check your oil or the air pressure in your tires. If they do, you should offer a small tip, perhaps 2 or 3 *pesos*.

And even though Pemex is building many more stations, it's still a good idea to fill up anytime your gas gauge registers half full.

TROUBLE ON THE ROAD

In the event that you do experience car trouble try to get off the road. If there's no shoulder do the best you can to get away from traffic. Raise the hood and settle in for a wait. On all main highways and many secondary roads the Green Angel repair trucks patrol constantly during daylight hours. You can either wait for them or call for assistance. If you've had your cell phone programmed to work in Mexico you may be able to call 066 for help. If not, and you can reach a land line dial the same number. This nationwide emergency number does not always work so you need these numbers for the 24 hour emergency hotline: 01 55 5250-0123 or 01 800 903-9200. If those don't get you through try 01 55 5250-8221 extension 130/297. You'll need to be able to tell the operator, who may not speak English, exactly where you are. Try this:

I don't speak Spanish.	*No habla Español.*
I have a problem with my car	*Tengo una problema con el coche.*
I can't drive it.	*No puedo manejarlo.*
The car is a black Jeep Cherokee	*El coche es un Jeep Cherokee negro.*
Send the Green Angels to:	*Envien ustedes los Angeles Verdes a:*
Highway (or tollroad) (57D)	*la autopista (cuota) cincuenta y siete*
10 kilometers N,S,E,W,	*Diez kilómetros al norte de; sur de, al oeste de; al este*
of (the name of the town)	*de Saltillo*

Toll roads are shown as numbers followed by a D. 57D is a toll road, called in Spanish a *cuota* (KWO-ta).

All Green Angel drivers are proficient mechanics and should have some English. They carry a full inventory of hand tools and a few common universal spare parts. If your problem is minor, and one of you has the needed spare parts, they can usually effect repairs on the spot. I suggest that you carry spare v-belts, a fuel filter, a thermostat and gasket, radiator hoses, and a funnel in case you need gas. Green Angel services are free, except for any parts, fluids, or gasoline they provide but a tip is always appreciated. And you can always offer a cold soda from your cooler.

And the Highway Patrol is out on major byways at all hours of the day and night.

Often another traveler or a nearby resident will stop and offer help before the Angels arrive. Breakdowns are fairly common so you won't be a novelty. If you believe it's necessary, you can ask for a tow truck (*grúa),* or a mechanic (*mecánico).* A breakdown might be your introduction to the world-famous Mexican friendliness and helpfulness. If help is provided always offer to pay afterwards, but be prepared to deal with a refusal. You can still offer that cold drink.

TRAFFIC STOPS BY THE MEXICAN ARMY

It's not uncommon to encounter roadblocks on some of the highways in Mexico. These are usually manned by Mexican soldiers in green fatigue-type uniforms. The soldiers are unfailingly courteous. They're also curious. The stops are made for several reasons. They are usually looking for guns or ammunition, drugs, illegal aliens, or other contraband. They pull vehicles out of traffic at random so don't feel threatened. Usually the soldier who approaches to speak wants to know where you came from (*de donde viene?)* and where you're going (*á donde va?)* The dialogues below will help you respond.

I am a tourist.	*Soy turista.*
I don't speak Spanish.	*No habla Español*
I am coming from Laredo (or Nogales, etc.)	*Vengo de Laredo*
I'm going to Chapala.	*Voy a Chapala*

The response will often be a smile, a nod, and *"Si, Jalisco!"*

They may or may not want to inspect your vehicle. In either case, cooperate. If they open your cooler it is not out of line to offer cold drinks to all of them if you have enough. It isn't a bribe; it's a gesture of appreciation to young men in the service of their country.

TRAFFIC STOPS BY OTHER AUTHORITIES

You may also encounter occasional temporary inspection stations set up by *Aduana,* Mexican Customs agents. They usually dress in civilian clothes but drive white pick-ups with their logo painted on the doors. At other times the Federal Judicial Police may stop you. These are not the dark green and khaki-clad Mexican Highway Patrolmen driving black and white sedans with light bars, but very serious "Men in Black" wearing black fatigues and baseball caps. Be *very* cooperative with these gentlemen. They are usually well armed, business-like, and very polite. Play it by ear when offering one of those sodas.

TRAVELING WITH CHILDREN

To prevent international child abduction, parents of minor children (under 18 years old) should carefully document their legal custody.

- If a minor child is traveling with only one parent, the absent parent should provide a notarized consent letter.
- If only one parent has legal custody, he or she should present proof of custody.
- If a minor child is traveling to Mexico alone or in someone else's company, both parents (or the sole documented custodial parent) should provide a notarized letter.
- If a child traveling to Mexico has a different last name from the mother and/or father, the parents should be prepared to prove to the airlines and Mexican authorities, with a birth certificate or adoption decree, that they are the parents.

Mexican entry regulations require Spanish translations of all legal documents, including notarized consent decrees and court agreements. Enforcement of this provision is not always consistent, though, and English-language documents are usually sufficient. If this proves not to be the case, translators and notaries are available near most border crossings.

DRIVING TO MEXICO WITH YOUR PETS

To legally import your pet you must have a U.S. Interstate and International Certificate of Health signed by a veterinarian. This document should show that the pet has been inoculated against rabies, hepatitis, pip, and leptospirosis. The U.S. Embassy website states that you must have this document issued within 15 days of crossing the border and it must show that the required inoculations have been given within that 15-day period. I've never been asked for any paperwork on my traveling companions but others, including Teresa, have been asked to show papers. This is usually not a problem but get the form anyway. Regulations limit you to one dog or cat when entering Mexico but Teresa and I have crossed with as many as three dogs and I made a crossing with two cats and a dog.

The biggest concern some have is which hotels in Mexico will allow pets to stay in their room. Jane Wilkinson at http://gringodog.home.comcast.net/pet-friendly.htm has the only list of hotels that I'm aware of and kindly gave permission for this referral. She's planning an update so if you have any questions or suggestions you can contact her at jrwilkinson@attglobal.net.

You can check for more information about driving in Mexico at www.customs.ustreas.gov/travel/travel.htm, http://aphis.usda.gov/oa/pubs/petravel.html, www.inspection.qc.ca, or http://canadaonline.about.com/cs/customs.

Once you're in Ajijic here's an excellent doctor. Look at http://animalcare.ws/news/petstomexico.htm. Dra. Luz Maria Pérez and husband Hugo Hidalgo take care of Pirata for me. Animal Care, Mobile phone 01 33 346-6024, Carretera Pte. #915-A, El Bajio, Ajijic.

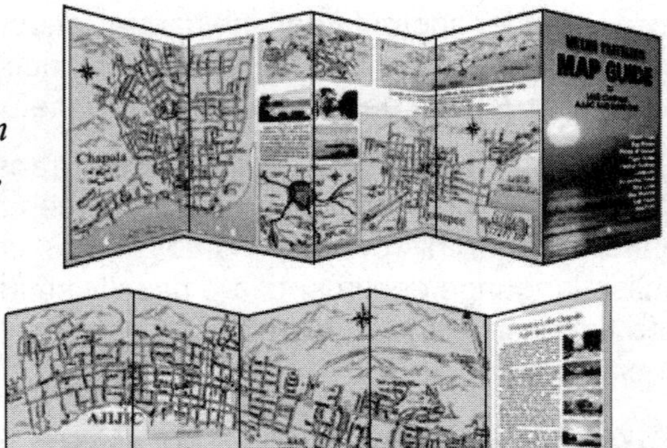

A map of the northshore of Lake Chapala, *adapted from Tony Burton's original, is included with this guide.*

MAPS AND DIRECTIONS

If your local bookstore can't provide you with an acceptable map of Mexican roads you'll be able to find maps, including the excellent Guia Roji brand, at Pemex stations and perhaps other places along the border. Also look on www.mexicomaps.com and www.maps-of-mexico.com

WHERE TO STAY IN MEXICO

The best resource for finding hotels in Mexico before you leave home is www.allmexicohotels.com. Type in the name of town you want and press the return key. A list will pop up with plenty of information including prices, location and so forth. If your car is fully loaded be sure the hotel offers secure parking or a night watchman. Take your electronics into your room and all original papers and passports. If something happens to your vehicle during the night you'll have all the paperwork in your possession.

CONSULATES AND CONSULAR AGENCIES ALONG YOUR ROUTE

Americans who need assistance enroute to the Lake Chapala area can contact agents in these cities.

Ciudad Acuña	877 772-8661
Ciudad Juárez	625 611-3000
Hermosillo	662 217-2375
Manzanillo	314 335-0605 or 334-0977
Matamoros	868 812-4402
Mazatlán	669 916-5889
Monterrey	818 345-2120
Nogales	631 313-4820
Nuevo Laredo	867 714-0512
Piedras Negras	867 788-0343
Puerto Vallarta	322 222-0069
Reynosa	899 923-9331
San Luis Potosí	444 811-7802/7803
San Miguel de Allende	415 152-2357/0068
Tijuana	664 622-7400

Canadians who need assistance enroute to the Lake Chapala area can contact these agents. The e-mail addresses are (name of city)@canada.org.mx. Website updates and names and fax numbers are available at www.canada.org.mx.

Guadalajara	33 3615-6215/6270
Mazatlán	669 913-7320
Monterrey	818 344-2753/3200
Puerto Vallarta	322 293-0098/0099
Tijuana	664 684-0461

Some of these contacts are not on direct routes from the border to the Lake Chapala area but since many visitors sightsee along the way, I've included some of the coastal contacts.

LEAVING MEXICO

Leaving Mexico and crossing the U.S. border requires that you have all of your immigration, pet, and vehicle documents in your possession. At the border you will turn in your vehicle sticker at a Banjercito facility before crossing into the U.S. You do not need to leave Mexico at the same port you entered. Failure to return the window sticker may prevent you from entering Mexico with *any* vehicle in the future and may result in a fine if you attempt to re-enter the country at a later date.

LEAVING MEXICO WITHOUT YOUR CAR

If you need to leave the country without your vehicle for any reason, contact an attorney who can write up a notarized letter stating that you have not left your car in Mexico illegally. In the event your vehicle was totaled in a wreck, get the section of windshield to which your permit is attached and take it with you.

U.S. AND CANADIAN CUSTOMS

Customs officials will want to verify your citizenship before allowing you to enter their country. They will ask you if you have anything to declare. If you're flying out of Mexico the flight attendant will give you a Customs Declaration Form to fill out. Keep all receipts for purchases made in Mexico. Certain U.S. states may charge a tax on alcoholic

> The numbers for the Guadalajara airport, 01 33 3688-5248 or 01 33 3818-6100 can be used to inquire if flights are arriving and departing on time. However, if your flight is national you probably won't get an English-speaking person on the line. You may, if the flight you're checking on is an international one, but don't count on it.

beverages you bring. These folks are doing a difficult and thankless job, so please cooperate with them. This is a non-threatening procedure. And very often you'll hear "Welcome home." I love that.

Entering Mexico by Air

If your ticket is booked to Guadalajara, you'll land at the Miguel Hidalgo International Airport between Guadalajara and Lake Chapala. This is not a huge airport so entry is almost foolproof. You'll deplane and board a bus which will take you to the terminal. Uniformed attendants will direct you through the doors leading to the *Migración* booths. Look at the signs to determine which line is for your status as a tourist. When you get to the booth, present the forms you filled out on the plane, along with your passport or other identification. Some agents will also ask for your return ticket so keep it handy.

After your FM-T is stamped and returned to you, step into the terminal. You'll be in a large room so you can't get lost. Directly ahead is the luggage carousel. You know what to do. After you claim your luggage head for the agents standing beside the traffic lights on short poles. There is a button on each pole that the agent will instruct you to push. If the light is green you'll be allowed to pass and you'll be free to exit into the main terminal where friends, family or car rental agencies are waiting. If the customs light shows red you'll be directed past it to a set of tables where your bags will be inspected. If you are carrying something that requires you to pay a duty, the customs agents will direct you to offices a dozen steps to the left. Pay the duty and exit into the main terminal. There will be baggage handlers there who can assist you with your bags. They will have uniforms, name tags hanging around their necks, and two-wheeled dollies. Tip them 5 to 10 *pesos* per bag, depending upon your nature and how helpful you feel they've been.

If you're not being met at the airport you can walk outside under the covered terrace and locate the taxi ticket booths. The fares are set by law and all drivers abide by them. Buy a ticket from the attendant and then board the taxi you're directed to. Give your receipt to the driver. Tips are not necessary but you may feel one is appropriate if the driver helps with your luggage or offers other assistance. If you do not have *pesos* there is a money exchange kiosk inside the terminal and an ATM machine that will dispense *pesos*. Don't tip with U.S. or Canadian coins because the recipient can neither spend them, nor exchange them at the bank.

Many of these drivers are not familiar with the Chapala area so if possible, have the B&B where you'll be staying provide you with directions to their front door in both Spanish and English. At the very least have the telephone number handy so you can call for directions if needed.

FLYING WITH YOUR PETS

There are a number of factors involved with this process so I suggest you call the airline as far in advance as possible to determine if this is an option for you. Some airlines provide this service and others don't. For more information go to the website of the Humane Society of the United States at www.hsus.org and also check out www.solutionsabroad.com/a_petsmexico.asp#airline. The only U.S. Interstate Commerce Commission licensed carrier of pets is:

Cosmopolitan Canine Carriers, Inc. 1-800-243-9105 fax 203 656-2527, petrelo@caninecarriers.com; www.caninecarriers.com

AIRLINE INFORMATION

I have an unproven suspicion that airlines change their numbers frequently. Each time I call I seem to get yet another set of numbers. Teresa checked these with Telmex information in late 2004. Note that these numbers are good during office hours. The 800 numbers may get you an agent after working hours but he or she may not speak English. Get a Spanish-speaking friend to help you if the language is out of your reach. Remember that you can always dial 040 for information. Ask "*Deme el número de teléfono de* Continental Airlines*, por favor*." When the operator asks, *"de donde?"* Say "Guadalajara." The system is automated so the number is repeated twice. If you're not comfortable with your level of Spanish you may want to write down the pronunciation of the numerals from 1 to 10. Dial these numbers if you are in Mexico.

Aero California	01 800 237-6200, 01 33 3616-2525
Aeromar	01 800 490-9090
AeroMexico	01 800 021-4000, 01 33 387-7000
Aerolineas Internacionales	01 800 465-2222, 01 33 3688-5817
Aeroliteral	01 800 711-3256
Air Alaska	01 33 3688-5403
America West Express	01 33 3688-5449

American Airlines	01 33 3616-4044
Aviacsa	01 800 007-4783
Continental Airlines	01 33 3647-4251, 01 33 3688-6134
Delta Airlines	01 33 3688-5772
Lineas Aereas Azteca	01 800 229-8322, 01 33 3688-5965
Mexicana	01 800 502 2000, 01 33 387-7070
United Airlines	01 33 3616-7993

AIRPORT CAR RENTALS

Avis	01 33 3688-5528
Optima Rent a Car	01 33 3688-5360
Hertz	01 33 3688-5403
Budget	01 33 3688-5531
Dollar Rent a Car (Limousines also)	01 33 3688-5659

LAKE CHAPALA AREA CAR RENTALS

Lakeside Car Rental
376 766-3732
Fernando@ajijiccarrental.com;
www.ajijiccarrental.com

Linea Professional
376 766-2555
fax 376 766-0066
letivera@laguna.com.mx;
www.fotolog.net/lineaprof
Recommended.

S&S Auto
376 765-4800
ssauto@laguna.com.mx

Sunset Rent-a-Car
376766-4771
sunset_rentacar@hotmail.com;
www.lakeside.com.mx

Immigration Photos

Studio Zaragoza
376 765-3495
376 765-4240

The best place to go for photos for official documents of all kinds: FM-2, FM-3, passports, etc. They also do black and white, and color photography, as well as videos of special occasions. Samples of sizes required for various purposes are displayed on their desk. Open Monday through Saturday 9 a.m. to 2 p.m., 4 p.m. to 8 p.m. López Cotilla #290, Chapala. *Highly Recommended.*

Ricardo Zaragoza
376 765-5442
Passport and document photographer. Open Monday through Saturday 10 a.m. to 2 p.m., 4 p.m. to 8 p.m., Friday 10 a.m. to 2 p.m. Miguel Martínez #534, Chapala.

Official Translators

These translators are certified to produce documents acceptable for use in any legal situation.

Ana Isabel Castellanos Aquilar
376 765-301
Translates legal documents from English to Spanish. Flavio Romero del. V. #393, Chapala.

Lorenza Castiello
376 765-4227
Av. de la Ribera #186-A, Riberas del Pilar. lorezac@prodigy.net.mx

Lisa Harrison
376 766-1459
angloazteca@yahoo.com; www.chapala.com/lisaharrison.html

Lic. Sergio A. Macias Aldana
376 765-2740
376 765-4510
Attorney and translator. Hidalgo 245-D, Chapala.

Facilitators/Interpreters

Ricardo Mendoza Gracian
376 766-4771
Bonded tour guide and help with interpretation, sunset_rentacar@hotmail.com; www.lakeside.com.mx

Justus Hauser
376 763-5333
fax 376 763-5335
Personal assistance and interpreter services for visits to notaries, the IMSS, doctors, mechanics, etc. Can arrange for U.S. notary service. English, Spanish, German spoken. justushauser@hotmail.com; www.all-in-1-services.com

Miguel Zamora Perez
376 766-3349
376 766-4082
01 33 3185-0392
This "Man Friday" can be hired to drive you to Guadalajara for a variety of errands, help you move furniture and appliances, assist you with negotiations and translations for IMSS applications, driver's licenses, DIF applications, business and consumer relat-

ed issues, and with the folks at the police department and city hall. He'll supply references.

Embassies and Consulates in Mexico

The Guadalajara consular region oversees citizens in the states of Jalisco, Colima, Aguascalientes and Nayarit.

American Citizens Services Section
01 33 385-2700

The American Citizens Services issues passports and registers the birth of children to U.S. citizens. They provide notary service for documents that need certification for business in the U.S. They handle the federal form needed to register to vote, and provide state voter information. This office will process a report of death, a federal requirement, used to settle estates. If the deceased has no heirs, the Consulate is required by law to take custody of the personal effects of the deceased and act as conservator of the property until a legal heir can be found. This section can also provide a list of physicians (not necessarily a recommendation) of English-speaking doctors in case of illness. If a citizen becomes destitute, they can help them contact family in the States to wire funds enabling them to get to the border by bus. This section also monitors any violent crimes against U.S. citizens. Victims of

Dale Hoyt Palfrey

crime must first file a report, a *denuncia*, to the local police and then give the official file number to the Consulate. If a citizen is imprisoned, staff will visit them regularly while they're incarcerated to relay information, but cannot interfere with the legal process. They can recommend lawyers, much like they do physicians.

The Federal Benefits Unit The Federal Benefits Unit handles Social Security, veterans' benefits, and several other pension-type programs. They recommend that you register with them but they keep all information strictly confidential. Services of other units are available Monday through Friday 8 a.m. to 11a.m., except on Mexican and U.S. holidays. Use the Lopez Cotilla entrance for both.

The U.S. Consular building is at the corner of Progreso and Lopez Cotilla in Guadalajara.

U.S. State Department Travel Website is at www.travel.state.gov. This website is easy to use to learn about what is required to travel to a foreign country and how to locate embassies. *Recommended.*

TO REGISTER YOUR TRAVEL PLANS ONLINE

To register your travel plans online go to:

U.S. citizens: http://travelregistration.state.gov

Canadian citizens: www.voyage.gc.ca/consular-e/sos/rocapage-.htm

If you lose your passport while traveling it is imperative that you immediately contact your embassy or the nearest consulate. When calling numbers in Mexico use this form:

From the U.S. or Canada:	011-52 + 10 digit number
Long distance from within Mexico:	01 + the 10 digit number
Local calling area:	the last seven digits or eight digits if you are calling in Guadalajara, Mexico City or Monterrey.

Consulate of Canada

Hotel Fiesta Americana #30, Lopez Mateos and Vallarta
Guadalajara, Jalisco, C.P. 44100 Mexico
01 33 3615-6270, 01 33 3615-5642, 01 33 3615-6266,
fax: 01 33 3615-8665; guadalajara@canada.org.mx

Consulate of Great Britain & Northern Ireland

Jesus de Rojas #20, Colonia de los Pinos
Zapopan, Jalisco
01 33 3432-2296; simon@cybercable.net.mx

Consulate of the United States

Progreso #175, Guadalajara, Jalisco
C.P. 44100 Mexico
01 33 3825-2700, 01 33 3825-2491, fax: 01 33 3826-5553
consuladousa@megared.net.mx; www.embassy-mexico.gov/guadalajara

Canadian Embassy in Mexico City

Schiller #529, Colonia Polanco
Mexico, D.F. 11560 Mexico
01 55 5724-7900, fax: 01 55 5724-7980; www.dfait-maeci.gc.ca/mexico-city/menu-en.asp

Embassy of the United States

Paseo de la Reforma #305, Colonia Cuauhtemoc
Mexico, D.F. 06500 Mexico
01 55 5080-2000, fax: 01 55 5511-9980; ccs@usembassy.net.mx
www.usembassy-mexico.gov

How Much Can I Bring in Duty-Free?

When entering Mexico by air or sea, customs allows each person to bring $300 US worth of gifts into the country in addition to personal items.

When entering Mexico by land, customs allows each person to bring $50 US worth of gifts into the country in addition to personal items.

How Much Can I Take Back Duty-Free?

When you leave Mexico and return to Canada you are allowed to take out $750 CAD worth of gifts duty free after 7 days or more out of the country. Do not count the day you left, but count your return day. Dates matter, not time of day. www.cbsa-asfc.gc.ca/E/pub/cp/rc4044/rc4044-.html#5174_20306

When you leave Mexico and return to the U.S. you are allowed to take out $800 US worth of gifts duty free per 30-day period. You have to have been out of the country for at least 48 hours. www.customs.gov/xp/cgov/travel/vacation/kyg/dutyfree_exemption.xml

Moving Companies

After experiencing the beauty and the great climate of the area many visitors decide to live here for extended periods of the year. Some want to move their possessions down. Here are several local companies that can help simplify that process for you. You can also arrange international moves through major carriers in the U.S. and Canada.

Strom Moving of Ajijic
376 766-4049

Kathy Strom wrote a booklet explaining every step of your move, including your responsibilities as well as theirs. They can also drive your vehicle into and out of Mexico for you. *Highly Recommended.* strom@laguna.com.mx; www.strommoving.com

The Movers Lakeside
376 766-3571

themoverslakeside@yahoo.com

Mendoza Balderas Moving, S.A.C.V.
01 33 3810-4859
01 33 3811-2541
01 33 3810-4133

Calle 7 #388, Colonia F.F.C.C., Guadalajara, Jalisco., C.P. 44440, Mexico, sales@marcelabalderas.com

Mundanzas Gou
01 33 3666-1404
fax 01 33 3666-1406

Calle Altos Hornos #1477, Guadalajara. gougdl@megared.net.mx

LOCAL MOVERS

Barbara's Bazaar
376 766-1824

Independencia #7, Ajijic.

Agustín Sanches Hidalgo #35, Ajijic.
376 766-1472
01 33 3489-2397

NOTES

Appendix

Important Numbers

TELMEX

Information	040
Time	030
Repairs	050
Ajijic Office	376 766-2131, 376 766-2132

EMERGENCIES

Emergency Number	066 (similar to 911). (080 is being phased out)
Green Angels Road Service	Cellular: 3668-1800, wait for recording, then 1+31489 Lakeside and the Guadalajara area (if calling from a non-cellular phone dial 01 33 3668-1800 and then the extension 1+31489)
Red Cross Emergency	065
Red Cross	376 765-2308, 376 765-2553

POLICE

Police Ajijic	376 766-1760
Chapala	376 765-4444, 376 765-2821
Jocotepec	387 763-0006, 387 763-0074
Police Investigation (*Agencia del Ministerio Público Investigadora general de justicia del estado de Jalisco)* Chapala 376 765-2267 376 765-2415 Jocotepec 387 763-1386	These detectives work out of the *Ministerio Publico* offices in Chapala & Jocotepec. Their job is to question suspects and witnesses, take fingerprints which are sent to Ocotlán for matching. After a robbery or a break in, once the police have been called, nothing should be touched until the

Not just the stuff of thriller novels, the International Criminal Police Organization (Interpol) was created in 1923, and is the world's largest police organization. Mexico is one of the 181 countries who are a part of Interpol's network. Based in Lyon, France, Interpol helps member countries combat world crime by maintaining a "watch list" of criminals, including terrorists (Osama bin Laden is one of them), and by tracking organized drug and weapons smuggling. In October 2004 Interpol reported that "women trafficking" is on the rise. Hundreds of thousands of women in Mexico, Latin America, western Europe and Japan are working involuntarily as prostitutes after being tricked into believing they would receive legitimate jobs, such as waitressing and babysitting. If you suspect that women are being duped in this way or that terrorists or other criminals are trying to cross Mexico's borders, call Interpol. If you should happen to sight bin Laden, call Interpol and then log on to www.rewardsforjustice.net and collect the U.S. State Department's $25 million reward.

Ministerio Público detectives arrive. From then on they are in charge of the case. Their hours are roughly 9 a.m. to 3 p.m., 6 p.m. to 8 p.m. Monday through Friday. In Jocotepec, they are open Saturday and Sunday from 10 a.m. to 2 p.m. for matters involving traffic accidents.

Traffic Police (*Tránsito*) 376 765-4747 Chapala

Livestock on Roadways 376 765-5600

Lake Chapala Harbormaster 376 765-2230 (Lopez Cotilla #191, Across from Cristianía Park).

CRIME HOTLINES

Interpol 01 55 5346-2541 Mexico City

PREVENTEL Security Hotline 01 800 713-2017 (in English, maybe). State hotline to report kidnappings, robberies, criminal gangs, sales of illegal drugs, prostitution, police who give inadequate or improper service, or

An Ajijic-Chapala Fireman relaxes at the station in Chula Vista.

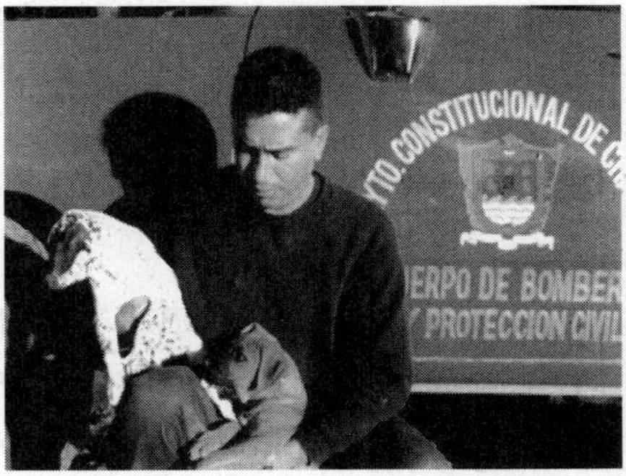

Dale Hoyt Palfrey

places where illegal merchandise might be stored. preventel@jalisco.gob.mx

FIRE DEPARTMENT AND RESCUE

Ajijic-Chapala Civil Rescue and Firemen/ *Protección Civil y Bomberos*

376 766-3615. Prominently located in upper Chula Vista, this branch of fire-fighters and rescuers respond not only to emergencies in Ajijic and Chapala, but also the villages that lie to the north: along the *Libramiento* to Atotonilquillo and northeast: Santa Cruz de la Soledad, San Nicolás, Tlachichilco, Mezcala. They're available 24 hours a day.

Jocotepec Civil Rescue and Firemen/*Protección Civil y Bomberos*

387 763-1804, Director Gerardo Camarena Sanchez directs this branch of service for emergencies. Their facility includes a fire truck, seven trained firemen and nine volunteers. Available 24 hours a day, 365 days a year.

When do I call Civil Rescue?

Civil Rescue and Firemen (*Protección Civil y Bomberos*) should be called for the following emergencies: accidents on highways or in the home, drownings, gas leaks, fires, bees nests and other natural disasters. They will administer first aid and help coordinate other officials.

Donato Guerra #4, just east of Hidalgo Sur and south of Vicente Guerrero, Jocotepec.

24-HOUR AMBULANCE

Chapala

Red Cross	376 765-2553, 376 765-2308
Clínica Ibarra	376 765-4805
Clínica Municipal	376 765-5421

Ajijic

Clínica Ajijic	376 766-0500, 376 766-0662

Riberas del Pilar

Clínica Máscaras	376 765-4805

Jocotepec

Clínica Municipal	387 763-1920

IMSS CLINICS

IMSS Clinic Chapala	376 765-2240, Niñoes Heroes #59
IMSS Clinic Jocotepec	387 763-0386, Donato Guerra #95. Four doctors service this branch of IMSS. It is suggested that patients arrive a half hour early for appointments. Small drugstore on premises. Open Monday through Friday 8 a.m. to 11 a.m., 2 p.m. to 5 p.m. Saturday and Sundays for emergencies only. Donato Guerra #95, south of Vicente Guerrero and west of Hidalgo Sur, Jocotepec. Some English spoken.

24-HOUR TOWING (*GRUA*)

Ajijic, Chapala	376 765-4280
Jocotepec	387 763-2767
Guadalajara	24-hour service. 01 33 3605-5086
Tonalá	24-hour service. 01 33 3602-0458

LOCKSMITHS(*CERRAJERIA*)

Ajijic	376 766-3003 for house calls
Chapala	376 765-3252
San Antonio Tlay.	376 766-1074
Jocotepec	01 33 3448-8253

ELECTRICITY

Electricity (CFE) Chapala	376 765-2509, 765-2389, 765-2337
Jocotepec	Call Chapala numbers above
Electrical Emergencies/Complaints	071, 765-3966, 765-3961 (Includes Jocotepec area)

ORDERING GAS

"Quiero ordenar gas, por favor."	I'd like to order gas, please
"Tiene un tanque estacionario?"	Do you have a stationary tank?
"Si."	Yes.
"Cual es su dirección?"	What is your address?
"En San Antonio, Banderas numero diez."	In San Antonio, Banderas #10.
"Vamos a pasar en la mañana (ó dos horas)."	We will come by in the morning (or in two hours.)

GAS FOR COOKING

Gas Licuado	376 766-0538. Call for delivery glicuado@gal.icanet.net.mx
Gas Sol	376 767-1060. Call for delivery
Gas Z	376 766-0790. Call for delivery www.grupozeta.com

If your gas is delivered in cylinders, post a sign saying "gas" on your door; trucks that patrol the streets will stop.

Propane Gas for Grills and Motor Homes

Gasolinera Guadalajara/ *Gas Licuado* 376 763-5089 (not long distance from Ajijic). Bring your small propane tanks for filling. Open Monday through Saturday 9 a.m. to 6 p.m., Sunday 9 a.m. to 3 p.m. Carr. Camino Antiguo Ixtlahuacan S/N (*sin numero*, no number). From the old railroad station in Chapala drive 3 miles toward Vista del Lago golf course. At 3 miles turn left on an unmarked road (just opposite the the *Acueducto Chapala,* Guadalajara Pumping Station). Go four tenths of a mile down a gravel/dirt road and turn left when you see big blue metal gates. Park and walk through the person door in the blue metal gates. The office is toward the end of the block of buildings on your right.

Propane Gas for Converted Autos

Z-Gas This 24-hour service station is across from El Torito grocers on the Carr. Pte. in Ajijic.

WATER

Bottled drinking water is delivered by truck. Post a sign saying "agua" or "Aga" the award-winning brand from Jocotepec, on your door and a truck will stop.

Water Commission (SIMAPA) 376 766-0423 Ajijic, 376 765-2926 Chapala. (Also offices in San Antonio Tlay., San Nicolás, Santa Cruz de la Soledad, Atotonilquillo.)

Pipa-Water Truck to fill household cisterns (*aljibes*) 376 765-2725. Miguel Angel Martinez. Call for delivery.

IMMIGRATION

Immigration/*Migración* 376 765-5600 (Main Number, City Hall). FM-2, FM-3, Visa Applications and

	Renewals, Chapala City Hall (*Municipio de Chapala*). Wednesdays 10 a.m. to 2 p.m., Madero #202, Chapala.

TRANSPORTATION

Taxi Ajijic	376 766-3662. 24-hour service from Samuel Reyes.
Taxi Stand at the Chapala Bus Station	376 765-4697
Taxi at the Chapala Plaza	376 765-3511 Hours: 6 a.m. to 9 p.m.
Taxi at the Plaza in Ajijic	376 766-0674 Hours: 7 a.m. to 8 p.m.
Taxi in Jocotepec	0133 3947-4952: 24 hours; 0133 3493-8901, 7 a.m. to 9 p.m.
Chapala Bus Station (*Central Camionera Chapala*)	376 765-2212
After Hours Private Driver	Francisco (Pancho) Miramontes 376 766-1142

PAYING BILLS - ELECTRICITY

Electricity (CFE) Chapala	Privada Zaragoza #3, Chapala (Hard right at Pemex gasoline station) Hours to pay: Monday through Friday, 8 a.m. to 2 p.m., other business until 3:30 p.m.
Jocotepec	Corner of Hidalgo Sur and Vicente Guerrero at traffic light in Jocotepec.
Ajijic, Bugambilias Plaza	Automated kiosk downstairs accepts your bill and money. Acts similar to an ATM machine.
Ajijic, Pinturas Prisa	An attendant will allow you to pay during midday hours. Ask what day she accepts bills from your area. Carretera Pte. #17, Interior 1, Ajijic.
Lloyd Fund Management	Account-holders may arrange for this service. Ajijic Branch: Carr. Chapala-Jocotepec #40; Chapala Branch: Madero #232.

Online	If you have an account with Banamex, Bancomer, Banorte, Santander Serfin, or Inbursa you may pay online by going to: www.cfe.gob.mx. Go to upper right hand corner and click on English. Register by giving your name, an email address and your electric bill number. You can ask questions and report problems. You can also check your current energy consumption.

TELEPHONE

Telmex in Person	Ajijic Office, Carr. Chapala-Jocotepec #113, Monday through Friday, 9 a.m. to 2 p.m.
Telmex Automated Kiosk	Outside the Ajijic Telmex there is an automated kiosk that accepts your bill. If you don't have a bill, key in your telephone number with area code. It acts similar to an ATM or parking machine.
	At local banks. If you have an account with the bank the service is free. If not, a charge of approximately 12 *pesos* is added. Online at telmexusa.com/explorer/servicios_linea/00_consulta_recibo.html

TOURISM

Chapala Dept. of Tourism	376 765-3141

HEALTH DEPARTMENT/*CENTRO DE SALUD*

Health Department Chapala	376 765-2623
Health Department Jocotepec	387 763-0230

DIF/SOCIAL SERVICES

DIF Chapala	376 765-3349, 376 765-2849
DIF Ajijic	376 766-0680

POST OFFICE

Ajijic Post Office	376 766-1888 Hours: 8:30 a.m. to 3 p.m. Monday through Friday.
Chapala Post Office	376 766-1888 (Same number and hours as Ajijic)
Chapala Telegraph Office	376 765-2181 Hours: 10 a.m. to 3 p.m. Monday through Friday.
Jocotepec Post Office	387 763-0322 Hours: 8 a.m. to 3 p.m. Monday through Friday.

CITY HALL

Ajijic Delegación Municipal de Ajijic	376 766-1760
Chapala Presidencia Municipio	376 765-2405, 376 765-3932 376 765-5600 through -09
San Antonio Tlay. Delegación Municipal	376 766-1287
San Juan Cosalá	387 763-0350
Delegación Municipal Jocotepec	Presidencia 387 763-0074 Jocotepec. Municipio 387 763-0006.

OTHER NUMBERS

IMSS Social Security Office Chapala	376 765-4990
***Hacienda*/Taxes**	376 765-2064 Juárez #575-A, Chapala
City Hall/ *Ministerio Publico*	376 765-2415 Chapala
***Derechos Humanos* (Human Rights)**	Guadalajara 01 33 3669-1101
Comisión Federal	376 765-3966 Chapala
SEMARNAT Environmental Regulation Office	376 765-3066 Chapala

CAR PAPERS

Car Papers/*Oficina de Recaudacion de Estado, Secretaria de Finanzas*	**Chapala**—376 765-2064, Juárez #575D. Monday through Friday 9 a.m. to 2 p.m. **Jocotepec**—Matamoros #80. Monday through Friday 9 a.m. to 2 p.m. **Ocotlán**—01 392 922-0713 Niños Heroes #152, Col. Centro. Monday through Thursday 9 a.m. to 2 p.m.

Everything to do with car papers is done in this office: new papers, renewals, car plates, change of ownership, registration and to *pay* for a new or renewed drivers license. The staff is helpful and some have a fair command of English.

DRIVER'S LICENSES

Driver's Licenses and Renewals

To test for or renew a Mexican driver's license you have several options:

State Office 01 33 3819-2431	Guadalajara. At Circunvalación and the corner of Alcalde. Open Monday through Friday 9 a.m. to 2 p.m.
Regional Office 01 392 922-0713	Ocotlán. At Niños Heroes #152, Col. Centro, Ocotlán. Open Monday through Thursday, 9 a.m. to 2 p.m.
Riberas del Pilar Office 376 765-4747	At Hidalgo #92, Riberas. Open Monday through Friday, 9 a.m. to 3 p.m. At this time, the schedule to pick up li-censes or to test is on Mondays. For foreigners, they're currently testing the last Monday of the month. However, schedule changes and technical problems are common. Check ahead of time for details.
Jocotepec Office	At Matamoros #80, Jocotepec. Open Monday through Friday 9 a.m. to 2 p.m. You may test here if you can show a Jocotepec address and can speak Spanish well.

PROPERTY TAXES/*PREDIAL*

Catastro (land registry)	The land registry counters are in the Chapala City Hall Foyer, Madero #202, Chapala. Open Monday through Friday, 9 a.m. to 3 p.m. Number pick up from 8:30 a.m. Pay in February for 15% discount (watch for notices in the Guadalajara Reporter). Bring the previous year or most recent tax receipt.

CONSTRUCTION PERMITS

Manifestación de Construción (construction declaration) for new/unregistered building improvements. Chapala City Hall, Madero #202, Chapala. Open Monday through Friday, 9 a.m. to 3 p.m.

WATER SERVICES/*AGUA POTABLE*

If you live in Chapala	SIMAPA office, Chapala City Hall, south wing, second floor.
If you live in Ajijic	Guadalupe Victoria #63, Ajijic.
If you live in Atotonilquillo, San Antonio Tlay., Santa Cruz, San Nicolás	Delegación offices. Offices are open 9 a.m. to 2 p.m. Pay yearly by the end of February for 15% discount (watch for notices in the Guadalajara Colony Reporter or other publications), or monthly. Be sure to bring your most recent receipt or property owner's name and address. Prices vary within municipalities and rates are determined by the size of the property; specifically by the size of the garden, number of bedrooms and bathrooms.

BUSINESS LICENSES/*LICENCIA MUNICIPAL*

Padrón y Licencias Office, Chapala City Hall, south wing, ground floor. Commercial licenses are valid for one calendar year, coming due as of January 1 regardless of the original date of issue. Open Monday through Friday 9 a.m. to 3 p.m. Pay by March 31 to avoid late Payment fine. Bring original registration form and most recent receipt for license renewal. Inquire about requirement for opening a new business.

AUTOMOBILE FEES/*REFRENDO Y TENENCIA*

Owners of Jalisco-plated cars pay a yearly flat registration fee (*refrendo*) to the state finance ministry (SEFIN). All 1995-2005 model cars are subject to a yearly ownership tax (*tenencia*) based on the vehicle's bluebook value.

Chapala

SEFIN State Tax Office, Hidalgo 212-6, at end of corridor next door to HSBC. Also handled by local banks.*(See note below)

SEFIN is open Monday through Friday, 9 a.m. to 2 p.m. Bank schedules vary. Pay by March 31 for 30% discount, May 31 for 15% discount, applicable only to flat 300 *peso refrendo* fee. Pay by June 30 to avoid late payment fines on *Refrendo* and *Tenencia*. Bring license plate number. *If paying at bank, ask for specifics.

Appendix

INDEX

A

C

D

F

I

J

K

L

M

Q

R

S

U

V

Making Real Estate
Real Easy.®
www.chapala.com
765-3676
765-2877
Each Office is Independently Owned And Operated
COLDWELL BANKER
Chapala Realty

Are you on Chapala.com?
(Over 2.5 Million Hits a Month!)
Advertise in the Ojo and get a FREE webpage
Lakeside's Best Publicaction

Let Me Help Make Your Real Estate Dreams Come True!
Dear Sid, You do your job...with honesty, integrity and a true southern hospitality. Michael M, Wauconda, IL
"I enjoyed our "tour" and your sharing of information... I want to thank you for your generous offer of the FIRST CLASS taxi ride to the aeropuerto! We both were overwhelmed by the kindness we received from you..." Rosemary W. – Michigan
"We could not get over your excellent service and your enthusiasm. We really appreciated the time you spent with us and the valuable information." signed, Helen and Henk B. of San Jose, California.
Elke G. writes, "You're the greatest! We never expected to receive such a welcome to the area! "
Buying or just looking, I want to be of service.
So, call Sid today!
COLDWELL BANKER
CHAPALA REALTY
Each Office is independently owned and operated.
Call: Office – (376) 765 –2877
elsidmx@yahoo.com USA
www.ChapalaRealEstate.com &
www.chapala.com/sid.html

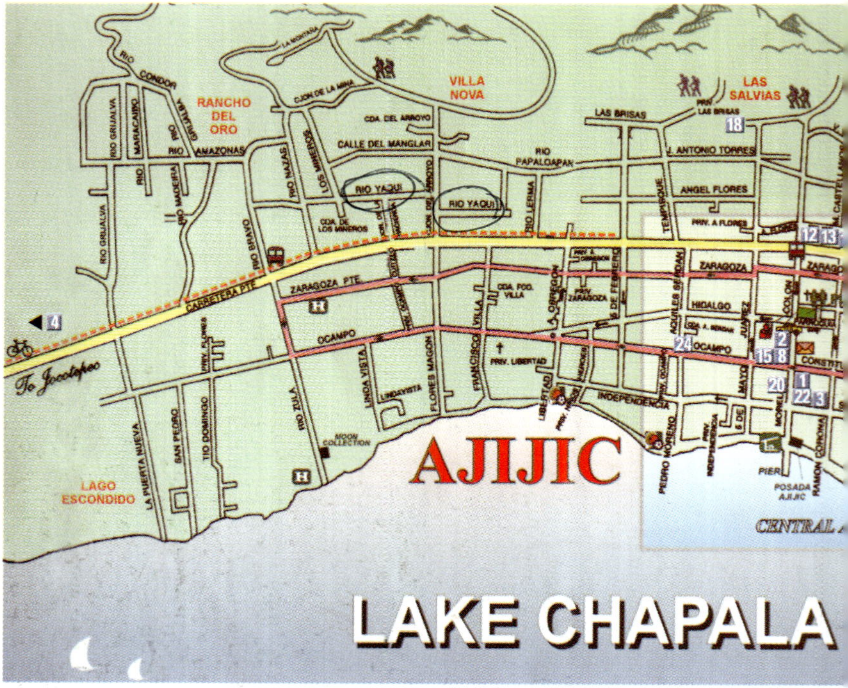

If calling from outside Mexico add 011 52 before local numbers.

1 **Georgette Richmond, Ajijic Real Estate** – Morelos 4, Ajijic, (376) 766-2077

2 **Ajijic Rentals** – Colón #1, Ajijic, (376) 766-1716

3 **Galería Maestros del Arte** – 16 de Septiembre #13, Ajijic. (376) 766-4133 or (376) 766-1089

4 **Animal Care–Ajijic** – Carretera Ajijic – Jocotepec #915-A, (376) 766-3062

5 **La Floresta Self Storage** – (376) 766-0661 or 766-1045

6 **La Paloma Bed & Breakfast** – Juan Alvarez #56, Ajijic, Toll free US & CDN: 1 (877) 237-1980, (376) 766-4140

7 **Linea Professional** – Carr. Ote. #33-C, Ajijic, (376) 766-2555

8 **Diane Pearl Colecciones** – Colón #1, Ajijic, (376) 766-5683

9 **Villas Eucaliptos Bed & Breakfast**– 16 de Septiembre #127, Ajijic, (376) 766-1400

10 **Coldwell Banker** – Hidalgo 223, Chapala, (376) 765-3676, 765-2877 Carretera 38-B, Ajijic, (376) 766-1152

11 **Sid Grosvenor – Coldwell Banker,** Hidalgo 223, Chapala, (376) 765-2877

12 **Canadians in Mexico** – Plaza Montaña Center, (376) 766-4828, www.canadiansinmexico.com

13 **Charter Club** – Plaza Montaña Center Main Hwy. at Colón, Ajijic, (376) 766-1777

14 **Rivas Auto Repairs** – Hidalgo #78, Riberas del Pilar, Cell: 01(333)197-3748

15 **AIG Insurance** – Colón #1, Ajijic, (376) 766-3975

16 **Lakeside Homes** – Carretera Ote. #5-B, Ajijic, (376) 766-5423, 766-5424

17 **Arellano Builder & Architect & Chula Vista Norte** – Libramiento, San Antonio Tlay., (376) 766-2177, Cell: 01(333)488-4476

18 **Villa Del Angel** – Juarez Privada #3, Ajijic, (376) 766-0783

19 **Roma Property Management** – Constitución #57-A, Ajijic, (376) 766-3163, Cell: 01(333)171-1514

20 **Arati** – Morelos #3, Ajijic, (376) 766-0130

21 **Eddy's & More** – Constitución #52, Ajijic, (376) 766-5040

22 **Ajijic Real Estate** – Morelos #4, Ajijic (376) 766-2077

23 **Media Luna** – Carretera La Floresta, Ajijic, (376) 766-0932

24 **Pedro's Restaurant & Bar** – Ocampo #71, Ajijic, (376) 766-4747

25 **Eager & Asociados** – Donato Guerra #16, Morelos #2, Ajijic, (376) 766-1617 or (376) 766-1918, 766-4465

Lagunanet – Within US: 1 956 242-0180, (376) 766-0297

Mexico Insights – www.mexico-insights.com

Call For Less – (376) 766-0517

Chapala.com – www.chapala.com

Strom Moving – (376) 766-4049

Head for Mexico – www.headformexico.com

Mexico Cultural Journeys – mexjourneys@prodigy.net.mx

Republicans Abroad – www.republicansabroadlakechapala.org

Western Mexico — A Traveller's Treasury – www.sombrerobooks.com

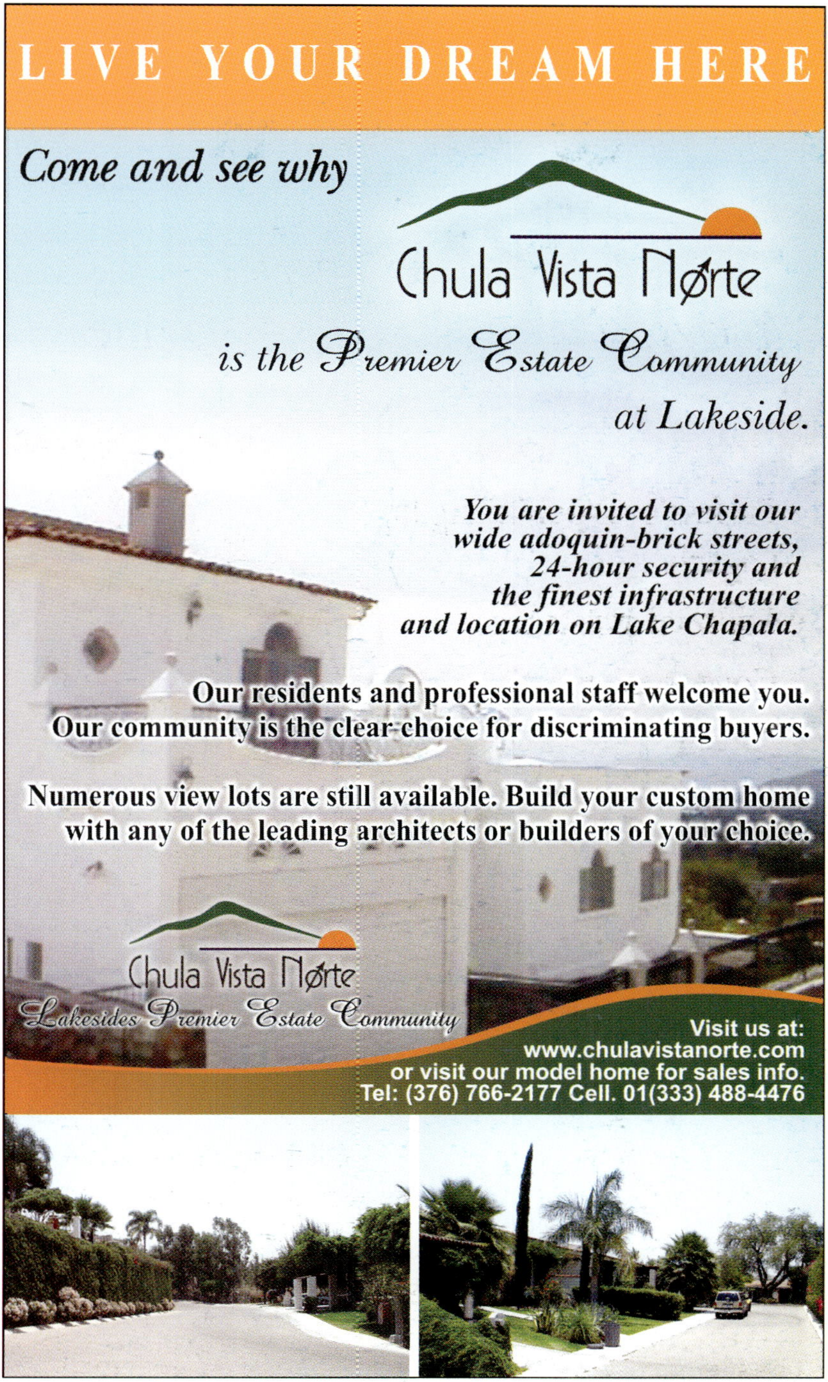
LIVE YOUR DREAM HERE
Come and see why
Chula Vista Nørte
is the Premier Estate Community
at Lakeside.
You are invited to visit our
wide adoquin-brick streets,
24-hour security and
the finest infrastructure
and location on Lake Chapala.
Our residents and professional staff welcome you.
Our community is the clear choice for discriminating buyers.
Numerous view lots are still available. Build your custom home
with any of the leading architects or builders of your choice.
Chula Vista Nørte
Lakesides Premier Estate Community
Visit us at:
www.chulavistanorte.com
or visit our model home for sales info.
Tel: (376) 766-2177 Cell. 01(333) 488-4476